Stephen Carey
US Household

S0-CFC-209

083-38-2312

HUMANITY AND MODERN SOCIOLOGICAL THOUGHT

NEW YORK   CHICAGO   SAN FRANCISCO   ATLANTA   DALLAS   MONTREAL

HUMANITY AND MODERN SOCIOLOGICAL THOUGHT

R. P. Cuzzort
University of Colorado

ORONTO   LONDON   SYDNEY   Holt, Rinehart and Winston, Inc.

Copyright © 1969 by Holt, Rinehart and Winston, Inc.
All Rights Reserved
Library of Congress Catalog Card Number: 69-14522
Cloth ISBN: **0-03-075465-8**
Paper ISBN: **0-03-081479-0**
Printed in the United States of America
34567890   071   9876

To Barbara

Barbara who?

PREFACE My formal introduction to sociology, anthropology, social psychology, and the other social sciences came immediately after the end of World War II. At that time social scientists were concerned, as I believe we still are, with promoting human welfare and with avoiding another inhuman display of man's inability to get along on this planet. The training I received twenty years ago was certainly well intentioned. At the same time it was, in a sense, naïve—it had the kind of naïvete that comes with youthful idealism and innocence; for then, as now, the social sciences were youngsters—upstarts in the academic world. They lacked established dignity and prestige. But things have changed considerably—a short span of time has seen psychology become both firmly established and extremely powerful as an academic discipline and science. Anthropology is growing lustily. Sociology is acquiring a sophistication that now marks it as a different breed of thought from what it was in the thirties and forties. If these fields have not yet become fully respectable, they have certainly lost some of their earlier innocence.

Today we cannot honestly present sociology or the other behavioral sciences the same way they were presented just a few decades ago. We cannot, for example, begin by defining sociology as a science and then, neatly sweeping all contrary arguments under the rug, blithely move on as if it were an effort properly housed in the campus physics building. Sociology, and the social sciences generally, operate within the fiery give and take of human values and human conflicts. Like the subject with which they deal, they are, when at their best, controversial in nature.

This book is predicated on the belief that the student should encounter immediately the controversial aspects of sociology —for these areas of discord give it an electric quality. I have, therefore, presented in this work men who stand as controversial figures in sociology and in social or cultural anthropology. None of these observers of the modern scene has lacked critics. Each has remained firm against his opponents and defended himself brilliantly and, at times, with charm. For me this has been the drama of social research and writing. I have tried to capture some of this drama, and I hope I have succeeded to some extent.

But I wish to do more than share with the reader some of the excitement I have found in the works of leading social scientists. I would also like to impress upon my audience the significance of what contemporary sociologists have to say about modern human conditions. Perhaps I am indulging in a paranoia common to my profession, but I fear the observations of social scientists are often casually dismissed as impractical or, worse yet, unnecessary. The ordinary man-in-the-street who sometimes finds the commentaries of television newscasters beyond him will not take kindly to the rarefied flights of someone like Max Weber or Emile Durkheim.

To make matters worse, the humanistic intellectual is inclined to discount the sociologist or anthropologist as an especially crude manifestation of the barbarous progress of science—a progression that has eclipsed an age of poetry, romance, and enchanted intellectualism. The natural scientist, on the other hand, grudgingly and occasionally admits a psychologist, anthropologist, economist, or sociologist into the general ranks of science. He usually feels, at the same time, that they are not really scientists.

This picture is probably overly pessimistic. However, I believe social scientists have been too eager to blame such criticism of their efforts and intellectual character on their limited ability to use exact scientific procedures. This criticism, to the extent it exists, may well reflect an attitude based not so much on the social scientist's restricted use of scientific method as it is on the pervasive feeling that he is not concerned with truly serious problems.

This book endeavors to show that sociologists are involved with profound problems of both a humanistic and a scientific variety. Moreover, their concerns and speculations are not without impact for the celebrated man-in-the-street. I have tried to show, in the writings of the social scientists discussed here, that the scientific concerns which led them down some interesting theoretical pathways were also major humanistic concerns.

The sociologist and anthropologist are, in their hesitating and faltering fashion, bringing into being a new rhetoric of man. Though some of my colleagues would be embarrassed—if not downright insulted—to have their work called "rhetoric" and though some humanists would snicker at the very idea, it is not as silly as it might seem. Whether I am right or wrong is for the rest of this book to determine. In any event, what I have tried to do, in addition to giving a sense of the excitement of social science, is to present a sense of its involvement with issues which have eternally puzzled man and which have been of dreadful and burning concern to him. Social science has not abandoned these concerns—it has only turned toward them with a new sense of hope and with a more intense reliance on logic, observation, and intelligence than man has dared or been able to employ in the past.

The content of this book consists, for the most part, of a discussion of the major works and ideas of fourteen men who have contributed to social thought. I will be called upon, I know, to justify my selection. Let me therefore attend to this matter now.

Anyone who is familiar with sampling procedures will notice that my sample of sociologists is quite biased. Had I wished to give the reader a more representative review, I could have drawn a perfectly random sample of names from the directory of the American Sociological Association. There would still be a slight bias in such a sample because it would include only those men who are members of the American Socio-logical Association and exclude those who are not. Still, in terms of representation, it would be a decided improvement over the grossly biased selection on which this book is based.

I do not, however, believe a random selection would be better than the one presented here. Such a technically repre-sentative sample would probably produce fourteen or fifteen men who, among them, have written less than any single one of the men whose works are discussed here. It should be immediately apparent that it is necessary to be biased. The question then becomes whether or not the form of the bias is appropriate.

I have selected men whose writings I think have a relevance for our times. I have selected men who, in their works, reveal both the variety and the consistency of modern social thought. It is, in my estimation, certainly unfair and perhaps unwise to provide an introductory student with a picture of sociology based on the formulations of a "unified" approach. It is unfair because it can lead the student into a deceptive sense of simplicity—it can produce an intellectual narrowness at best and scornful rejection at worst. A unified approach may appeal to a small segment of students at the possible cost of alienating the remainder.

A review of the works of the men considered in this book should offer the student some idea of the diversity of modern social thought. At the same time, in the course of his read-ing, the student hopefully will encounter at least one approach with which he "resonates." If his interests are mathematical, then possibly he will find Richardson worth further investiga-tion. If his interests are historical, he might find Weber to his liking. If his interests are psychological, he should find Goffman's work something to think about. If he is of a literary bent, Riesman or Berger might offer him stimulation. If he has religious concerns, Durkheim should lead him on into deeper thought.

I am not afraid of diversity in teaching sociology—it should, I believe, be welcomed. At the same time, to permit diversity to grow without limit is to encourage chaos and confusion. Intellectual dazzle sets in. There should be an apparent thread or two of consistency to help us make contrasts and see the relationships which exist among the various observers of the social world.

The writers I have chosen deal with modern society. They are analytical rather than descriptive; that is to say, they are more concerned with the "why" of social happenings than the "what." Though their subject matter ranges from the social adjustments of the epileptic to the origins of modern capitalism, they reveal a common reliance on an intelligent use of what Mills called the "sociological imagination."

Most significantly, each of the men I have selected deals with a broad humanistic concern. These men share not only the professional training and imagination of the competent social scientist, they also share involvement with some of the great problems that have concerned men since the beginnings of history.

Of course, I could have selected differently and still have arrived at the same effect. There are many superb social analysts writing today. I have chosen from those I know best and from those who appealed most to my students. This is, admittedly, very personal and arbitrary. But possibly sociology is a more personal experience than we, as academicians and dispassionate researchers, would like it to be.

This book is an attempt to repay, in very small part, the great debt I owe to sociology, to many professional colleagues, and to several thousand wonderfully patient students who have been kind enough to remain attentive and questioning in my classes as I explored some puzzling and not always clear ideas.

It is traditional in prefaces to books of this sort to mention certain selected individuals to whom one is especially indebted. Only tradition could impose such an impossible task on a writer. My indebtedness seems, to me, to be virtually without limit. I must, however, recognize the encouragement and support of Prof. Jean Phillips and Prof. Daniel Glaser of the University of Illinois. Their kindness was never in doubt; yet they could be trusted to be cruelly critical if they felt it was necessary to save me from some folly to which I had become attached.

Prof. Charles K. Warriner, Chairman of the Sociology Department of the University of Kansas, provided unusually detailed and perceptive commentaries on some of my ideas. I would like to express my special thanks to him. Prof. Paul Meadows of Syracuse University and Prof. Jack Don C. Gibbons of the University of California, Santa Barbara, were simultaneously critical and encouraging—I am grateful.

Though they have no direct involvement in the writing of this book, I would like to express my gratitude to the following men: Prof. James A. Quinn, University of Cincinnati; Prof. Donald J. Bogue, University of Chicago; Prof. Otis D. Duncan, University of Michigan; Prof. Don Martindale, University of Minnesota; Prof. Gustav Carlson, University of Cincinnati; Prof. William Stephens, Florida Atlantic University; Prof. Philip Mitterling, University of Colorado; and Prof. Carroll D. Clark, University of Kansas. From these men I learned much.

I would also like to express my gratitude to those men and women whose nearly futile task it was to try to educate me as I progressed from grade school through graduate school. Often, in the confusions of youth, I repaid their efforts with ingratitude and, at times, open hostility. I cannot undo what has been done. However, the model of their patience, tolerance, and determination to educate me despite myself stands me in good stead now that I am engaged in trying to educate others.

I must also mention here Mr. Fred Pomeranz and Mr. Terry Hutton who provided me with much assistance in checking sources and handling various routine matters.

Books have a way of impressing upon their authors the fact that we human beings are discouragingly fallible creatures. I must therefore atone in some way for the inevitable errors which doubtless appear here and there throughout the following pages. I will decline to apologize for grammatical or stylistic errors because sociologists are supposed to be notoriously insensitive to matters of style. Substantive errors are another thing. Wherever I have made an error of fact or an error in interpretation I must take sole responsibility. I do this without hesitation. At the same time, I am grateful to those who have given me less to apologize for than would have been the case had I not received their help.

R.P.C.

Boulder, Colorado
October 1968

CONTENTS

✓ = READ

wed.

T. S. Elliot
The Hero Cheering

"The Unheroic Trag.
Hero" by

The Nulliable Othello
by Bradely *

HUMANITY AND MODERN SOCIOLOGICAL THOUGHT

1   Varieties of Courage: An Introduction to Social Thought

We have come, in recent years, to rely on intelligence as the most important part of intellectual effort. If we have oversubscribed intelligence—and I believe this is so—then it is an unfortunate thing. There is a great deal more to creative intellectual work than intelligence. Too many bright people are walking around who never accomplish much of anything to let us honor any other conclusion. Intelligence is obviously necessary to attain profound insights—it is the *sine qua non* of intellect; but it is not, in itself, sufficient for highly innovative and daring work. In addition to intelligence, an outstanding intellectual must possess endurance, tolerance, a sturdy sense of humor and perseverance, a goodly amount of courage, and a strong faith in his own worth. These attributes, which so often count for so much, are surprisingly easy to overlook in an age of talent. Yet they are attributes which separate the productive artist or scientist from the man whose singular strength rests in his high IQ.

The social scientists whose writings and ideas form the foundations of this book demonstrate the overriding importance of possessing more than intelligence. All of these men have unusually keen minds and sensitive powers of observation. However, each in his own way reveals as well his humor, affection, tolerance, and courage as he brings these qualities together in an effort to grapple with and comprehend the irrationalities of man.

C. Wright Mills, for example, did not possess the profound genius and meticulous attention to detail that characterized the work of, let us say, Max Weber. Even so, he held strengths which enabled him to attain a large following among American and European intellectuals. He was, above all, a man of courage and affection. The more he devoted himself to his work, the more he became emotionally and intellectually involved with his society—a society

3

which seemed to him bent on the most insane forms of self-destruction. C. Wright Mills was a social scientist, but he was a scientist in love with his subject—and in his love he unveiled the concern a doting parent might reveal when he sees his dull but darling child playing happily in a nest of vipers. There are times when the expression of love is an act of courage; C. Wright Mills provides us with a case in point.[1]

Another man, whose work appears later in this book, offers an example of a different kind of quality. Lewis F. Richardson must have experienced the discouragement that comes when an intellectual finds himself alone with his convictions. Richardson was among the first to believe there was some value in trying to apply modern mathematical reasoning to human social and economic activities. But few of his colleagues were willing to encourage or support him in this belief. It was necessary for Richardson to publish his early works on mathematical studies of human conflict at his own expense. Some of his friends told him candidly they thought his ideas were amusing. Nonetheless, his was a serious effort; Richardson was, after all, a competent and reputable natural scientist. Despite the cool reception his effort received, he continued his work on human conflict and maintained the same devotion to rigorous thought in these studies that he had given to his researches in meteorology. Only later, after his death, was the value of what he had done more widely conceded. The disparaging opinions of his friends faded. But they were opinions against which Richardson in his lifetime had to assert himself. We, who can view his work from today's vantage point, tend to dismiss too casually the fact that Richardson had to persevere under discouraging and depressing conditions.

The "character" of social science

Each of the men presented in the following chapters stands as an example of what, for want of a better word, I shall have to refer to as the "character" of social science. All occupations suffer, more or less, from stereotypes. Librarians, for example, are always supposed to be dried-up, sallow-skinned, watery-eyed souls whose timidity is exceeded only by their lack of worldly

---

[1] Presthus makes the following interesting comment concerning Mills: "The implications of academic organization and its claims for appropriate professional behavior are suggested by the fact that several reviewers of Mills' work concluded: 'Here is a man who will never be president of the American Sociological Society.'" Robert Presthus, *The Organizational Society* (Vintage Books; New York: Random House, Inc., 1962), p. 13.

experience. We know, or at least we ought to know, that this stereotype is unrealistic—there are too many exceptions to it.

Social scientists are also stereotyped. One common denominator attributed to social scientists is a somnambulant dullness combined with a wordy concern for things everybody else already knows.[2] If nothing else, the men presented in this book stand as a refutation of this stereotype. They are, singly and together, neither dull nor given to elaborating the obvious. They offer revelations of what it means to mature as a social scientist. They are not only men who gather social facts; they are also men who attempt to make sense of the facts they have been able to obtain. For Max Weber this effort meant persevering despite severe nervous disorders that incapacitated him throughout his lifetime. For Robert K. Merton it has meant, and continues to mean, a devotion to work and self-discipline that is found only among the most dedicated of artists and scientists. For George Lundberg it meant a life-long attempt to ascertain the place of science in an examination of human affairs. For Leslie White it means a willingness to make explicit and direct those idiocies which he finds in officially sanctioned superstition and tradition. For C. Wright Mills it meant pursuing his individual conception of what was most needed in sociological literature—regardless of whether this would result in a loss of reputation among his professional colleagues.

So it is with the other men whose works appear in this volume. Each is included because he has contributed to the multihued character of sociology and the social sciences. He has contributed not only a valuable book or theory, but he has contributed something of himself. He did not, in other words, function mechanically as a social scientist—he did not simply follow the rules and prescriptions for success as a sociologist or anthropologist. He went further; he followed his own conscience and his own knowledge when he felt this would benefit man's understanding of himself. This, in part, is what I mean when I say these men provide us with an insight into the character of sociology.

But social science obviously is not entirely a matter of character. Many men, throughout the course of history, have made social pronouncements. They have done this in good faith and have often shown great courage.

---

[2] A very articulate and amusing employment of professorial stereotypes appears in the tongue-in-cheek novel *Purely Academic* by Stringfellow Barr (New York: Simon and Schuster, Inc., 1958). The characterization of sociologists by Barr is a more thorough development of a nasty stereotype than I can afford to present in this chapter. I recommend this novel to you, but suggest that you read it as it was written—with tongue-in-cheek. This is not, incidentally, a bad attitude to assume in reading many novels.

Nonetheless, they did not serve as social scientists. The men included in this book identify themselves professionally as social scientists.[3] We need to pause for a moment and consider, generally, what such a commitment means.

The "craftsmanship" of social science

A dedication to social science implies, first of all, a sense of "craftsmanship." As craftsmen, these men are aware of and interested in the latest and best modes of understanding ourselves and our social systems. It often impresses me as regrettable that some of my students, especially men, may be knowledgeable about craftsmanship in cars or "hi-fi" equipment and yet gullibly accept the shoddiest and most antique of social theories. I cannot help wondering what becomes of the man who skillfully masters complex forms of modern machinery while carrying in his head ideas about himself and others which were beginning to show signs of decay several centuries ago.

This matter of craftsmanship has several aspects. One of these, as C. Wright Mills refers to it, is a matter of "sociological imagination."[4] It is not the task of the social scientist to conserve ancient and hallowed conceptions of the social and political realm. He is expected, instead, to bring to his studies the disciplined use of imagination. I mention this because there are some people who look upon the social scientist as an unimaginative clod—evidently they believe that the use of imagination is confined to artists, writers of fiction, and others who have freed themselves from the more taxing empirical demands of science. Perhaps I am reacting to the occasion when I was introduced as a social scientist to the director of an art museum on a midwestern campus. "Ah," he said, as he shook my hand, "You are one of those fellows who counts pigs and alcoholics and things like that." I replied that I hoped I knew more about art than he appeared to know about social thought. Certainly the social scientist is more than a counter of pigs and alcoholics. It is true that empirical work of this sort occupies a great deal of the time of social scientists throughout the country. It is equally true that much work of this kind is dull and routine—the collection of factual material

---

[3] There is one exception. Lewis F. Richardson was a meteorologist and acquired considerable acclaim as a natural scientist before turning his attention to an analysis of social conflicts. His work is so interesting and relevant, however, that I felt it would be a grave injustice to him and his work to hold his lack of proper academic credentials against him.

[4] See C. Wright Mills, *The Sociological Imagination* (New York: Oxford University Press, 1959). Mills spells out in greater detail than I can manage here what the term "craftsmanship" ought to mean to a social scientist.

in any science is often dull.[5] But the thinking that takes place before and after the "facts are in" does not have to be and should not be dull.

Later in this book one of the most imaginative of contemporary sociologists will be introduced. Erving Goffman, now Professor of Sociology at the University of California, exemplifies, par excellence, what I mean when I talk about imagination as an element of craftsmanship. This kind of imagination, in a different form, appears in the writings of Jules Henry, David Riesman, and, indeed, all of the others who appear in the following pages. Without the use of imagination a social scientist—no matter how impeccable his social data, no matter how rigorous his logical reasoning—is something less than complete as a craftsman. He may be a skilled technician, but he is not truly a master.

Craftsmanship involves the disciplined use of imagination. It also involves the ability to set forth one's ideas in language which is clear and persuasive. I have tried, in discussing the ideas of these different writers and thinkers, to retain the clarity of expression which their original works possess. Again, I think this is worth mentioning because each of these men refutes the notion that the social scientist is a fellow whose ideas are so weak and commonplace that he must fill out their emaciated forms with obscure terminology and obfuscating phrases. Among the men presented here the most obscure, stylistically, is Max Weber. But Weber wrote the scholarly prose of the German academician and while his style is not as simple and direct as that of Riesman or Goffman, it is surprisingly precise and devoid of excess fat.

I have said that these men are men of intellectual character and I have referred to them as men who exemplify the "craftsmanship" of social science. But these qualities, even yet, do not specifically set them apart as social scientists. The diversity of thought which appears in the following pages is sufficient, I believe, to lead the reader to the conclusion that these men share very little in common. If this is the case, then what, specifically, is a social scientist? Is he someone who takes an odd assortment of courses in college and then, when the time comes, merely hangs up a shingle and proclaims himself to the world as a social scientist? If so, then the status of the social scientist is in sad condition.

---

[5] A fictional account of the routine nature of much scientific work appears in Mitchell A. Wilson, *Live with Lightning* (Boston: Little, Brown and Company, 1949). C. P. Snow also comments on this in some of his novels. A novel that greatly romanticizes the work of sociologists is Eugene Burdick's *The 480* (New York: Dell Publishing Co., 1964). Even this unrealistically romantic novel—which I recommend only to someone going into the social sciences—comments on the routine nature of much research.

Common perspectives

I want the reader to see that social science offers various perspectives on man. Yet, at the same time, despite their variety, social scientists share common fundamental points of view. What are these basic commonalities?

First, and without doubt foremost, they all accept a naturalistic view of man. By this I mean they believe human events can be best analyzed and best understood by attempting to find the natural "causes" or natural circumstances associated with such events. Man is not something set apart from nature. He is not endowed with some special spirit or some special portfolio from heaven which removes him from nature's processes. Drop a human being from a cliff and he falls with the same acceleration as a rock, a massive piece of wood, or a hog. Man does not, by virtue of being a man, find himself exempt from any of the influences of nature, be they chemical, electrical, physiological, neurological, psychological, or social and cultural.

This naturalistic position, endorsed by all of the writers discussed in this book, has gained overwhelming popularity among modern intellectuals. It is the most fundamental premise of a scientific perspective. In its most extreme form it is the argument that any mysterious event, any miracle, can ultimately be found to have its origins in natural conditions available to man's observation and understanding. Naturalism does not preclude the existence of mysteries; but, where mysteries exist, it attributes them to man's ignorance of how things "work" in the real world. Mysteries and miracles are not the product of some divine force teasing man with a dramatic display of magical happenings.

The first common thread, then, which runs through this book is that of naturalism. The implications of a naturalistic position are not always palatable and not always comforting—especially when employed in an attempt to comprehend human social and cultural systems. For example, a scientist who would not think of using divine intervention to explain reflexive actions in a frog's muscle will sometimes find this same idea perfectly acceptable in discussions of the development of religious institutions, the progress of nations, or why some people are successful and famous while others are not—in each instance it is a matter of being in God's favor. The position taken by the writers surveyed in this book is that if something is happening in the course of human development, we can best understand whatever it might be by a careful analysis of its relationship to events in the observable world. Whether the writer is a down-to-earth scientist (as exemplified in the chapter on how to lose at games) or a more speculative and freewheeling commentator on humanistic questions (the chapter presenting David Riesman's views exemplifies this approach), there is agreement on taking a naturalistic perspective toward man and his history.

There is a second perspective or point of view which social scientists have in common, regardless of their specific treatment of man. This second perspective is largely a matter of emphasis on the significance of man's existence as a social being. Indeed, social science, in its different forms (such as anthropology, sociology, social psychology) might be defined as an attempt to trace the implications of the fact that man must exist within human social systems. These implications can be traced in various ways. Some social scientists may focus on a rather narrow segment of social activity—marital happiness, for example. They may then spend a good part of their professional lives attempting to find the natural correlates of such happiness. Work of this sort is often characterized by a highly factual quality. Studies have been conducted showing marital happiness to be associated with realistic sexual education in childhood, good marital adjustment among parents, the religious affiliation of the couple, complementarity of needs, social class, educational level, occupational status, and any number of other factors. The point is, however, that each of the factors mentioned here is a *social* factor. Each one involves the fact of social membership. None deals with the individual as something isolated, independent, autonomous, or removed from the associations in which he is involved with others.

Other social scientists may concern themselves with "broader" issues. C. Wright Mills, for example, takes on the problem of war and the struggles between nations. His articles and books lack the factual quality—the numerous tabular presentations of statistical data—which are likely to be found in works concentrating on more specific and "narrow" problems such as marital happiness. Even so, the effort is still one that concentrates on the social causes of social conditions. It is possible to ascribe social conflicts to such unsocial factors as instincts, climatic conditions, and biological factors like population growth. Social scientists, however, are becoming more and more inclined to find the answer to human social concerns in the social nature of man himself.

Two of the more extreme representatives of this point of view are Leslie White and Emile Durkheim. Both White and Durkheim, using somewhat different language, say that the causes of a social or cultural condition (such as crime, for instance) cannot be understood independently of the social context within which the condition occurs. This is neither a simple point nor a trivial one. We have, down to the present time, emphasized an individualistic approach to many problems or concerns which cannot be resolved in such an elementary fashion. The criminal, for example, is still looked upon as a person with a perverted or distorted personality; all that is needed to set him straight is extensive psychiatric treatment.

Or, as another example, there are still many persons naive enough to believe that a superior society will be created by producing a biologically superior stock of people. Both White and Durkheim, and virtually all the other authors considered here, would point out that regardless of genetic stock, granting a minimal level of average ability, we would still find ourselves making the moral discriminations and the social and economic differentiations which have characterized human society throughout the ages.

Let me quickly indicate the essential basis of such reasoning. Regardless of the genetic qualities of their constituents, most groups and organizations must make a distinction between leaders and subordinates. Just this one distinction raises many problems, but—and this is the important thing—these problems stem from an organizational concern and not from problems of personality, body build, diet, skin color, body odor, intelligence levels, or anything else. A myth may arise that supports the leader, but the myth can take many forms. In one place the leader may point to the cleft between his teeth as a sign of his right to leadership. In another place he may point to his blond hair and blue eyes. But the social scientist takes a different point of view. A sociologist would claim that social demands require leadership, and whether the leader has blond hair is beside the point—someone will have to occupy that role.

Great leaders have been of all races. Some have been men of unusual physical strength and others have been slight. Some have been undoubtedly brilliant, others were men of average intelligence. The one thing they shared in common was occupancy of a leadership position. This fact causes the social scientist to focus his attention on social roles and how they are created and integrated with one another, how they are sustained, and how people become motivated to occupy various roles. But as we become more concerned with roles and their organization, we must become more concerned with a mode of analysis that always involves at least two kinds of persons in interaction. Try, for example, to consider the role of a teacher without having to take into account the tangential roles of students, school administrators, parents, and others.

The social scientists in this book, then, share in common a social orientation toward man. Whether the author is Richardson, examining through the cold equations of mathematical logic the development of an arms race, or Jules Henry watching a group of children in an American classroom, the emphasis is on determining who is doing what to whom and why they are doing it. The emphasis is a social emphasis. So, social scientists share naturalism and a concentration on social causes in their approach to understanding man.

A third common factor in the writings of social scientists is a dedication to intellectual abstraction or generalization. Regardless of whether it is an empirically oriented sociologist doing factual studies of the journey to work, or an anthropologist examining kin structure among the Potawatomie Indians, the final objective of each effort is the development of a synthesizing generalization. Social scientists want to make broader sense out of the specific facts they have accumulated.

In some instances the generalizations achieve stunning effects. Merton is able, after sifting through a mass of historical information, to demonstrate a relationship between Puritan religious ideology and the rise of science. Riesman is able to relate broad social trends to changes in individual character. He suggests that as America moved from an expansion toward the west to the establishment of a more settled nation-state, American character changed accordingly. Pioneers who migrated westward, as well as eastern industrialists and capitalists, were men of "inner-direction" and strength of convictions who dared, like Vanderbilt, to say aloud, "The public be damned." Today, as organizations insist on smoothness of operations, American character has become more sensitive and responsive to the desires, tastes, and needs of others.

Such generalizations are not necessarily "truth." They are, instead, devices that make an otherwise overwhelming mass of facts manageable to the limitations of the human mind. This is why statistics is so popular among social scientists today. If social conditions can be translated into numerical values, then all that is necessary to bring them together and simplify them is statistics. However, although statistical generalizations may help to organize and make sense of thousands of individual facts, they nonetheless do not refer to anything existing in the real world. An elementary example will illustrate what I mean: Statisticians found, after obtaining census information from the population, that the average American family in the early sixties was made up of 3.2 people living on an annual income of $5557. Their religious affiliation was Protestant and they possessed 1.4 automobiles. Some of this sounds reasonable and "true," except for the 3.2 people and the 1.4 cars. These figures give the game away, and we understand immediately that our typical American family is not a reality but a statistical artifact or construction. After all there is no such thing as one-fifth of a person or four-tenths of a car.

But even though these artifacts are not "true" in the sense that they refer to nothing in the real world, such generalizations still have great utility and value. A statistical average is a generalization that enables us to comprehend quickly the typical condition of things. We could, if we desired, compare the average white adult American male with the average nonwhite adult American male and, by comparing two nonexistent or "unreal" or "untrue" statements, come to some very realistic conclusions regarding the relative status of whites and nonwhites in this country.

Regardless, then, of whether the social scientist is working with numerical data of a statistical variety or with historical data of a more qualitative variety, the dominant interest is not in the specific case—it is in the generalizations that may be obtained from a number of specific cases. When Max Weber, for example, talks about an "ideal type" of bureaucracy, he is not talking about any specific bureaucracy. He is referring, instead, to a general conception of the nature of bureaucracy based on an examination of many such organizations.

The relationship between observations and generalizations is a tricky one in the social sciences—as it is in any other science—and has led to an intensive and almost morbid interest in what is called "methodology." We will not focus on the methods of the men whose works are introduced in the pages that follow. But I would like to enjoin you to consider two possible sources of error in any author's work as you read the rest of this book.

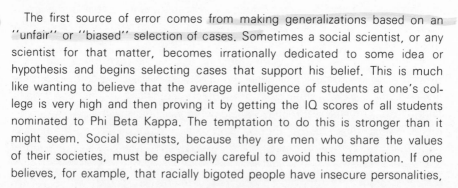

The first source of error comes from making generalizations based on an "unfair" or "biased" selection of cases. Sometimes a social scientist, or any scientist for that matter, becomes irrationally dedicated to some idea or hypothesis and begins selecting cases that support his belief. This is much like wanting to believe that the average intelligence of students at one's college is very high and then proving it by getting the IQ scores of all students nominated to Phi Beta Kappa. The temptation to do this is stronger than it might seem. Social scientists, because they are men who share the values of their societies, must be especially careful to avoid this temptation. If one believes, for example, that racially bigoted people have insecure personalities, it becomes surprisingly easy to overlook people who are secure and yet bigoted, or people who are insecure and yet not bigoted.[6]

A second source of error consists of generalizing beyond known cases. This is something like having five observations with values of 1, 2, 3, 4, and 5, and then saying the average for all the cases in the world is 3. This kind of error is difficult to make when dealing with statistical data.[7] It is surprisingly easy to make when dealing with historical data. A classic case in point was Freud's generalization of the Oedipus complex to all cultures on the basis of his observations of the mother-son relationship in western European cultures.

It is not generalization itself which is "bad." Indeed, and this is the point of the argument here, generalization is essential. Valid and useful generalizations are the goal of scientists in any field of endeavor. What we must guard against, however, are generalizations coming from biased samples or generalizations which do not recognize their own observational limits.

We have now identified three central characteristics of social scientists: they are naturalistic in their approach to man; they concentrate on the social character of man; and they seek generalizations that create unity and understanding amidst the bewildering variety of daily human activities. There is yet another quality I must include here. The social scientist must be willing to prepare his ideas, his observations, and his generalizations so that they can be subjected to critical review. Social science, like any other science, is a public effort. One may make all the clever observations it is possible to imagine, and one may construct elaborate theories which integrate into a magnificent pattern the manifold schemes and practices of man; but this means nothing until the effort has been presented before a humanely hostile community of scholars and fellow social scientists. It is this feature of social science which often inhibits many an otherwise ambitious young aspirant from joining the ranks of the expert. Social science is a public activity. Consequently, the social scientist must be willing to work within a system of evaluations that openly elevate or depress the worth of his efforts. A new ob-

---

[6] Even when working with nonhuman subjects, a scientist can distort his findings. There have been instances reported where researchers have been gentle with rats that behaved according to theory and unwittingly mean toward rats that did not. For example, in returning the animals to their cages the researcher would be likely to toss the nonconforming rat more roughly into his cage. This different treatment of the animals was sufficient to influence the outcome of some experiments using rats as subjects.

[7] The reason for this involves some rather complicated technical arguments. However, they boil down to the fact that one of the first things that an embryonic statistician is required to learn is that he *never* knows the value of a statistic for a population from which he has only sample data.

servation or a new mode of integrating older observations may make a man's life work obsolete. Yet, despite the strong egos which exist among many social scientists, there is a willingness to accept this feature of science.

The public character of science means it is not an occult mystery to be presided over by members of a priestly caste. It is available to all—it is democratic in spirit. Today's foremost theory may be overthrown tomorrow by some radical group. Even so, it takes a bit of daring to place before one's colleagues an idea which one knows will probably go against their grain. With possibly a few exceptions, most of the men discussed in this book have done this. Henry, for example, wrily comments on the fact that he was turned down by foundations from whom he sought support as often as he was aided by them.

Objectivity

One last feature of social science which I must mention, and which will come up a number of times later in this book, is the dedication to objectivity which has more and more become the hallmark of the social scientist. Objectivity in social science refers to the belief that it is the duty of the social scientist to make no moral pronouncements. He is not to evaluate the ethical character of the people whose behavior he observes. He is not, in other words, supposed to use terms like bad, evil, pervert, good, nice, wonderful, proper, or worthless. It is astounding how the removal of such terms from one's writing saps it of stylistic vigor. As a consequence, social scientists in general and the sociologist in particular have been pointed to as good examples of what not to do when writing.

Objectivity means, for the social scientist, that a Nazi is no better nor any worse than a Quaker; a homosexual is ethically on the same plane as a saintly hermit; a murderer is as proper a subject for contemplation as a factory manager; a bitter divorce case is not "bad" and a wedding anniversary celebrating fifty years of married bliss is not "good." Man's ethical nature is a concern for the social scientist only insofar as it might have an influence on human behavior. Or, a social scientist might be interested in the extent to which ethical pronouncements reflect the struggles that take place between competing groups in a society. For example, a social scientist, when acting as a scientist, cannot endorse the Lord's Prayer.[8] He might, however, show con-

---

[8] It is necessary to mention here that I am speaking of the social scientist in his capacity as a scientist. As a citizen, or in his other capacities, a social scientist certainly has the right, like any man, to express his values.

siderable interest in different versions of the prayer that have been used. One version of the prayer, as a case in point, uses the term "trespassers" while another uses the term "debtors." Does this tell us something about the struggles that have taken place between landed and commercial interests in our society? Are ethical phrases the debris that remains after a great power struggle has taken place within a society? A question like this makes morality a subject for analysis rather than development—and we need to wonder if analysis, like that of the frog in a biology laboratory, is more likely to lead to the demise than to the good health of its subject.

This problem of objectivity in the social sciences is an extremely knotty one; and it is one that social scientists have not been able, as yet, to handle in a truly satisfactory fashion.[9] The whole issue is discussed more thoroughly in the chapter dealing with George Lundberg and his work. Lundberg believed there really was no issue—one could function as a behavioral scientist only if he maintained the most rigorous devotion to the canons of objectivity. One has to assume something of the character of the proverbial man from Mars. Personal values, sentiments, ethical considerations, and moral judgments must be kept out of the task of reporting the nature of human nature. C. Wright Mills, on the other hand, took the behavioral sciences to task for abdicating one of the purposes they could best serve—that of helping man find not only why he does some of the things he does, but of helping him as well to discover newer and better goals in life. But, as soon as one suggests new goals for man, he is beginning to function in a moral capacity. Does the social scientist have this right?

Although the writers in this book are, to a man, naturalists; although each strongly emphasizes man's social character; although each presents powerful and carefully thought out generalizations; and although each is willing to make his arguments public—they begin to separate and move along different and somewhat antagonistic paths when it comes to what should be done with their ideas, with social science, and with man's moral character.

The strongest proponents of objectivity in this book are Lundberg, Weber, Durkheim, Richardson, and perhaps Merton. Several authors move over to the other side and advocate that the social scientist be willing to take sides on ethical issues. Most blunt in this matter is C. Wright Mills; others are

---

[9] Social scientists are not the only ones who are concerned with the relationship between a commitment to scientific objectivity and a commitment to human values. One of the best known efforts to cope with this problem is the series of essays by J. Bronowski, *Science and Human Values* (see footnote 10). Is it sufficient, or—more extremely—is it the finest form of dedication to claim that one must seek that truth which is independent of our failings as humans? Is this what science is?

David Riesman, Peter Berger, and Jules Henry. Sorokin is indirect in his criticisms of modern society—but it is clear that he is critical, and to this extent he violates the canons of objectivity. The position that a few of these writers take is not always completely clear. Goffman, for example, achieves a unique effect by writing with such perfect detachment and objectivity that it seems, at first, he has stripped man of his last veils—after Goffman one cannot easily pretend he is without blame in the human conspiracies which daily take place. But if objectivity of this kind can lead us to wonder about the value of our actions toward others, then it is writing which is not devoid of ethical commitment.

The applications of social science

Whether it is ethically neutral or ethically committed, there is still the problem of what one does with social science. After all, with electronics one can build radios and pinball machines; with chemistry one can create plastics and nerve gases; with behavioral psychology one can teach pigeons to play Ping-Pong. But what does one do with social science? A flippant reply would be that one can use social science to become a social scientist, and I fear this is the greatest utility seen in the field today. Before we examine the specific writings of social scientists, I believe it is worth a few moments to attempt to make the point that social science—of all fields of intellectual effort—is fraught with the greatest practical consequences.

But what do I mean when I say social science is "practical"? I shall define practicality—and I concede this definition is both arbitrary and elusive—as any effort which results, after a time, in the lowering of human fears and discomforts. It is quite difficult, in many instances, to determine just how practical some of our seemingly very practical inventions have been. For example, it is not easy to ascertain whether the motorcycle—that currently popular mode of local transportation in campus communities—has decreased or increased the general level of human fears and discomforts. The practical value for the rider of not having to walk is balanced by the nuisance value for hundreds of people of being subjected to a flatulent noise. The practical values, and there are many obvious ones, of nuclear power have been balanced by a pervasive fear that has spread throughout the world. So, this business of determining practicality is not simple, but there is a lesson to be learned. If the practicality of obviously practical devices is not easy to ascertain, it is also true that the impracticality of impractical efforts is sometimes equally hard to demonstrate. We should not be hasty in designating something impractical.

However, for some people the social sciences are impractical. The social sciences seem to achieve little in the way of an obvious and demonstrable reduction of human fears and discomforts. Or, it may seem that the social sciences are not able to attain these ends any better than already established competitive systems. After all, the social sciences exist to provide us with knowledge about our social character; but we also get such information from novelists, religious thinkers, political demagogues, astrologers, and, above all, from our friends and from our own personal experiences with innumerable others whom we encounter in the course of a lifetime. It is not easy to reject the opinions of our friends—even though in their ignorance they may do more to exaggerate our fears than to allay them. It is not always easy to accept the carefully established findings of a social scientist when we believe, on the basis of our own personal observations and encounters, that he is dead wrong. In such circumstances the social sciences seem like the sheerest folly—the heightened caricature of a very impractical kind of business.

A first comprehension of the practicality of the social sciences comes from a recognition that the cumulative ignorance of our friends and associates and the narrow range of experience which is afforded us as individuals is the foundation upon which injurious ideas and policies may be founded. Our friends and our experiences encapsulate us and build around us a protective shield of limited observations and understanding within which we can acquire a distorted sense of security and comfort. Perhaps I can illustrate my meaning with a quotation from Bronowski.

> The gravest indictment that can be made of our generalized culture is, in fact, that it erodes our sense of the context in which judgments must be made . . . When I returned from the physical shock of Nagasaki . . . I tried to persuade my colleagues in governments and in the United Nations that Nagasaki should be preserved exactly as it was then. I wanted all future conferences on disarmament, and on other issues which weigh the fates of nations, to be held in that ashy, clinical sea of rubble. I still think as I did then, that only in this forbidding context could statesmen make realistic judgments of the problems which they handle on our behalf. Alas, my official colleagues thought nothing of my scheme; on the contrary, they pointed out to me that delegates would be uncomfortable in Nagasaki.[10]

In this quotation Bronowski poignantly describes a plight similar to that confronting the social scientist. Social science, to use Bronowski's phrase, is an effort to stave off the erosion of our sense of the context within which judgments must be made. It is an attempt to prevent, in our complex day and age, having men destroy each other because of fears arising from ignorance.

---

[10] J. Bronowski, *Science and Human Values* (Torchbooks, rev. ed.; New York: Harper & Row, Publishers, 1965), p. xiv. I strongly urge anyone going into science, either natural or social, both to read and to ponder Bronowski's essays.

It is an attempt to maintain a strong factual basis for decisions involving our-selves. Just as physical science is a network of judgments concerning physical reality, so is social science a network of judgments concerning social reality. To the extent these judgments are valid and to the extent they deal with sig-nificant and crucial aspects of our social environment, to that extent social science is as practical as all other forms of intellectual enterprise—perhaps more practical.

In a few instances the practical consequences of a program of research in the social or behavioral sciences have been dramatic and immediately ap-parent. A classic example of this is the Hawthorne Plant studies conducted in the 1920s by the Western Electric Company. The researchers were con-cerned with factors promoting worker efficiency. They speculated, since the work involved assembling small electrical relays, that a certain optimum level of illumination would be most conducive to high levels of worker productivity.

They improved lighting conditions for an experimental group in the factory and found, not to their surprise, that worker efficiency improved. Then, as they increased and decreased lighting conditions far beyond reasonable op-timums, they were astonished to observe that worker efficiency continued to increase. They then played with various levels of lighting and found worker efficiency remained extremely high—even when the level of illumination began to approach that of a full moon on a clear summer's evening.[11] After search-ing about for some factor which had to be upsetting the whole program of research, someone suggested it might be the social influence of the research activity itself that was causing things to go awry.

This proved to be the case. The experimental workers in the factory had developed feelings of being special—after all, they were being observed by college-trained scientists. The particular social treatment given the workers in the experiment led to increased morale and increased productivity. The practical consequences of this were immediately apparent. Management began, after the Hawthorne Plant studies, to focus on promoting worker morale. The value of the social status of the worker, vis-à-vis physical work settings, was reconsidered.

But the practical consequences of social science are not always so dramatic and overwhelmingly obvious. In fact, there are many occasions when the social scientist seems to be making assertions which are not only impractical

---

[11] See F. J. Roethlisberger and W. J. Dickson, *Management and the Worker* (Cambridge, Mass.: Harvard University Press, 1941).

—they appear to be attempts to rend the fabric of society. Take, for example, Emile Durkheim's assertions on the normality of crime. What practical value can be given to the claim that crime is normal? Worse yet, the whole thing sounds like an apology for crime. If crime is normal, why try to stop it? I do not want to go too far with all of this. Durkheim's conceptions and their practical value are discussed more fully in the next chapter. But it serves to highlight the problem under discussion. I would like to suggest, and this will have to suffice, that Durkheim's conception of crime is highly practical insofar as it provides us with a more realistic understanding of the setting within which crime occurs. It may be comfortingly simple to believe that crime is the product of an evil personality or a perverted mind. But such a notion isolates us from an understanding of the context in which crime occurs. In a sense, by misleading us, such ideas function to create the very conditions they are supposed to explain. Durkheim, though presenting a complex conception of the social world of man, winds up giving us one which is more practical than many simpler ideas.

The practicality and the novelty that natural science brings to mankind come out of technology. By means of technology the scientist has been able to produce machines and creations which have no resemblance to anything arising from "natural" processes. We are awed by the slamming thunder of a sonic boom and we are impressed by the spectacle of a man living on blood being circulated through his system by the heart of another person. These are not "natural" occurrences. Their man-made character is obvious.

When we come to the realm of human behavior, however, a curious turpitude sets in. The "unnatural" modifications of human nature that may be socially produced, the reforms in character which might be instituted by social science, come to be seen eventually as a normal and "human" manner of behaving. Physical science, through its machines—and art, through its various manifestations of technique—can demonstrate the contrast between man and nature. The social scientist has no machines to speak of. He has little technique. Yet his influence has produced modifications in human character perhaps as significant as those brought about by the jet plane or the invention of the incandescent light bulb.

The only problem is that social modifications, once introduced, become such an integral part of human social meanings and definitions that people remain unaware of the extent to which the social philosopher or scientist has had an influence. For this reason, perhaps, Americans are more aware of the part that Thomas Edison plays in their lives than they are of the part played by Karl Marx.

About the men in this book

Now I must turn from the practicality and influence of social thought to the fourteen men whose writings and characters constitute the subject matter of this book. Most identify themselves professionally as sociologists. Two are anthropologists and one, during his lifetime, was a meteorologist. But all of them show a concern for humanity and the enigma that is mankind. To use an expression cited by C. Wright Mills, they all ". . . did their damnedest with their brains." Most importantly, they all, in varying degrees, remain within the social scientific boundaries prescribed by naturalism, social determinism, generalization, and objectivity. These qualities, as I have already indicated, distinguish the work of a social scientist from that of a novelist or journalist. There is a very apparent difference between the way a sociologist handles, for example, the issue of racial discrimination and the way a sensitive novelist like James Baldwin handles it.

This book is not an effort to drive further boundary stakes into the ground of intellectual endeavor in an attempt to specify the lines which separate the domain of the sociologist from that of the humanist. Nor is this book an attempt to suggest that sociologists and social scientists are no different from novelists, artists, or romantic philosophers—they are different! Moreover, it is a difference which makes a difference.

Though there are considerable differences between humanistic and social science perspectives, I would like to see greater recognition given to the fact that each has much to gain from the other.[12] It is possible today for a pro-

---

[12] The rifts which exist between the humanities and the social sciences are the result of both sides' denigrating the other. A great humanistic critic such as Edmund Wilson displays a haughty contempt for sociological literature. E. E. Cummings sees scientists in general as "oneeyed sons of bitches." Auden would add to the list of commandments one more: Thou shalt not commit a social science.

On the other hand, social scientists have not always been kind in their appraisal of what they feel to be the fanciful and cheaply bought worlds of the imagination produced by the humanist. Lundberg, for example, is highly skeptical of the value of novels as a means of getting at the truth of human nature.

But the attack on the humanist has taken place at deeper and more seriously wounding levels. For the psychoanalytically oriented anthropologist, literature or art is to be taken as a datum—as a revelation of the ego of the author or the ethos of the culture—but it cannot be accepted for what it is trying to appear to be. It is surprising that psychoanalysis, which divests art of its meaning more thoroughly than any other behavioral science perspective, is more acceptable to the literary humanistic set than is, say, sociology. The reason for this probably resides in the fact that psychoanalysis still permits the cultivation of style while sociological writing virtually destroys any sense of humanistic style.

fessor of English to bring further meaning to a body of literature by using some of the theories, observations, and concepts of the social scientist.[13] It is also possible for a sociologist to use literary examples very effectively as a way of teasing further meaning out of formal sociological concepts.

Sometimes, in an effort to divorce himself from his humanistic origins, the social scientist has gone to great lengths to hide from others, and perhaps from himself, the fact that he is interested in matters which, for thousands of years, have interested the philosopher, the novelist, the poet, or the artist. In his struggles to achieve scientific respectability the social scientist has, for example, disclaimed an interest in evil—after all, it is an extremely difficult term to define and it certainly lacks objectivity. He is, instead, concerned with crime and delinquency—defined in strictly operational terms. Rather than show an interest in the "art" of love, he is concerned with family disorganization—measured by divorce rates. Rather than endow man with dramatically heroic or antiheroic qualities—which is the eternal humanistic effort—the social scientist seems to prefer talking in terms of bloodless abstractions which remove man, as a being, from the scene.

But language is often misleading. When a sociologist talks about family disorganization he is describing, in his own rhetoric, a process which is terribly human and, no matter how objectively described, painful to those involved. The sociologist is touching a subject which he must always share with the novelist and the artist. The clinical studies of divorced women by Goode are, in some ways, more revealing of the realities of human suffering than Albee's turbulent description of married life in the home of an associate professor of history.[14]

In this book I have tried to make explicit the implicit humanistic concerns of social scientists. Each of the fourteen men considered in the following pages touches on some problem which has already been deeply examined in humanistic literature—but the social scientist brings a new view. Emile Durkheim, in his own work and in works which later evolved from his ideas, looked at faith—particularly religious faith—and attempted to give it a secular place in human affairs. Max Weber examined the loci of power and, when he was

---

[13] A recent and very engaging case in point is the analysis of Victorian pornography by Steven Marcus. See Steven Marcus, *The Other Victorians* (New York: Basic Books, Inc., 1964).

[14] *Who's Afraid of Virginia Woolf* is an eloquent and dramatic statement of what is involved in the act of loving. But it is Albee's statement. W. J. Goode's *Women in Divorce* (New York: Free Press of Glencoe, 1956) is not so eloquent, but it is no less enlightening. A compilation of the experiences of a great number of people can, if ordered by a competent and thoughtful social scientist, have a different but equally profound impact.

done, the myth of the hero had lost some of its vigor. Merton examines the relationship between religion and science and concludes, interestingly enough, that the latter is a special manifestation of the former. Lundberg raised the question of duty—is it necessary for some men to respond mechanically to the tasks assigned them in order that the greater number may benefit? Lewis F. Richardson raised the issue of whether or not we are free and, more significantly, if we are free, does this mean we can never understand our natures? David Riesman forces us to examine some modern questions concerning the nature of individual integrity. Goffman presents some novel observations concerning hypocrisy. Peter Berger is concerned with the extent of social constraints on individual actions and how man may free himself from some of these constraints. Leslie White is concerned with the possibility that man may some day become unable to adjust to the cultural world he has created. Pitirim Sorokin finds modern society lost in sensationalism and attempts to ascertain why this is so and what the implications might be. Jules Henry is concerned with the extent to which modern culture represses man's ability to understand himself and live creatively. Albert K. Cohen takes up the old humanistic issue of the origins of evil. Finally, Theodore Caplow, in a brief and clever analysis, touches on the topic of man's rationality.

This quick run-through can only sketch some of the different humanistic themes which these social scientists have developed in their own way. The list is certainly not exhaustive and it suffers from the drawback that several writers may deal, in unique ways, with the same general humanistic concern. In radically different terms, for example, Lewis F. Richardson, C. Wright Mills, and Albert K. Cohen have something to say about the problem of individual responsibility.

The great concentration on methods which has characterized social science down to the present has caused the sociologist to eschew the nonscientific humanistic approach to man's problems. Often, in this effort to place barriers between the social scientist and the literary person, the social scientist has lost sight of the fact that actually there is little difference between the central concerns of sociology and those of humanistic literature. This book tries to indicate these common concerns without, at the same time, making any claims that social science is the only way to approach them. We have spent too much time, I believe, trying to resolve the problem of whether social science *or* literature should be turned to for inspiration and guidance in our lives. This way of phrasing the question, so typical of western forms of thinking, is unfortunate. A more profound question is to ask how we can use both sociology *and* the various humanistic pursuits to improve our condition. Each chapter in this book, therefore, attempts to point up the nature of the human-istic concerns of each of the social scientists considered here.

Let me warn the reader once more, before he continues, that it is impos-sible in a work of this kind to give any realistic presentation of the richness of thought contained in the works of men like Durkheim, Weber, Merton, or any of the others presented here. Therefore, I have had to be content with the hope that I have been able to catch something of the ''spirit'' of any given author. If I have been successful in this, then I remain confident the reader will wish to find out more about these men by turning to their original works. Only by going to the source can one understand the full extent to which these men have given of themselves and displayed the courage necessary to remain locked in a struggle with profound questions until the question began to ''give a little.''

2   The Sacred and the Profane: An Introduction to Emile Durkheim

The social world is largely invisible. That is to say, social relationships are usually not perceived directly by any of our senses; they can only be known by learning the meaning of the relationships to the participants. To a surprising extent many people, including some who should know better, think they can "see" social happenings. For example, when I ask students in introductory courses if they have ever seen a family, they quickly, and with few exceptions, reply in the affirmative. Of course they have "seen" families— after all, have they not lived in one for the past eighteen or nineteen years?

Although my students think they know a family when they "see" one, I have to inform them that they do not. The point is simple to make and its implications, as we shall presently note, are quite profound. Suppose we observe a young man walking down the street with his arm around the waist of a charming young woman, and, toddling behind them, are several children. In this situation we are immediately inclined to think we are looking at a "family." However, this collection of individuals might in no way constitute a family. Perhaps we are looking at an unmarried boy and girl who have been baby sitting for some neighbor; or, these people might be related or unrelated in a variety of other ways, none involving kin associations. We have no way of knowing whether they constitute a family unless we ask someone or unless we examine those credentials which certify them as a bona fide family.

Observation of the invisible

It comes as a mild shock to most people to be told that the entire web of human social interrelations is founded on many invisible and indirect meanings which we bestow on various individuals. Not only have we never seen a family, we have never seen a student. Nor have we seen a teacher. Nor have we ever seen a scientist, a saint, or a sinner. So it is with all socially defined statuses. We can observe the people who occupy such statuses;[1] but, until we are informed in some fashion that they occupy a certain status and are expected, as a result, to behave accordingly, we cannot respond in any appropriate manner.

The fact that the sociologist is confronted with the task of interpreting socially given meanings puts him in the position of being a kind of semanticist. Thus, although the sociologist might say he is studying the "status" of the Negro in modern America, he could equally well say he is studying what the "word" Negro means to Americans and what happens when they apply this word to a class of people.

The social world is, then, largely an invisible world. This constitutes a major methodological problem for the sociologist.[2] Sociology is supposed to be a science; and science, after all, is based on observation. What kind of science is it that devotes itself to an examination of events which are, by their very nature, not directly observable? I shall not belabor this question for long. Let it suffice, for the moment, to mention that many sciences, high energy physics for one, believe that it is valid to rely on indirect observations. The problem which the invisibility of social identities poses for scientific sociology should be left to weightier methodological treatises.[3] We will pass it by and move into the more engaging substantive implications of the invisible nature of the social world.

Social influences: effects and interpretation

Let us begin by establishing two fundamental and realistic principles. The first of these is that social influences, though not directly observable, may have observable effects. We cannot, for example, directly observe those ideas and those involvements which lead men into wars, but we can observe the

---

[1] Some epistemologists and philosophers would even dispute this contention, but we do not need to go into such cloudy flights here.

[2] This, of course, is not only a problem for the sociologist—every social scientist must cope with it. The cultural anthropologist, for example, is concerned as a scientist with the meanings which different events and things have for men in primitive societies. A true understanding of these can come only from an extensive "immersion" in the culture. One cannot merely observe what is happening at a physical or behavioral level and fully comprehend its anthropological value.

[3] Sociology certainly cannot be said to suffer from a lack of investigations into methodology; it perhaps suffers from an excessive concern with methods. As one writer commented, sociology is a field with the most methods and the fewest results. If this condition is so, it is a testimonial to the problems that exist in observing what we think we are observing when we talk about human social behavior.

aftermath of a bombing raid. We can say, then, that even though social forces remain hidden, they are nonetheless "real." They are real because they are real in their effects. If the invisibility of social forces appears to deny validity to the efforts of the social scientist, the real consequences of social involvements give his work a scientific justification. Science, after all, is the serious examination of what is real.

It is necessary to mention this first principle because some people want to deny the reality of social forces.[4] Apparently they go by the old maxim that sticks and stones can break one's bones but social meanings will never hurt anyone. We are saying, quite to the contrary, that society, though "invisible" and indirect, is powerfully real—it can be malignant as well as benign. It is real because it is real in its consequences.

The second principle we must develop before going on is that the invisible and indirect nature of the social realm makes it subject to considerable interpretation. Social influences daily confront us with the equivalent of "black box" problems. "Black box" problems are those given to students in electronics who observe the electrical energies going into and coming out of a mysterious black box—they must then determine what is in the box on the basis of this information. So it is in society. We are given various kinds of information and, more importantly, misinformation about people and we must reach some conclusions about what makes them tick the way they do. This second principle—that social behavior is subject to interpretation—is significant because, paradoxically enough, the form which the interpretation of social forces will take comes from society itself. It is this feature of society which gives it a power over the individual that it would otherwise lack.

Let me briefly illustrate what I mean when I say that society provides the form of its own interpretation. In earlier times, when a person behaved in a peculiar fashion he was likely to be accused of harboring demonic spirits. This was in keeping with the religious temper of the times. Today, we would be more likely to say that such a person is "sick." There is surprisingly little difference between the two interpretations of what is going on inside the "black box." Both kinds of interpretations are ways of legitimizing the use of repressive sanctions against the individual. Both interpretations provide society with a justification for imposing penalties on the person who is violating proper standards of conduct. Both interpretations are capable, to a sur-

---

[4] A debate has gone on for years among sociologists as to whether or not society is "real." A very popular technical treatment of this argument appears in a paper by Charles K. Warriner. See "Groups Are Real: An Affirmation," *American Sociological Review*. 21 (October 1956), 549–554.

prising degree, of blinding us to the moral or external or normal qualities of the behavior of the person we have believed to be possessed of the devil or of "sickness." In this fashion we are armed by socially authorized forms of interpretations with the rationale for injuring others in the name of keeping them in their proper social place. The surprising thing is that this occurs in even the most sophisticated and knowledgeable of social orders.

If the fact that the social world is veiled or hidden behind meanings creates problems for the social analyst living in an age of modern sophistication, how much more so must it generate difficulties for men living in primitive social systems. How does primitive man respond to the social "black box" problem? How does primitive man come to grips with the extremely complex, indirect, powerful, and invisible forces of social influence? According to our second principle he must endow these forces with properties he understands—he must reduce them to terms that fall within the rhetoric of his culture. Even as we, in a scientific age, attempt to reduce social forces to the rhetoric of science, so must primitive man rely on his beliefs, his culturally given awareness, for social understanding. The end product of the primitive effort is often a mythology populated by supernatural beings or powers. The mechanism inside the "black box" is a spiritual force. This, in a very brief and inadequate condensation, is the argument made by Emile Durkheim in *The Elementary Forms of the Religious Life*.[5] This book is considered by some writers to be his finest work.[6]

Religion as a form of sociology

What Durkheim suggests is that religion is actually a primitive form of sociology; religion is an interpreter of the social order and, as such, also its fountainhead.

It is a consistent part of Durkheim's conception of religion that a deity expresses in a personal form the power of the society, a power clearly felt, though not so consciously defined. God is society "apotheosized"; society is the real God. This identity is adumbrated in the totem animal, a "sacred object"; and more clearly shown in the personal deity, Jahveh, or Zeus. The tribal god is, like the totem

---

[5] Emile Durkheim, *The Elementary Forms of the Religious Life,* translated by J. W. Swain (New York: Free Press of Glencoe, 1954). Durkheim's other major works, all published by Free Press of Glencoe, are *The Division of Labor in Society,* translated by George Simpson (1964); *Education and Sociology,* translated by S. D. Fox (1956); *Moral Education: A Study in the Theory and Application of the Sociology of Education,* translated by E. K. Wilson and H. Schnurer (1961); *The Rules of Sociological Method,* translated by S. A. Solovay and J. H. Mueller (1950); *Suicide, A Study in Sociology,* translated by J. A. Spaulding and G. Simpson (1951).

[6] See Harry Alpert, *Emile Durkheim and His Sociology* (New York: Columbia University Press, 1939). Alpert's work is one of the better reviews of Durkheim's contributions to modern social thought.

animal, often confusedly conceived of as a member of the group; another evidence of the close relationship between group and deity.[7]

Durkheim, despite his agnostic and scientific mentality, held that society could not exist independently of religious forms of sentiment and action. Into any social event there will intrude religious forms of expression. Even science, that most secular and skeptical form of human enterprise, is not immune to religious modes of thought and conduct. Indeed, to the extent science grows and acquires the character of a "community," we might expect to find it incorporating more of the characteristics of a religious institution.[8]

But what are these characteristics? The most essential, in Durkheim's thought, is the quality of sacredness. Every society distinguishes between the sacred and the profane. This distinction is crucial and highly relevant to sociological understanding, for it is essentially a distinction between the social and the nonsocial. That which is considered sacred in a society is given its awesome sacred qualities by virtue of its capacity to represent values, sentiments, power, or beliefs which are shared in common—the sacred object comes out of and is supported by the total society. The profane object, on the other hand, is not supported in this manner. It may have considerable utility, but it gains its value primarily from the extent to which it is useful to some individual—it has little or no public relevance.

An illustration will clarify what Durkheim is saying. When Babe Ruth was a living idol to baseball fans, the bat he used to slug his home runs was definitely a profane object. It was Ruth's personal instrument and had little social value *in itself*. Today, however, one of Ruth's bats is enshrined in the Baseball Hall of Fame.[9] It is no longer used by anyone. It stands, rather, as an object which in itself represents the values, sentiments, power, and beliefs of all members of the baseball community. What was formerly a profane object is now in the process of gaining some of the qualities of a sacred object.

I purposely selected an illustration here which leads us away from traditional conceptions of sacred objects. Durkheim extends the concept of sacredness in such a manner that we come to see the process whereby the profane is transmuted into the sacred in a wide variety of realms. In the case of the bat in the Baseball Hall of Fame we have a profane object undergoing a mild

---

[7] Charles Elmer Gehlke, *Emile Durkheim's Contributions to Sociological Theory* (New York: Columbia University, Longmans, Green & Company, Agents, 1915), p. 39.

[8] A recent sociological investigation of science as a community has some pertinent observations. See Warren O. Hagstrom, *The Scientific Community* (New York: Basic Books, Inc., 1965).

[9] The introduction of religious elements into a secular pastime provides some insight into the nature of traditionally religious structures. Such "shrines" as the Baseball Hall of Fame take on some of the qualities of parareligious systems.

and limited form of transmutation into the sacred—it is being changed from a private object to a public object. In the process it is becoming distinctive in a very special way.

The difference between sacred and profane objects has much to do with a comprehension of the nature of religious institutions. The definitive feature of a church or religious institution resides in the fact that the church is an organized body of people concerned with maintaining and responding to sacred objects.

> Thus a definition of religion exists: ". . . an interdependent system of faiths and practices relating to things sacred—that is, to such things as are separate and proscribed, faiths and practices uniting all their adherents in a single community, known as a Church."[10]

We respond to the sacred object with a sense of awe and respect. This response may, on occasion, be so overwhelming that we think our feelings come from the sacred object itself. This, argued Durkheim, would be a mistake. The reason is fairly simple—anything and everything imaginable has, at one time or other, served the purpose of being a sacred object. An object that invokes mysterious and serious feelings in one man can generate laughter in another.

Because such a variety of objects may serve as sacred things, the awesome character of the sacred object must come from outside itself. The sacred object represents or symbolizes some force which is capable of inducing submission, awe, a sense of personal impotence, humility, and powerlessness. The force which is capable of achieving this, in relation to the person, is society. Thus, Durkheim comes to the conclusion that the sacred object is actually a symbolic representation of social force.

Following in Durkheim's footsteps, a modern sociologist, Guy Swanson of the University of Michigan, has carried the argument further. [11] If the sacred object is a representation of society, and if societies differ in the way they

---

[10] Maurice Halbwachs, *Sources of Religious Sentiment* (New York: Free Press of Glencoe, 1962), p. 23. Halbwachs was one of Durkheim's most brilliant students. In this book he carefully summarizes, mostly in Durkheim's own words, the central thoughts contained in *The Elementary Forms of the Religious Life.* I would recommend that a student interested in this subject read Habwachs and then turn to the more elaborate discussion by Durkheim.

[11] Guy E. Swanson, *The Birth of the Gods: The Origin of Primitive Beliefs* (Ann Arbor: The University of Michigan Press, 1960). Swanson's argument, and more significantly his data, reveal the current vitality of Durkheim's thinking in modern sociology. I should add here that I once gave a talk about Swanson to a church study group and the Episcopalian priest who led it. The conclusions of the work angered some of the audience who considered them a threat to their beliefs. However, the priest, a man thoroughly trained in Freudian psychoanalytic theory, said to me, "Very interesting; now I am aware that God works through society as well as through the mind."

are organized, then some of the socially held conceptions of the nature of the sacred should vary systematically with the way in which the society is ordered. Regrettably, we cannot explore all of the ideas and facts which appear in Swanson's work. We can indicate something of its spirit and its connection with Durkheim's thinking, however, by concentrating on how Swanson demonstrates the connection between monotheistic religious beliefs and a particular type of social structure.

God and the symbols associated with God fall in the realm of the sacred. In fact, it is not especially rare to find religions in which even the name of God is so sacred it may not be uttered aloud. What accounts for the form which these ideas take? If Durkheim is correct, there must be some association between a given social structure and the conception of God which exists in that society. Swanson presents the idea that religions organized around the concept of a single God are associated with organizational difficulties which develop as a society becomes more complex.

At this point, before we can begin to understand something of the Durkheim–Swanson argument, it is necessary to introduce a qualification. When we talk of monotheism we must be aware that we are rarely talking about spiritual conceptions which involve only one God and no more than one God. Usually we are referring to religions which involve a number of gods, spirits, and heavenly beings with a supreme God or heavenly being standing above this spiritual host. Instead of using the term "monotheism," Swanson prefers to use the term "high-god" religions. Our own Judaic-Christian religious beliefs provide us with a "high-god" religion of this type. There is not only the supreme God, but there is Satan, also a powerful god, who rivals the ultimate forces of the spiritual world. More significantly, and more notable to the sociologist, Satan is essentially a disruptive force—a constant threat to the solidarity and smooth operation of the community. The intercession of God Himself is usually required to keep Satan from wrecking the life of any individual and the community which that individual serves.[12]

Now we can come back to Swanson's work and rephrase our question slightly: At what point in a society's development does the concept of a high-god begin to appear in its religious beliefs and practices?[13] Swanson, again

---

[12] I concede that Satan is a more complex personality than I have made him out here. He may not always be directly disruptive. For example, in the story *The Devil and Daniel Webster*, Satan offers wealth, position, and a life of happiness for Webster's soul. Presumably Satan may thereby build up his power within the spiritual realm and then prove even more disruptive later on.

[13] I have used the phrase "At what point in a society's *development* . . ." This makes Swanson sound more evolutionary than the specific facts of his study would warrant. I have done this in the interest of making a very complicated point in a relatively brief space. Technically speaking, Swanson's study is cross-sectional rather than longitudinal.

on the basis of an extension of Durkheim's thinking, suggests that a high-god will appear when organizational elements within a society begin to conflict with each other and bring about the demand for a higher authority which can resolve these conflicts. Thus, a society organized on a strictly kinship basis, where the family is the principal organizing agency and has no other agencies conflicting with it, will have no conception of a high-god. The character of the society would not require it. Such a society might believe in a diffused spiritual force, sometimes called *mana*,[14] or it might have other religious conceptions, but the idea of a high-god will not appear.

Also, for theoretical reasons too involved to go into here, a society comprised of two major organizational groupings would not have a conception of a high-god. However, when we get into the realm of three or more major organizational groupings, we move into a situation where one of the groupings must become dominant over the other two and must function to resolve conflicts between subordinate major components of the society. Thus, a society organized into kinship units which, in turn, are parts of tribes which, in their turn, are parts of a still higher level of organization—such as a kingdom or nation—will be likely to have a religion which involves the idea of a high-god. The concept of a high-god is a manifestation of the organizational characteristics of the society.

All of this has been highly speculative and abstract. We are still left with the question: Is there any way of demonstrating whether this is true or not? Swanson's work indicates that there is a way and, moreover, that such a demonstration suggests Durkheim was correct in his speculations.

To test the Swanson–Durkheim theory concerning high-god religions Swanson obtained data from 39 primitive cultures and examined their social structure and their religious beliefs. With the aid of several assistants, Swanson divided the 39 cultures into those which had religions involving the concept of a high-god and those which did not. The 39 cultures were also divided into those having a "simple" social structure involving only one or two sovereign groups and those with "complex" structures involving three or more sovereign groups.

According to the theory, the idea of a high-god should appear only in the cultures with complex social structures. Cultures with simple social structures should not have high-god religions. When Swanson ordered his facts he obtained the following distribution of cultures:[15]

---

[14] Swanson, *The Birth of the Gods,* pp. 6–10.
[15] *Ibid.,* p. 65. This is a slightly modified version of Swanson's table; original copyrighted 1960 by The University of Michigan Press.

HIGH-GOD	NUMBER OF SOVEREIGN GROUPS	
	(Simple) One or two	(Complex) Three or more
Present	2 (against theory)	17 (for theory)
Absent	17 (for theory)	3 (against theory)

So, out of the 39 cultures examined by Swanson, 34 conformed to the theory and 5 deviated. Statistical tests by Swanson indicated that the amount of conformity to the theory was much greater than we might reasonably expect simply by accident. Therefore, the facts do not give us cause to reject Durkheim's general theoretical position.

Swanson, advancing further the theoretical perspectives of Durkheim, investigated such other aspects of religious belief as the idea of a morally concerned God, witchcraft, the existence of the soul, and similar concepts. He found them also to be related to different features of the social structure. We cannot go into these demonstrations here. Exciting as Swanson's research is, we must leave it and return to Durkheim.

Moral order and social structure

We have begun with Durkheim's speculations on religion because they quickly lead us to the heart of his understanding of society. For Durkheim, the only legitimate approach to a comprehension of the nature of social order is by an examination of morality. Because morality and religious thought are so closely conjoined in primitive societies, the investigation of primitive religious thought can be especially revealing to the sociologist. In modern society the relationship between moral order and religious practice is more tenuous, but this does not diminish the value of examining moral force as a means of comprehending human social nature.

> But if there is one fact that history has irrefutably demonstrated it is that the morality of each people is directly related to the social structure of the people practicing it. The connection is so intimate that, given the general character of the morality observed in a given society and barring abnormal and pathological cases, one can infer the nature of that society, the elements of its structure and the way it is organized. Tell me the marriage patterns, the morals dominating family life, and I will tell you the principal characteristics of its organization.[16]

[16] Emile Durkheim, *Moral Education: A Study in the Theory and Application of the Sociology of Education*, translated by E. K. Wilson and H. Schnurer (New York: Free Press of Glencoe, 1961), p. 87. In 1887 Durkheim began his distinguished thirty-year-long career at the University of Bordeaux. This was the first time a French university offered a course in social science. Five years later he moved to the Sorbonne—the University of Paris—where he spent the remainder of his life. Durkheim taught not only social science but pedagogy, and he taught these subjects jointly throughout his career. (See Alpert, *Emile Durkheim and His Sociology*, p. 43.)

In his doctoral dissertation, published ten years before the above state-ment appeared, Durkheim presented, at great length, the rationale under-lying his claim. This work, entitled *The Division of Labor in Society*, reveals that a superb sociologist can hold views of society as radically different from those of the common man as the views of physical reality held by the best physicists. We can give some hint of the radical nature of Durkheim's thought by presenting his views on crime.

Crime, for Durkheim, is a natural consequence of the existence of a col-lectively supported morality. Crime is therefore a natural part of *any* social order because any social order requires a collectively supported morality. In itself this does not seem radical or inventive—but it rather quickly leads to a more comprehensive understanding of the nature of criminal action than we can acquire through biological or even psychological approaches to criminal behavior.

One of the perplexing aspects of criminal action noted by Durkheim is the fact that it is often behavior which is not directly harmful to society or to any individual. As Durkheim notes,

> What social danger is there in touching a tabooed object, an impure animal or man, in letting the sacred fire die down, in eating certain meats, in failure to make the traditional sacrifice over the graves of parents, in not exactly pronouncing the ritual formula, in not celebrating certain holidays, etc.?[17]

We cannot, then, simple-mindedly define crime as behavior which is directly injurious to the physical safety of the members of a society. There are too many exceptions to such a definition. Even more notably, there are many cases of crimes which, though physically injurious, are less seriously punished than crimes which violate an exotic code—and Durkheim makes much of this fact. A modern example of what we are talking about is the fact that a white man, in the United States of America, who kills a Negro is likely to be less severely punished than a Negro who rapes a white woman.

We have to give up the whole idea that crime is a simple form of injury to society when we consider further that some actions which are capable of completely disrupting the entire society often carry no criminal onus at all. A stock market collapse, for example, can disorganize the social body over-whelmingly—but it is not viewed as a criminal act.[18] A man may give serious

---

[17] Reprinted with permission of The Macmillan Company from *The Division of Labor in Society* by Emile Durkheim, p. 72. © The Free Press of Glencoe 1960.

[18] *Ibid.*, p. 72. This is Durkheim's example. The objection might be raised that a market collapse does not involve intent to engage in crime. Durkheim would reply that in all probability most societies have not, throughout history, been concerned with intent in reacting to criminal action.

consideration to an action which he has some reason to believe might result in the deaths of thousands of people and yet be applauded as a hero rather than a potential criminal of fantastic magnitude.[19] Crime is not, then, something which is actually or potentially physically harmful to society. Durkheim asks,

> Shall we say [in modifying our conception of crime] that criminal acts are those which *seem* harmful to the society that represses them, that penal rules express, not the conditions which are essential to social life, but those which *appear* such to the group which observes them?[20]

This would seem to be an easy way out of the matter—but Durkheim refuses to accept the gambit. There is more to it than that. This solution, appealing though it is, does not really get us anywhere because it does not tell us why societies have introduced rules which are apparently useless. The important thing is to find out why various rules are considered vitally necessary— even when no direct connection between the rules and the viability of the society can be ascertained. Why, for example, was the Medieval Church so morbidly interested in sexual delinquency? Anthropological studies have revealed numerous societies that sustained themselves admirably with sexual patterns which the church would have condemned as highly perverse and disruptive.[21]

The problem is resolved if we can comprehend the extent to which Durkheim is able to distinguish between the form and the content of social action. Though many rules may seemingly have little connection with the efficient operation of a society, they may, through the possibility of their violation, remain as standards of the effectiveness of the moral force of the total society. In this respect, it makes little difference what the rule might be. Indeed, the more powerful the moral force of the total society, the more arbitrary the rules of the system can be and still serve as standards of the strength of that force.

It is this kind of reasoning which enables Durkheim to make an unusual observation concerning the nature of crime. He asserts,

---

[19] I am thinking, here, of the following news item which appeared in the May 13, 1967, issue of the *New York Times.* "Washington, May 12.—It may have sounded ominous, but to the White House it was just a regrettable coincidence that no amount of explanation could overcome . . . What had been for months President Johnson's personal story . . . suddenly broke into print today . . . On the women's page of the *Washington Post*—a staple in the news diet of every foreign diplomat here—[a news item] read, 'President Johnson told his daughter, Luci, last June, "Your daddy may go down in history as having started World War III. . . ."' He felt he had no alternative, he said . . . and he felt he had taken all possible precautions to limit the effects, but there was reason to worry."

[20] Durkheim, *The Division of Labor in Society*, p. 73.

[21] Mead and Calas cite a study which reports the marriage of a Chuckchee shaman to another male in the tribe. The institutional incorporation of homosexual relations did not destroy Chuckchee society. See Margaret Mead and Nicolas Calas, *Primitive Heritage* (New York: Random House, 1953).

. . . we must not say that an action shocks the common conscience because it is criminal, but rather that it is criminal because it shocks the common conscience. We do not reprove it because it is a crime, but it is a crime because we reprove it.[22]

Murder classically illustrates Durkheim's argument. Murder receives whatever criminal status it acquires according to the extent to which it is reproved by society—not because murder in itself calls for its own evaluation as a moral affront. There are occasions, even in our own contemporary society, where murder, broadly defined as taking the life of another against that person's will, is not reproved and is not, therefore, criminal. Police have, at times, beaten prisoners to death without arousing any great sense of moral indignation in the community they served.

Thus, criminality does not inhere within the specific form of an illegal action but rather in the content of that action when viewed in terms of the affront it offers to the moral conscience of the entire society. Curiously enough, according to Durkheim, the stronger the moral conscience of a society, the more likely we are to find murder less reproved than are acts against the body of rules which exist as the moral authority of the society. Durkheim states,

> Thus, in lower societies, the most numerous delicts are those which relate to public affairs, delicts against religion, against custom, against authority, etc. We need only look at the Bible, the laws of Manou, at the monuments which remain of old Egyptian law to see the relatively small place accorded to prescriptions for the protection of individuals, and, contrariwise, the luxuriant development of repressive legislation concerning the different forms of sacrilege, the omission of certain religious duties, the demands of ceremonial, etc. At the same time, these crimes are the most severely punished. Among the Jews, the most abominable attacks are those against religion. Among the ancient Germans, only two crimes were punished by death according to Tacitus: treason and desertion. According to Confucius and Meng-tseu, impiety is a greater crime than murder. In Egypt, the smallest sacrilege was punished by death.[23]

Crime is behavior which has its meaning only because it violates the moral sentiments of society. It is a threat to the integrity of those sentiments and, as a consequence, produces a reaction. It is in the reaction that Durkheim comprehends the distinction between collective force and the nature of the individual. The general reaction to crime is punishment; but the significant thing about punishment is the extent to which it is carried.

Capital punishment is a case in point. If a criminal were to "pay society" for his misdeeds by giving his life, then it would seem sufficient merely to

---

[22] Durkheim, *The Division of Labor in Society*, p. 81.
[23] *Ibid.*, p. 93.

take his life in the simplest and most direct manner possible. But this is not done, even in modern and presumably enlightened cultures. There is an institutionalized form of harassment that goes with taking the criminal's life. There are demeaning actions which seem to have the purpose not only of taking the criminal's life but of taking his humanity as well. He may, for example, have to spend his last hours in a cell which is lighted twenty-four hours a day. He may have to remain in the continuous presence of a guard. His head may be shaved. He has to wear shabby clothes and experience other forms of humiliation. The taking of life is not enough.

A Durkheimian view suggests that our judicial system possibly errs on the side of oversentimentalism in some matters. There is a peculiar illogic in taking two men convicted of the same crime and placing one of them in a hospital because he is ''insane'' and the other in a prison because he is ''normal.'' What we are doing in such instances is confessing that, since one individual is ''normal,'' what brought about the commission of the crime is not evidently an inherent serious defect in character. It must, therefore, have been something else, and the only other reasonable thing left is social circumstance. But social circumstances cannot be held culpable and it is necessary to assess culpability. Therefore, because he is guilty of being normal, the sane person may be executed while the insane person is sent to an asylum.

It would seem, if we were being reasonable about this matter, that a person's normalcy would stand as the greatest argument for not punishing him. Current thinking is evidently based on the idea that a presumably normal person who violates the existing social code threatens, more so than an insane person, the viability of that code. Our reaction is not one which is concerned with the welfare of the person who broke the code. Instead, we are concerned with the welfare of the code itself. To the extent the violator is considered ''normal'' yet subjected to punishment he must be seen as a sacrifice for the welfare of the many. Durkheim would suggest this is characteristic of all societies.

The extreme and ''irrational'' qualities of punishment are a clue, for Durkheim, to the nature of collective sentiments. We are not only concerned with making the criminal ''pay,'' when we punish him, but we are concerned with making him an embodiment of suffering which balances the affront to the moral order.

It is certain that at the bottom of the notion of expiation there is the idea of a satisfaction accorded to some power, real or ideal, which is superior to us. When we desire the repression of crime, it is not we that we desire to avenge personally, but to avenge something sacred which we feel more or less confusedly outside and above us. This something we conceive of in different ways according to the time and the place. Sometimes it is a simple idea, as morality, duty; most often we represent it in the form of one or several concrete beings: ancestors, divinity. That is why penal law is not alone essentially religious in origin, but indeed always retains a certain religious stamp. It is because the acts that it punishes appear to be attacks upon something transcendent . . .[24]

The power of the moral order comes from the fact that it is a collectively held set of beliefs. That is to say, it is a set of strongly held beliefs shared in common by a large number of people—it lies within the public as well as the individual domain. It is essential to understand that it is the collective nature of the moral order which gives it tremendous influence and which elevates it above any single individual. Indeed, the moral order acquires a solidarity *sui generis* (of its own kind). For this reason, crimes are more than an affront to the individual—they are a threat to the solidarity of the moral order, and the reaction is beyond anything which might seem reasonable to a dispassionate observer.

Thus it is that we, from our present disengaged vantage point, can feel a sense of horror when we read the punishment prescribed by the ancient Germans for damaging a tree,

Sacred groves were common among the ancient Germans, and tree-worship is hardly extinct amongst their descendants at the present day. How serious that worship was in former times may be gathered from the ferocious penalty appointed by the old German laws for such as dared to peel the bark of a standing tree. The culprit's navel was to be cut out and nailed to the part of the tree which he had peeled, and he was to be driven round and round the tree till all his guts were wound about its trunk.[25]

Whether anyone actually had to suffer this dreadful punishment I am not able to say—certainly history offers us countless examples of people who were made the objects of obsessive punishments. Even if no one actually experienced this gruesome punitive measure of the ancient Germans, it exemplifies what Durkheim is trying to say. From a modern perspective it seems unthinkable that anyone could want to disembowel a man merely because he damaged a tree. And that is Durkheim's point! The reaction hinted at in this old punishment transcends a rational, objective, and individualistic consideration of the matter. The threat is not to an individual sentiment but to a collectively shared sentiment—and the reaction stems from that collective source,

---

[24] *Ibid.*, p. 100.
[25] Sir James G. Frazer, *The Golden Bough* (New York: The Macmillan Company, 1922), p. 127. Note the discrepancy between Frazer's comment and Durkheim's reference to Tacitus cited earlier. According to Durkheim, only treason and desertion were punishable by death among the ancient Germans.

not from an individual source. So it is that we must come to understand crime and punishment as actions and reactions taking place at a collective level.

Durkheim's considerations of crime are actually a means of entering into a greater matter—an examination of the changing nucleus of social order. Repressive punishment occurs when the solidity of a society comes from its collective commitment to a moral order of some kind. By sharing similar beliefs, traditions, and moral sentiments men are kept together. But this form of social integration is in the process of being supplanted by another. The key to this is the fact that repressive punishment has been steadily declining in severity. Taking its place is punishment more concerned with the attainment of restitution than with making an example through torture.

The division of labor and social structure

If this is so—if we are witnessing the decline of social organization based on moral consensus—then what is the basis of the newer forms of social order? The answer, says Durkheim, is social order based increasingly on a complex interweaving of highly specialized and discrete units which, together, make up an organic whole, somewhat as the separate and specialized organs of the body make up an individual.[26]

Such a society, organized on the basis of the division of labor, acquires an increasing amount of differentiation between its parts.[27] As this division occurs, the moral basis which forms the common sentiments underlying the society grows broader but does not cease to exist. The violent forms of reaction which characterize its existence in primitive cultures give way to reproval of a more feeble sort. A congressman who violates the codes of ethics of Congress, such as they are, is not drawn and quartered and his head placed on a pike for all to witness. He may receive a censure or, at most, be ousted from office. Of societies organized on the basis of a division of labor Durkheim says,

---

[26] Durkheim is careful to probe further than a simple physiological analogy would suggest. Indeed, he went to great lengths to show the limitations of a biological model for the analysis of society. Durkheim stated, ". . . the division of social labor is distinguished from the division of physiological labor by an essential characteristic. In the organism, each cell has its defined role, and cannot change it. In societies, tasks have never been so immutably distributed." See *The Division of Labor*, p. 329.

[27] Some idea of the extent of this differentiation in the modern United States can be ascertained by a quick reference to the *Dictionary of Occupational Titles*. It currently lists more than 35,550 job titles.

. . . even where society relies most completely upon the division of labor, it does not become a jumble of juxtaposed atoms, between which it can establish only external, transient contacts. Rather the members are united by ties which extend deeper and far beyond the short moments during which the exchange is made. Each of the functions they exercise is, in a fixed way, dependent upon others, and with them forms a solidary system. Accordingly, from the nature of the chosen task permanent duties arise. Because we fill some certain domestic or social function, we are involved in a complex of obligations from which we have no right to free ourselves. There is, above all, an organ upon which we are tending to depend more and more; this is the State. The points at which we are in contact with it multiply as do the occasions when it is entrusted with the duty of reminding us of the sentiment of common solidarity.[28]

The division of labor, specialization, the integration of highly differentiated parts—this is a later basis of social solidarity which comes out of and moves alongside the older moral basis. The division of labor is a second ring of force in a nucleus which has the moral order at its core.

This theme, the reality and force of the collectively supported moral order, is dominant in Durkheim's thinking and appears throughout all of his work. This theme provides the foundation for his masterful investigation into the nature of suicide. So brilliantly did Durkheim execute this combination of theory and research that it is even today lauded as a model of investigation in social science—though Durkheim published this work in 1897.[29]

Suicide and its relation to social forces

But why would Durkheim, a man interested in the nature of social organizations, be concerned with something as individualistic as suicide? The answer is that suicide provided Durkheim with a subject matter which permitted him to carry off a *tour de force*. If Durkheim's sociological perspectives permitted him to bring new understanding to that most individualistic of all acts— suicide—then sociology would be forcefully established as a perspective for examining other features of human behavior. How did Durkheim accomplish this demonstration?

---

[28] Durkheim, *The Division of Labor*, p. 227.

[29] Emile Durkheim, *Suicide* (see footnote 5). For a work published in 1897 concerning human social nature, this book is astonishingly sophisticated. One only needs to compare it with more run-of-the-mill social research conducted at the time to see how advanced Durkheim's thought was. This does not mean, however, that Durkheim did not make some serious methodological errors. For a balanced review of Durkheim's effort see Hanaan C. Selvin, "Durkheim's *Suicide:* Further Thoughts on a Methodological Classic," in Robert A. Nisbet's *Emile Durkheim* (Englewood Cliffs, N.J.: Prentice-Hall, Inc., 1965), pp. 113–136.

It would appear, from a commonsense perspective, that when one kills himself he has engaged in an act which is about as private and as removed from social approval as can be imagined—and in some instances this is probably so. For Durkheim, however, the issue was whether or not the intrusion of social influences could be found even here—in this most personal and final moment. If the intruding social forces could be found, then a nice case had been made for seeing man as more than the sum of his biological and psychological natures; he would have to be viewed also as a captive of social forces extending beyond him and shaping his private fate.[30]

Durkheim began his argument by suggesting that perhaps suicide is such an individualistic act it might not be of interest to a sociologist. Anything which would make suicide demonstrably a result of individualistic conditions would, therefore, negate a sociological consideration of the matter. So, it was necessary at the outset to consider all individualistic factors to determine whether or not they could account for self-inflicted deaths.

> But is [suicide] of interest to the sociologist? Since suicide is an individual action affecting the individual only, it must seemingly depend exclusively on individual factors, thus belonging to psychology alone. Is not the suicide's resolve usually explained by his temperament, character, antecedents and private history?[31]

Note here that Durkheim began by recognizing the theoretical position he intended to oppose. He was aware that he had to develop it thoroughly before he could enter into a discussion of the social perspective he endorsed.

The first psychological argument he took into account was the possibility that suicide is a product of insanity, of mental imbalance, of some derangement of a person's abilities. To refute this argument, Durkheim obtained data from hospitals for the mentally ill. He observed that the proportion of women in such hospitals was very slightly greater than the proportion of men. This being the case, he argued, we ought to expect suicide resulting from insanity to occur as often among women as among men. Suicide rates indicated, however, that men are between three and four times as prone to commit suicide as are women.[32]

---

[30] Durkheim is often viewed as an "anti-psychological" writer. This is not entirely correct. It is more fair to say he was concerned with getting people to recognize the value of social as well as biological and psychological factors in human affairs.

[31] Emile Durkheim, *Suicide, A Study in Sociology* (New York: Free Press of Glencoe, 1951), p. 46.

[32] Durkheim relied to a great extent, in this study of suicide, on what are today called "ecological" correlations. These are very tricky measures of association. See W. S. Robinson's article, "Ecological Correlations and the Behavior of Individuals," *American Sociological Review*, 15 (June 1950), 351–357.

Durkheim then examined the extent to which the incidence of insanity varied among Protestants, Catholics, and Jews. He found that people of Jewish faith were more likely to experience mental disorders than Protestants and Catholics. However, despite this, the Jewish people had lower suicide rates. From this Durkheim concluded that suicide varies in inverse proportion to psychopathic states rather than being consistent with them.[33]

But insanity is only one individualistic possibility. There are others. Perhaps, suggested Durkheim, alcoholism is a factor in suicide. Durkheim quickly discounted this by comparing maps of the distribution of suicides in France with maps showing the distributions of prosecution for alcoholism—there was no relationship between the two.

If abnormal psychological conditions and alcoholism do not account for suicide, perhaps there are yet other nonsocial influences which do. Race, for example, might have an effect on suicide. Durkheim did not have much racial variation among the nationalities he studied, but he showed great ingenuity in his analysis of the facts which were available at the time. Taking the Germans as a racial type,[34] he observed that in different Austrian provinces the proportion of Germans varied—ranging from very high to very low proportions. If the racial factor were important, Durkheim said, then suicide rates should vary along with the proportions of Germans in the provinces. But the suicide rates behaved very erratically in conjunction with Durkheim's "racial" factor. For example, provinces with very high proportions of Germans had both high and low suicide rates. Provinces with very low proportions of Germans also had high and low suicide rates. Durkheim concluded that race did not affect suicide.

Yet another class of nonsocial influences remained to be considered. Perhaps the physical environment had an effect on suicide. Possibly climate or weather might determine or at least be associated with self-destruction. Here Durkheim ran into a problem because the facts did support a relationship between seasonal changes in weather and the occurrence of suicide.

> . . . the monthly variations [in the incidence of suicide] obey the following law, found in all European countries: Beginning with January inclusive, the incidence of suicide increases regularly from month to month until about June and regularly decreases from that time to the end of the year.[35]

---

[33] This is Durkheim's wording. See *Suicide*, p. 72.

[34] Durkheim is using what would today be considered an "ethnic" or national type and not a racial type. Germans are part of a broader "Caucasian" racial grouping which includes most of the people of Europe who were included in Durkheim's data.

[35] Durkheim, *Suicide*, p. 111.

But any number of other social activities follow the same law. Railroads receipts are greatest in the summer and lowest in the winter. Accidents increase in the summer and decline in the winter. Crime increases in the summer and decreases in the winter.[36] Durkheim admitted there was a relationship but then discounted its significance by claiming that weather is simply associated with human activity in general. Because suicide is one form of human activity, it happens to vary with the weather.

Finally, Durkheim considered the possibility that suicide is a product of imitation or of mass contagion—one commits suicide because it is a fad. The evidence and arguments Durkheim used to dispense with this suggestion are too lengthy to dwell upon here. However, he made a comment which sums up his rejection of imitation as an explanation of suicide. He said,

> Certain authors, ascribing to imitation a power it does not possess, have demanded that the printing of reports of suicides and crimes in the newspapers be prohibited . . . Actually, what may contribute to the growth of suicide or murder is not talking of it but how it is talked of. Where such acts are loathed, the feelings they arouse penetrate the recital of them and thus offset rather than encourage individual inclinations. But inversely, when society is morally decadent, its state of uncertainty inspires in it an indulgence for immoral acts frankly expressed whenever they are discussed, and which obscures their immorality. Then example becomes truly dangerous not as example but because the revulsion it should inspire is reduced by social tolerance or indifference.[37]

What Durkheim is saying is that people do not blindly imitate actions which occur around them. Instead, people are more likely to follow or try to imitate behavior which is highly valued. But this changes the character of the problem. If this is so, then we must ask why societies come to value some forms of behavior and not others. We must also consider the position of the individual with respect to the possibility of attaining valued forms of social behavior. What happens, for example, when a man endows his life with meaning in terms of some code of conduct and then is not permitted to live in the manner which he has come to feel is important to him? If, under these circumstances, he commits suicide, it is certainly not imitative. It may, to the contrary, be a reaction to a denial to conform to a socially prescribed code.

We have not, in the above paragraphs, done justice to the patience and thoroughness of Durkheim's consideration of views which he felt were in

---

[36] Someone once observed that sex crimes were associated with ice cream consumption, that is, the more ice cream consumption in a community during a month, the larger the number of sex crimes. The explanation, of course, is that both ice cream consumption and sex crimes are associated with warmer weather.

[37] Durkheim, *Suicide*, p. 141.

error. We have, through his example, made one point, however. In the examination of human social conduct it is necessary to be as aware as possible of all existing relevant arguments and know the evidence which supports them.

Having considered positions contrary to his own, Durkheim went on to develop his sociological interpretation of suicide. Durkheim believed that the cause of suicide lay somewhere in the relationship which existed between the individual and the moral order constituting the society of which he was a member. This relationship can vary in nature and, accordingly, the individual is variously subject to inclinations toward suicide.

First Durkheim considered the case where the individual is related to the moral order in a normally binding way, but the moral order itself contains within it ideas which make the individual see himself as separated from it. For example, it is possible for some forms of moral order to place greater reliance on the individual—to make the individual responsible for his own affairs. In this event, the person does not have recourse to the community when things go wrong. He is personally accountable. Such a person, said Durkheim, will be more likely to commit suicide than will one who believes more readily he can turn to the community for support when he makes errors. Suicide coming from this sense of individualism—of a belief in freedom from the constraining moral order—Durkheim called *egoistic suicide*. Durkheim felt he had evidence to support this position by observing that suicide rates were higher among Protestants than among Catholics. The former religion placed the individual more on his own—freeing him from institutional constraints to a greater extent and making him vulnerable to the limitations of his own ego.

A second kind of relationship between the individual and the moral order that Durkheim considered was one in which there was an intense binding of the individual to society. In this instance the person is so closely tied into the social group and is so much a part of the moral order that he is willing to give his life for it. Suicide of this kind, Durkheim noted, still exists in the army and in those cultures which impose ancient forms of obedience. The rite of *hara-kiri* exemplifies this form of suicide. Durkheim used the term *altruistic suicide* to refer to this phenomenon.

The best example I can relate of altruistic suicide is a celebrated incident in Japanese history which occurred early in the 17th century and is known as the "Tale of the Forty-seven *Ronin*." This incident involved forty-seven *samurai* warriors who cunningly avenged the death of their master, a minor lord, who had committed *hara-kiri* after being insulted by an official in the *shogun's* palace. The *samurai* retainers of the *daimyo* killed the official of the *shogun* and then, according to their code, met together in a grove after the assassination. There each of the forty-seven men killed himself.

The distinction between egoistic and altruistic suicide is not always a clear one, yet it seems necessary. The suicide of a man who feels despondent and guilty because he believes he personally has done a wrong and there is no absolution seems different in kind from that of the *samurai* warriors who found honor in death.

Finally, Durkheim isolated a third form of suicide which he called *anomic suicide*. Anomic suicide, described in quite unacademic terms, is suicide resulting from the pain or disorientation which comes when we are pushed out of whatever social rut we have fallen into. As a person matures within a society he comes to develop a social character which is comfortable to him. He acquires a conception of the moral order that gives stability and meaning to his life. Various things can disrupt this. A poor man, for example, might suddenly fall heir to great wealth. Rather than finding the riches a blessing, the man might find himself alienated from his former impoverished friends while remaining unacceptable to the established rich—the classical Eliza Doolittle bind. This condition Durkheim referred to as *anomie*—a state of normlessness, of being pushed into a realm where the rules are either ill-defined, contradictory, or lacking. In such circumstances a person, torn away from the regulative influences of society, finds life unbearable. The result is anomic suicide. Durkheim felt that the higher rate of suicides found in times of economic crisis and among divorced persons supported his contention.

By relating suicide to social systems, Durkheim validated the sociological perspective in an almost sensational manner. He was wrong in many particulars, but the *tour de force* was accomplished nonetheless. After Durkheim it became impossible to view man as an autonomous being or society as merely man's biological nature extended over the landscape. Society had peculiar qualities which came about from the nature of social organization itself. Society was a condition *sui generis*. While society was, in general, beneficial to man and had enabled him to survive and achieve a dominant state on this planet, it still exacted a cost for some. Society enabled the majority to live, and, paradoxically, was the cause of death for a minority.

Durkheim in perspective

Durkheim worked at the end of a century of magnificent scientific achievements, two of which should be mentioned here. Above all, the end of the 19th century was the age of Darwin and, as a result, it was an age when humanity was being placed in truer biological perspective. But the obsession to divest man of his angelic origins led to excesses until virtually every feature of human endeavor was believed to have its origins in strictly biological conditions. Durkheim's contribution is, then, all the greater when we recognize the extent to which he was moving against a scientific perspective of great respectability. If Durkheim seems excessive today, it is perhaps because he was attempting to counter another excess—that of biologism.

The second scientific feature of Durkheim's era was the value given to observable facts. The scientific ethic of the time was moving radically toward getting people to "put their money on" whatever could be demonstrated to be observably true. Durkheim's contribution is all the greater, therefore, when we understand he was working within and against the handicap we mentioned at the beginning of this chapter—the fact that the social world is not directly observable. By taking observable forms of behavior, such as suicide or crime,[38] and revealing their connection with social identities, Durkheim gave sociological investigation a new basis in fact—and, at the same time, laid a course for social investigation that has continued down to the present.

The humanistic implications of Durkheim's work are not easy to assess. To an age which idealistically extolled democratic virtues and the autonomy of the individual, Durkheim gave the tempering concept of anomie—the price of individualism might be anxiety and death. Man required social regulation and order. Anomie was the other face of freedom.

In a century which saw the church being rudely elbowed aside by science, Durkheim further undermined the sanctifying rationalizations of religion by saying God was simply a personification of social force. Yet, at the same time, he also provided the greatest justification for religious doctrine ever granted by a social scientist when he claimed that all societies must have religious commitments. Without religious dedication there is no social order.

For the humanist concerned with the problem of evil Durkheim offered little hope. Even a society of saints, he suggested, would identify among its body of holy men some who violated the high standards of that saintly group. Social organization, a necessity of life for human beings, has as one of its properties the differentiation of its parts into the moral and the immoral. As there cannot be a success without those who fail, there cannot be a good without those who are evil. The moral order which is the nuclear force binding society together creates, in itself, the evil that is necessary to sustain it. Durkheim's message to the humanist concerned with evil is to recognize that

---

[38] We cannot really observe a suicide or a criminal directly either. But Durkheim was working with data that revealed some of the relatively more concrete effects of social force.

somehow we all share in the process. To the extent we are human, we are social. To the extent we are social, we share. Though the judge who condemns an evil man to die cannot legally condemn himself as well, he should never lose sight of the greater matrix of involvements that brought about the evil and in which we all participated and conspired.

Durkheim devoted his life to the endeavor that men should not lose sight of that greater matrix which he called the moral order or the collective conscience. For that reason, if no other, humanists as well as social scientists will long be indebted to him.

3   Power, Bureaucracy, Money, and Religion: The Views of Max Weber

If there is a bridge between American and European sociology, it is made up in large part of the works of two men. One of these men was Emile Durkheim—a Frenchman; the other was Max Weber—a German. Both men were born at about the same time: Durkheim in 1858 and Weber in 1864. Each reached the height of his active career in the times just preceding World War I. Durkheim died in 1917. Weber died in 1920.

Despite their different national identities, Weber and Durkheim shared much in common. Both men gave paramount significance to religion as a historical and human force. For Durkheim religion was a logical necessity. One is forced to recognize and accept its existence not because religion is an historical fact but because it is logically a social necessity. For Durkheim the argument went, essentially, "If society exists, then religion must exist." Beginning with a logical consideration of the matter, Durkheim could then investigate religion from a logically preestablished point of view. Weber, with the German scholar's regard for history, approached religion by studying its historical forms in great detail until he reached the point where he could begin to develop synthesizing generalizations.

If Weber is less exciting than Durkheim, he is more versatile. Durkheim was more narrowly dedicated to sociology. Weber's comprehension ranged across economics, sociology, political science, anthropology, history, and philosophy. Even so, the differences between the character and intellect of the two men are perhaps less significant than the similarities. Both were thoroughly committed intellectuals and both were extremely contemptuous of simplistic answers to human affairs. More significantly, both turned to the moral order as the fountainhead of social analysis. Both saw religion as the key institution in the understanding of the social order.

Weber was concerned with the specific political and economic consequences of religious doctrine. He concluded, in what is generally recognized as his most influential work,[1] that capitalistic economic practice is an outgrowth of ideas contained within Protestant religious doctrine. Weber examined the pervasive effects of religious thought within the social structure and traced in great detail the many unanticipated consequences of particular religious beliefs.

Weber's career is all the more remarkable when we note that he spent nearly twenty years of his adult life disabled by emotional disorders which, at times, left him so enervated that he would sit by the window for hours picking his fingernails. He would tell his wife it felt good to do nothing.[2] The contradictions in Weber's nature and the complexity of the man are summarized in the following quote from Gerth and Mills,

> Throughout his life, Weber was a nationalist and believed in the mission of the *Herrenvolk*, yet at the same time he fought for individual freedom and, with analytic detachment, characterized the ideas of nationalism and racism as justificatory ideologies used by the ruling class, and their hireling publicists, to beat their impositions into weaker members of the polity. . . . He was proud of being a Prussian officer, and yet asserted in public that the Kaiser, his commander-in-chief, was something of which all Germans should be ashamed . . . A model of the self-conscious masculinity of Imperial Germany, he nevertheless encouraged the first woman labor official in Germany and made vital speeches to members of the woman's emancipation movement of the early twentieth century.[3]

Weber's scholarship is as complex as his character. Any brief attempt, such as this, to outline the significant ideas in his writing must preface the effort

---

[1] Max Weber, *The Protestant Ethic and the Spirit of Capitalism*, translated by Talcott Parsons (New York: Charles Scribner's Sons, 1930). Weber's publications are numerous. The following references include those which indicate the breadth of Weber's interests and studies and, at the same time, might be of interest to students who want to pursue Weber's ideas further. *Ancient Judaism*, translated and edited by Hans H. Gerth and Don Martindale (New York: Free Press of Glencoe, 1952); *Basic Concepts in Sociology*, translated and with an introduction by H. P. Secher (New York: Citadel Press, Inc., 1964); *The City*, translated and edited by Don Martindale and Gertrude Neuwirth (Collier Books; New York: The Macmillan Company, 1962); *From Max Weber: Essays in Sociology*, translated, edited and with an introduction by H. H. Gerth and C. Wright Mills (New York: Oxford University Press, 1946); *Max Weber on the Methodology of the Social Sciences*, translated and edited by Edward A. Shils and Henry A. Finch (New York: Free Press of Glencoe, 1949); *The Rational and Social Foundations of Music*, translated and edited by Don Martindale, Johannes Riedel, and Gertrude Neuwirth (Carbondale, Ill.: Southern Illinois University Press, 1958); *The Religion of China*, translated and edited by Hans H. Gerth (New York: Free Press of Glencoe, 1959); *The Religion of India*, translated and edited by Hans H. Gerth and Don Martindale (New York: Free Press of Glencoe, 1958); *The Sociology of Religion*, translated by Ephraim Fischoff (Boston: Beacon Press, 1963); *The Theory of Social and Economic Organization*, translated by A. M. Henderson and Talcott Parsons (New York: Free Press of Glencoe, 1964).

[2] Gerth and Mills (eds.), *From Max Weber: Essays in Sociology*, p. 12.

[3] *From Max Weber: Essays in Sociology*, translated, edited and with an introduction by H. H. Gerth and C. Wright Mills (New York: Oxford University Press, 1946), pp. 25–26.

with an apology. Yet, it is necessary to make the attempt, for modern sociological thought is grounded, in large part, in the numerous writings of Weber.

Weber lived in a time and place dominated—or at least strongly affected—by the theories and writings of Karl Marx. There was the hope that just around the corner lay a new Utopia—founded in material plenty and a classless society. A politically astute person had to know and had to react to Marxist thought—and Weber was a political man. Much of Weber's thought flowed from his reaction to the writings of Marx. It is certainly an oversimplification, but it is also an aid in reading Weber, to view his writing as an attempt to refute the emphasis Marx gave to material economic concerns. Where Marx saw the church as the apologist for capitalistic exploitations, Weber saw the church as the matrix of ideas from which capitalism was to evolve. Marx claimed that without capitalism the church was not necessary. Weber argued that without a particular type of religious thought capitalism could not have come into existence.

Relationship between economic and religious systems

It is apparent, in this day and age, that both Marx and Weber viewed the historical process too narrowly. Religious and economic systems are not perfectly distinct entities. They are merged and their boundaries are ill-defined. It is not really possible to say that one "determines" the character of the other. They both influence each other and, further, they are both simultaneously affected by changes taking place in the other institutions that make up society. Even so, it is instructive to examine Weber's work; it stands as an antidote to the popularity of materialistic interpretations of history.[4]

Weber began his speculations on the relationship between economic and religious systems by considering observed differences in economic productivity in Protestant and Catholic districts of Europe. If the former were more productive, he argued, it was not because they had been "freed" by the Protestant Reformation. Quite the contrary, they had been placed under closer religious control. Moreover, it was not possible to say that the Protestant districts were more economically industrious because they were more materialistic and less "ascetic" than the Catholics in their interests. There were too many exceptions. Some Catholic districts, in France or Italy for example,

---

[4] Materialistic interpretations of history are sometimes thought to be the unique eccentricity of Marxists and, more specifically, Russian Marxists. Yet it should be apparent that materialistic interpretations of history and humanity are also very popular in America. When General Electric says "Progress Is Our Most Important Product" they are equating the elevation of humanity with the distribution of a "product." Such crassness cannot be claimed to be the unique *Weltanschauung* of either the Russians or the Americans—it belongs to both.

revealed a lusty interest in life and its enjoyments. Protestant areas, the Mennonites in Germany, for example, were possessed of an austere other-worldliness. It was, said Weber, too simple to say that religious attitudes and economic effort were combined by ascetic motives.

Yet the economic picture remained clear—the Catholic areas were less economically progressive. One could not readily forego the idea that religion had something to do with economic effort. The problem was to find the hidden connection. To do so required a more intensive examination of the nature of capitalist doctrines and Catholic and Protestant philosophy.

To summarize the nature of the capitalist spirit Weber turned to the writings of Benjamin Franklin. Here was capitalism in its most naive and open form of expression—an economic spirit which Europeans found repulsive. One European of the times, writing of Americans, said, "They make tallow out of cattle and money out of men."[5] But the important thing in Franklin's expressions of the spirit of capitalism, Weber held, was to see the *moral* nature of his economic advice. In capitalist economies the making of money took on the character of a purpose rather than a necessity. It became a value rather than something that happens by chance or something which wells out of the avarice of a particular individual. There develops a collective "spirit" which advocates the idea that each person is called upon to make the utmost of his life and, furthermore, the form this should take is devotion to industry in this world. Weber examined such statements of Franklin's as the following:

> For six pounds a year you may have the use of one hundred pounds, provided you are a man of known prudence and honesty.
>
> He that spends a groat a day idly, spends idly above six pounds a year, which is the price for the use of one hundred pounds.
>
> He that wastes idly a groat's worth of his time per day, one day with another, wastes the privilege of using one hundred pounds each day.
>
> He that idly loses five shillings' worth of time, loses five shillings, and might as prudently throw five shillings into the sea.
>
> He that loses five shillings, not only loses that sum, but all the advantage that might be made by turning it in dealing, which by the time that a young man becomes old, will amount to a considerable sum of money.[6]

Weber's point, as he examined the writings of Franklin, was that here was something new. There have been wealthy men in the past and there have been men of ambition and avarice. But Benjamin Franklin has set forth a

---

[5] Ferdinand Kürnberger, as quoted by Max Weber in *The Protestant Ethic and the Spirit of Capitalism*, p. 51.

[6] Benjamin Franklin, quoted by Max Weber, in *The Protestant Ethic and the Spirit of Capitalism*, p. 50.

moral treatise which takes the individual to task for not minding to matters of business. To tend one's groats is also to tend to the interests of one's soul. Western religion had not advocated such a prosaic sentiment prior to the Reformation. Indeed, as Weber commented, such a state of mind would, in the medieval period, have been viewed as the lowest kind of avarice and usury.

This is a very important point and we must understand it if we are to appreciate the subtlety of Weber's observations. First of all, capitalism must not be viewed simply as the desire to make money—such a desire in some individuals, Weber claimed, is as old as the history of man.

> The *auri sacra fames* is as old as the history of man. But we shall see that those who submitted to it without reserve as an uncontrolled impulse, such as the Dutch sea-captain who "would go through hell for gain, even though he scorched his sails," were by no means the representatives of that attitude of mind from which *the specifically modern capitalistic spirit as a mass phenomenon* is derived, and that is what matters. At all periods of history, wherever it was possible, there has been ruthless acquisition, bound to no ethical norms whatever. Like war and piracy, trade has often been unrestrained in its relations with foreigners and those outside the group.[7] [Italics mine, R.P.C.]

Capitalism must be understood as a mass phenomenon. It is a culturally prescribed way of living; it is a complex of ideals; it is a change in the older moral order. Weber's first point, then, is that we must see capitalism as a moral prescription, widely binding on all members of the society, to advance their individual material interests.

The second important feature of Weber's argument was that capitalism must be seen as a massive encroachment on what might be called a traditionalistic sense of effort or the value of work. It is worth noting that Weber was well aware, before American industrial psychologists documented the matter further, that workers are not always motivated to produce in terms of self-interest. Instead, they will often accept a certain traditionally given standard as sufficient and produce enough to meet such a standard. Weber summarized the matter nicely by saying,

> A man does not "by nature" wish to earn more and more money, but simply to live as he is accustomed to live and to earn as much as is necessary for that purpose.[8]

So it was that Weber revealed himself to be concerned with a specific form of a broader problem that has interested anyone seriously involved in the social sciences: How does social and economic change occur? How do

---

[7] *The Protestant Ethic and the Spirit of Capitalism*, translated by Talcott Parsons (New York: Charles Scribner's Sons, 1930; London: George Allen & Unwin Ltd.), p. 57.
[8] *Ibid.*, p. 60.

the massive forces of culture come to be modified? Like other modern social scientists, Weber concluded that the answer lies within the nature of the social order itself. To understand social and economic change we must consider the preexisting social and economic order. It is the social order which changes itself.[9] Any existing social and economic system contains not necessarily the seeds of its own destruction but rather forces which change its character to the point where it is almost no longer recognizable.

From Weber's perspective, the growth of capitalism as an economic system was also the growth of capitalism as a moral system. To recapitulate briefly, the problem of the capitalistic transition was (1) to make the acquisitive motive more than a personal eccentricity—it had to be elevated to a moral principle; (2) to destroy reliance on traditional forms of economic satisfaction and replace those forms with the rational calculation of returns coming from the investment of given amounts of labor and capital. So the question is raised: How was capitalism able to arise out of a preexisting moral order which held the acquisitive motive to be base and vulgar and which accepted traditional standards of consumption and production? This was Weber's concern.

Behavioral implications of Protestant thought

To resolve the problem Weber turned to an examination of some of the behavioral implications of Protestant thought. Protestant thought arises out of and is, quite literally, a "reforming" of doctrines that had long been held by the Catholic Church. Weber presumed that if a man takes his religion seriously, then to some extent at least his behavior will be affected by it. If this is so, then an examination of the moral directives of religion can help us understand how certain kinds of behavior came into being. What, then, were the implications of Protestant thought in its relation to capitalism? Weber turned first to an examination of Luther's concept of the "calling."

Luther set forth the idea that one should accept his "calling," his position within temporal society, so long as the calling is legitimate. The idea of the calling served one major purpose. Prior to the Reformation those activities which most magnified man in the eyes of God were efforts which, essentially, involved a withdrawal from the world. In the exercise of monastic asceticism and priestly celibacy, the individual found closer identity with Christ and with

---

[9] This position, in different forms and versions, is endorsed by a number of modern social writers. Among those appearing in the present book who subscribe to this view are Leslie White, Pitirim Sorokin, Jules Henry, Robert K. Merton, and, of course, Emile Durkheim.

God. Luther suggested, to the contrary, that all legitimate enterprises were equal in the eyes of God and that man could enhance his own state of grace by meeting the demands of his temporal or worldly calling. Luther was, in a sense, paving the way for the value which we, today, give to professionalism. Weber was concerned with the extent to which this theological concept and religious argument would have consequences for the economic realm. He suggested that what Luther did was to bring work into the secular realm— worldly duties were no longer, after Luther, subordinated to spiritual or ascetic ones. It was the necessary first move toward capitalistic morality. Weber said,

> The effect of the Reformation as such was only that, as compared with the Catholic attitude, the moral emphasis on and the religious sanction of, organized worldly labour in a calling was mightily increased. . . . Everyone should abide by his living and let the godless run after gain . . . But in the concrete calling an individual pursued he saw more and more a special command of God to fulfill these particular duties which the Divine Will had imposed upon him . . . The individual should remain once and for all in the station and calling in which God had placed him, and should restrain his worldly activity within the limits imposed by his established station in life.[10]

Luther provided a justification for involvement in worldly affairs, but did little more than that. To see the more profound connection between Protestant thought and capitalistic enterprise it is necessary to turn to the writings of Calvin.[11]

Calvinism, following the momentum established by Lutheranism, continued the process of providing religious justification for worldly concerns and effort. Luther supplied the concept of a calling. Calvin supplied an interest in predestination. If man was placed on this earth as God's creature, and if God stood infinitely beyond man's limited intellectual capacities, then it would be foolish to presume that any kind of effort on man's part would place him in a state of grace with God. Only God would know and God, being far beyond man's mind, would not tell. Thus, man's fate was predestined in the sense it was out of his own hands and in the hands of God. Just as a man could

---

[10] Weber, *The Protestant Ethic and the Spirit of Capitalism*, pp. 83–85.

[11] It is necessary to introduce an antidote to the oversimplifications that characterize any attempt to summarize Weber's work in a brief space. Weber was not saying that Protestantism, and only Protestantism, is the necessary condition for capitalism. Rather, he was concerned with the extent to which some kind of religious moral order is necessary for the development of particular kinds of economic order. Weber stated, ". . . we have no intention whatever of maintaining such a foolish and doctrinaire thesis as that the spirit of capitalism . . . could only have arisen as the result of certain effects of the Reformation, or even that capitalism as an economic system is a creation of the Reformation . . . On the contrary, we only wish to ascertain whether and to what extent religious forces have taken part in the qualitative formation and the quantitative expansion of that spirit over the world." See page 91 of *The Protestant Ethic and the Spirit of Capitalism*.

not know the specific nature of his own worldly demise—the form of his own death—he could not know, in advance, the form of his relationship with God. At the same time, Calvin claimed that some men—a few—would be among the saved. The rest would fall among the damned.

Thus, Calvinism provided the world with a new variation on the older Christian notion of damnation and salvation. Calvin carried the idea of an omnipotent God to its extreme and concluded that salvation was already determined by God and there was nothing the individual could do about it. More importantly, there was nothing the church could do about it! The complete elimination of salvation through the sacraments of the church formed the absolutely decisive difference between Calvinism and Catholicism.[12] Weber then went on to say,

> The great historic process in the development of religions, the elimination of magic from the world which had begun with the old Hebrew prophets and, in conjunction with Hellenistic scientific thought, had repudiated all magical means to salvation as superstition and sin, came here to its logical conclusion. The genuine Puritan even rejected all signs of religious ceremony at the grave and buried his nearest and dearest without song or ritual in order that no superstition, no trust in the effects of magical and sacramental forces on salvation, should creep in.[13]

Not only were magical means useless in the attainment of salvation, but so were any and all other means. It then becomes a curious matter to determine how such an ethic, such a religious point of view, could come to be associated with the worldly, acquisitive and accumulative spirit that characterizes capitalism. The principal effect of this idea, said Weber, was to throw people into a state of brooding individualism. Torn from the security of the church, of traditionalism, of magic and ritual, man stood alone before his God. He was more vulnerable than ever before. His ignorance was a source of torment. His fate was unknown. Thus it was that individualism became a common affliction and not a specific eccentricity.

But if this idea were carried to its *reductio ad absurdum*, it would produce unbearable anomie. Rather than stimulating communal development and economic order, it would produce a highly disruptive disengagement of the individual from the affairs of the community. Something had to balance out the individualism of Calvinistic Puritanism by retaining the individual within the communal order. Weber resolved this problem by considering the Calvinist's conception of the ultimate purpose of life.

---

[12] *Ibid.*, pp. 104–105. This is a slightly modified version of Weber's statement to the same effect.

[13] *Ibid.*, p. 105.

The world exists to serve the glorification of God and for that purpose alone. The elected Christian is in the world only to increase this glory of God by fulfilling His commandments to the best of his ability. But God requires social achievement of the Christian because He wills that social life shall be organized according to His commandments, in accordance with that purpose.[14]

Weber's picture of the Calvinist is that of a man tormented with a concern over his fate. He stands alone, yet bound to the community by his sense of God's omnipotence. He cannot distinguish the saved from the damned and he cannot rely on any device to assure his own salvation. Yet there remains a very dim light in this ideological darkness. Though the Calvinist cannot achieve salvation he can, through the extent to which he is able to manifest God's glory, convince himself of his own membership in the elect. He can seek external signs of inner grace. These signs cannot assure him of salvation, but they can help convince him he is among the saved.

The achievement of Calvinism was that it explicitly brought the religious struggle into this world. No longer need the fully dedicated religious man retreat into monasticism to test his commitment. He could test it in his work, in his calling, in his daily activities. Weber commented that the effect of the Reformation was to make every Christian a monk all his life.[15] More significantly, he was a monk who lived and dwelled within the community, within industry, within the school and the family. These and other institutions were to be affected accordingly.

It remains, now, to make the connection between the asceticism of Protestant ideology and the development of capitalism as an economic practice flowing from the greater moral order. The connection is not obvious because Protestant asceticism, reflecting the more pervasive asceticism of Christianity in general, was inclined to view the acquisition of wealth as morally suspect. One's dominating concern should be the Kingdom of God and not the acquisition of wealth. However, the fear of wealth coming from Protestant asceticism lay not in the fact that wealth itself is corrupting but that it promotes a moral relaxation. If one can remain dedicated to the principles of good works and the fulfillment of the glory of God and not be tempted into leisure, then wealth is, in no way, evil. Indeed, and this is significant, it may function as a sign of success in one's calling.

It is not wealth which is evil but rather the waste of time which is the true evil.

---

[14] *Ibid.*, p. 108.
[15] *Ibid.*, p. 121.

Waste of time is thus the first and in principle the deadliest of sins. The span of human life is infinitely short and precious to make sure of one's own election [into the ranks of the saved]. Loss of time through sociability, idle talk, luxury, even more sleep than is necessary for health . . . is worthy of absolute moral condemnation . . . [Time] is infinitely valuable because every hour lost is lost to labour for the glory of God. Thus inactive contemplation is also valueless, or even directly reprehensible if it is at the expense of one's daily work. For it is less pleasing to God than the active performance of His will in a calling.[16]

Thus, Protestantism, with its derivations rooted in early ascetic Christianity and Judaism, latched onto work as an ascetic exercise. In this respect it differs from almost all other monastic rules the world over, according to Weber.[17] Work was elevated to a moral principle and, moreover, a principle binding on all who aspire to the Kingdom of God. Work was made a direct expression of religious fervor. Still more significantly, not any kind of work could satisfy the demands of the Protestant Ethic. Only that work was acceptable which directly served the glory of God—and the glory of God was manifested in the ongoing community and its legitimate interests.

Furthermore, work which is sloppy and ill-conceived, even though taxing and tiring, is not sufficient. It might try the soul, but it cannot work for the glorification of God. That work is best which is conscientiously planned, thorough, and methodical. In a word, work was given a *rational* quality through an irrational process—the religious mysticism of Luther, Calvin, and other Protestant leaders generated the idea of rationality in work. The foundations were thus laid for capitalistic modes of thought. Capitalism, if it meant nothing else, meant the rational use of wealth and the rational use of labor. Men had sought wealth before and men had worked before—there was certainly nothing new in this. But with capitalism men were set to the task of calculating gains. Rationalism in determining the worth of an enterprise achieved the level of a socially supported value. How, said Weber, could capitalism have come into being unless some kind of moral basis was laid for it in advance? Because this moral basis was lacking in the religions of other countries—even though they were rich in resources and labor—their economies did not and could not move toward the capitalistic form.[18]

What has happened to the Protestant Ethic? Observers of the present scene find it suffocating from the crushing weight of its own successes. It is ironic, if Weber's thesis is correct, that capitalism not only became independent of

---

[16] *Ibid.*, p. 158.

[17] *Ibid.*, p. 158.

[18] Some writers have speculated that the code of Bushido in Japan was influential in promoting the technological and industrial modernization of Japan. I am indebted to Professor Joyce Lebra of the University of Colorado for bringing this to my attention.

its Protestant origins but eventually reached the point where it could challenge values dearest to the heart of the Puritan individualist. The challenge,
when it came, had its origins in two sources. One of these was the rise of
the large organization—the development of modern bureaucracy. The other
source of the challenge was modern science. In many ways science is the
most rational and possibly the purest extension of ideas contained in the
Protestant Ethic.[19] At the same time, it stands as the most secular of human
institutions and the greatest barrier to a collective return to religious mysticism.[20] In any event, as Weber conceded, once the process leading toward
capitalistic morality had begun, it eventually reached the point of an autonomous system—a system no longer reliant on the older morality that brought
it into being.

The nature of bureaucratic organization

Weber was concerned with the subtleties of the connection between religious
and economic moralities. He was also concerned with the consequences of
social organization. In particular he was involved with questions concerning
the nature of bureaucratic organization. No sociologist today can discuss this
topic without paying his respects to Weber. Indeed, Merton claims that
Weber may properly be regarded as the "founder of the systematic study of
bureaucracy."[21] Weber was interested in bureaucracy because it represented
another facet of the process of rationalization—a process which seemed, to
him, to characterize modern society in contrast to "traditional" forms of society. A rational ordering of the economy brought along with it a rational
ordering of social relations. The efficiency that came to characterize the productive process also came to characterize social organization. Men, in their

---

[19] Robert K. Merton has attempted to show the relationship that exists between Protestant
religious thought and the rise of scientific thinking in Western culture. If Protestantism promoted
rationality in business, it seems reasonable to conclude that it promoted rationality in other
spheres of human activity. Essentially, the argument is that if God is all-rational and if God made
the world, then the rationality of God will be found in His works. Early scientists of the 17th
century were, according to Merton, predominantly Protestant and were, by virtue of religious
training, more congenial to the idea of finding rationality within nature itself. This thesis is explored at some length in the next chapter.

[20] It is interesting to note, in this instance, the bad press which the "Hippie" movement received in recent years. The Hippie emphasis on subjectivism and mysticism stands more as a
threat to the institution of science than it does to the values of the American middle classes.
If science is often ignored in discussions of power in the modern world, it is probably because
science is held to be beyond the mundane and arbitrary value interests that are so integral a
part of the political scene. This, of course, is a mistake. Science, per se, is a political force
and it is as politically significant in our time as the Holy Roman Catholic Church was in its time.

[21] Robert K. Merton, et al., Reader in Bureaucracy (New York: Free Press of Glencoe, 1952),
p. 17. Copyright 1952 by The Free Press a Corporation.

social lives, were processed as impersonally and as efficiently as were the material resources which were also necessary for production.

Capitalism solved the problem of tearing men away from traditionalistic economic motives[22] and traditional patterns of production. Bureaucracy, in essence, solved the problem of breaking men away from a reliance on traditional modes of power. To see this, we need to consider briefly Weber's conception of the nature of power in its traditional forms and in its bureaucratic forms.[23]

Power, very broadly defined as the probability of having a command obeyed by others when they are resistant, can be dealt with in two very distinctive ways. First of all, power can be seen as having its locus in the person or individual. By this Weber meant only that certain features may give a person a commanding appearance and cause others to accept his dictates as necessary ones to follow—the individual is felt to be blessed with extraordinary powers. Power that emanates from such a source was called "charismatic" power by Weber. The individual having such power is believed to be divinely inspired, possessed of sacred qualities, capable of prophecy, and otherwise set apart from the ordinary run of men.[24] A second form of power is that which has its locus not within the person but within the office or status the person occupies.

Charismatic power

Charismatic power, as Weber considered it, is reliant on the expressive qualities of the individual. It resides in the flashing eye, the powerful voice, the jutting chin, or some other sign which identifies its possessor as a "born leader." The significance of these signs can be suggested by imagining the incongruity arising from casting a midget as a biblical fiery prophet instead of a more imposing-looking figure. Because charismatic power rests, ultimately, on the unique impressions of the individual, it has an arbitrary and eccentric quality about it which makes it a potential source of disruption to more ra-

---

[22] This is relative, of course. Modern America, for example, though less traditionalistic than is, say Egypt, in its labor practices, is still not 100 percent efficient in this respect.

[23] The concept of power is extremely difficult to define in a social context; no one has achieved a truly satisfactory definition. If we define power as the capacity to make people do things they do not want to do, we have to establish the fact that they do not want to do what we are demanding of them.

[24] From the extent to which intelligence is idolized in America, I would suggest that it is a modern form of the quest for charisma. However, the intelligence test has routinized this form of charisma. In fact, it has gone so far as to lead to a number of people with high intelligence quotients organizing themselves into a group known as *Mensa*. Weber, I like to believe, would have been amused.

tional forms of power utilization. The charismatic leader, as Weber nicely put it, is not congenial to the idea of routine. To the contrary, because his power is lodged within his personal qualities, he exists as a threat to routine and to the established order.

The unstable, eccentric, and individualistic character of charismatic power must be regulated somehow if a permanent and stable power system is to be developed within the community. Weber held that purely charismatic power exists only in the originating moments of new social forms. The need for stability leads to the regulation of charisma or, as Weber put it, the "routinization" of charisma.

The necessity for stabilizing power based on the eccentricities of the individual can be quickly seen. If the followers of a charismatic leader are dependent on him for guidance, how are they to cope with the problems that arise when the leader dies or is incapacitated? How is the quality of charisma to be given continuity beyond the life-span of the individual who possesses it? How is the magic of charisma to be retained when the magician has gone? The problem thus becomes one of somehow taking the power-giving qualities of charisma out of the ephemeral nature of the individual and bringing them into the stable and continuous structure of the community. Sources of power that were once the property of a charismatically endowed individual must become the property of the community; they must somehow be incorporated into the routine of communal living. Weber referred to the process whereby this took place as the "routinization of charisma."[25]

The problem of "routinizing" charisma can be solved in a variety of ways. Weber listed the following as among the more common and significant ones:

1. A search can be initiated for persons who possess signs of charisma similar to those possessed by the leader. If the leader had a cleft between his teeth, then perhaps people with cleft teeth will also possess some of the charismatic qualities with which the leader was endowed. Weber referred to the search for the Dalai Lama as an example of this kind of solution. In this instance a search is initiated for a child with characteristics which identify him as a reincarnation of the Buddha.

2. The new leader can be sought by divine judgment, revelation, through oracles or the casting of lots. In such instances, the selection procedure is given a legitimacy—an acceptance by the community—and the person who is thus selected is endowed with charismatic qualities.

---

[25] Weber, *Theory of Social and Economic Organization*, pp. 364–373.

3. A very simple and common solution to the problem is to rely on the judgment of the charismatic leader himself and have him select his successor. The magician is the man best qualified to select the magician who will follow in his stead.

4. A new leader can be established through selection by a council which is qualified both to determine the charismatic leader and to endow him with qualities of leadership by means of special ceremonies. Legitimacy of power rests, in this instance, on the acceptance of a charismatically qualified council and on the impressive and ritualistically correct procedures of ceremony.

5. Another means of routinizing charisma exists in the simple assumption that it can be biologically or hereditarily transmitted. Therefore, the charismatic leader can be replaced by his son, who will be possessed of similar qualities. It should be noted here that such an assumption functions to solve a social problem in the transfer of power and that it has only a very tenuous connection with reality. The community may possess any number of people who are better qualified, in terms of talent and energy, for the tasks of leadership than is the present leader's son. However, to ascribe such qualities to the son simplifies what otherwise might prove to be a communally disorganizing process by attempting to rediscover "true" charisma.

6. Finally, the problem of stabilizing charisma can be met by ritualistic transmission. Weber exemplifies this by saying,

> The most important example is the transmission of priestly charisma by anointing, consecration, or the laying on of hands; and of royal authority, by anointing and by coronation.[26]

Charisma which is individualistic, disturbing, revolutionary, and eccentric cannot long remain the organizing force within a community. It calls for routinization; but routinization, whether of a traditional form or a more modern bureaucratic form, introduces a conservative, stable, and collective structure.

Bureaucratic power

Whereas the above forms of routinization of charisma are attempts either to find someone who is charismatic or to transfer charisma to someone who is not, bureaucracy solves the problem by investing not the person but the office he occupies with power. It is this relatively profound accomplishment of bureaucratic forms of organization that provides bureaucracy with both its

---

[26] *The Theory of Social and Economic Organization*, translated by A. M. Henderson and Talcott Parsons (New York: Free Press of Glencoe, 1964), p. 366.

stability and its capacity to maintain consistent control over its membership. The powerful man no longer needs a flashing eye and a booming voice; he needs only the credentials that qualify him to occupy a particular position of authority.

Weber was concerned with the ideal forms of bureaucracy: What are the essential features of a rational, large-scale, and efficient social organization?[27] Weber saw bureaucracy as a form of social organization which constrained the personal and eccentric qualities of charismatic leadership. But how does bureaucracy operate? In essence, suggested Weber, bureaucracy depends on the relationship that exists between a set of formal regulations and a set of offices. The offices are so organized as to maximize the controlling efficiency of the regulations.

To see what this means we need to turn to Weber's listing of the essentials of bureaucratic organization.[28] Because Weber's formulations are extremely abstract, I have attempted to illustrate them with examples drawn from the realm of higher education in the United States—a realm that is now well bureaucratized and a realm that is also familiar to the student. Bureaucracy, as seen by Weber, involves the following mutually interdependent ideas:[29]

"1. . . . any given legal norm may be established by agreement or by imposition, on grounds of expediency or rational values or both, with a claim to obedience at least on the part of the members of the corporate group." The important qualification in this statement appears in the use of the term "expediency." Thus, higher learning, as a bureaucratic process, comes to abound in "legal" rules and regulations which specify the form—and to a considerable extent the content—of education. It becomes expedient to differentiate, in a legalistic sense, the study of psychology from the study of literature; and it becomes expedient to distinguish the study of literature from the study of anthropology. So it goes. Moreover, whatever one is studying, it is expedient to study the subject in terms of an intellectual bookkeeping system that assigns credits for what amounts, on the student's part, to maintaining a sense of bureaucratic propriety. That is, if the student functions according to the norms binding on a proper bureaucrat, he will be moved through the career system.

---

[27] For a penetrating statement of Weber's ideas concerning charisma and bureaucracy, the student should read Reinhard Bendix, *Max Weber: An Intellectual Portrait* (Anchor Books; Garden City, N.Y.: Doubleday Company, Inc., 1962).

[28] This list is set forth in *The Theory of Social and Economic Organization*. The particular quotations presented here were taken from Merton *et al., Reader in Bureaucracy* (New York: Free Press of Glencoe, 1952), pp. 18–27. Copyright 1952 by The Free Press a Corporation.

[29] It is necessary to mention here that Weber viewed bureaucracy as a form of organization which has appeared in a variety of historical settings. It is not uniquely or specifically modern.

Critics who are concerned with the extent to which students are motivated by expediency perhaps miss the point. From Weber's perspective, a student who recognizes the need for expediency will be conforming more to the character of the educational bureaucracy than the student who does not.[30] Such a student will be highly rewarded by the bureaucracy—at least in terms of the intellectual bookkeeping system which doles out grades to those freshmen and sophomores and upperclassmen who retain some sense of their bureaucratic nature. The freshman bureaucrat who recognizes the value of expediency will be resonating to a sentiment that is dominant within the greater organizational structure.

"2. [*Within bureaucracy*] *administration of law is held to consist in the application of . . . rules to particular cases; the administrative process is the rational pursuit of the interests which are specified in the order governing the corporate group within the limits laid down by legal precepts . . .*" Weber's point here is perhaps the most profound among the many he made concerning the character of bureaucracy. The effective bureaucrat is, from the perspective of Weber, a person who pursues the interests of the corporation as these appear in legal precepts. As a consequence, in specific instances, the individual is dealt with legalistically rather than personally. His actions are measured against the interests of the corporate group and are thereby evaluated. The legal system that makes up the structure of the interests of the bureaucracy is taken as given.

It is this feature of bureaucracy that has resulted in much criticism from existential novelists such as Camus and Kafka.[31] In the clash of the person and the structure, it is the person who is evaluated against the background of the legal system of the structure. Recently, for example, student protesters at the University of Colorado demonstrated against the appearance, on campus, of a Central Intelligence Agency recruiter. In the application of the general rules to the specific action, virtually no discussion took place concerning incongruities between norms of scholarship and intellectual activity and the morality underlying the activities of the CIA. Instead, university administrators moved quickly and suspended the protesters—thereby protecting the "image

---

[30] The student motivated by expediency is the eternal concern of the pedagogue. It was Jacques Barzun, I believe, who commented to the effect that, granted the nature of graduate school organization today, the student motivated by expediency is superior to his idealistic counterpart. A very ingenious discussion of the transformation of idealism into technical competence by forcing the student to be expedient appears in Howard Becker, E. C. Hughes and B. Geer, *Boys in White* (Chicago: University of Chicago Press, 1961).

[31] Franz Kafka's *The Trial* (New York: Alfred A. Knopf, Inc., 1937) is one of the better known fictional depictions of the point being made here.

and reputation of the university." Weber's point is that in bureaucratic administration, the administrator identifies with and protects the interests of the bureaucracy and does so in a relatively uncritical manner.[32]

"3. [Within the bureaucracy] the typical person in authority occupies an 'office.' In the action associated with his status, including the commands he issues to others, he is subject to an impersonal order to which his actions are oriented." The concept of "office" is important in grasping a deeper understanding of the nature of bureaucracy. It enables us, perhaps, to see professors somewhat differently if we recognize them as intellectual officials; or, to put it another way, as officials who are intellectuals. College students acquire a different character when we view them as minor officials—junior bureaucrats within the educational bureaucracy.

Because an office requires relatively uncritical acceptance of one's official duties, and because being an intellectual demands a critical sensitivity, the college professor of any intelligence sooner or later experiences the conflicts that come from the opposing demands of bureaucratic passivity on the one hand and intellectual rebellion on the other.

The professor who is a good bureaucrat will, with considerable pride, boast to his students that he has eliminated all personal allusions and anecdotes from his lectures. In such an instance the professor is openly recognizing the prior claims of office over any other kind of experience—especially the more disorganizing and less legalistic experiences that well from one's personal encounters with life.

"4. . . . the person who obeys authority does so, . . . only in his capacity as a 'member' of the corporate group and what he obeys is only 'the law.' " The educational bureaucracy runs into more problems with this aspect of bureaucratic structure than just about any other. Weber is merely pointing out that bureaucracy has a tendency to restrict performance to the demands of the office. What someone does on "his own time" is his business. This, again, characterizes an "ideal" bureaucracy. If, for example, the chairman of the physics department is the greatest physicist in the world, then why

---

[32] Though this statement is severe, it is warranted. There is a tendency for the critical evaluations of the administrative official to take the form dictated by the interests of the bureaucracy rather than the interests either of the individual or of broader moral issues. Thus it is that a federal court recently supported the employment of loyalty oaths for schoolteachers in Colorado with the assertion that such oaths promote a recognition that this is a nation of laws and not of men. It strikes me as peculiar that the judges were not willing to make explicit the possibility that this is a nation of laws *and* of men. Presumably a complete dedication to law has an administrative cleanness that a dedication to humanity does not have.

should it concern anyone that he spends his off-duty hours passing out ban-the-bomb leaflets or conducting experiments in the application of certain tenets of a philosophy of free-love?

A more aggravating problem arises from the extent to which this feature of bureaucracy, within an educational setting, produces "compartmentalization." A student—and students, generally speaking, make very good bureaucrats—is all too willing to function in his capacity as a member of a corporate group. When this means he must study English 101, Chemistry 201, Sociology 111, and Modern History 202, he does so. Each course is taken, the requirements met, and the credits are entered in the bookkeeping system. The possibility that there might be a connection between all four courses and that each could be profitably examined from the perspectives of the others is not considered. Reality reflects the offices of bureaucracy and is subordinated to them, despite the resulting strain.

"5. . . . members of the corporate group, insofar as they obey a person in authority, do not owe this obedience to him as an individual but to the impersonal order . . ." Weber suggested that within a bureaucracy allegiance becomes more abstract. College students might, for example, assert their willingness to do or die for old Siwash, but they would consider it absurd to be willing to do or die for President Jones of old Siwash. I found it interesting to observe, in 1966, that over a third of the students in my social science classes were unable to identify Ho Chi Minh when asked to do so in tests. He was referred to variously as "a Chinese leader," "a South Vietnam political leader," and "an oriental." The enemy is no longer personalized. Instead, the enemy is looked upon as an abstract condition located somewhere in a misty "they." "They" are held to believe in an equally misty and ill-understood set of ideas called "communism," or "capitalism," or some other "ism," which "they," in a manner never well-defined, will somehow impose on all the mistily "free" people of the world. Weber, had he lived in present times, would have been interested in the extent to which human conflict has become an abstracted process.

"6. [Within a bureaucracy] the organization of offices follows the principle of hierarchy; that is, each lower office is under the control and supervision of a higher one." This is a fairly obvious comment and does not require, in this context, much further elaboration. Whether it is a military, political, industrial, educational, or religious bureaucracy, the fact of hierarchy is evident. There are points in the hierarchy, however, that produce interesting situations. The graduate student, for example, stands between the student body and the faculty in the academic hierarchy. He is not really a faculty member and yet he is very close. This poses a problem for the graduate student. Should he treat his teachers as colleagues or as his professors? He can easily seem either too formal or too casual. Some students, to avoid the problem, elect to greet their teachers with a noncommital "Hi" or "Good morning" rather than to commit themselves with a "Hello, Professor Johnson" or a "Howdy, Jack."

"7. . . . only a person who has demonstrated an adequate technical training is qualified to be a member of the administrative staff of [a bureaucratically] organized group, and hence only such persons are eligible for appointment to official positions." The role played by technical competence in bureaucracy is an especially significant one and wells from the more pervasive concern that is given to the rational pursuit of the ends of the organization. If the organization is to attain its goals, then it is paramount that its personnel be as efficient and as competent as possible. Their efficiency is dependent on the extent to which they possess technical competence. The consequence, in an ideal bureaucracy, is personnel selected on the basis of examinations.

Within the bureaucracy of higher learning it is hardly necessary to point to the prevalence of examinations as a means of determining the right to continue in a "career." However, some interesting observations have been made concerning the manner in which men are selected for positions in universities when their records are equivalent. Under these conditions, extraneous features are allowed to sway the choice. Usually these features will take into account the extent to which the "personality" of the candidate will be such as to assure a "smooth" operation of the department.[33]

"8. In the rational type [of bureaucracy] it is a matter of principle that the members of the administrative staff should be completely separated from ownership of the means of production or administration . . . There exists, furthermore, in principle complete separation of the property belonging to the organization, which is controlled within the sphere of office, and the personal property of the individual, which is available for his own private uses. There is a corresponding separation of the place in which official functions are carried out, the 'office' in the sense of premises, from living quarters." Weber touches, here, on a property of bureaucracy which has far reaching ramifications. He is suggesting, albeit somewhat indirectly, that Marxist doctrines concerning the social employment of property may be only the ideological reflection or after-

---

[33] This has been documented by Theodore Caplow and Reece McGee, *The Academic Marketplace* (New York: Basic Books, Inc., 1958). At one point in the interviews carried out by McGee a faculty member said, "He played the recorder. That was the reason we hired him." [Interviewer]: "Because he played a recorder?" [Respondent]: "Yes, we thought that would be nice." There is a strong hint here that the respondent, rather unbureaucratically, was pulling the interviewer's leg.

effect of a process that had already been established by the bureaucratization of society.[34]

This point, though very profound, hardly needs elaborate documentation or illustration here. It is of more interest to pursue some of the possible implications of the point. For example (still within educational bureaucracy), what are some of the effects of this on the political and social ideology of professors? Is there a liberalizing effect? Does lack of ownership bring about a lowered sense of identification with the institution and a greater willingness to function as a more cosmopolitan intellectual? Does the complete, or nearly complete disengagement of the student, *qua* student, from ownership and the acquisition of goods produce a feeling that what he is doing is not concrete or personally meaningful?

"9. Administrative acts, decisions, and rules are formulated and recorded in writing, even in cases where oral discussion is the rule or is even mandatory. This applies at least to preliminary discussions and proposals, to final decisions, and to all sorts of orders and rules. The combination of written documents and a continuous organization of official functions constitutes the 'office,' which is the central focus of all types of modern corporate action." Weber is referring here to what Mills referred to as the "enormous file." Not only does the bureaucracy record actions taken and the resulting consequences; it also keeps records of policies formed, and it keeps carefully preserved the rules and regulations which give form to the system. All of this constitutes the "file."

While such files, records, and formally expressed legal definitions of the regulations defining each office provide for a high degree of continuity, they also introduce an impersonal and rigid element into the conduct of office. Paradoxically, it becomes a mark of the good bureaucrat to know how and when to violate the demands of the formal system.[35] An interesting case in point is the following solution to a vexing bureaucratic problem by a colleague of mine.

---

[34] A particularly interesting treatment of this theme can be found in Adolf A. Berle, Jr., *Power without Property* (New York: Harcourt, Brace & World, Inc., 1959). See also James Burnham, *The Managerial Revolution* (New York: The John Day Company, Inc., 1941). Galbraith points out that the meaning of property, where large-scale industrial concerns are involved, is extremely complex. Governmental and industrial interests are so interrelated it is difficult to establish where the public domain begins and the private ends. See John Kenneth Galbraith, *The New Industrial State* (Boston: Houghton Mifflin Company, 1967).

[35] This point has been amply documented by sociologists. See A. W. Gouldner, *Patterns of Industrial Bureaucracy* (New York: Free Press of Glencoe, 1954), and Erving Goffman, *Asylums* (Anchor Books; Garden City, N.Y.: Doubleday & Company, Inc., 1961). I understand that postal workers in Britain go on strike by following, to the very letter, every regulation required of postal employees; the resultant mess is sufficient to foul up the delivery of mail. I have also heard the same story told of French bureaucrats.

The situation consisted, for my colleague, of having to teach classes in an old wooden building that was once used as a military barracks during World War II. The building was a fire hazard and the classroom itself, with a single exit, was a serious potential catastrophe. My colleague was reasonably concerned. He sent several letters to administrative officials who stood above him in authority. His request that something be done to alleviate the situation was ignored. At the same time, the demands of office called for this professor to teach his class three times a week for a period of fifty minutes each time.

Instead of lecturing, the professor instituted a program of training in fire drills and fire safety. He then spent ten to twenty minutes of each class period taking his students outside the building to a safe place and then returning. This activity was sufficiently disorganizing to call for action on the part of the administration. They could have done several things—one being to chastize or otherwise bring sanctions against the instructor. However, because he was engaging in an action obviously designed to promote the safety of the students,[36] the administration was forced to capitulate. The episode ended happily with a set of fire escapes being constructed for the classroom.

I will have to bring this discussion of Weber to a close at this point. Weber has been criticized for presenting what amount, in the final analysis, to broad historical speculations and hypotheses. He has been accused of using such general and ideal conceptions that we are made unwarrantedly secure in our feeling that we understand. For example, when we get down to the specifics of a particular bureaucracy we may find that it deviates considerably from the picture given us by Weber. But even if we grant the validity of these criticisms, they still do not detract from the stature of Weber or the value of his work. Weber remains a significant beginning point for the humanist or social scientist who is seriously concerned with understanding the character of modern society. Few other writers—if any—have so magnificently comprehended the workings of religious, political, economic, and social organizations. The student should note, as he continues through this book, the extent to which many contemporary sociological writers have been influenced by Weber. Only to the extent that we perceive this influence can we have a basis for evaluating the fullness of Weber's contribution to social thought.

---

[36] Alvin Gouldner, in *Patterns of Industrial Bureaucracy* (p. 197), points out that administrative officials deal seriously with safety regulations. Gouldner says, "In the main, however, management felt that the most convincing justification for a safety program was the interdependence of safety and production . . . the *major* legitimation of safety work . . . was its usefulness to production."

4 The Unanticipated Consequences of Human Actions: The Views of Robert King Merton

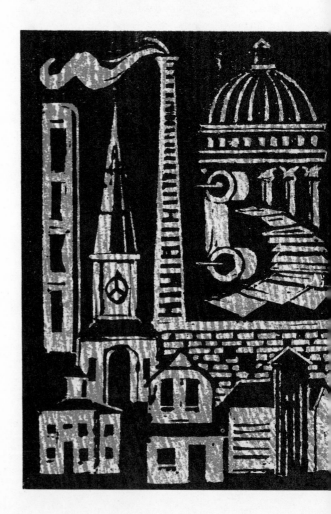

By the time America entered the 1960s sociology had achieved enough notoriety to be of some interest to the general public. Popular writers were producing, here and there, magazine articles concerned with the problem of what sociology really is and what sociologists are like. The opinions expressed were not always flattering—and even when flattering were sometimes back-handed.

In 1961 *The New Yorker* published a biographical profile of one of America's leading sociologists. The tone of the article leaves the reader with the feeling that its subject is a man regrettably squandering himself in a profession which, at best, is simple and gross.[1] The sociologist profiled in the magazine article was Robert King Merton—then, as now, one of America's foremost living sociologists.[2] The article describes Merton as a

---

[1] See *The New Yorker* "Profile" by M. M. Hunt, *The New Yorker* (January 28, 1961), pp. 39–40+.

[2] The following selected listing of Robert K. Merton's works will provide an indication of the extent and variety of his contributions to sociological thought. *Contemporary Social Problems; An Introduction to the Sociology of Deviant Behavior and Social Disorganization,* edited by Merton and R. A. Nisbet (New York: Harcourt, Brace & World, Inc., 1961); *Continuities in Social Research: Studies in the Scope and Method of "The American Soldier,"* edited by Merton and Paul F. Lazarsfeld (New York: Free Press of Glencoe, 1950); *The Focused Interview; A Manual of Problems and Procedures,* with Marjorie Fiske and Patricia L. Kendall (New York: Free Press of Glencoe, 1956); *Mass Persuasion; The Social Psychology of a War Bond Drive,* with the assistance of M. Fiske and Alberta Curtis (New York: Harper & Row, Publishers, 1946); *On the Shoulders of Giants; A Shandean Postscript* (New York: Free Press of Glencoe, 1965); *Reader in Bureaucracy,* edited by Merton and others (New York: Free Press of Glencoe, 1952); *Social Theory and Social Structure* (rev. and enl. ed.; New York: Free Press of Glencoe, 1957); *The Student-Physician; Introductory Studies in the Sociology of Medical Education,* edited by Merton, George G. Reader, and Patricia Kendall (Cambridge, Mass.: Harvard University Press, 1957); *Sociology Today; Problems and Prospects,* edited by Merton, L. Broom, and L. S. Cottrell, Jr. (New York: Basic Books, Inc., 1959).

. . . tall, hollow chested man of fifty . . . thin lipped, rimless spectacled and earnestly talkative as the Hollywood stereotype of a minister, but with a quizzically twisted smile as a giveaway . . . Socially . . . an agreeably convivial fellow, who, despite his somewhat austere appearance, steadily and tirelessly does away with Scotch . . .[3]

The author registers the same feeling toward sociologists that a college student shows toward his professor when he discovers, in the course of growing up, that the man has human as well as intellectual qualities.

Merton's career spans a crucial period in the development of American sociology—a period during which sociology in this country moved from rather simple factual conceptions of the social order to more abstract and sophisticated conceptions of human society. European sociology, typified in the works of Durkheim and Weber, was rooted in an examination of the moral order. American sociology, up to the time of World War II, was engaged in an indirect idealization of the American family farm and the small, semirural American community.[4] For many American sociologists the problem confronting modern man was how to regain a rural paradise lost. Sociological studies took the form of elaborate comparisons between rural and urban modes of living.[5] The rural mode, somehow, more often appeared as the better way of life.

But this naive and pastorally romantic sociology had to give way before more analytic forms of sociology—forms of sociology which attempted to identify and then relate the most fundamental, and therefore the most abstract, conditions of society. This approach to sociology is not especially concerned with such specific social problems as rural-urban contrasts in divorce rates. It turns, instead, to a consideration of what is meant by a social system.[6] What are the properties of any social system? How are the elements within the system interrelated to form a structure? How do the parts, and the manner

---

[3] *The New Yorker,* p. 39.

[4] Much of the sociology of the 1930s consisted of elaborate distinctions between what were essentially rural and urban modes of living. To a surprising extent, even as late as the forties, American sociology classes could be found that ignored both Durkheim and Weber.

[5] A recent highly developed study of this type is Harald Swedner, *Ecological Differentiation of Habits and Attitudes* (Lund, Sweden: CWK Gleerup, 1960.)

[6] There is an important *caveat* to enter here. The structural-functionalist often presents the appearance of being a scientist analytically examining the parts of society in much the same manner as the biologist examines the functioning of the organs of a dog or monkey. Merton even relies on such an example in defining what he means by function. However, unlike the biologist, the sociologist *never* has an opportunity to observe the whole of society. He works, instead, with the idea or concept of a society. Or, as Roger Wade has put it, "Sociologists never collect actions, they collect only words about actions." (Mr. Wade is presently a graduate student at the University of Colorado. The quotation came from a conversation we had concerning the nature of sociological studies.) The sociologist, to a greater extent than he would like, is placed in the position of a semanticist—though by inclination he would prefer to be in the position of the naturalist afield.

of their relationship, bear upon the performance of the entire system? What are the functions of the different parts? What are the consequences of a given structure for the people who move within it?

The structural-functional approach

Sociologists taking this approach to the study of human social organization call themselves "structural-functional" sociologists. By the end of World War II structural-functional analysis was an extremely active, if not dominant, school of thought within the sociological community of theorists and scholars. In 1949 the publication of *Social Theory and Social Structure* placed Robert Merton at the forefront of those who advocated structural-functional approaches to the study of society. To understand Merton's thought requires, then, that we turn to an examination of structural-functionalism.

The term "function" refers to the extent to which some part or process of a social system contributes to the maintenance of that system. It is necessary, if we are going to gain a clearer conception of Merton's use of this term, to note that function does not mean exactly the same thing as purpose or motivation. It means, instead, the extent to which a given activity does, in fact, promote or interfere with the maintenance of a system. As Merton puts it,

> Social function refers to <u>observable objective consequences, and not to subjective</u> dispositions (aims, motives, purposes).[7]

[handwritten annotation: involves not only purposes but consequences.]

It is one thing, for example, to speculate on the aims, motivations, and purposes underlying advertising in modern America and another to see it from a functional perspective. If we ask an advertising man to tell us the aims or purposes of his profession, he might mention several things:[8] Advertising exists to improve the level of living of Americans. Advertising seeks to make Americans aware of the wealth of goods and services that American industry has the capacity to provide. Advertisers are motivated to sell their clients' products. Advertising seeks to upgrade the consumer tastes of people. Advertising keeps alive the American dream of happiness through possessions. We could continue this list further.

A functional analysis promotes a different way of looking at advertising.

---

[7] Reprinted with permission of The Macmillan Company from *Social Theory and Social Structure* (rev. and enl. ed.) by Robert K. Merton, p. 24. © The Free Press, a Corporation 1957.

[8] For an extensive and engaging listing of the values of advertising see Kenneth M. Goode and Harford Powel, Jr., *What About Advertising?* (New York: Harper & Row, Publishers, 1928), pp. 29–32.

What does advertising in fact _do?_ Further, what are the consequences of what it does for the greater society? Compare the following functional evaluation of advertising with the above motivational evaluation of advertising.

It is well known that one of the things advertising does is to pretend to make significant differences out of what are known to be virtually identical products. It has been factually established, for example, that most consumers cannot tell a Chesterfield cigarette from a Pall Mall when blindfolded.[9] Most beer drinkers cannot distinguish between one brand and another. By creating differences where none in fact exists, advertising serves the function of enabling a variety of cigarette manufacturers, brewers, and other companies to survive where there is no utilitarian basis for their survival.[10] Thus, a functionalist would claim that one of the functions of advertising is to maintain a form of industrial pluralism. Along with this, advertising sustains the belief that such a pluralistic system does encourage true competition—that is to say, competition which leads toward improved products. The belief may or may not be true. The point is that one of the functions of advertising is to support this belief by encouraging industrial pluralism.

Manifest functions and latent functions

Merton makes a distinction between two forms of social function. One of these he refers to as "manifest functions" and the other as "latent functions." Manifest functions are objective consequences for some person, subgroup, or social or cultural system which contribute to its adjustment _and were so intended._ Latent functions are consequences which contribute to adjustment but were not so intended.[11] The distinction is a valuable one and it is one which makes clear the nature of sociological investigation as perhaps few other distinctions do. Manifest functions are essentially the official explanations of a given action. Latent functions are the sociological explanations of a given action.

A variety of examples will help make the distinction and indicate its socio-

---

[9] The irrationalities in consumer preferences are summarized in Vance Packard, _The Hidden Persuaders_ (New York: David McKay Co., Inc., 1957), pp. 13–23.

[10] This is very similar to the argument made by Emile Durkheim in _The Division of Labor in Society,_ translated by George Simpson (New York: Free Press of Glencoe, 1964). The function of the division of labor, said Durkheim, is to provide conditions whereby a greater variety of life can be supported within the same ecological space. In a sense, then, advertising could be said to be a vital ecological process.

[11] It should be noted here that the basis for this distinction is a subjective one—that is, intention. Sociologists sooner or later find themselves having to rely on the subjective meaning of a given action in order to give the action wider value in their theoretical formulations. This is frustrating to thinkers who are seeking to produce an empirically oriented theory which is objective and not subjective.

logically heuristic value. An example used by Merton is the Hopi Indian rain ceremony. The manifest function—the intended use of the ceremony—is to bring rain. At the same time it is scientifically evident that such ceremonies do not bring rain. Even the Hopi who had participated in such ceremonies over the long generations must have observed that there was little connection between annual levels of rainfall and the conduct of the rain ceremonies.[12] Yet the ceremony persisted and there was sufficient reason for it to persist; so the Hopi retained the ceremony regardless of its bearing on actual rainfall levels. The reason for such persistence, Merton claims, is that the ceremony performs other functions for Hopi society than merely bringing rain. To examine only the manifest functions of a ceremony, a tradition, a social group, or a particular role is to examine it at the most superficial level. The beginnings of sociological understanding often are found in a consideration of the latent functions. Referring to the Hopi rain ceremonies, Merton goes on to say,

> . . . with the concept of latent function, we continue our inquiry, examining the consequences of the ceremony not for the rain gods or for meteorological phenomena, but for the groups which conduct the ceremony. And here it may be found, as many observers indicate, that the ceremonial does indeed have functions —but functions which are non-purposed or latent.

> Ceremonials may fulfill the latent function of reinforcing the group identity by providing a periodic occasion on which the scattered members of a group assemble to engage in a common activity . . . such ceremonials are a means by which collective expression is afforded the sentiments which . . . are found to be a basic source of group unity. Through the systematic application of the concept of latent function, therefore, *apparently* irrational behavior may *at times* be found to be positively functional for the group.[13] [Italics Merton's.]

One other example, drawn from more contemporary circumstances, may help further in revealing the usefulness of the manifest–latent function distinction. Consider the following item taken from the morning's newspaper.

> After 40,000 miles or more, a baker's dozen countries and innumerable speeches to Communist audiences, Stokely Carmichael, the Black Power advocate, announced his odyssey would end with his return to Hell.

> "I shall return to Hell—that is, the United States," said Carmichael, according to . . . the press in Stockholm . . .

> Carmichael's journey began in July, his first stop England. The Daily Sketch, calling for expulsion of the 26-year-old visitor, quoted him as telling a British

---

[12] When a latent function is important, even though the manifest function is not being met, there is a tendency to rationalize social action. Thus, when a rain ceremony does not produce rain, it is not considered the fault of the ceremony. Instead, the fault is likely to be found in the incompetent performance of one of the participants.

[13] Merton, *Social Theory and Social Structure*, pp. 64–65.

audience: "It is time to let the whites know we are going to take over; if they don't like it, we will stamp them out, using violence and other means necessary."

Carmichael left England for Fidel Castro's Cuba and a conference of Latin-American Communists weighing prospects for hemisphere-wide revolution. Now the Communists were including the United States in calls for "liberation struggle."[14]

Granting the accuracy of the reporting and recognizing also that Carmichael's comments have been taken out of context,[15] we can look at these statements first from the point of view of their manifest functions and then from the point of view of their latent functions. At the manifest level Carmichael seems to be making highly irrational and ineffective threats. After all, even superb organization and armament could not enable the blacks of America—or of the world, for that matter—to stamp out the whites. In some ways, the scientific correspondence between Carmichael's ceremonial chants and the desired effects is about as remote as that of the Hopi rain dancer. But the concept of latent functions leads to further consideration of the matter. Carmichael's statements have received widespread coverage in the press and they have been heard around the world by large numbers of people. There must be more to it than the irrational mouthings of an alienated American black man. The concept of latent functions asks for a thoughtful consideration of other possible social consequences coming from Carmichael's actions. Let us speculate on a few.

First of all, it is obvious that Carmichael is engaged in an extreme and vitriolic condemnation of the United States. Further, he is a black man. Moreover, he is being rewarded with publicity and worldwide attention for his audacity. One of the latent functions of Carmichael's behavior, then, is to provide a model for men who have believed for generations that to insult a white man means immediate and personal catastrophe. Even nonwhites who might sincerely and thoroughly repudiate the radicalism of Carmichael's position cannot help being affected by the public performance they actually observe. Carmichael is a social fact and not a social aspiration. His actions have consequences, and a sociological examination of these requires that we distinguish between what Carmichael appears to be and what he is actually achieving.

Another possible latent function of Carmichael's actions might be to bring moderate nonwhite and white leaders together in attempts to forestall vio-

---

[14] From an article by Special Correspondent William L. Ryan, appearing in the December 2, 1967, issue of *The Rocky Mountain News*, p. 68. Reprinted by permission of The Associated Press.

[15] It is enlightening to compare what newspapers have to say about Carmichael and what Carmichael has to say. See Stokely Carmichael and Charles V. Hamilton, *Black Power: The Politics of Liberation in America* (New York: Random House, Inc., 1967).

lence. If so, then the actual consequence of Carmichael's call for revolutionary violence would be a *détente*. Nonetheless, the consequence would serve the interests of the social system.

It becomes quickly apparent, from these illustrations, that the concept of latent function has some of the qualities of an after-the-fact rationalization or excuse for the way things are. The functionalist seems to be saying, ''Well, if something exists in the social order, there must be a pretty good reason for it—otherwise it would not exist. Therefore, let us think long and hard on the matter and sooner or later the reason for its existence will come to us.''

Is a latent function an apology for the status quo? We found ourselves running into much the same problem when we considered Durkheim's discussion of crime (see Chapter 2). After all, when Durkheim said crime is necessary to any society, he was providing crime with a latent function. Now the structural-functionalist appears to be excusing superstitious rain dances and radical revolutionaries as functional features of the social order. Merton was aware of this disturbing feature of structural-functionalist thought and tried to get around it by introducing yet another idea—the idea of dysfunctions.

The dysfunctional process

Dysfunctional events lessen the adjustment of a social system. Dysfunctional features of a society imply strain or stress or tension. Society tries to constrain dysfunctional elements somewhat the same way an organism would constrain a bacterial or virus infection. If the dysfunctional forces are too great, the social order is overwhelmed, disorganized, and possibly destroyed.[16]

One of the clearest examples I know of a dysfunctional feature in a social system was the Catharist heresy in Europe in the 12th century. The Cathars were of the opinion that affairs of the flesh were damning to the spirit. As a consequence, they concluded that the ideal relationship between a man and a woman was that of brother and sister. They advocated brother-sister relationships in marriage. So extreme were their views that they would eat no food which they considered the product of a sexual union. They would not, therefore, eat eggs, milk, meat, or cheese. They married, but ideally did not consummate their marriages sexually. Feudal leaders in provinces where such heretical views existed recognized fully the implications of such a point of view—it meant, if followed through, an attrition of population. Had the Cathars been completely successful, the consequence would have been the loss, in

---

[16] It is worth noting in Merton's work that the idea of function is used more often than dysfunction. In *Social Theory and Social Structure*, for example, a book of over six hundred pages, the index mentions dysfunctions only three times.

a generation or two, of the total society—a painless, perhaps, but certain loss. Despite their peaceful and gentle nature the Cathars were too threatening. They were destroyed. Their elimination from society was thorough; the only evidence we have of their existence is indirect, consisting for the most part of allusions to the Cathars in church records.

The next example, illustrating the possible dysfunctional use of prisoners as slaves in ancient Rome, is an engaging one.[17]

Lead poisoning, according to Dr. Gilfillan, killed off most of the Roman ruling class and damaged the brains of Commodus, Nero, and all those other mad emperors. Such poisoning became common, he points out, about 150 B.C., after the wealthy Romans began to use Greek prisoners of war as their household servants. These slaves brought with them the Greek custom of using lead-lined pots for cooking, especially for warming wine and for concentrating honey and grape syrup, the sweeteners most popular at that time. Nobody realized that food cooked in such utensils became highly toxic—although the Greek upper classes probably had been decimated by the same slow-acting poison a few generations earlier. Alexander the Great, for example, quite possibly died of it, rather than of alcoholism.

Writing in the *Journal of Occupational Medicine*, Dr. Gilfillan notes that fashionable Roman matrons began to drink wine at about the same time they acquired Greek cooks; and that they soon began to show the classic symptoms of lead poisoning—sterility, miscarriages, and heavy child mortality. Their surviving children often suffered permanent mental impairment. As a consequence, he estimates, the aristocracy lost about three-quarters of its members in each generation. As evidence he cites both census statistics and the heavy deposits of lead found in bones taken from the more splendid Roman tombs of the period.

The poor people, meanwhile, were spared—because they cooked in earthenware pots, and couldn't afford to drink much wine in any case. Moreover, they did not use the lead water pipes and lead-based cosmetics which the wealthier classes enjoyed. "The brightest and winsomest from the poorer class" did occasionally climb to positions of power and wealth—whereupon they too fell victim to the rich man's scourge. The result, Dr. Gilfillan argues, was a systematic extinction of the ablest people in the Roman world. He does not, however, draw any conclusions about later cultures which might have poisoned themselves—with tobacco, air pollution, radioactive fallout, or whatever—without realizing what they were doing.

Let me suggest one more illustration of a dysfunctional process. Some demographers are of the opinion that medical technology may have dysfunctional effects for modern social systems if it succeeds in creating disproportionately greater numbers of old people than have existed in the past. A so-

---

[17] John Fischer mentions this interesting theory in *Harper's Magazine*. Copyright © 1967, by Harper's Magazine, Inc. Reprinted from the December, 1967 issue by permission of the author. Pp. 16 and 18.

ciety that requires the flexibility and adaptability of youth and which, at the same time, is made up of relatively inflexible older people, might suffer as a consequence. That is to say, strain might be introduced into the system leading to disorganizing conflicts, breakdowns in communication, and inflexible ways of thinking about national and international problems.

Values of functional analysis

The point of these illustrations is that functional analysis orients thought toward the social consequences—intended and unintended—of a particular action. Merton claims functional analysis has the following virtues:

First of all, it inhibits the tendency to dismiss a seemingly irrational social event with the casual observation that it is merely superstition, foolishness, or craziness. For example, a superficial response to a campus "panty raid" might be to dismiss it as "kids blowing off steam" or as "youthful foolishness and exuberance." A functionalist, on the other hand, is concerned with the form of the action—why a panty raid and not some other form of foolishness? He is also interested in the functional nature of the raid—what is the relationship of the raid to other features of the campus social structure?

Second, the concepts of manifest and latent function provide the sociologist with a means of probing into those features of social behavior which are more theoretically valuable. The sociologist can, for example, study the effects of a war bond propaganda campaign to determine its effectiveness. At the manifest level he can consider its avowed purpose[18] of stirring up patriotic fervor. Such an investigation is of primary value to administrators and others who are interested in producing an effective propaganda campaign. The latent consequences of the campaign can carry the sociologist further into the matter. Merton investigated the appeals used by Kate Smith during a war bond campaign in World War II. One of the latent consequences of the campaign was to stifle expressions of difference toward official policy.[19]

Third, a functional approach to social action has ethical and moral implications. Essentially, such an approach brings a more sophisticated awareness to the moral issues involved in a particular situation. Merton puts it this way,

The introduction of the concept of latent function in social research leads to conclusions which show that "social life is not as simple as it first seems." For as

---

[18] Merton uses the term "purpose" here. This is confusing because Merton has gone to considerable pains to make the distinction between function and purpose.
[19] See Robert K. Merton, *Mass Persuasion.*

long as people confine themselves to *certain* consequences (e.g. manifest consequences), it is comparatively simple for them to pass moral judgments upon the practice or belief in question. Moral evaluations, generally based on these manifest consequences, tend to be polarized in terms of black or white. But the perception of further (latent) consequences often complicates the picture. Problems of moral evaluation (which are not our immediate concern) and problems of social engineering (which are our concern) both take on the additional complexities usually involved in responsible social decisions.[20]

Thus, to return to an earlier illustration, at the manifest level the prolongation of life is an obvious moral good. At the latent level we need to consider the matter further. Could such a program lead to a society where a youthful minority might have to go to the extreme of considering ways of killing off their elders in order to avoid the repressive effects of their presence?[21]

A fourth value of structural-functional analysis, somewhat similar in nature to the last mentioned value, is that it replaces naive moral judgments with sociological analysis. Merton illustrates his meaning, in this instance, with a reference to political "machines." Traditionally the political machine in America has been viewed as an evil: It is a source of graft. It is corrupt, and it is a perversion of democratic processes. The political boss buys votes instead of earning them through public service. The machine protects criminal elements rather than exorcising them. The machine gives public jobs and offices to loyal members of the organization rather than to men best fitted to the task. So the criticisms continue. A functionalist, however, argues that the extensive development of such machines and their continued existence over relatively long periods of time suggests that they are serving social ends that other, morally approved, organizations have abdicated. Merton says,

> Examined for a moment apart from any moral considerations, the political apparatus operated by the Boss is effectively designed to perform [various] functions with a minimum of inefficiency. Holding the strings of diverse governmental divisions, bureaus and agencies in his competent hands, the Boss rationalizes the relations between public and private business. He serves as the business community's ambassador in the otherwise alien (and sometimes unfriendly) realm of government. And, in strict business-like terms, he is well-paid for his economic services to his respectable business clients.[22]

---

[20] Merton, *Social Theory and Social Structure*, p. 68.

[21] In a similar vein, Dick Gregory commented recently on the present trend toward organ transplant surgery. Referring to the fact that the only present living heart transplant patient is relying on the heart of a colored man, Gregory said he hoped white people were not thinking of using blacks as their general source for spare parts.

[22] Merton, *Social Theory and Social Structure*, pp. 75–76. This point is nicely illustrated in the movie *The Last Hurrah*. In this film the political boss is sympathetically portrayed as a man to whom the people come for real help rather than bureaucratic pretenses at helping.

This statement should not be read as an apology for bossism and the political machine system of municipal or local government. Merton hastily goes on to state,

> To adopt a functional outlook is to provide not an apologia for the political machine but a more solid basis for modifying or eliminating the machine, *providing* specific structural arrangements are introduced either for eliminating [certain] demands of the business community or, if that is the objective, of satisfying these demands through alternative means.[23]

If we wish, then, to operate either as relatively detached social analysists or as social and political activists, a structural-functional point of view is necessary.[24] It inhibits a tendency toward naive moralizing about social issues and it places any given social action within the greater context of the total social structure.

The nature of deviant behavior

Of the various contributions to social thought by Merton, perhaps the best known and most generally applied has been his consideration of the nature of deviant social behavior. Rather than view such behavior as the product of abnormal personalities, Merton was concerned with the extent to which it might, at least in some considerable part, be a result of the structural nature of society itself. In this respect Merton knowingly endorsed a position which, by the middle of the 20th century, had become a labored cliché. However, Merton was concerned with more than merely stating a truism of the order that delinquents or social derelicts are the sorry products of the society that spawned them. He was, instead, interested in specifying the process whereby deviant action is generated within a social structure.

Deviant behavior presents a critical problem to men who accept a sociological perspective. The problem is this: On the one hand the sociologist is well aware that society and culture have an almost crushing capacity to induce conformity on the part of the individual. On the other hand, innovation does exist. The directives of the culture may be challenged or modified. How can deviation occur within a system which has so much power to prevent it?

---

[23] Merton, *Social Theory and Social Structure,* p. 76.

[24] Kingsley Davis reacts to this argument in an interesting article. See "The Myth of Functional Analysis as a Special Method in Sociology and Anthropology," *American Sociological Review,* **24,** 6 (1959) 757–772. Davis points out that structural-functional analysis is actually just another way of talking about sociological analysis. In other words, whether sociologists call themselves structural-functionalists or something else, they still use the same basic approach.

Merton dealt with this problem in the following manner, using American culture as the basis for his observations.

To begin with, he developed the reasonable argument that American culture places great emphasis on the value of individual attainment of success. At the same time, and this is quite significant, the means of achieving success are left pretty much up to the individual. Institutional means for attaining success—the legitimate pathways to money, fame, or power—are not given any special emphasis or consideration. The man who attains success by relying on quasi-criminal devices may be as admired, or even more admired, than the man who employs the legitimate structure. Having established this beginning point, Merton raises a more fundamental question. He puts it this way,

> What . . . are the consequences for the behavior of people variously situated in a social structure of a culture in which the emphasis on dominant success-goals has become increasingly separated from an equivalent emphasis on institutionalized procedures for seeking these goals?[25]

Merton was concerned, here, with the problem of how people adapt to society and the ways in which the structural features of society affect the form the adaptations might take. In his approach to this problem Merton decided to strip social structure down to two elemental conditions that hold for any society. He did this by making a distinction between the goals of a culture and the means the culture provides for achieving those goals.[26]

If we grant the existence of these conditions—that society encourages an interest in certain goals and, at the same time, provides certain sanctioned means for attaining such goals, then the alternative forms of adaptation are limited to how the person responds to these goals and the means provided for their attainment. One may accept the goals and the means, or he might accept the goals and reject the means. Or, he might accept the means while rejecting the goals. Merton summarized the five forms of adaptation possible in the form of the following table:[27]

---

[25] Merton, *Social Theory and Social Structure,* p. 139.

[26] On the surface, the distinction between goals and means seems simple and clear; in practice it is not. This is probably the major limitation to the utility of Merton's scheme or "social action" theories. To take a very homely example, grades may be viewed simultaneously as a means and as an end to a college student. At one level they are a means of getting through school and getting into a profession. At the same time they may be a goal for which the student must prepare himself. In the final analysis, the extent to which something exists as a goal or as a means is subjective. In the realm of human conduct the external classification of an action as goal oriented is not possible. This, in part, was one of the main contributions of Freudian thought. A man who is ambitious and successful in his work would, from a Mertonian standpoint, be occupationally goal oriented. Freud would suggest, on the other hand, that maybe such an effort is really only a means of getting even with his wife by asserting his superiority. This example suggests the further possibility that the term "latent function" is actually a device to cope with the problems of determining human goals when using structural-functional theories.

[27] Merton, *Social Theory and Social Structure,* p. 140.

A TYPOLOGY OF MODES OF INDIVIDUAL ADAPTATION

Mode of Adaptation	Culture Goals	Institutionalized Means
I. Conformity	+	+
II. Innovation	+	−
III. Ritualism	−	+
IV. Retreatism	−	−
V. Rebellion	±	±

The nature of these alternative modes of adaptation can be illustrated by a brief examination of goals and means in institutions of higher learning. One of the legitimate goals of the system is the attainment of a high grade-point average.[28] The institutionalized means for achieving this is by study, hard work, and taking tests and examinations. If the student accepts both the goals and the means, then, according to Merton's scheme, he is a conformist—and this is one way of defining conformity.

A student might, however, seek the goal of getting good grades but resent the means available for the attainment of such a goal. He could then respond by employing some kind of innovation. That is to say, he might use unacceptable means to attain an acceptable goal. He might cheat or have someone else take his examinations for him. Or, as has occurred in rare instances, he might attempt to gain access to the office of records and alter his grade report. If the pressure toward institutional goals is great enough, says Merton, while at the same time there is less emphasis placed on the value of legitimate means, such innovative forms of adaptation will proliferate.

A ritualistic form of adaptation is one in which the student rejects the idea of grades but latches onto the means employed to get grades as a way of life. Reading, study, and the taking of examinations become sufficient. Every campus has its academic "bums" who make good enough grades to remain in college and who have little other aspiration than to hang around college, go to classes, and live a student's life. The professor who reads from yellowed notes the obsolescent ideas of another era is a ritualist. The students who come to class and then write letters home—these are ritualists. The school administrator who demands signatures on loyalty oaths—regardless of more concrete manifestations of loyalty—is a ritualist. In all of these instances we have people placing emphasis on the means of attaining some end, often to the detriment of attaining the goal itself.

---

[28] For purposes of exemplification, we will simply assume that grades can be dealt with as a desired goal and ignore the possibility of looking on them as means.

The fourth category of adaptive modes refers to the retreatist. The retreatist in college would be the student who cares nothing about grades and, furthermore, sees little point in studying for or taking examinations. In effect, he withdraws from the system. He is a dropout.

Merton's discussion of rebellion is more brief than we would like it to be and it is surprisingly vague. Yet rebellion is distinct from any of the other forms of adaptation. The rebel, unlike the retreatist, is not apathetic about the situation in which he finds himself. Instead of passively withdrawing, he concludes that the system is sufficiently important to warrant being reformed. He is sufficiently caught up in the goals and the means of the culture to seek to change them. The rebel finds the system frustrating enough to cause him to wish to change it, but not so frustrating that he seeks to withdraw from it. Most importantly, Merton suggests that the distinguishing characteristic of the rebel is a belief that the source of social problems lies within the social order itself rather than within the individual. His aspiration becomes one of changing the system. The rebel is idealistic enough to believe in the higher aspirations of his culture, but pragmatic enough to conclude that greater effort is necessary to move closer to those ideals. Current examples of the rebellious mode of adaptation on the campus might be the Students for Democratic Society or the student-supported Free Speech movement at Berkeley.

By making these distinctions Merton is attempting to establish more than a simple typology of different forms of behavior. He is not only developing a distinction between the conformist and the innovator, for example; he is also attempting to locate the social conditions that increase the likelihood of getting one kind of behavior over the other. In effect, Merton claims that in those social circumstances where social goals are highly valued and the means for obtaining the goals are not as highly valued, the likelihood of innovation is increased. Criminal behavior, which is one kind of innovative action, is more likely in a society which places great emphasis on individual success, wealth, and power, and which, at the same time, does not emphasize the value of the legitimate means for obtaining these goals. Merton argues that such a situation exists in the United States.

It is necessary, if we are to grasp the significance of Merton's thought, to recognize the extent to which Merton is giving culturally established, collectively held, value priorities a place in the interpretation of individual conduct. A culture which, for example, values cleverness over the dignity of work will likely find itself peopled with clever loafers. The source of the condition is, however, within the manner in which the culture establishes the balance between means and goals—not in the individual.

The sociology of science

At a less abstract level, one of Merton's strong interests has been a consideration of the sociology of knowledge and, more narrowly, what might be called the sociology of science. The emergence of science, the development of science as a massive and powerful institution, poses a great variety of sociologically valuable questions. Science is not, certainly, a simple response to the demands of a growing and expanding population. It is not a simple product of man's intelligence. It appears, rather, to be a way of viewing the world that has emerged from culturally established attitudes which were somehow conducive to its development. Merton, more specifically, claims that science is an outgrowth of world views contained in early Protestantism. Weber saw capitalism coming from Protestantism; Merton sees science as yet another contribution of the Protestant Ethic.

Merton summarizes the character of his argument with the following statement,

> It is the thesis of this study that the Puritan ethic, as an ideal-typical expression of the value-attitudes basic to ascetic Protestantism generally, so canalized the interests of seventeenth-century Englishmen as to constitute one important *element* in the enhanced cultivation of science. The deep-rooted religious *interests* of the day demanded in their forceful implications the systematic, rational, and empirical study of Nature for the glorification of God in His works and for the control of the corrupt world.[29] [Italics Merton's.]

Merton isolated several facets of Puritan thought and practice and concluded that scientists of the 17th century were functioning as innovators. While they still held to the ethical, moral, and spiritual goals of Protestant-Christian doctrine, they were engaged in a modification of the means whereby such goals were to be attained. Specifically, they were in the process of turning to nature itself rather than to theological inspiration or speculation as a means of attaining Puritan goals.

Foremost among these goals was the endeavor to serve and glorify God. If Puritanism instilled in man the desire to glorify God, and if Puritanism had some bearing on the development of early science, then the 17th-century scientist would evaluate his work in terms of the extent to which it worked toward the greater glorification of God. This, claims Merton, is what did in fact

---

[29] Merton, *Social Theory and Social Structure,* pp. 574–575. Pitirim Sorokin argues, more broadly, that both science and capitalism grew out of a movement toward "sensatism." This movement had an influence on all of the institutions of Western European society. See Chapter 12 of this work for more details.

happen. Seventeenth-century scientists not only prefaced their works as being dedicated to the greater glory of God but saw the true ends of science to be the glorification of the Creator.

> In his last will and testament, Boyle echoes the same attitude, petitioning the Fellows of the Society in this wise: "Wishing them also a happy success in their laudable attempts, to discover the true Nature of the Works of God; and praying that they and all other Searchers into Physical Truths, may cordially refer their Attainments to the Glory of the Great Author of Nature, and to the Comfort of Mankind." John Wilks proclaimed the experimental study of Nature to be a most effective means of begetting in men a veneration for God. Francis Willughby was prevailed upon to publish his works—which he had deemed unworthy of publication— only when Ray insisted that it was a means of glorifying God. Ray's *Wisdom of God* . . . is a panegyric of those who Glorify Him by Studying His works.[30]

The Puritan Ethic was also strongly utilitarian—that is to say, it emphasized social welfare. The early scientist was as eager to indicate the social merit and worth of his work as he was to make it an effort dedicated to God's glory. Moreover, scientific studies promoted discipline, work, and serious rather than idle thoughts—all Puritan values. There is, then, a congruence between some of the basic tenets of Puritan thought and those of the early men of science. We are thereby brought before the irony, if this interpretation of the origins of science carries any validity, of observing a religious ethic bringing into being (or at least serving as the midwife of) an ideology which, in its extreme forms, has produced religion's most serious opposition and intellectual challenge.

Puritan values provided the sanction for science. The scientist could feel justified in the belief his work was meaningful, not only to him as an individual but also in a much greater context—science was an entry into the works of God. There was a greater end to a scientific formulation than the mere statement of an empirical regularity.

The fact that Protestant thought emphasized individualism, rationality, utilitarianism, and empiricism might have had only a fortuitous relationship to the development of science. Merton suggested that a significant test would be to determine whether or not Protestants, in the early days of scientific discovery, were more often found within the ranks of scientists than we would expect on the basis of their representation in the total population. To determine this, Merton investigated the membership of the Royal Society, an "invisible college" of scientists, in its early formative years. He commented,

> . . . of the ten men who constituted the "invisible college," in 1645, only one, Scarbough, was clearly non-Puritan. About two of the others there is some uncertainty, though Merret had a Puritan training. The others were all definitely Puritan.

---

[30] Merton, *Social Theory and Social Structure*, pp. 576–577.

Moreover, among the original list of members of the Society of 1663, forty-two of the sixty-eight concerning whom information about their religious orientation is available were clearly Puritan. Considering that the Puritans constituted a relatively small minority in the English population, the fact that they constituted sixty-two per cent of the initial membership of the Society becomes even more striking [31]

This disproportionate representation of Protestants within the ranks of science has occurred, as well, in present times. Merton cites the observations of Knapp and Goodrich to the effect that some Protestant denominations are proportionately several hundred times more strongly represented among lists of meritorious American scientists than we would expect on the basis of their representation within the general population. On the other hand, representation by Catholics is excessively low—although in other professional categories, such as law, the Catholics more than hold their own. [32]

One of the consequences, one of the latent functions of the Puritan form of Protestantism in the 17th century, then, was to set the stage for the development of rational and empirical science. Merton summarizes his argument by making four principal observations.

First, the relationships between emerging science and religion were indirect and certainly unintended.

Second, science, once the ideological orientation necessary for it was set, acquired a degree of functional autonomy—it acquired a character of its own which, eventually, would lead to the point where science would appear to be completely removed from religious modes of thought.

Third, Merton suggests that the process of institutional modification of thoughtways and the development of new institutional forms may be so subtle as to occur below the threshold of awareness of many of those involved in it.

Fourth, the more dramatic conflict between science and religion—particularly in the 19th century—has possibly obscured the more significant relationship which exists between the two. [33]

Merton was explicitly aware that his study follows in the path of Max Weber. Weber was concerned with the influence of Protestant thought on the development of capitalism. Weber also suggested, in a very sketchy manner, that Protestantism had a similar influence on the development of science. However, Merton elaborated what Weber left implicit.

---

[31] *Ibid.*, pp. 584–585. Merton cites Dean Stinson as the source of his data.
[32] *Ibid.*, p. 602.
[33] *Ibid.*, pp. 605–606.

Merton increasingly became interested in the idea of the unanticipated consequences of social action until, eventually, it formed one of the most resonant underlying themes of his work. Out of Puritan religion, unexpectedly and without design, appears science. From propaganda campaigns designed to solicit money come unanticipated and subtle constraints on democratic political ideology. From fears of loss of freedom come repressive measures to assure that liberty will be preserved. It is this feature of human social conduct which requires, if man is to make the best social use of his reason, a constant and subtle examination of the functional aspects of any given social action. To evaluate a policy only in terms of its apparent or official objectives is to see considerably less than half of what is taking place.

There is a presumptuousness in Merton's writing. He makes much of the fact that men are not always aware of the ways in which they are shaping their own destinies. He then enjoins the sociologist to correct this situation by considering the latent functions of human endeavors. One wonders what the latent functions of a completely successful sociological enterprise of this kind might be. Would an accurate manifest and latent transcription of all his plans make the world a better place for man? Is it better not to know?

The question is not purely academic. Sociology, like any other scientific or humanistic effort, will never be perfectly successful. Yet, through the efforts of men like Merton, it has achieved today a sufficient level of success to make it an effective force in modern social life. It therefore becomes a humanistic question to inquire into the latent functions of men who pursue the quest for latent functions. Do they jeopardize the tenuous hold that official interpretations of reality have on men and thereby dissolve the social bond? Or do they aid us in the comprehension of our most serious irrationalities? It is a question for a structural-functionalist to consider.[34]

---

[34] Sociologists certainly have not ignored the question of the social functions of sociology. For some interesting discussions of this matter see Maurice Stein and Arthur Vidich, editors, *Sociology on Trial* (Englewood Cliffs, N.J.: Prentice-Hall, Inc., 1963).

5 Can Science Save Us? The Question of George A. Lundberg

No field of study, scientific or nonscientific, is without consequences for the study of man—in this sense we can claim all human intellectual endeavor is geared ultimately toward understanding ourselves. Men specialized in the study of electronics have now turned toward developing electronic models of the human brain. Field research of the geologist has resulted in archeological findings that give man increasingly earlier prehistorical origins. And some of the most abstruse theoretical physics has led to perspectives that eventually spill over into humanistic concerns. A recent example was the debate and furor created by the principle of indeterminancy. Although Heisenberg probably never intended to have it used as such, the principle of indeterminancy was seen by many exponents of free will as a physical or scientific argument supporting their contention that man is morally responsible for his actions. The field of biology, and genetics in particular, is so rife with political overtones that a number of governments have been unable to avoid the temptation to tamper with it—and the results, on occasion, have been scandalous.

Fields like geology, chemistry, theoretical physics, electronics, or microbiology are only indirectly involved in the study of man. For example, while nuclear fission has obvious manifold implications for the future course of history, a knowledge of nuclear physics is not directly transferable to the study of society or an examination of human emotions. In fact, a specialist in one of these fields may express an open pride in the insulating ignorance of the humanities which his intensive specialization offers him. But such a view is terribly narrow. Knowledgeable and liberal men in these spheres of intellectual activity are likely to claim that their work is related to broader philosophical, sociological, humanistic and even theological concerns.

If we may accept, for the moment, the idea that even the most specialized

91

natural sciences have at least an indirect bearing on the study of man, then we can begin to see how truly varied and competitive are the arguments which promise to shed light on human social and psychological understanding. The variety is overwhelming. Man's attempts to account for himself have ranged from the charmingly bizarre religious conceptions of the medieval Cathars, who believed men were fallen angels wrapped in garments of flesh,[1] to the icy speculations of modern behaviorists who view man, along with all other creatures, as a delicate response mechanism.[2]

With few deviations, every conception of man ever devised has also been the basis of a scheme for promoting his improvement.[3] Religious conceptions of man offer spiritual exercises designed to strengthen moral character. Materialistic conceptions of man attempt to advance human welfare by producing faster autos and bigger airplanes, and by installing better plumbing. Psychoanalytic conceptions of man see progress coming through a fuller understanding of ourselves and through the eventual attainment of a tolerance of our intolerable natures. Racists argue that great civilizations are the product of genetic superiority; that the way to further the progress of mankind is to purify the bloodstock of the leading culture, that is, the one to which the racist happens to belong at the time. Health food faddists claim wonders for their diets. Intellectuals, especially academic ones, argue that man is a product of his training and then, rather naturally, espouse education as the way to solve the ills of the world.

What are we to do in the midst of all this clamor and confusion? Is there some single criterion by which these varied claims can be evaluated? Is there some way man can approach the complexities of himself and his society and, at the same time, avoid falling into the dogmatic faiths which, so far, have been the only means whereby he has been able to sustain himself in the face of such confusion?

---

[1] I encountered this bit of information in Denis DeRougement, *Love in the Western World* (New York: Pantheon Books, Inc., 1956). Perhaps the Cathars are right.

[2] A leading exponent of this point of view, though not himself an icy person, is B. F. Skinner. See his *Science and Human Behavior* (New York: The Macmillan Company, 1953). Viewing man as a delicate response mechanism may seem cold and analytical; even so, Skinner believes such a perspective could pave the way toward a more Utopian and full life for man. He expressed this belief in the form of a novel. See B. F. Skinner, *Walden 2* (New York: The Macmillan Company, 1962). I highly recommend this novel to anyone considering a career in the modern social sciences.

[3] One of the few exceptions, to my knowledge, is G. K. Zipf, *Human Behavior and the Principle of Least Effort: An Introduction to Human Ecology* (Reading, Mass.: Addison-Wesley Publishing Co., Inc., 1949). At no time, if I remember properly, does Zipf advance a way in which his analysis might be used to improve the lot of mankind. This, if nothing else, makes Zipf one of the most unusual social theorists of the thirties and forties—a time that abounded in social reform schemes.

Social science and social myth

We cannot ignore this question. Is man required by the nature of things to rely always on some blind faith? Can we give meaning to life only by feeding on the delusions offered by some uncritically accepted ideology? Is, as a conservative acquaintance of mine once put it, an open mind an empty mind? Are various forms of intellectual bigotry the only way to avoid confusion and meaninglessness?

It was this issue which George A. Lundberg attacked and attempted to resolve. Lundberg sought to provide us with an approach to human problems that does not lean on emotional surrender to an established ideology; nor does it force us to respond with a hopeless shrug of the shoulders as we retreat into a modern cult of despair. Quite simply, Lundberg suggested that we acquire faith in a form of reasoning which is itself constantly skeptical of faith. We can be confident only of the method we use; we can never be confident of our conclusions. This is the paradox of the position taken by the modern social scientist—and it is one we shall examine through Lundberg's writings.[4]

Only science, suggested Lundberg, possesses the ability to bring order into disorder without having to rely on myths and delusions. It has done this in the physical and biological realms. Now we must accept the logic and general analytic procedures of science and apply them to our psychological and social natures. Anything else will result in deception, error, and confusion. Because this position is so fundamental to the social sciences—anthropology, economics, political science, social psychology, and sociology—we must give it some attention here.

Lundberg begins by suggesting that of all the different ways of coming to grips with nature man has tried so far, the most successful has been science. Science, after a rough and often bitterly vituperative struggle for survival among ideas, won out over religion, magic, and tradition as a means of bringing nature under man's control. It has not yet, however, won out over

---

[4] The following brief bibliography of George A. Lundberg's works refers only to his major writings. *Sociology* (New York: The Macmillan Company, 1939); *Leisure, A Suburban Study,* with Mirra Komarovsky and Mary A. McInerny (New York: Columbia University Press, 1933); *Social Research, A Study in the Methods of Gathering Data* (2d ed.; New York: David McKay Company, Inc., 1942); *Can Science Save Us?* (2d ed.; New York: David McKay Company, Inc., 1961). This chapter is based primarily on materials appearing in *Can Science Save Us?* and extracts are reprinted by permission of David McKay Company, Inc. This small volume had a great impact on me when I was just beginning studies in the social sciences. I still strongly recommend it to undergraduates—and, though now outdistanced by more sophisticated treatments of the same issues, it still merits review from those of us who have greater experience.

these less effective thoughtways when it comes to an understanding of man. In this realm preference is still given to customary forms of thought, to religion, or even to reliance on magic.[5] When we can see how successful science has been in bringing about control over physical reality and, to a lesser extent perhaps, over biological reality, why do we not apply it directly to human political, economic, and social concerns?

The reason we do not allow science to enter human affairs more extensively, says Lundberg, is because most people feel they already know the answers to problems of social relations.[6] The man who places his faith in the slower but more certain logic and rigor of science is at a disadvantage in the human realm because here he must compete with a variety of charlatans who provide quick and superficially reasonable answers. Lundberg sees the social scientist in a position similar to that of honest physicians who were at one time disadvantaged in their competition with snake oil practitioners.[7] The "snake oil practitioners" in the human realm are the astrologers, fanatics, and lonely hearts columnists who, though they give enough occasional good advice to remain successful, rely in the final analysis on their own prejudices. The major distinction between idealistic charlatans who are ignorant of the limitations of their knowledge and the old-fashioned snake oil man is that at least the snake oil man knew he was a fraud.

But is it not equally a form of ignorant and idealistic faith to rely on science as the savior of humanity? Only, says Lundberg, if we force science to give us quick and ready answers.

I know that the method I propose is scoffed at in some quarters on the ground that, while it may be the solution for the long run, life is a short run. Whose life? Human life in its collective aspect stretches backward at least a million years and may reach much farther into the future. Throughout the ages it has been regarded as the mark of the intelligent and the civilized man that he has the power to feel and plan beyond the immediate situation. In any case, what choice have we? The proximate and immediate solutions which all desire are themselves dependent upon the development and use, in however modest degree, of scientific knowledge. Whether we look at it from the long or the short perspective, certain social

---

[5] Even an advanced civilization is not without its exponents of magic. I just recently talked with a woman who is working toward a graduate degree in the field of anthropology. With great seriousness we talked about a time when she exorcised a devil from the mind of a disturbed girl by using mental force. Several quite intelligent and charming people have confessed to me that they are witches and have done so, I now discover, in all sincerity. Witchcraft evidently means something to them and they accept it as a working principle—a way of getting things done. I had been inclined, at first, to presume my leg was being pulled.

[6] Lundberg, *Can Science Save Us?*, p. 5.

[7] *Ibid.*, p. 13.

problems have arisen as a result of science, and in our struggle with these problems science alone can save.[8]

Lundberg tells us, in this passage, that we really have little choice in the matter. The development of a social *science*, regardless of the extent to which such an endeavor falls short of pure scientific ideals, is necessary and inevitable. Now what we must do, says Lundberg, is come to a full understanding of what this means for all of us. Lundberg entreats the layman, on the one hand, to develop greater understanding of and patience with the behavioral scientist. On the other hand, he takes social scientists to task for not being sufficiently dedicated to science as a way of life or, at least, as a way of developing knowledge. Although the social scientist cannot be as rigorous in his work as the chemist, physicist, or biologist, he is nonetheless morally called on to act as scientifically as he can and he must not relax in this effort.

Lundberg does not equivocate in his defense of the social sciences as sciences. They are, in his estimation, legitimate sciences in every respect. The ideal social scientist is an objective observer and writer whose own values and emotions do not intrude into his quest for decisive facts—facts that will either lend further support to a theory or weaken it to the point where it is no longer acceptable. The scientist Lundberg offers us is a detached, dispassionate, and thoroughly rational intellectual. He offers no panaceas. He does not plead for some reform or social movement. He can tell you with equal effectiveness how to stimulate a race riot or operate a bakery. His duty is not to tell you where to go; only how to get there.

> My point is that no science tells us *what to do* with the knowledge that constitutes the science. Science only provides a car and a chauffeur for us. It does not directly, as science, tell us where to drive. The car and the chauffeur will take us into the ditch, over the precipice, against a stone wall, or into the highlands of age-long human aspirations with equal efficiency . . . the scientist who serves as navigator and chauffeur has no scientific privilege or duty to tell the rest of the passengers what they *should* want.[9]

For Lundberg, the social scientist is a man who can, with some accuracy, make conditional statements about the outcomes of given policies—but he may not himself formulate the policy. He can say, with all of the neutrality of an electronic computer, ". . . at the technical level alone, exemplary central nuclear attacks offer significant advantages. The problems of com-

---

[8] George A. Lundberg, *Can Science Save Us?* (2d ed.; New York: David McKay Company, Inc., 1961), p. 16.
[9] *Ibid.*, p. 38.

mand, control, and communications, which are very great in sustained high-intensity nuclear wars, are much reduced in slow-motion exchanges that are limited and deliberate.''[10] He must not, however, if he follows the ideal described by Lundberg, indicate any personal preference for one alternative over the other.

The "scientific" social scientist

This characterization of the social scientist which Lundberg draws for us is not especially attractive. After all, many people come into the social sciences because they are discontented with the way things are in the world today. They want to improve conditions—and this desire for reform means that one is permitting an intrusion of his values into his work as a social scientist. Yet, one does not become a criminologist in order to amass knowledge that may be sold with equanimity to police officials or gangsters. We do not devote our lives to the development of theories of conflict only to have them, when published, used by national or community leaders as a means of suppressing an exploited population. But Lundberg has a reply for this kind of warmhearted approach to social science.

In the first place, argues Lundberg, the desire to reform people or impose our values on others interferes with the validity of our scientific findings. Social science can be respectable in the eyes of the world only if its findings are as accurate and as unemotional as it is possible to make them. One of the things that makes the quotation from Kahn just cited as sobering as it is, is the fact that Kahn maintains an attitude of not caring. If he were a pacifist, people would be inclined to discount his statement—thinking, perhaps, that he was writing satire. If he were a militarist, people might wonder whether he was trying to "whitewash" the use of thermonuclear devices in warfare. But Kahn has the virtue of being able to maintain a disinterested attitude. Lundberg claims that only by this kind of dispassionate presentation of arguments can the findings of social science come to have any effective application in the attainment of whatever values we hold dear.

In the second place, says Lundberg, the cold objectivity of the scientist does not mean that values and sentiments are to be done away with. To the contrary, only by having scientists assume this cool and detached attitude can we hope to maintain some semblance of a democracy and avoid a dic-

---

[10] Herman Kahn, *Thinking About the Unthinkable* (New York: Frederick A. Praeger, Inc., 1965).

tatorship of pseudoscientific frauds. The scientist may legitimately attempt to ascertain the prevailing values of his society. He might, for example, poll people and determine how they value equality of opportunity for all people in the United States. Once the values are ascertained, he can then suggest ways of efficiently achieving them. In a word, Lundberg advocates a democratic system of determining values through scientific means. If, for example, polls indicated that the majority of the population wanted to destroy some minority, then, though the scientist might personally disagree with this policy, if he wishes to continue to function as a social scientist, he is obligated to seek the most efficient ways available for achieving this end. Lundberg's social scientist begins to look like Dr. Strangelove—with the addition of a heavy trace of Adolph Eichmann. If we dislike this characterization, we must consider the alternative. The alternative is a world in which scientists themselves establish values. But there is nothing in science which gives it moral insight—it is fraudulent to pretend science can provide us with moral directives.

If we are to avoid situations in which the masses of men become dedicated to inhuman values, we cannot do it by giving the scientist moral power. We can do it only by giving greater freedom to men whose task it is to concern themselves with human values—writers, theologians, philosophers, artists, poets, and politicians. The scientist does not dare step into the moral arena; the moment he does so his scientific character becomes blemished. His facts become suspect. His arguments and his writings are directed not toward scientific truths but toward what he believes ought to be, or what he would like to think, is man's condition.

The radical quality of Lundberg's proposal appears most explicitly in the following quotation. In reading this quotation, keep in mind it is being made by a man who is a liberal advocate of democratic government; moreover, he is presenting this argument to colleagues who, almost to a man, are of similar political persuasion.

> The services of *real* social scientists would be as indispensable to Fascists as to Communists and Democrats, just as are the services of physicists and physicians. The findings of physical scientists at times also have been ignored by political regimes, but when that *has* occurred, it has been the *regime* and not the *science* that has yielded in the end.[11]

As Lundberg views it, the only way the social scientist can increase his utility and enhance his status as a scientist is by sticking to his job *as a*

---

[11] Lundberg, *Can Science Save Us?*, p. 57.

scientist. Whether he operates within a fascist, communist, or democratic regime, he should tend to the development of scientific knowledge and ignore the broader issues of values and policy formation. Lundberg reduces the central tasks of the social scientist to three general concerns.

> Social scientists, as scientists, had better confine themselves to three tasks: First and foremost, they should devote themselves to developing reliable knowledge of what alternatives of action exist under given conditions and the probable consequences of each. Secondly, social scientists should, as a legitimate part of their technology as well as for its practical uses, be able to gauge reliably what the masses of men want under given circumstances. Finally, they should, in the applied aspects of their science, develop the administrative or engineering techniques of satisfying most efficiently and economically these wants, regardless of what they may be at any given time, regardless of how they may change from time to time, and regardless of the scientist's own preferences.[12]

Although superficially it seems prosaic, this is nonetheless a daring manifesto and an extremely controversial one. Behavioral scientists are still not agreed on it, and every person who considers entering the social sciences as a profession should seriously come to his own conclusions concerning the merits of this proposal. The most controversial proposition in the above statement is the one suggesting that the social scientist should develop techniques for satisfying the wants of the masses economically and efficiently regardless of what those wants might be at any given time. Is the man who refuses to do this when he cannot agree with the desires of the masses violating his commitments as a social scientist? If we accept Lundberg's arguments literally, the reply to this question has to be affirmative.

The character and division of education

Now let us consider another feature of this discussion. If science is the hoped-for savior of modern mankind, education is the medium within which a proper scientific spirit is sustained. Lundberg examines the character of education in modern society and concludes it may properly be divided between the arts and the sciences. The humanities should be incorporated into one or the other of these two central divisions. Philosophy, for example, is one of the humanities. It must, however, be taken apart, says Lundberg, and its different pieces should be placed either within the sciences or within the arts. For example, logic is more a scientific concern than a humanistic one; therefore, we ought to place the study of logic within the sciences. Also, those portions of philosophy which deal with ideas about man or nature belong in

---

[12] *Ibid.*, pp. 59–60.

the sciences so long as they represent historical efforts to achieve valid forms of understanding. But when philosophy is concerned with esthetics, it belongs among the arts. It has been extremely confusing, argues Lundberg, to lump diverse intellectual efforts together in a fusion of arguments that become tangled simply because man is unwilling or incapable at times of distinguishing between scientific and artistic thought.

In his proposal Lundberg does not give priority to science over art. Indeed, he claims only to seek to free both for the fullest achievements of which they are individually capable. He makes this clear in the following comment.

> A reasonable content for general education today, then, seems to me to be as follows: first, a command of the principal linguistic tools essential to the pursuit of either science or art. Second, a familiarity with the scientific method and with its principal applications to both physical and social problems. And third, appreciation and practice of the arts, including literature. Furthermore, these three fields should be so integrated toward a common purpose that the question of their relative importance would not even arise. One does not ask which is the most important leg of a tripod.[13]

The Middle Ages were able to unify education through theology. No such unifying principle exists today unless it is science. But science is not, as students so often believe it to be, a particular subject matter. It is, instead, a method of study and it is applicable to the study of man as well as to the study of nature. If science as method can become a unifying theme within education, then many of the ills of contemporary education may be resolved. But what is this scientific method that Lundberg speaks of? He gives a relatively clear and brief statement. Science, says Lundberg, is a form of behavior having four parts. It consists of

1. Asking clear and answerable questions.
2. Making pertinent observations in an unprejudiced manner.
3. Reporting these observations clearly and accurately.
4. Revising previously held assumptions and beliefs in the light of our reported observations.

If we approach the study of man from this methodical base, then we must revise the curricula of our schools. Many educators believe the best form of education is one which begins with the old established classics and works its way into the problems of modern times. Lundberg is extremely skeptical of such a procedure and suggests that it might be better to ignore the classics for a while and first concentrate on contemporary events; then, when one

---

[13] *Ibid.*, pp. 74–75.

Lundberg
says:

has established via science a sufficient understanding of modern problems and modern man, he may be ready for the classics. The classics are not relevant to modern problems because they are located in the past. More significantly, they must be examined with great caution because they are often the fascinating and unwitting fables of men who were capable of telling lies with incomparable genius.[14]

We ought to note here that Lundberg dismisses the classics by using a very nonscientific device—the testimony of a famous man. He quotes Jefferson's opinion of Plato in which Jefferson says the following about the Greek philosopher: ''. . . His foggy mind is forever presenting the semblances of objects which, half seen through a mist, can be defined neither in form nor dimensions. Yet this, which should have consigned him to early oblivion, really procured him immortality of fame and reverence . . .''[15]

It is difficult to avoid the feeling that Lundberg, in his defense of science, is using a number of nonscientific devices to achieve the effect he is seeking. We shall want to keep this in mind when we evaluate his efforts more broadly near the end of this review. At the moment, we will simply make note of the fact that Lundberg is behaving like the spokesman of any faith—that is, he is relying on authority, rhetoric, tradition, and, perhaps, an essentially personal hope to generate the argument that science is the way we *should* develop an understanding of ourselves.

Lundberg is opposed to displays of reverence for established bodies of works that have been elevated to the status of classics. Science, however it is defined, always retains a high degree of skepticism—and in the social sciences this skepticism must be directed against official, traditional, accepted, or ''classical'' interpretations of human character. The story is told of two scientists who were riding through the countryside and, in the course of their tour, passed by a flock of grazing sheep. One of the scientists commented to the other that it seemed the sheep had just been sheared. The other laconically replied they did in fact appear to be sheared—at least on the side he could see. This degree of skepticism is required of all scientists, but we should especially reserve such skepticism for observations having to do with man. Yet, obtusely enough, people generally seem more willing to direct critical skepticism against the findings of the social scientist while accepting the more casually developed generalizations of the novelist or armchair philosopher; a factually supported generalization is no more likely to be accepted than any other kind.

---

[14] *Ibid.*, p. 85.
[15] *Ibid.*, p. 86.

Science and art

Will science supplant artistic, literary, and spiritual ways of life? If it does, says Lundberg, then the cost of science has been great—certainly greater than he would be willing to bear. Is the physical or social scientist a barbarian incapable of any "real" feeling? Is he like the man in E. E. Cummings' poetry who appears in the lines

> (While you and i have lips and voices which
> are for kissing and to sing with
> who cares if some oneeyed son of a bitch
> invents an instrument to measure Spring with?[16]

Does science deaden esthetic and spiritual sensitivity? Lundberg replies persuasively. In brief, Lundberg says that without scientific understanding we cannot have a heightening of esthetic and spiritual sensitivity. How does he make his point?

First of all, says Lundberg, some people claim that spiritual sensitivity is created by a sense of mystery. They further argue that science reduces the mysteries of nature and thereby robs man of an enjoyment of its beauties and spiritual qualities. A knowledge of astronomy takes from us the ability to wander into the "mystical moist night air, and from time to time, look up in perfect silence at the stars." This is an unfortunate notion, because there is nothing in astronomy that prevents a person from achieving an emotional appreciation of the stars. If anything, an astronomer can see more to be awed by than can an ignorant man. Who is more awed, the man who believes, in a primitive manner, that the stars are light shining through holes punched into the umbrella of the sky; or the man who is aware of the magnitude of intergalactic distances and the forces that radiate throughout space? Lundberg sees no reason why the first man should have greater spiritual or esthetic strength than the latter. Science does not reduce spirituality by reducing mystery because science is as capable of generating mystery as it is of reducing it. Even as science resolves certain questions it raises an even greater number of other questions—and the process is endless.

In the second place, says Lundberg, some people believe that scientific sophistication overly commits one to analysis. As a result, men lose their appreciation of esthetic, ethical, literary, and artistic concerns. A physicist who gives a discourse on the physics of an especially beautiful sunset may be

---

[16] From *Poems 1923–1954* by E. E. Cummings. Reprinted by permission of Harcourt, Brace & World, Inc., Publishers.

pitied because his audience feels that the poor man is so busy analyzing the event he has little chance to appreciate it. People may wonder if someone who knows as much about the physiology of sex as, let us say, Johnson or Masters,[17] can enjoy love. Lundberg dismisses this attitude toward science in much the same manner as he dismisses the first.

> Ask the musician if his study of harmony and counterpoint has decreased his enjoyment of music and he is likely to go to the other extreme and assure you that without these studies you can't *really* enjoy things musical. But he may feel quite concerned about the esthetic life of our physicist and almost certainly about the esthetic experience of the botanist and the sociologist.[18]

It is, perhaps, true that ignorance can generate a certain kind of reaction to an event that sophistication cannot offer. A person who, for example, is ignorant of how to fly an airplane will find his first experiences at the controls more thrilling than those which come after he has had several hundred hours in the air. In a similar fashion, a person's ignorance of an ethnic or religious or racial group can produce a sense of excitement—the kind of thrill that comes with feelings of fear and uncertainty. The acquisition of sound and reliable knowledge is likely to change this.

Lundberg spends time with this issue because it is important and because it is, despite the seeming obviousness of a plea for knowledge, an extremely difficult argument. There is strong resistance to the idea that knowledge is worth the effort it takes to obtain it. This is the "I like what I have now, why should I change?" kind of attitude. How can one answer this? How can one demonstrate—how can one convince another—that the accumulation of knowledge can improve one's life?[19] We grant a certain value to knowledge, but usually it is a cash value—a college education means more money in the bank. Or, we evaluate knowledge in terms of the extent to which it can be translated into technology. The pragmatic test of knowledge is whether we can do something with it, earn something with it, build something with it, or, in a military state, destroy something with it.

Lundberg's plea for social science is at bottom a pragmatic one. He says we can engineer society closer to our desires if we emphasize the accumulation of better social knowledge, that is, more scientific knowledge. However,

[17] See William Masters and Virginia Johnson, *Human Sexual Response* (Boston: Little, Brown and Company, 1966).

[18] Lundberg, *Can Science Save Us?*, p. 99.

[19] In a movie I saw a few years ago the leader of a rebellious gang of motorcycle toughs was asked what he sought in life—what were his goals? He arrogantly replied that he wanted to be free, to have fun, to ride his machine, and to have a ball. As I watched, I placed myself in the position of having to rebut this scheme for life. I found it hard to do. How can one demonstrate—empirically, logically, or any other way—that there might be more?

it is not easy to sustain this argument. It is possible, when it comes to human social organizations, to make as much pragmatic use of a myth or lie or common sense as it is to make use of scientifically valid knowledge. Santa Claus is not without utility—and Madison Avenue has shown that mythical imagery sells more produce than symbolic logic ever could. Charlie Brown in the comic strip *Peanuts* has been more influential than many college professors.

The value of good knowledge, whether social or physical, is ultimately a matter of personal recognition, mature taste, and a matter of faith. All one can do who has the knowledge is reiterate that it means something—it is valuable. The person who masters musical theory knows its value for the appreciation of music, but he cannot communicate this value to a person ignorant of the theory. So too, the social scientist would like to communicate the value of his knowledge to the person who is ignorant, but it cannot be done. One has to be willing to find for himself whether the game is worth the candle.

Lundberg asserts that the knowledge we acquire about ourselves must be valid knowledge. We cannot achieve understanding and mastery over the world around us and over ourselves if we indulge in delusions. He cites the case of a British social scientist who doubts the validity of cinematic depictions of social mobility in America by referring to novels that reveal a different picture. Then Lundberg goes on to say,

> . . . while most people in Europe get their ideas about America from the movies, this "social scientist" is not so gullible. He checks on the reliability of the movies by reading novels. In short, if we really want to know how things are at the bottom of a rabbit hole, read a work by Lewis Carroll for the report of an eyewitness named Alice. Or, if you want to check the reliability with which the English novel portrays English life, visit the English movies.[20]

We must reject the distortions of society brought to us by men whose job it is to entertain us. These men are spinners of myths and masters of deception. We must rely, for serious work, on science and reason.

This appeal to reason, this request for faith in scientific procedures lies at the heart of modern social science. And it places the social sciences in a peculiar position. After all, the social sciences deal with a subject—man—which has been the traditional subject of humanistic studies. At the same time, they attempt to employ a method—that of science—which has become the hallmark of the natural sciences. This situation has made the social sciences particularly vulnerable to criticism. If they succeed as sciences, then they are apt to be scorned by humanists; on the other hand, if they succeed

---

[20] Lundberg, *Can Science Save Us?*, p. 103.

as humanistic studies, they are apt to be scorned by the scientist. This vulnerability cannot be overcome simply by protesting greater faith in science. Instead, we must, as social scientists, attempt to evaluate as honestly and as completely as possible what a subscription to science has meant for the social sciences.

What does faith in scientific method mean for the social sciences? A recent work by William Stephens deals with this question more openly and specifically than any other I have seen. Stephens, to an extent not developed by Lundberg or any other positivist, wrestles with the problem of truth in social and psychological studies. He concludes that propositions which can be validated most completely are, at the same time, of least social or human value. If we put all of our money on scientific skepticism, as Lundberg would have us do, we might find ourselves in the position of having to live on the basis of validated knowledge which is of little utility to us as men. This is a messy paradox for the social scientist and one which he does not, I believe, yet know how to handle. The problem, in a word, is to balance probably valid trivia against possibly delusional profundity.[21]

Let me illustrate what is being discussed here with two quotations. One is taken from a social science journal and the other from the writings of an astute humanist.

> . . . There is a very high correlation, as might be expected, between intimacy of family life and fondness for the parents, although the correlation is not quite as high as was found to prevail among a sample of University of Minnesota students. (From an article appearing in *Child Development*.)

Compare the above statement, made by a social scientist, with the following, made by a humanist.

> . . . When I first read D. H. Lawrence's novels, at the age of about twenty, I was puzzled by the fact that there did not seem to be any classification of the characters into "good" and "bad." Lawrence seemed to sympathise with all of them about equally and this was so unusual as to give me the feeling of having lost my bearings. Today no one would think of looking for heroes and villains in a serious novel, but in lowbrow fiction one still expects to find a sharp distinction between

---

[21] Stephens puts it yet another way: "The proper scientist finds, when he leaves his laboratory, that well-documented hypotheses will not take him very far. In his everyday activities and in his private thoughts—outside the laboratory—he must be almost as credulous and superstitious as the rest of us. Likewise, the more sophisticated speculative writer has some understanding of scientific procedures and the demands of evidence. He can, perhaps, temporarily suspend this awareness, in order to free himself to speculate. But this awareness, no matter how it is handled, must be with him, and it must affect the way he feels about his work." From William N. Stephens, *Hypotheses and Evidence* (New York: Thomas Y. Crowell Company, 1968), p. 209.

right and wrong and between legality and illegality. The common people, on the whole, are still living in the world of absolute good and evil from which the intellectuals have long since escaped. (From an essay by George Orwell.)

The point is not so much that one statement is based on a careful and extensive collection of scientific data and the other is not. The point is that Orwell's comment offers us greater insight. We can fit Orwell's observation into a number of contexts and acquire at least the illusion of understanding. For example, Orwell sheds some light on the recent popularity, in America, of Batman. His observation, taken from literature, also seems to apply to the simple romances and adventures that make up most of the entertainment offered by television. The social scientist offers us a more carefully validated statement—we can be more confident that it is so. At the same time, it is not an especially exciting statement. That is to say, once one is given this information, he finds it difficult to do much with it. Lundberg seems to overlook this sometimes very glaring difference between fact and utility.

Lundberg gives us the impression, although he probably would not endorse this idea, that any scientifically established proposition is superior to any non-scientifically asserted proposition. For example, the scientifically demonstrable fact that white populations have longer life expectancies in the United States than do nonwhite populations is superior to the proposition that Santa Claus uses LSD. However, as obvious as this argument seems, when we get into the realm of human behavior the situation is not so clear as it looks at first.

Let us consider, for just a moment, the use of astrology as a means of finding oil wells and as a means of attending to personal affairs of the day. In the first instance we are likely to find that, compared with scientific procedures, astrology is not competitive; scientific methods work better when it comes to oil wells. But what happens when we use astrological procedures for our personal affairs? Suppose the stars ''tell'' us that today we will be in an unusually social mood and we should take advantage of the ''fact'' to make friends and influence people.

In this case the astrologer is not only providing us with a means (sociability) but also with the end toward which the means should be employed (making friends). If we follow the statement provided by the astrologer, it is likely to work. We have a kind of self-fulfilling prophecy here which acts to validate the statement. After following the astrological advice we have received, we are able to validate it. Thus, astrology can work in the field of human affairs to an extent not possible in the physical world. I must add that I am not attempting to justify astrology as a way of handling social problems. I merely want to point out that astrology can be relatively more useful in human social affairs than in the physical domain. In other words, astrology can compete more effectively with psychology and sociology than it can with geology or physics.

The blending of ends and means

It is possible, then, when working with humans, to blend together ends and means. The reason that lonely hearts columnists, politicians, writers, demagogues, or any other nonbehavioral science figure can be effective in persuading others of the "rightness" of their assertions is that the assertions have a self-validation built into them. If, for example, I say, "You're great!," I have not only made a statement concerning a goal toward which you might aspire, *I'm glad someone thinks so.* but the statement itself helps serve the attainment of that goal.

We have, then, a situation in which quite nonscientific assertions may have a degree of social utility and thereby prove competitive with the assertions of social science. On the other hand, we find that some of the facts of the social scientist may contain an implicit, if not explicit, moral commitment. When, for example, a social scientist recently commented on the ten billion dollars per year that young people in America have to spend, he was not able to avoid clucking a little over the "fact" that most of this money is spent for trash that would not appeal to a mature taste.[22]

When we add to all of this the fact that there is considerable debate among social scientists themselves regarding the extent to which social science should be objective and value free, we have come back to the point where we began this discussion. What are we to do? Once more we are subjected to a confusing clamor of contradictory claims and opinions. There are men who want to underscore the word *science* and men who want to underscore the word *social* when we talk about the social sciences. Despite this confusion and debate, there is, within all the social sciences and among most of its leading spokesmen, a common set of aspirations which give unity to their efforts. I discussed these common factors—naturalism, generalization, an emphasis on social causation, and objectivity—in the first chapter of this book and do not need to elaborate on them further at this point. Whether or not the dedication that social science has given to these ideals will result in a

---

[22] Professor Warriner, of the University of Kansas, has correctly admonished me to be careful about differentiating between the extent to which a moral commitment is contained *within* a fact and the extent to which an interpreter places a commitment *upon* a fact. This distinction, in a sense, sums up the problem of objectivism in the social sciences. If we say, for example, that young people spend their money on "trash," have we expressed a fact or are we making an interpretation? The issue is not perfectly clear-cut.

"superior" knowledge of man remains to be seen. Certainly large-scale organizations cannot be run by the stars and survive for very long. The demand for social science comes out of the needs of big social organizations. Whether social science is useful to the individual is a more difficult matter. Many people survive with only the most minimal awareness of the findings and arguments of the social scientist. Personally, I believe a knowledge of social science is able to reduce fears and to expand awareness and understanding. It is, therefore, of value to the individual. But this belief is largely a matter of faith grounded in my own experiences. Each of us must find for himself whether or not science is able to save him.

Two implications of the social scientific ethic

Before we leave this topic we must consider, at least briefly, the broader implications of the social scientific ethic. I think there are two issues worth mentioning. One of these has to do with the place of faith in human affairs. The other has to do with the conflict between scientific and humanistic interpretations of man and his nature.

It is difficult to examine Lundberg's writing or that of the men who preceded him, like Comte and Spencer, without recognizing that a plea is being made for the acceptance of a new faith. Any human activity must be grounded, in the final instance, in beliefs which are not, in themselves, subject to any form of test. These beliefs we take at face value and endorse them and act on them without critical examination. Often the elements of faith become so thoroughly a part of our intellectual and emotional baggage that we come to believe they are instinctive features of men in general—they are simply human nature. We may take on faith the idea that progress is good. We might accept on faith the idea that sex is dirty. Faith may lead us to believe that work is a test of an individual's spiritual worth. We may, through faith, become followers of men who range in thinking from the fundamental evangelism of Billy Graham to the racial vituperations of George Lincoln Rockwell. It is a matter of faith.

But if faith is a necessary and central feature of being human, what happens when an idea appears on the scene which tells us to reject faith as a basis of action? As I said before, the paradox of scientific thought is that it claims you must be faithful to skepticism. But skepticism is a rejection of faith. This sounds like a clever trick—if it can be done. What have been some of the consequences of man's attempt to live within a skeptical ideology whose force cannot be ignored and which, at the same time, deprives him of the comforting illusions of older faiths?

One response has been to perceive nature as "meaningless" and man as a puny and insignificant element within it. As skepticism has torn away many of the ancient conceits man gave himself, it has led some men to react with a moan of anguish and self-pity. Others have attempted to replace the old conceits with new ones even more arrogant and irrational. The current vigor of racism, for example, seems to be historically associated with a decline in the salience of a number of Christian moral doctrines.

Another kind of response to skepticism—one which both social scientists and humanists have hoped for—is a recognition of the freedom and the responsibility which it gives the individual. The skeptical and knowledgeable man—the sophisticated person—is freer to do with himself what he will. The man who is aware of many of the subtle forces brought to play on him by society has an advantage the unaware man lacks. The knowledgeable person has the potential for using rather than being used by the social situation in which he finds himself. In this sense, then, we can agree with Lundberg when he suggests that science can save us. It can free us from the binding constraints of blind tradition. We have been saved insofar as we have been freed. But, in our freedom, we must find in our own way the best use to which we can put our lives—and in this effort science cannot help us. Here the responsibility is ours alone and we cannot blame physics, psychology, economics, or any other science if we fail.

The second humanistic concern I wish to touch on, before leaving the subject of faith in science, is the one that has to do with the rivalry which exists between humanistic and scientific conceptions of man. I have already alluded to this with a quotation from an eminent humanist, E. E. Cummings. The scientist, as Cummings sees him, is a myopic and sickly fellow who tries, all too often, to measure things which are better not measured. Measurement and quantification seem to be at the heart of the issue between the humanist and the scientist. When the social scientist attempts to measure marital happiness or group morale the humanist can be heard snickering in the background. But when the social scientist attempts to develop a measuring instrument of this kind he does so with the end in mind of furthering communication between men. Men can discourse reasonably with each other only if the terms they use have some kind of common meaning. A measuring instrument provides this commonality. A measuring instrument is not, as E. E. Cummings sees it, something that takes the spring out of spring and the life out of living. Indeed, it is something of a paradox that humanists who shout most loudly for better communication between men can, at the same time, deride a certain kind of communication—the scientific measuring instrument.

I have tried, in this chapter, to make the student or the general reader aware of some of the pervasive problems which appear when one argues for a science of man. I have not been able to present any clear answers to these questions because I do not believe there are any. A commitment to science is a personal thing—not too distant in nature from a commitment to religion. I have seen too many steely-eyed men of faith in both science and religion, however, to want to present a one-sided argument for science. This chapter will have been successful in its intentions if it causes the reader to examine further and steadily the personal implications and the social values of science in our time. Lundberg stated the question simply: Can science save us? Let us think a while longer before we try to answer with a muted yes or no.

6 Statistics of Deadly Quarrels: The Logic of Lewis F. Richardson

By the end of the 18th century thoughtful men were beginning to appreciate the power of mathematical reasoning. Newton's mechanics were forcing intellectuals into new ways of seeing the world—and a few thinkers were on the threshold of trying to bring order to an understanding of man by applying mathematical logic to human affairs. The 17th-century philosopher Spinoza, for example, set forth a system of ethics intended to rival geometry in its regularity and consistency of logical development. But it was not until the beginning of the 19th century that a very simple, yet frightening, mathematical argument locked man into a logical equation from which he has, ever since, found it difficult to extricate himself.

Malthusian reasoning

In 1798 the Reverend Thomas Robert Malthus suggested that two factors in nature are associated with each other in a particular manner. Moreover, the inevitable and natural outcome of this association will be miserable and wretched deaths for the greater mass of mankind. The somber equations of Malthusian thought placed man and food on one side of an equal sign, and death, poverty, famine, disease, war, and misery on the other.

The alarmed reaction of the world was immediate and widespread. Even today, the 18th-century ideas of Malthus have such a compelling nature about them that it might be profitable to consider briefly the character of his reasoning before turning to more complex equations. We can learn a great deal about the power of logical reasoning in human affairs by examining this early and very elementary form of mathematical argument. After spending a little time with Malthus, we can then turn to a more sophisticated form of mathematical conceptions of human relations—the human conflict models of Lewis F. Richardson.

The first thing about Malthusian thought we need to notice is its abstract character.[1] Malthus was not concerned with the nearly infinitely varied details which distinguish man from man and culture from culture. He was, instead, concerned with human populations. But talking about populations has the effect of transforming people into digits. To characterize several nations by saying that one has a population of 100 million and the other a population of 80 million bleaches out all of those social details that make national characterizations so unique—at the same time, however, it has the advantage of enabling us to talk in the language of numbers.

Human populations, said Malthus, have one very interesting mathematical property: they grow in a geometric fashion. In fact, all populations, whether human or not, have this property—they grow geometrically. Malthus meant by this that organic populations, including populations of human beings, double in size over a given interval of time and continue to double with each succeeding interval.

We might stop at this point and, if we had never heard of Malthus or the present concern over the world's "population explosion," we could, even if we were only slightly arithmetically inclined, trace out some of the implications of this statement. Suppose, for example, that human populations doubled every fifty years. We could begin at the time of Christ with two people and see how long it would take to reach the present world population of roughly three billion souls. The arithmetic is so elementary we can, with pencil and paper and a small amount of patience, determine the answer in a few minutes—sometime between the year 1500 and the year 1550. By the middle of the 20th century we would, at this rate, have a world population of over one trillion people—a figure three hundred times greater than the present world population.

We can, if we wish, change the interval of time. How many people would we have in the world today if we began with two people at the time of Christ and their numbers doubled every twenty-five years? Malthus made the cal-

---

[1] The abstract wonderland quality of mathematical symbols is nowhere better illustrated, to my way of thinking, than in the following anecdote related by Aaron Sayvetz. "The blissful dream of one or a few unifying principles for all of knowledge was rudely punctured for me one day by Professor Arthur Constant Lunn, a sort of one-man department of applied mathematics who roamed restlessly about on the upper floors of Eckart Hall on this campus for many years. Professor Lunn, all unawares of the effect he was to have, one day removed the chalk from his mouth where it usually was poised like a cigar, and said, 'I can represent all of the wisdom of the world by a single letter.' With bated breath, we waited. Shuffling to the board, he wrote, 'Let W stand for all of the wisdom of the world.'" From a mimeographed paper entitled "Subject Matters and Disciplines in the Natural Sciences," by Aaron Sayvetz, 1963, p. 12.

culation and his answer was startling. We would have enough people to place four persons on every square yard of habitable ground on this planet. Even so, there would be a surplus! Enough people would be left over to populate all the planets in the solar system in a similar fashion. And yet there would still be a surplus. We would have enough remaining to place four humans on every square yard of all of the planets of all of the stars visible to the naked eye at night—assuming each to have as many planets as our own sun. And we would still have a surplus!

This is, of course, a fantastic figure—a purely mathematical fantasy: Nonetheless, it fires the imagination and leads immediately to speculation about what "really" is happening. Since the doubling of human populations every twenty-five or fifty years is not unreasonable, what has happened to the large numbers we might arithmetically expect? Obviously something controlled or checked the growth of population. Malthus was led to conclude that devastating checks on population growth were necessary, natural, and inevitable. Since the checks involved reduction of population through famine, disease, war, and misery, Malthus came to the logical and rational conclusion that misery is man's unavoidable destiny. He did not, incidentally, believe that population growth could be effectively checked by contraceptive practices.

This is the essence of Malthusian thought. Now we need to pause, for a moment, and see how Malthus developed his logic and used his mathematical fantasies as the basis of a compelling moral argument. First of all, Malthus concentrated on several numerically or quasi-numerically defined variables— population size was one and means of subsistence another; the degree of human happiness was a third. So, the first step in the construction of a mathematical conception of human affairs is to isolate some conditions which may be presumed to exist in varying amounts. When we have done this, we have isolated or identified those variables whose nature we want to understand.

The second thing Malthus did was attribute certain dynamics or mathematical properties to the variables he isolated. In his consideration of organic populations, for example, he gave them the property of doubling in size over some interval of time. Please note that much of what is being done at this stage is very abstract and imaginative or speculative. The idea of doubling can be toyed with in various ways. We could pretend that human populations double every five minutes if we wished. We would arrive at very large population figures in a very brief period of time. We could, if we desired, assume they double every 1000 years. Then, of course, it would take longer to get large numbers, but even at this slower pace they would eventually move into the same crushing magnitudes. At this stage of thinking we are free to play with our conceptions as we desire. Generally, though, we will try somehow to fit the conception to reality and use, in this case, something like a twenty-five- or fifty-year interval.

The third thing Malthus did was to postulate a relationship between population growth and growth in the means of subsistence. The essence of this relationship was that population growth would always move up to and then be checked by limitations in the growth of the means of subsistence. The relationship between the growth of human population and growth in the means of subsistence was such that population growth was a simple function of growth in subsistence.

The fourth feature in Malthus's conception of the world was the tracing of some of the implications of the relationship between the variables involved in this conception. Malthus was not especially concerned with a purely mathematical statement of the consequences of the relationships he developed. Instead, the implications of these relationships were directed toward depicting a bleak and calamitous future for humanity as a result of man's procreative powers. Malthus was as much a moralist as economist and his simple mathematics were never very far removed from his moralistic sentiments.

Finally, a fifth element in the Malthusian argument which we must consider is its degree of correspondence with events in the real world. Malthus spent a great deal of time demonstrating that a doubling of human populations in a period of twenty-five to thirty years is not unreasonable. He attempted, in other words, to show that his logic was not entirely unrelated to the world around us.[2]

The model of the world Malthus offers us is a compelling one. The fateful consequences of Malthusian logic depend, of course, on whether or not some of the conditions ascribed to the variables used in the model are, in fact, true. For example, do human populations necessarily tend to increase in a geometric fashion until checked by the means of subsistence? Have we, today, through the use of sophisticated contraceptive devices reached the point where population growth will decline to zero and population size will remain constant? In our own business-profit economy, population growth might reflect the need for growing markets more than biological necessity—an expanding population helps industry expand. There are a number of other inter-

---

[2] Thomas Robert Malthus, *An Essay on the Principle of Population; Or a View of Its Past and Present Effects on Human Happiness* (7th ed.; London: Reeves and Turner, 1872). Seven editions, each enlarging and refining the original essay published in 1798, attest to the concern Malthus gave his argument and the care he took to meet the criticisms leveled against him by hostile intellectuals.

esting questions we might ask, but we cannot go into them here. We have been concerned with Malthus because he illustrates a particular way of thinking about humanity—a form of thought that tries to apply mathematical logic to human problems.

Now we will examine a more sophisticated example of this kind of thinking. Although it is somewhat complex, it still corresponds in many ways with the simpler and more worldly reasoning of Malthus.

"Quantitative history"

Near the close of World War I a mathematician and meteorologist named Lewis F. Richardson became concerned with the forces that lead to conflicts between nations. He developed some of his central ideas while serving as an ambulance driver with the Allied forces. His first efforts were published at a personal cost of £35 and Richardson gave away nearly 300 copies to his friends. Richardson commented about this,

> Some of my friends thought it funny, but for me it was quite serious, and was the beginning of the investigations on the causes of wars which now occupy me in my retirement.[3]

While historians were struggling with the innumerable complicated details and facts of the war, Richardson went in another direction. He constructed a a logical "model" of how human conflicts might lead to circumstances where the spiraling exchange of hostilities eventually precipitates a conflict of catastrophic proportions. He referred to his effort as "quantitative history."[4] Only after he had considered the "logics" of struggle was he ready to examine the facts to see if they supported his reasoning. His ideas were sufficiently imaginative and daring to be called a pioneering work of the first magnitude by one of America's leading economists.[5] We can benefit from an examination of them.

Stages in the development of a mathematical model

From now on, when we talk about Richardson's work, we shall use the term "mathematical model." By this we will mean an attempt to describe a pro-

---

[3] Lewis F. Richardson, *Arms and Insecurity,* edited by N. Rashevsky and N. Trucco (Pittsburgh, Pa. 15213: Boxwood Press, 1960), p. 287. Most of the materials in this chapter are based on arguments appearing in this work.

[4] Richardson, *Arms and Insecurity,* p. xx.

[5] Kenneth E. Boulding, *Conflict and Defense* (New York: Harper & Row, Publishers, 1962), p. 25.

cess in the real world by means of mathematically defined terms and relationships. How did Richardson do this? Before we go further, let me mention that Richardson's thought will be presented largely through illustration. If you wish to gain a more comprehensive and technical understanding of Richardson's work, it will be necessary to turn to his major writings.[6]

The construction of a mathematical model requires first, as was the case with the Malthusian model, the identification of those variables or conditions that happen to concern the builder. Richardson was interested in human conflicts and, in the model being shown here, settled on five variables as the basis of his model:

Variable 1. The expenditure in any given year for arms in Country X. This will be symbolized by x.

Variable 2. The expenditure in any given year for arms in Country Y. This will be symbolized by y.

Variable 3. The grievances that Country X has against Country Y. This will be symbolized by g.

Variable 4. The grievances that Country Y has against Country X. This will be symbolized by h.

Variable 5. The passage of time. Time will be symbolized by t.

At this point we actually have only three factors to contend with: arms expenditures, grievances, and time. Only two countries are involved. We now have the basic ingredients of the model—the pieces, as it were—that will form the finished product. With the five variables x, y, g, h, and t, the first stage of the model is finished.

It is now necessary to make some reasonable assumptions about the nature of these variables. The second stage in building a mathematical model is to attribute certain dynamics or mathematical properties to the variables. Richardson assumed that arms expenditures and grievances for Country X or Country Y would tend to remain stable or constant over time unless external circumstances intervened to bring about changes. He suggested that the external circumstances most important in affecting the quantity of arms expenditure in either country are the ways in which the two countries, X and Y, perceive each other and how they respond to these perceptions. This is examined further in the next stage of development.

---

[6] See especially, *Arms and Insecurity* and *Statistics of Deadly Quarrels,* edited by Quincy Wright and C. Lienau (Pittsburgh: Boxwood Press, 1960). Another relevant work by Richardson is *Generalized Foreign Politics* (Cambridge: Cambridge University Press, 1939), 91 pp.

The third step in constructing a mathematical model is to postulate certain relationships between the variables. Because we want to examine the extent to which Country X and Country Y are making changes in expenditures for arms, let us first introduce some measure of change in x and y before we continue.

Suppose that Country X spent ten billion dollars on arms in 1963. In 1964 it spent twelve billion dollars on arms. There is a change here in the amount spent on armament amounting to two billion dollars. We will call this change in Country X's armament expenditures dx/dt. We will call Country Y's change dy/dt. Here dx merely stands for a difference in x for a given difference in time or dt. In other words,

$$dx = 12 \text{ billion} - 10 \text{ billion} = 2 \text{ billion},$$

$$dt = 1964 - 1963 = 1,$$

$$dx/dt = 2 \text{ billion}/1 = 2 \text{ billion increase per year.}$$

So, dx/dt is a measure of change in armament expenditures. The same is true for dy/dt. If Country Y spent 15 billion dollars on arms in 1963 and 15 billion dollars in 1964, the value of dy/dt would be

$$dy = 15 \text{ billion} - 15 \text{ billion} = 0,$$

$$dt = 1964 - 1963 = 1,$$

$$dy/dt = 0/1 = 0, \text{ or no change during the year.}$$

From this example we can see that when dx/dt or dy/dt equals zero, *no additional* expenditures are being put into arms.

This is a crucial step. What we are very interested in is whether or not Countries X and Y are increasing their rate of expenditures or decreasing their rate of expenditures. If the value of dx/dt is increasing, then Country X is putting more and more money into its armaments. If Country Y is doing the same thing, that is, if dy/dt is increasing each year, then we have both countries building up their arms and we have the condition that leads to an arms race.

Now we may come back to the task of considering some possible relationships between the variables in the model. We can begin by thinking about what might influence the value of dx/dt and dy/dt. Richardson suggested that the rate at which Country X is going to build up its arms will be influenced by the level of armament expenditure taking place in Country Y. For the purpose of the model we will say the rate of armament expenditure in

Country X is some proportion of the level of armament expenditure in Country Y. This would give us the following relationship,

$$dx/dt = ay.$$

In other words, the rate of change in armament expenditure in Country X (dx/dt) is equal to some proportion (a) of the level of armament expenditure in Country Y (y). The same relationship pertains to Country Y. Thus,

$$dy/dt = bx.$$

Here the letter b stands for the proportional effect of the level of armament in Country X on the rate of armament in Country Y.

We have now postulated a reasonable relationship between some of our variables. We have a relationship that fits our intuitive understanding of events and, at the same time, is capable of being expressed in mathematical language.

The following table shows how armament would be affected by this condition. (See Table I. The reader is encouraged to check a few of the figures in the table to see how they are generated.) Note, in this table, that the

TABLE I

We will substitute, *arbitrarily*, the value of .15 for a and .25 for b. Thus,

$$dx/dt = .15y,$$

and

$$dy/dt = .25x.$$

We will assume that armament expenditures begin with Country X at 15 billion per year and Country Y at 25 billion per year and follow the computation through a decade.

Year	x^*	dx/dt	y	dy/dt
1950	15.00		25.00	
1951	18.75	3.75	28.75	3.75
1952	23.06	4.31	33.44	4.69
1953	28.08	5.02	39.21	5.77
1954	33.96	5.88	46.23	7.02
1955	40.89	6.93	54.72	8.49
1956	49.10	8.21	64.94	10.22
1957	58.84	9.74	77.22	12.28
1958	70.42	11.58	91.93	14.71
1959	84.21	13.79	109.54	17.61
1960	100.64	16.43	130.59	21.05

* The large figures involved in dealing with billions were rounded for purposes of simplification.

values of a and b have been arbitrarily assigned. Here we are doing the same thing as we might have done in the Malthusian model by arbitrarily deciding that a human population doubles every five minutes or that it doubles every one thousand years. The point is that even though neither of these figures is realistic, the general consequences of the model remain much the same. It is this characteristic of mathematical models that keeps them from becoming purely empty logical exercises. The arbitrary figures used in these illustrations do not alter the general implications of the model.

As we observe the increasing amounts of money going into armaments in Table I we begin to wonder what might hold back or "brake" these escalating values. So, let us consider the possibility that the larger these values get, the more they tend to sap the economy of the arming country. In other words, the more a country is putting into arms, the less capable it will be of drastically increasing its own rate of armament. Thus, we might claim for Country X the following kind of situation,

$$dx/dt = ay - mx,$$

where mx is a braking factor. Note here that we have not added a new variable to the model. The level of arms expenditures, variable x, is being used as a braking element.

So, the rate of increase in armament expenditures in Country X is affected positively by the level of armament of Country Y and negatively by some proportional influence that comes out of the level of armament in Country X— we call this latter influence a "braking factor" because it has a tendency to reduce the value of dx/dt. We will go on and postulate a similar situation for Country Y, that is,

$$dy/dt = bx - ny.$$

In these last two equations the letters m and n stand for the proportional influence of the braking effect of each country's armament levels. How this equation works is shown in Table II.

So far, all we have said is that when the braking effect is greater than the arming effect (when the product of mn is greater than the product of ab) we get a negative set of values for dx/dt and for dy/dt, and armament expenditures decline.

Now, to complete the third stage of this model, all we need to do is introduce the effects of grievance, symbolized by g and h. We will assume that if the grievance factor is positive, it will add to the rate of armament increase; if it is negative (that is, friendly relations exist), then the rate of armament

TABLE II

Arbitrarily we will let $m = .35$ and $n = .45$. Thus,

$$dx/dt = .15y - .35x,$$

and

$$dy/dt = .25x - .45y.$$

As in Table I, we shall begin with $x = 15$ billion and $y = 25$ billion.

Year	x	dx/dt	y	dy/dt
1950	15.00		25.00	
1951	13.50	−1.50	17.50	−7.50
1952	11.40	−2.10	13.00	−4.50
1953	9.36	−2.04	10.00	−3.00
1954	7.58	−1.78	7.84	−2.16
1955	6.11	−1.47	6.21	−1.63
1956	4.90	−1.21	4.95	−1.26
1957	3.92	−0.98	3.95	−1.00
1958	3.14	−0.78	3.15	−0.80
1959	2.51	−0.63	2.52	−0.63
1960	2.01	−0.50	2.02	−0.50

increase will be lowered. The basic set of relationships used in the model can now be stated and appear as follows,

$$dx/dt = ay - mx + g,$$

and

$$dy/dt = bx - ny + h.$$

The third stage is now complete. We have postulated a set of relationships between the variables used in the model.

The fourth development of this model requires that we derive some inferred conclusions or implications from the postulated equations. This is done mathematically. In the case of the Richardson process model equations presented here, it is possible to derive four general logical conclusions. We will not go into the mechanics of the mathematical derivations. It will suffice merely to present and illustrate the conclusions to which our logic brings us. Students of mathematics are encouraged to check the following arguments.[7]

---

[7] This presentation is a modification of one appearing in a book by Anatol Rapaport entitled *Fights, Games, and Debates* (Ann Arbor: University of Michigan Press, 1960).

Case 1.—THE STABLE BALANCE. This takes place when the braking influence is relatively high and the grievance factors are positive. In other words, both Country X and Country Y will approach a situation where armament expenditures will not increase or decrease ($dx/dt = 0$ and $dy/dt = 0$) when mn is greater than ab and both g and h are greater than zero.

We have such a situation in Table III. Here we have allowed

$$dx/dt = .15y - .35x + 5,$$

and

$$dy/dt = .25x - .45y + 3.$$

Thus, mn is greater than ab,

$$mn = (.35)(.45) = .1575,$$

and

$$ab = (.15)(.25) = .0375.$$

Also, g and h are both positive values, that is, each country harbors grievances against the other.

Table III illustrates the fact that no matter where armament expenditures begin, the amount spent on arms will level off at 22.5 billion for Country X and at 19.2 billion for Country Y. Note that though the grievance factor is positive, a stable balance of power has been attained. The model says that if internal economic brakes are strong enough, external grievances will not necessarily lead to an arms race. Nothing in common sense could as clearly lead us to this conclusion. The mathematical model provides an exact logical

TABLE III

| | $dx/dt = .15y - .35x + 5.$ | | | |
| | $dy/dt = .25x - .45y + 3.$ | | | |
Year	x	dx/dt	y	dy/dt
1950	15.00		25.00	
1955	21.63	0.28	18.43	0.08
1960	22.23	0.07	18.90	0.07
1965	22.41	0.02	19.08	0.03
1970	22.47	0.01	19.14	0.01
1975	22.49	0.00+	19.16	0.00+
1980	22.50	0.00+	19.17	0.00+

instrument for a hypothetical consideration of *possible* relations between variables. Note, however, that it is a hypothetical consideration. The precision of the model lies in its logical structure and not in its realism or in its ability to mirror factual events.

Case 2.—THE ARMS RACE. This occurs when the braking factor (*mn*) is low and all other factors are relatively high. In other words, an arms race will begin when *ab* is larger than *mn* and both *g* and *h* are positive. This is rather obvious. Common sense would suggest that an arms race is likely when two nations are very sensitive to each other's levels of armament, both are hostile toward each other, and armaments are not being slowed down by internal economic brakes. At least, however, our model does not violate what seems to be a reasonable evaluation of conditions.

We will pass on to the next case.

Case 3.—DISARMAMENT. Disarmament occurs when grievances are below zero (that is, a state of friendliness exists) and the braking power of the economies is high. This, like the second case, is fairly obvious and it corresponds with commonsense notions. Friendly nations with strong economic checks on arms developments will probably not be as likely to indulge in an arms race.

We may now turn to the fourth case which is the most interesting of all, because its conclusions cannot be readily drawn from commonsense ways of thinking about conflict situations.

Case 4.—THE UNSTABLE SITUATION. This is the most intriguing case of all. It specifies that when the braking power is low and grievances are low, we may have a runaway arms race or, on the other hand, we may have a disarmament race! This will happen when *ab* is larger than *mn,* and *g* and *h* are less than zero. Whether or not we will have an arms race or a disarmament race depends on the initial level of armament expenditures! This has been illustrated by the figures in Table IV. Note here that only the initial level of armament expenditures makes the difference between an arming or disarming movement in the two countries. Once again, notice in this table that the braking power is low and so are the grievances. In fact, friendly relations exist between the countries. Nonetheless, this can eventuate in an arms race. Richardson came to the conclusion that an unstable situation like that depicted in Table IV existed in Europe prior to World War I, and that had armament expenditures been only slightly lower the war might not have taken place.

We have considered some of the logical consequences of the model and, though they are interesting, they must remain mathematical fancies unless they have some bearing on the world in which we live. So, now we must turn

TABLE IV

$$dx/dt = .35y - .15x - 5.$$
$$dy/dt = .45x - .25y - 3.$$

Year	x	dx/dt	y	dy/dt
		Disarmament		
1950	15.00		18.00	
1951	14.05	−0.95	17.25	−0.75
1952	12.98	−1.07	16.26	−0.99
1953	11.72	−1.26	15.03	−1.23
1954	10.22	−1.50	13.54	−1.49
1955	8.43	−1.79	11.75	−1.79
1956	6.28	−2.15	9.60	−2.15
1957	3.70	−2.58	7.02	−2.58
1958	0.60	−3.10	3.93	−3.09
1959		−3.71	0.22	−3.71
1960				−3.06
		Armament		
1950	23.00		26.00	
1951	23.65	0.65	26.85	0.85
1952	24.50	0.85	27.78	0.93
1953	25.54	1.04	28.86	1.08
1954	26.81	1.27	30.13	1.27
1955	28.33	1.52	31.66	1.53
1956	30.16	1.83	33.49	1.83
1957	32.36	2.20	35.69	2.20
1958	35.00	2.64	38.33	2.64
1959	38.17	3.17	41.50	3.17
1960	41.97	3.80	45.30	3.80

to the fifth and final stage in the development of a model[8]—we must find out how well it jibes with reality. Here we begin to see why this can be a highly captivating form of thinking about human events. For, if reality does not match a carefully developed and well-reasoned idea, that is cause for thought; if it does, well, that is also cause for thought!

Richardson's application of his model

We must now investigate how Richardson matched his models with the world. We will concern ourselves with just one such matching because of limitations

---

[8] This fivefold development of a mathematical model is a slightly modified version of a discussion of such models presented by James Coleman, "The Mathematical Study of Small Groups," in *Mathematical Thinking in the Measurement of Behavior*, edited by Herbert Solomon (New York: Free Press of Glencoe, 1960), pp. 1–149. Reprinted with permission of The Macmillan Company. Copyright by The Free Press, a Corporation 1961.

of space. But do not conclude that Richardson was inclined to neglect this aspect of model construction. On the contrary! He made a great effort to bring reality and model together, using both to understand each. The European arms race of 1909, continuing through 1914, provided an especially interesting and significant statistical test of the value of the model.

In this arms race France was allied with Russia. Germany was allied with Austria-Hungary. Neither Italy nor Britain was especially involved. To use this arms race as a test of his equations, Richardson first simplified them by assuming that the coefficients a and b are equal. He also assumed the coefficients m and n to be equal. Thus, we now have

$$dx/dt = ay - mx + g,$$

and

$$dy/dt = ax - my + h.$$

We may now combine these two equations into one by addition, and get the following equation:

$$d(x + y)/dt = (a - m)(x + y) + g + h.$$

This equation tells us that the amount Countries X and Y are spending on armament jointly will determine the amount of increase in arms they jointly spend the next year.

Once we have an equation that enables us to predict the change in joint armament expenditures on the basis of existing joint armament expenditures, we can determine the extent to which these values are associated. For the arms race of 1909–1914 we obtain the values shown in Table V.

TABLE V

Defense Budgets of Countries Involved in the Arms Race
of 1909–1914 Expressed in Millions of Pounds Sterling

Country	1909	1910	1911	1912	1913
France	48.6	50.9	57.1	63.2	74.7
Russia	66.7	68.5	70.7	81.8	92.0
Germany	63.1	62.0	62.5	68.2	95.4
Austria-Hungary	20.8	23.4	24.6	25.5	26.9
Total $= x + y$	199.2	204.8	214.9	238.7	289.0
Time rate $= d(x + y)/dt$	5.6	10.1	23.8	50.3	
$x + y$ at same date	202.0	209.8	226.8	263.8	

Source: Lewis F. Richardson, *Arms and Insecurity*, ed. by N. Rashevsky and N. Trucco (Pittsburgh, Pa. 15213: Boxwood Press, 1960), p. 32.

According to Richardson's equations, the change in armaments, $d(x + y)/dt$, should be closely related to the total amount spent on armaments, $x + y$, at the same date. The data in Table V support this contention to a surprising extent. If we correlate the values in the bottom two lines of the table, they reveal a high degree of association. The nature of this association is shown graphically in the following figure. Obviously four points along a line do not provide sufficient evidence to prove a theory. But the regularity is striking enough to make us see some promise in mathematical modes of thinking about human behavior.

Richardson develops further aspects of this basic model and supports them with more complex data. At one point, for example, he compares ten nations in "warlike worktime" and develops models going far beyond the simple two-nation rivalry developed here. Unfortunately, we cannot pursue these elaborations any further. It will suffice if the reader now has some understanding of what is meant by mathematical models and if he has some comprehension of their role in the study of human social behavior. Most of all, because many students have a dread of mathematics, it is hoped that this brief presentation

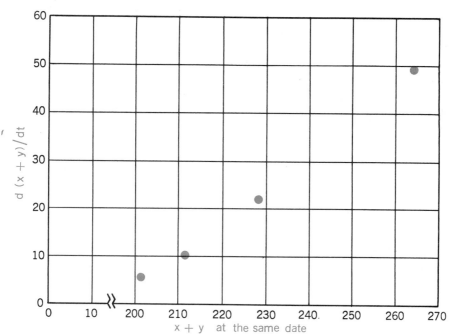

Source: Lewis F. Richardson, *Arms and Insecurity*, ed. by N. Rashevsky and
N. Trucco (Pittsburgh, Pa. 15213: Boxwood Press, 1960), p. 33.

has led the reader to the conclusion that mathematical thinking is neither supreme wizardry beyond mortal ken nor an occult exercise to be feared and avoided. It is, quite simply, an attempt to lay out in bare abstract terms the elements of a logic and then develop as carefully as possible the strictly logical implications of these elements. When we do this what have we gained and what have we lost? Before leaving the mathematical model we must evaluate it in general terms.

Simplicity and neatness versus "unreality"

Men who sharpen their reasoning with mathematical terms and arguments, such as Malthus and Richardson have done, present some of the clearest and most compelling theories in the literature of social philosophy. The vigor of the attacks directed against such theoretical formulations has come, in good part, from the fact they were developed with sufficient clarity to invite equally clear criticism.

The clarity of mathematical models rests upon their simplicity. Although some of Richardson's models seem extremely complex, they are really more simple than most of the other ideas appearing in this book. The simplicity of mathematical models is, at one and the same time, the joy and the sorrow of such thinking. We are reminded of the costs exacted by this form of thinking by Arthur Lunn's suggestion that all of the world's wisdom can be easily represented in mathematical form by a single letter—all we have to do is let W represent all of the world's wisdom. When a mathematical sociologist says, "Let S stand for society . . ." we may feel unhappy because the analysis of social events is not that easy; analysis is being achieved by a *fait accompli*. When a physical scientist says, "Let M equal mass . . ." we are not as disturbed. The condition referred to by the symbol is, in itself, homogeneous, quantitative, and abstract. Society, on the other hand, though abstract, is neither homogeneous nor quantitative. There is a difference between letting S stand for solar energy and letting S stand for the esthetics of a sunset. Or, imagine if you will, letting H stand for a novel by Hemingway. We could do it, but what would it mean?

The equations developed by Richardson, more so than those developed by the physical scientist,[9] have an "unreal" quality about them. Richardson was

---

[9] I should mention here that Richardson was, in fact, an excellent physical scientist and a Fellow of the Royal Meteorological Society. In his attempts to apply equations to human conflict he is functioning, however, as a social scientist, and it is as such that we view this aspect of his work.

not unaware of this and made the following comment about the "dreamlike" nature of his equations:

> . . . the equations have some analogy to a dream. For a dream often warns an individual of the anti-social acts that his instincts would lead him to commit, if he were not wakeful.[10]

Another feature of the equations, besides their dreamlike quality, is their "neatness" of proof. The simplicity of the model gives it a compelling quality that other forms of theorizing may lack. Social scientists who fault members of activist social movements for using easy solutions of social problems will, nonetheless, turn around and build a mathematical model even more severely simple. For example, it is obvious to a literate human being of the 20th century that Nazidom's emphasis on world Jewry as a cause of human suffering was a gross and erroneous attempt to oversimplify national and world problems. Its appeal derived from the fact that it was such a simple-minded solution. Even so, Nazi ideology is more complex than Richardson's mathematical models.

The appeal that mathematical models have for some social scientists may stem from the promise of neatness and simplicity which they offer. If war can be reduced to a set of simultaneous equations, then all that is necessary is to feed the appropriate parameters to a computer and determine who will win. A warning against the desire to reduce social forces to a set of equations is sounded by a writer and thinker who is himself highly laudatory toward Richardson and toward mathematical forms of thought. Kenneth Boulding comments,

> . . . Our failure to find stable difference equations in social systems is not merely because we have not looked hard enough or because our techniques of analysis are not refined enough. Our failure is due to the fact that the equations do not exist; that is, social systems are not stable dynamically in the small, as most physical systems are. This does not mean that they are purely random or haphazard; it means, however, that the classical apparatus of physical mechanical systems, the system of simultaneous differential equations, has only a very limited applicability to social systems . . .[11]

The mathematical model is simple and concise. It may, in varying degrees, match the reality it is designed to summarize. It has a very abstract quality which gives it a dreamlike character. As a consequence, even the finest and most useful mathematical representations of reality do more violence to it

---

[10] Richardson, *Arms and Insecurity*, p. 12.
[11] Boulding, *Conflict and Defense*, pp. 23–24.

than any dream. For example, as I sit in my study I can see outside my window puffy cumulus clouds being formed in a hot summer sky. The trees seem to be wilting in the heat and the campus is deserted. Can I represent this reality with a formula like

$$E = Mc^2,$$

or with any other formula; or, indeed, with any kinds of symbols, words, gestures, or expressions?[12]

Although a formula does not directly match the reality I perceive, it nonetheless cannot be said to lack truth. Nor does it lack utility. Is this also the case with mathematical models developed by social scientists such as Richardson? To a more limited extent, I believe the answer must be an affirmative one.

If nothing else, the quest for mathematical forms of expression has led to greater attempts to clarify the meaning of terms. Richardson's critics, even his most friendly critics, have questioned the manner in which he dealt with the problem of "grievances" in his equations. One of the more stunning logical derivations of Richardson's equations was the conclusion that an arms race can develop and get out of control under conditions where the grievances are not only low but negative, that is to say, a state of friendship exists. Richardson measured the degree of grievance or lack of grievance in terms of the amounts of international trade taking place between countries. If two countries were engaging in large amounts of international trade, then grievances were low. If grievances were high, presumably little or no international trade would take place between the countries. We do not want to get too embroiled in the problem here—it will be sufficient merely to raise the issue. What do we mean by grievances? When we speak journalistically of animosities between nations, how do we come to such conclusions? In general discourse we are likely to accept the assertion that America has a pathogenic fear of the Soviet Union.[13] Presumably America does have a grievance against Russia and vice versa. But, on the other hand, we note the warm treatment paid by the people of either nation to visitors. The Ballet Russe was very warmly received here, and Van Cliburn was idolized in Russia before Amer-

---

[12] This is expressed more forcefully by Weston La Barre, who puts it the following way: "Is it not convenient to know that matter is only action divided by its own squared absolute speed? What hath our grammar wrought?" See La Barre, *The Human Animal* (Phoenix Books; Chicago: The University of Chicago Press, 1960), p. 205.

[13] See, for example, Henry's assertion that America's fear of Russia is the most important single fact in American history since the Revolution and the Civil War. Jules Henry, *Culture Against Man* (New York: Random House, Inc., 1963), p. 100.

icans came to know of him. If this can happen, wherein does the locus of grievance lie? The g factor in the equation

$$dx/dt = ay - mx + g$$

begins to raise some questions. How do we define it in real terms? It is an old problem in the social sciences, but it is a problem which is more directly raised by mathematical models than other forms of expression.

The greatest strength of the mathematical model rests ultimately in the exercise it is able to give to the precise utilization of logic. Although the mathematical model takes us into a kind of Alice-in-Wonderland world of abstractions, it holds us fast in a network of "If this, then that" kinds of statements. If grievances and armaments are related as we have specified, then arms races will take a form dictated by logic. Here is imagination, but imagination disciplined carefully by adherence to the rules of logic. Richardson, unlike a Christian optimist, cannot conclude from his logic that love is enough to save nations from each other. Unfortunately or fortunately, as the case may be, the utilization of mathematical models in the social sciences is still not sufficiently accurate to permit us to give greater validity to Richardson than we would to the Christian optimist. Both work within a world of dreams. But Richardson's dreamworld is logically systematic.

Humanistic implications of mathematical models

What are the humanistic implications of mathematical models? These models cope with an ancient issue in human thought. The issue is whether or not man is free to will his destiny or is, instead, caught like a robot within great forces that determine his fate. If, as Richardson suggests,

$$dx/dt = ay - mx + g,$$

then the activities of our diplomats, statesmen, militarists, and businessmen are simply special individual efforts that finally fit into the catastrophic consequences of the over-all equation.

Richardson was aware of this and states it in an imaginary dialogue between himself and a critic:

Critic: I still don't like the fatalistic look of your mathematics. The worst disservice that anybody can do to the world is to spread the notion that the drift toward war is fated and uncontrollable.

Author: With that I agree entirely. But before a situation can be controlled, it must be understood. If you steer a boat on the theory that it ought to go toward the side to which you move the tiller, the boat will seem uncontrollable. "If we threaten," says the militarist, "they will become docile." Actually, they become angry and threaten reprisals. He has put the tiller to the wrong side. Or, to express it mathematically, he has mistaken the sign of the defense coefficient.[14]

But, if the militarist recognizes the sign of the defense coefficient, then the equation loses its validity. It is an old issue in modern form. Throughout this book the problem of human freedom and human constraint intrudes itself time and again. Mathematical models are most meaningful when men are least free.

Richardson was not able to ascribe a strict determinism to human affairs. On the other hand, he was not able to view man as completely free from deterministic influences. The equations to which he so carefully and thoughtfully gave his attention were not, in his final estimation, science. Like some latter-day social scientists, Richardson viewed his work as partly art and partly science—reflecting the deterministic and nondeterministic elements in human behavior. He stated, as he viewed his work in perspective,

> Nearly all statistical inquiries resemble cookery in so far as they involve discretion, which is akin to art. You must not put a bad egg into a cake nor a suspect number into a fine distinction. These arms races exhibit, I believe, characteristics intermediate between those of machine-like determinism and those of freely willed choice.[15]

In a day and age when human conflict has become so globally threatening, we must give it our most considered thought. Mathematical models are not the final resolution of the problems engendered by human conflict, but they do manage to provide a view afforded by no other means of thinking. For this reason, the student who sets himself the task of understanding man and, at the same time, evades obtaining even an elementary understanding of mathematical models is certainly ill-equipped for his work.

---

[14] Richardson, *Arms and Insecurity*, p. 226.
[15] *Ibid.*, p. 203.

7   The Sociologist
in Anger:
The Views
of C. Wright Mills

Sociologists can follow either of two separate paths during their professional lives. The first path moves toward a sense of detachment from social affairs—greater quantities of social knowledge, and the comfortable jobs that can be obtained with such knowledge, elevate a person until he is looking down on the world. He loses any strong sense of involvement with it. In this instance, the acquisition of social sophistication produces the feeling this is the best of all possible worlds. Or, if it is not, then certainly it is a world so big and so massively organized that there is not much anyone can do about it.

The second path—and one down which many a sociologist has traveled—leads to a very personal anger and sense of frustration. The more one becomes aware of human irrationality and self-deception, and the more one becomes aware of the extent to which man could spare himself much of the suffering he has had to endure, the more it seems necessary to lash out at human folly. This second pathway is, in some respects, professionally unbecoming. It means, to use nonacademic terms, that one has blown one's professional cool. But for the sociologist who cannot help being personally dismayed by what he learns about man, it may only mean he is more emotionally committed to all of humanity than he is to the small segment of it which forms the professional community of sociologists.

To elect one path or the other establishes how one will express whatever power he possesses as an intellectual. For Mills, the first path meant an abdication of responsibility. It led either to the cult of alienation or the fetish of objectivity. It led to the sentiment that the social scientist may have the right to analyze but not the power to criticize.

C. Wright Mills went down the second pathway. His work began with several relatively objective and empirical studies. Gradually, toward the end of his career,[1] his writing became more vehement and took on the character of moral sermonizing. He became famous as a young man with a rather "cool" examination of the white-collar worker. He closed his career with violent denunciations of the clergy,[2] American culture, and the historical drift toward war. The more heated his accusations became, the less he was tolerated by some of his colleagues. Even so, he earned the attention of students and humanistic intellectuals who were looking for men with sociological sophistication to give them new critical perspectives. C. Wright Mills did just that.

Mills' career was brief. His first essay was published when he was twenty-five.[3] His work ended twenty years later when he died from a coronary condition. During the last years a friend happened to visit Mills and candidly told him that he looked terrible. Mills replied, "Yes, I know. But God, how I have lived."[4] Perhaps it was this zest for living as well as his social criticism that made Mills the idol of young liberal intellectuals of the fifties.

The question of power

Though social change is so rapid today that social commentary becomes dated as quickly as the news, Mills' observations have retained much of their original relevance. There is a good reason for this. Mills was concerned with one aspect of society which never loses its significance—the question of power. His work remains centered on power—the nature of power, the distribution of power, the uses and abuses of power, the man of power, the power of organizations, the myths of power, the evolution of power, the irrationality of power, and the means of observing and comprehending power in the vastness of modern society.

---

[1] A very comprehensive listing of the works of C. Wright Mills appears in *Power, Politics and People: The Collected Essays of C. Wright Mills*, edited by Irving Louis Horowitz (New York: Oxford University Press, 1963), pp. 614–641. This list by Horowitz also includes various reviews and essays which have taken the work of Mills as their subject. It will suffice to list here some of the more important or well-known of Mills' works. *The New Men of Power: America's Labor Leaders*, with the assistance of Helen Schneider (New York: Harcourt, Brace & World, Inc., 1948); *White Collar: The American Middle Classes* (New York: Oxford University Press, 1951); *The Power Elite* (New York: Oxford University Press, 1956); *The Causes of World War III* (New York: Simon and Schuster, Inc., 1958); *The Sociological Imagination* (New York: Oxford University Press, 1959); *Listen Yankee: The Revolution in Cuba* (New York: McGraw-Hill Book Company, 1960).
[2] Both *The Causes of World War III* and *Listen Yankee* illustrate the "preachiness" of Mills. Mills himself referred to his work as "preachings." See Horowitz (ed.), *Power, Politics and People*, p. 2.
[3] C. Wright Mills, "Language, Logic, and Culture," *American Sociological Review*, IV (October 1939), 670–680.
[4] I acquired this anecdote from a conversation with William Bruce Cameron, Professor of Sociology and Dean, Liberal Arts College, University of South Florida.

In his writings Mills concentrated particularly on power elites within business. He was concerned with both the business executive and the labor leader. He was interested in the political influence of business and labor, and he examined the extent to which business elites were tied in with military and governmental elites. The observation that the leaders of various sectors of the society are rubbing elbows with each other is not, as one British review of Mills' work put it, very shocking. It has been going on for years in all civilized countries. But this criticism misses the point. It was not the relationship between the elites per se that was the motivation behind Mills' effort. He was interested in the relationship because of its historical and political significance in a nation which subscribes to an ideology of democracy and to the separation of administration among the various parts of the system. The most notable of these "separations," of course, is the constitutionally authorized guarantee of separation of church and state—a separation that Americans have never been able to achieve with complete comfort and satisfaction.[5] But the American system, in its ideal form, also seeks to hold military authority in a position subordinate to and somewhat independent of civilian governmental authority. It is similar with government and business.[6]

A more realistic view, however, concedes the close alliance that exists between these various sections of the society and the elite that governs them. Mills gave us a broadly delineated awareness of this relationship while, at the same time, functioning as a critic of it. We are, he suggested, now caught in the disastrous drift of a merging power elite which, in the name of "crackpot realism," is carrying us ever closer to catastrophe.

It is important, in grasping Mills' conception of power, to know that he located power, much as Weber did, within an institutional context. In order to have power one must, as it were, be able to tap the power of something greater than himself. This "something greater" consists of the collective power of an institution. This is practically tautological; yet, in a society that goes so far to celebrate the individuality of the man of power, it is a necessary corrective. Mills said,

> If we took the one hundred most powerful men in America, the one hundred wealthiest, and the one hundred most celebrated away from the institutional posi-

---

[5] Despite a Supreme Court ruling to the contrary, many schools throughout the country, with the tacit support of state and local authorities, still have prayers in class. The same authorities reveal a certain hypocrisy, I believe, in wondering at times why "other" people are lawless.

[6] The conservative idea, of course, is to keep government out of business. The position with respect to keeping business out of government is less clear. As Galbraith has observed, however, existing tax structures, transportation regulations, antitrust laws, the need for governmentally supervised inspection procedures, and the like have led to a situation where the distinction between private and public industry is becoming increasingly hard to establish.

tions they now occupy, away from their resources of men and women and money, away from the media of mass communication that are now focused upon them—then they would be powerless and poor and uncelebrated. For power is not of a man. Wealth does not center in the person of the wealthy. Celebrity is not inherent in any personality. To be celebrated, to be wealthy, to have power requires access to major institutions, for the institutional positions men occupy determine in large part their chances to have and to hold these valued experiences.[7]

The man of power must be understood, then, as deriving his power from an institutional base. This means, very broadly, that the exercise of power cannot be simply the exercise of individual eccentricity but must, to a considerable extent, run parallel with the "grain" of power that characterizes the institutional source. This is obvious in the case of political and church leaders where adherence to the policies of the system is a *sine qua non* of an individual's ascendancy in the hierarchy.. The study of power, then, becomes the study of institutions, the power relations between institutions, and the men who represent the expressions of those institutions.

Although Mills claimed that power has its locus within supporting institutions, he still was concerned with the fact that it is individuals who make decisions and are responsible for the consequences. Mills was torn on the one hand by an analytic perspective that properly locates the individual within the broader system and, on the other, by a humanistic sensitivity that made him critical of an apparent inability of the man of power to assert himself as an autonomous person.

The Power Elite

In *The Power Elite*, first published in 1956, Mills made explicit his belief that the American doctrine of balances of power or of "checks and balances" is an ideal showing less vigor today than was true in the past. Particularly significant in this respect has been the very recent and very noticeable ascendancy to power of the military in American life. In the 19th century the American military establishment was relatively weak, subordinate to civilian authority, and even respectful of civilian values and lifeways. Today, primarily because of the growth of military technology—a truly devastating technology with implications that cause civilian politicians to shy away from decisions involving its use—the military elite is acquiring greater authority in nonmilitary contexts. If the military has acquired a greater voice in American affairs than has previously been the case, it has not been because the military man has aggres-

---

[7] C. Wright Mills, *The Power Elite* (New York: Oxford University Press, 1956), pp. 10–11.

sively sought political power. It has been, instead, because of civilian political default.[8] Mills viewed this state of affairs with open dismay.

Once war was considered the business of soldiers, international relations the concern of diplomats. But now that war has become seemingly total and seemingly permanent, the free sport of kings has become the forced and internecine business of people, and diplomatic codes of honor between nations have collapsed. Peace is no longer serious; only war is serious. Every man and every nation is either friend or foe, and the idea of enmity becomes mechanical, massive and without genuine passion. When virtually all negotiation aimed at peaceful agreement is likely to be seen as "appeasement," if not treason, the active role of the diplomat becomes meaningless; for diplomacy becomes merely a prelude to war or an interlude between wars, and in such a context the diplomat is replaced by the warlord.[9]

Although Mills viewed the ascendancy of the military in modern America with a sense of dismay, he did not limit his concern only to the military man. If there is a military ascendancy—and Mills very openly and very vehemently believed this to be the case—then it extends beyond the confines of our military institutions. It is more than simply the rising power of a military clique. The various institutions of our society have, through the rise of modern technology, the practices of big business, and the irresponsibilities of American politics, found a military posture socially expedient. It is expedient with regard to our international image; it is expedient with regard to internal control and management.[10]

Internal control or management means, essentially, handling a large and amorphous mass of people who take on the character of a market. The mass market exists not only with respect to the sale of Mustangs and motorcycles but also with respect to the "sale" of opinions. Thus the people become a *media market*.[11] This "media market," this mass of people, stands passively at the bottom of American society. Just above it is an increasingly ineffective and fragmented middle level of professional people, politicians, educators, and intellectuals who are alienated from the lower levels and not a part of the power elite. At the top stands an increasingly unified and coordinated elite of power. This, as Mills saw it, is the trend in American social structure. It is a trend which, as he put it, is moving

---

[8] *Ibid.*, p. 205.

[9] *Ibid.*, p. 206.

[10] An exclusive concentration on this point is made in Fred J. Cooke's *The Warfare State* (New York: The Macmillan Company, 1962). A better treatment of the economic factors involved in the ascendancy of the military in America can be found in Seymour Melman, *Our Depleted Society* (New York: Dell Publishing Co., Inc., 1965).

[11] Mills, *The Power Elite*, p. 304.

. . . a considerable distance along the road to the mass society. At the end of that road there is totalitarianism, as in Nazi Germany or in Communist Russia. We are not yet at that end. But surely we can see that many aspects of the public life of our times are more the features of a mass society than of a community of publics.[12]

The impact of *The Power Elite*, then, comes not from the observation that the "high and the mighty" share clubs and secrets, profits and power. The impact comes from Mills' insistence that the extent to which this is so is increasing in America. Moreover, this is a trend which violates the liberal democratic traditions of the society.

White Collar

The Power Elite, when viewed from the vantage point of the present, seems like a very natural development in Mills' thinking. Five years earlier Mills had published *White Collar: The American Middle Classes* and gave Americans a not very flattering look at themselves. Most significantly, Mills saw the middle stratum of American society as people who had gained economic security and material advantages and had lost just about everything else. Above all, they had lost any sense of personal power or the sensible use of power. If *The Power Elite* is a discussion of the locus of power in America, *White Collar* is a discussion of those Americans who, like Sinclair Lewis's Babbitt, are losers and really never know it—they are the unwittingly passive voice in American politics. They suffer from the illusion of having power while, in fact, they have none. Mills made this very explicit from the beginning. He said,

> The white-collar people slipped quietly into modern society. Whatever common interests they have do not lead to unity; whatever future they have will not be of their own making. If they aspire at all, it is to a middle course, at a time when no middle course is available, and hence to an illusory course in an imaginary society. Internally, they are split, fragmented; externally, they are dependent on larger forces. Even if they gained the will to act, their actions, being unorganized, would be less a movement than a tangle of unconnected contests. As a group, they do not threaten anyone; as individuals, they do not practice an independent way of life.[13]

It is extremely difficult, indeed impossible, to ascribe a unitary character to

---

[12] *Ibid.*, p. 304.

[13] C. Wright Mills, *White Collar: The American Middle Classes* (New York: Oxford University Press, 1951), p. ix. Political leaders I have talked with are well aware that today the masses no longer consist of the disgruntled poor. They consist of the more or less disgruntled middle-income elements.

that segment of American society which refers to itself as "white collar." The training of such people can vary from a few days to twenty or more years. Income of the white-collar worker can vary from minimal wage levels to high five-figure salaries. The white-collar worker can be occupied with work which is physically exhausting—as is much clerical work in department stores—or work which places modest demands on mind and body. The white-collar worker can be an aggressive salesman or a retiring laboratory technician. He can operate within a system which nearly guarantees him the opportunity to rise to higher levels or he can be caught in a cul-de-sac. His work can be clean or it can involve an element of dirtiness—as is the case with technicians who must examine specimens of excrement.

Yet, despite this tremendous variety of social character, the term "white collar" has a special significance for American culture. Migrants to this country saw white-collar employment as a hope for their children if not for themselves. It was an ambition worthy of self-deprivation and suffering toil. The most vulgar form of the American dream has been to strike it rich—to stumble on an oil well, or to inherit an astounding fortune from a distant relative. The realistic American dream has been to find a good white-collar job—to work, if necessary, but to work "respectably." It was the aspiration of people who sought to disengage themselves from their peasant status— it was the collective impetus of people who were being subjected to the pressures of urbanization. City life was better than country life—and within the city, white-collar status was better than blue-collar status. To understand the white-collar class, then, requires a comprehension of the quest for prestige in America. It requires, as Mills put it, an examination of the "status panic."

In traditionalistic societies, prestige claims are relatively easily recognized and the person making the claim is likely to have it honored. In our society the situation is more anomic. A person cannot be certain that his claims for prestige will be honored and, if they are, he cannot always be certain that they are being honored for the proper reason. Although not all the way there yet, America is moving in the direction of becoming a society where

> All the controlling devices by which the volume and type of deference might be directed are out of joint or simply do not exist. So the prestige system is no system, but a maze of misunderstanding, of sudden frustration and sudden indulgence, and the individual, as his self-esteem fluctuates, is under strain and full of anxiety.[14]

The "status panic," the drive for prestige, is a central, though not all encompassing characteristic of the white-collar worker. Some white-collar workers

---

[14] *Ibid.*, p. 240.

experience less "panic" than others. Even so, concern with status is probably more characteristic of the white-collar worker than the blue-collar worker. Mills observed that the blue-collar worker's greater concern with the immediate necessities of living—a fair day's pay for a fair day's work—made him easier to organize in the labor movement. The white-collar worker has had a tendency to feel that such organization is degrading—it results in an association with the tactics of blue-collar workers.[15]

It is this feature of the prestige quest among white-collar elements that Mills found especially intriguing. Prestige, or lack thereof, does not particularly come from the value or lack of value of the work performed. Instead, to a great extent, it comes from the real or imagined associations of the white-collar worker. He obtains his prestige from his capacity to identify with some source which does, in fact, have recognition. The mechanic in the shop might be making a good income and performing miracles in the way of taking apart and putting together complex machinery. The minimal wage, forty-words-a-minute, fresh-out-of-high-school typist in the front office may, however, feel her's is the more prestigeful work. The reason is apparent—it is easier to associate one's self with the management when working in the front office. The prestige of the white-collar worker is often a "borrowed" prestige.

In surveying the "status panic" Mills looked to the future and reached a grim conclusion. One of the features offering greater status to the white-collar worker has been the fact that often his work identifies him as a person of superior education. By virtue of being a bank clerk one can be more readily associated with people of some education than would be the case if he were a filling station attendant. At the same time, in the driving surge for better positions, national educational levels have been rising. As national educational levels have been rising, the educational demands of most white-collar positions have, according to Mills, been falling.

> As the general educational level rises, the level of education required or advisable for many white-collar jobs falls. In the early 'twenties, personnel men said: "I think it has become a principle with the majority of our progressive offices that they will not take into the office any person or candidate who has not had the benefit of at least a high-school education." But soon they began to say that too much education was not advisable for many white-collar jobs.[16]

If this is so, then the disparity between the reality and the ideal—the hope

---

[15] College professors, until recently at least, have been very sympathetic with the labor movement in the United States. This sympathy, however, has been restricted pretty much to intellectual support. Unionization among college professors is not popular with the possible exception of those who occupy the lowest-income ranks.

[16] Mills, *White Collar*, p. 247.

education offers and the actuality it brings—may produce profound disillusion-ment. At best, said Mills, it opens the white-collar worker to a precarious psychological life.

The white-collar mentality—combined with the vastness of the white-collar element in American society—makes it a key to the understanding of Amer-ican character. For this reason Mills devoted much effort to an attempt to fathom the nature of this class of Americans. His conclusions seem to be as valid today as they were when written in 1956. In sum, Mills said: (1) white-collar workers are being squeezed economically and in terms of real power by the unionized blue-collar wage-earning workers; (2) white-collar status claims are becoming more precarious and unrealistic; (3) the threat of growing discontent and frustration among white-collar workers is enhanced by the flood of educated young people coming into the labor market and the in-creasing simplification of routinized clerical work; (4) the lack of political identity among white-collar workers makes them a politically malleable group for the power elite; and, finally, (5) the traditional signs of success will be increasingly evaluated in an ambivalent or confused fashion—is it worth it to fight one's way to the top? Of these possibilities, the political malleability of the white-collar class and the psychological strains of what Mills termed the "status panic" could produce a strain toward authoritarianism—the quest for clearly delineated status in a nation-state geared to attain goals of sim-plistic and readily determined worth.

If there is a strain toward authoritarianism in America today, then one form it might be readily expected to take would be an acceptance of military regi-mentation. Thus, Mills' concern with *The Power Elite* was a logical extension of observations made during the preparation of *White Collar*. His interest in the "power elite" increased further his concern that America was indeed moving in the direction of a capitulation to the simplicity and formality of military regulation and military thought. This capitulation, he felt, was thrust-ing the world ever closer to World War III.

The Causes of World War III

In *The Causes of World War III* Mills recapitulated the central ideas of his earlier works. He noted again the ineffectiveness of the white-collar element and he commented on the solidarity of the power elite. But in this work he was more concerned with the historical implications of these observations. What are the possibilities for the future? The possibilities that seemed most clear to Mills were those leading toward war. Moreover, the historical pos-sibilities were leading us toward war of a new kind—war which promoted efficiency and impersonality in much the same manner that a large industry promotes impersonal and efficient production. Mills, long before the Vietnam War forced greater consideration of moral issues and split the nation into "doves" and "hawks," was saying,

> In the expanded world of mechanically vivified communication the individual becomes the spectator of everything but the human witness of nothing. Having no plain targets of revolt, men feel no moral springs of revolt. The cold manner enters their souls and they are made private and blasé. In virtually all realms of life, facts now outrun sensibility. Emptied of their human meanings, these facts are readily got used to. In official man there is no more human shock; in his unofficial follower there is little sense of moral issue. Within the unopposed supremacy of impersonal calculated technique, there is no human place to draw the line and give the emphatic no.
>
>   This lack of response I am trying to sum up by the phrase "moral insensibility," and I am suggesting that the level of moral sensibility, as part of public and of private life, has sunk out of sight. It is not the number of victims or the degree of cruelty that is distinctive; it is the fact that the acts committed and the acts that nobody protests are split from the consciousness of men in an uncanny, even a schizophrenic, manner. The atrocities of our time are done by men as "functions" of a social machinery—men possessed by an abstracted view that hides from them the human beings who are their victims and, as well, their own humanity. They are inhuman acts because they are impersonal. They are not sadistic but merely businesslike; they are not aggressive but merely efficient; they are not emotional at all but technically clean-cut.[17]

The driving energy which employs moral insensibility and uses it in the working out of man's fate comes primarily from our conceptions of the realities of our circumstances. If, for example, we are walking past a graveyard on a dark and eerie evening and we begin to walk faster and faster and then break into a run, the driving energy which impels us comes from our conception of the "reality" of the situation. If we believe we are in a dangerous setting, then we react accordingly—regardless of the "realities" surrounding us. Men of power, like umpires at a baseball game, must give their conceptions of the complex interplay between nations the imprimatur of realism. They must refer to themselves as "realists" and as men who see the situation "realistically." A seat of power is no place for idealistic indulgences. And so it comes to pass that from the offices of the high and the mighty come supposedly "hardheaded" and realistic appraisals of world tensions. But just as an individual walking past a graveyard can be unrealistic in his appraisal, so can men of power collectively become deceived while, at the same time, patting each other on the back for their "realism." This, says Mills, might better be termed "crackpot realism."

---

[17] C. Wright Mills, *The Causes of World War III* (New York: Simon and Schuster, Inc., 1958), pp. 78–79. © 1958 by C. Wright Mills. Reprinted by the permission of Brandt & Brandt.

"Crackpot realism"

Among the features of "crackpot realism" that define world realities today are the following salient elements:[18]

1. The belief that war, rather than peace, is the natural character of man and nations; it is only realistic to assume as belligerent and as potentially destructive a posture as it is possible to assume.

2. It is only realistic to assume that the "other side" is as anxious to see us fail as we are to see him fail. National paranoia, suspicion, and ill-will are universal, permanent, and part of the primitive and unalterable nature of man.

3. It is simpler and more realistic to prepare for war than to prepare for peace. The problems of preparing for peace are more complicated and abstract than those involved in the preparation for war. It is, therefore, more realistic to solve human problems by resorting to military coercion.

4. Since war is natural, suspicion and ill-will universal, and a military posture the simplest solution, then it follows that our military leaders are the most qualified to cope with the complexities of the modern world situation. It is only realistic to give over to the warlord the control of enlarged and centralized means of violence. To be realistic is to give the generals free rein in the conduct of war.

5. It is, if the preceding "realities" are reasonable, only a matter of being realistic for politicians to encourage the growth of a military bureaucracy rather than the building of a civilian civil service of real integrity.

6. For the businessman, given the preceding set of realities, it is only hardheaded business realism to take advantage of the situation. This means the exploitation of circumstances in which there is profit in the manufacture of the means of violence and profit in the use of government supported research that comes from the quest for ever greater sources of destructive power.

7. It is also realistic and simple, indeed it is a cliché, to recognize that the economy is supported by the war effort—whether the effort is sustained in a shooting war or a "cold war."

8. The very simplicity and "reality" of the situation has led to a circumstance where the different political parties have accepted a common definition of the world situation. The consequence is a political climate in which there is no real choice—despite presidential candidate Goldwater's contentions to the

---

[18] This list of the features of crackpot realism is a highly modified version of one which appears in Chapter 13, pp. 81–89, of *The Causes of World War III*.

contrary during the 1964 campaign. It is realistic to have a political directorate composed of former generals and former corporation men—whose world appraisals share so much in common.

9. The massive hold of this "reality" has been overwhelming for both the general public and for members of the leading intellectual, scientific, and religious circles. For the general public the "realistic" response is that of moral insensibility. For the intellectuals and scientists the "realistic" response has been to echo and endorse the confused reality of officialdom. The intellectual's greatest moral failure has been his incapacity to propose alternatives and to retain his tenacity in the support of alternatives.

10. "Crackpot realism" replaces the goal of an anxiously held and frustratingly established state of peace and balance of power with the idea of "winning." One is never told what is won. It is sufficient simply to seek to win. To desire to win, even without knowing what it is that one is to win, is more "realistic" and sensible than to abdicate the concept of winning.

11. The general product of "crackpot realism" is a slow movement toward World War III. The individual consequences of such "realism" are, generally speaking, beneficial. People are rewarded for endorsing these conceptions of the world situation—they benefit individually. But the collective and historical thrust of these opportunistic views of world reality will be toward total military engagement.

And so, in the name of realism, men behave unrealistically. It was a view that Mills could not reflect on and, at the same time, not call absurd.

If the view of world realities as seen by men of power today, whether in Peking, Washington, or the Kremlin, is appropriately termed "crackpot realism," then what does it mean, given present world conditions, to think in a manner that can be called hardheaded realism? We must recognize, perhaps above all else, that war and war alone is the greatest enemy confronting mankind today. We must come to see world reality in other terms than those imposed by a military metaphysic. Industry must be used as a means of coping with world problems rather than as a means of buoying further the consumptive egos of those countries which have achieved industrialization. Finally, using Mills' phrasing, "The world encounter of coexisting political economies must be conducted in cultural, political, and economic terms."[19]

We must, as individuals, never lose our commitment to humanity. We must not allow ourselves, individually, to represent the broader trend of moral insensibility. Mills expressed this preachment eloquently by saying,

---

[19] *Ibid.*, p. 98.

What scientist can claim to be part of the legacy of science and yet remain a hired technician of the military machine?

What man of God can claim to partake of the Holy Spirit, to know the life of Jesus, to grasp the meaning of that Sunday phrase "the brotherhood of man"— and yet sanction the insensibility, the immorality, the spiritual irresponsibility of the Caesars of our time?

What Western scholar can claim to be part of the big discourse of reason and yet retreat to formal trivialities and exact nonsense, in a world in which reason and freedom are being held in contempt, being smashed, being allowed to fade out of the human condition?[20]

An academic sociologist might shake his finger at Mills and chastize him not for his eloquence but for his presumption—and eloquence often flows from presumption. After all, can we reasonably conclude that reason and freedom are being held in contempt? How can we be sure? How does one measure reason and freedom? How rapidly are they fading out? Are things really as bad as Mills said they are? Was Mills crying out against injustices and human circumstances that came more from his own fears and anxieties than from the world itself? Certainly the strong possibility of this would seem to be sufficient to incline us to ignore Mills when we settle down to the task of creating a serious sociology.

Mills would reply, I believe, somewhat as a meteorologist might: In predicting storms it is better to say that one is coming when, in fact, it might not be. The other kind of error is more disastrous. We leave ourselves defenseless when we conclude that a storm is not on the way—even as it bears down on us.

If Mills erred, he erred on the side he believed to be morally more defensible. The sociologist is involved in the system he is writing about and attempting to fathom. Mills saw the sociologist as a person morally encumbered to provide social knowledge which is significant. Because society is essentially a moral order, as Durkheim had already noted, this means that significant social knowledge must be morally significant. The sociologist must attempt by his writing as well as his observations to prevent men from falling into patterns of belief and action that appear catastrophic from a sociological perspective.

Mills functioned as a critic of the greater society and, as a critic, expressed great concern over the role of the intellectual. More specifically, he was concerned with the duties and character of the social scientist. He was quite unappreciative of the sociologist who teased at trivialities in a pseudo-scientific mumbo-jumbo jargon. His irritation with the work of some of his colleagues

---

[20] *Ibid.*, p. 125.

appears in nearly all of his works. However, it is elaborated and expressed most fully in *The Sociological Imagination*.

The Sociological Imagination

This book, as is true of Mills' other works, reveals a man exasperated by the discrepancy between the potential value of a human effort and its actual value or attainment. If Mills lambasted some features of sociology, it was because he felt they deserved criticism. Sociology is too important to be ignored and it is not beyond the need for some reforms. It is the intellectual who stands as one of the constraints against the abuse of power—but only for so long as he retains his sense and sensibility.

The importance of sociological thought comes out of the fact that it is not something limited to professors of sociology or courses in modern society on the campuses of American colleges. Instead, it is an exercise which all men today must attempt with more or less success. For Mills the difference between effective sociological thought and that which fails rested upon the use of imagination. This would not seem especially radical were it not for the fact that Mills' assertion appears as a reaction against the sociology of the thirties and forties which argued, in effect, that worthwhile sociological thinking comes mostly from facts. Theory is supportive, but its main function is to lead to further facts. The product of this kind of sociology, said Mills, is factual, in a sense, but lacking imagination. More importantly, it often, in the quest for factual information, bypasses problems that are more centrally significant. Speaking of studies of voting behavior—an area of interest which has lent itself to empirical or factual examinations of opinion—Mills said,

> It must be interesting to political scientists to examine a full-scale study of voting which contains no reference to the party machinery for "getting out the vote," or indeed to any political institutions. Yet that is what happens in *The Peoples' Choice*, a duly accredited and celebrated study of the 1940 election in Erie County, Ohio. From this book we learn that rich, rural, and Protestant persons tend to vote Republican; people of opposite type incline toward the Democrats; and so on. But we learn little about the dynamics of American politics.[21]

There is the suggestion in Mills' criticism of what he refers to as "abstracted empiricism"[22] that sociological research is guided more by the requirements

[21] C. Wright Mills, *The Sociological Imagination* (New York: Oxford University Press, 1959), pp. 52–53. Mills was critical of both narrow factual scientism and grand theory. The former gets lost in trivialities and the latter gets lost in its word play. Because of space limitations I have emphasized Mills critique of empiricism. It should be kept in mind that he was as critical of men like Talcott Parsons as he was of men like George Lundberg.

[22] See Chapter 5 of this work for a more detailed statement of the position which Mills is here criticizing. Lundberg was a leading exponent of what Mills referred to as "abstracted empiricism."

of administrative concerns than by intellectual concerns. The "scientific method" followed by the contemporary empirical sociologist is actually more an administrative method than a scientific one. Certainly, Mills suggested, it is more an administrative method than an intellectual one. The results of an opinion survey or a political preference poll can be of inestimable value to an official running for office. At the same time, it has relatively restricted scientific value. Because administrative concerns are virtually infinite and can penetrate into the most trivial aspects of organization, the kinds of research that can come out of an administrative interest will be infinitely varied and range from that which has some possible promise as an intellectual interest to that which will have none whatsoever.

The narrow concern with "factual science" which attracts many sociologists today, said Mills, has produced a very constrained view of man. It is a view which, incidentally, would be in keeping with an "administrative view" of man. That is to say, abstracted empiricism fits nicely into a research program geared toward the more effective control of human beings. Indeed, sociologists such as Lundberg have specifically stated that the goal of science—and they include sociology here—is to achieve prediction and control. With respect to human behavior this means controlling the lives and actions of men—and this concern is the paramount concern of the administrator.

The field of demography offers us an example of research which has great administrative value. No administrator can function very well without reliable census information concerning his organization and the community and state within which it operates. At the same time, the scientific character of demography suffers from a peculiar constraint—there is only so much one can do with census data. Usually academic or scientific considerations of census data prove to be elaborate exercises in the use of statistical devices. So severe is the problem with respect to population studies that some of the finest demographers and human ecologists in the country have seriously dealt with the issue of whether or not there is such a thing as population theory and what theory means in the field of population studies. Demography is preponderantly the accumulation of facts for the purpose of facilitating administrative or political decisions.[23]

It is elementary but necessary to remember that sociological writing, like any other, is concerned with convincing others. Convincing others involves at least two rudimentary and important considerations. First of all, we need

---

[23] Population studies received their initial impetus from political and military concerns. The development of census data in the United States came originally from the need for population data to determine the distribution of representation in Congress.

to convince others that what we have to say is significant and worth the effort of their review. Secondly, we must convince others that what we are saying is valid. The empiricist has concluded that the only form of validity is that established through fact and, moreover, that validity provided through fact is more important than any other consideration in the communication process. The result, Mills wryly observed, is thin.

But there is more to it than that. It is not so much that the empirical sociologist has become bogged down with statistics; this in itself is not a completely hopeless situation. A man living under a haystack of facts and figures might reasonably be expected to dig his way out to a point where he could see clearly the outlines of what previously had only been a dark and suffocating pressure. The serious problem, as Mills viewed it, is that the empiricist, even as he suffocates, thinks that building haystacks is the best of all possible lives. But perhaps this figure of speech goes too far. Mills put it this way,

> What has happened in the methodological inhibition is that men have become stuck, not so much in the empirical intake, as in what are essentially epistomological [sic] problems of method. Since many of these men, especially the younger, do not know very much about epistomology [sic], they tend to be quite dogmatic about the one set of canons that dominate them.[24]

But if facts are not enough—if the empiricism of modern sociological research is producing inconsequential and "thin" results—then what is one to do? Mills set forth his own conception of how a social scientist should undertake his work. He endeavored to convey a sense of what it means to be an intellectual who concentrates on the social nature of man and who seeks that which is significant. (It is worth a parenthetical comment here to observe that Mills recognized that one can make a significant statement which is not necessarily factually valid. For example, the philosopher Karl Jaspers, in an essay on the nature of totalitarianism, comments that totalitarianism cannot be destroyed from within; it must be destroyed from without.[25] It is difficult to assess whether historical records will back up such a statement. Nonetheless the statement is significant when we wish to consider the nature of the completely autocratic state. Jaspers is correct in a logical or definitional sense, though he might be subjected to criticism from an empiricist.)

Mills was critical of textbooks used in sociological courses. In his criticism he indicated the direction he thought contemporary sociology should take. Sociological texts suffer from being overly concerned with settled conceptions

---

[24] Mills, *The Sociological Imagination*, p. 74.
[25] Karl Jaspers, "The Fight Against Totalitarianism," in *The Dilemma of Organizational Society*, edited by Hendrik M. Ruitenbeek (New York: E. P. Dutton & Co., Inc., 1963), p. 6.

and from ignoring the possibilities of new ideas. The textbook provides the student with old ideas supported by new facts. New ideas might endanger the number of adoptions of the text.

Mills illustrated his point with a consideration of the concept of "cultural lag." This concept, popular in sociological thought down to the present time, has achieved an almost venerable position in the lexicon of sociological terms. The concept of cultural lag claims, essentially, that there are two aspects of culture. One aspect is the immaterial—consisting of ideas, sentiments, beliefs, values, interests, meanings, and other facets of a subjective or mental character. The other aspect consists of the material features of the culture—such as tools, artifacts, equipment, hardware, produce, chemicals, and other directly observable and "touchable" features of the culture. The concept of cultural lag then goes on to suggest that the immaterial aspects of culture "lag" behind the development of the material aspects of culture. We have a 20th-century technology, for example, embedded in a moral, religious, and legal system that has its roots in a Mediterranean pastoral society that existed 3000 years ago. We have the atomic bomb and, at the same time, a conception of warfare and conduct between nations more in keeping with the ideas of warfare held by Napoleon.

It is not so much that the concept of cultural lag is "bad" as it is that the sociologist tends to use it in an uncritical, unexamined, and unimaginative way. All too commonly the notion of cultural lag is used as a simple-minded "scientific" justification for a progressive ideology which holds that the problems of the present lie in the moral inadequacies of the past. The concept of cultural lag enables us to make value judgments about where we ought to go and what ought to lead our movement—namely technological advancement and physical science—while at the same time disguising the fact we have been making value judgments.

But it is not the naive hypocrisy of the sociologist who thinks in this fashion which bothered Mills the most. Certainly it is inconsistent to claim to be making objective statements about the social order which are, by their very nature, moral judgments. However, as Mills viewed it, this is not the most serious fault of sociology. The most serious fault is the lack of imagination and the dullness of thought which characterizes much sociological work. There is, said Mills, quite a difference between the way the sociologist uses an idea like cultural lag and the way a thinker of the magnitude of Thorstein Veblen uses the same idea.

In contrast to many sociologists' use of "lag," Thorstein Veblen's phrase "lag, lead and friction" led him to a structural analysis of "industry versus business." He asked: where does "the lag" pinch? And he attempted to reveal how the trained incapacity of businessmen acting in accordance with entrepreneurial canons resulted in an efficient sabotage of production and productivity. He was also some-what aware of the role of profit-making within a system of private ownership, and he did not especially care for the "unworkman-like results." But the great point is that he revealed the structural mechanics of "the lag." Many social scientists, however, use the politically washed-out notion of "cultural lag," which has lost any such specific and structural anchorage: they have generalized the idea in order to apply it to everything, always in a fragmenting manner.[26]

But what, in more specific terms, did Mills have to suggest? How, if it is so, is the sociologist to break away from the "washed-out" usage of social concepts and ideas? In answer, Mills provided some guidelines[27] which he be-lieved led toward a greater sense of intellectual craftsmanship.

Guidelines for intellectual craftsmanship

First of all, a good scholar or intellectual does not split his work from his life. Both are part of a seriously accepted unity. Life experience can be used in one's work, and the fruits of one's work can be used to enrich life. The sociologist must not "bureaucratize" his work and conclude that his is a "nine-to-five" business, to be abandoned with a sense of relief when the whistle blows in the late afternoon.[28]

Second, a good scholar must keep a file. This file is a compendium of personal, professional, and intellectual experiences. Such a file promotes organization, the preservation of experience, and the discipline of writing.

Third, a good intellectual engages in continual review of his thoughts and experiences. He does not write for the moment—he does not wait until the pressures of professional advancement call for writing up a request for govern-mental or foundation funds and then sit down and think up a "project."

Fourth, a good intellectual may find a truly bad book as intellectually stimu-lating and conducive to thinking and effort as a good book. But reading, whether it is a good book or a bad one, must be an intense experience and one which has relevance for the "file." But, at the same time, reading is a matter of balance—one should know when to read and when not to. To soak up too much literature is to risk being drowned by it.

---

[26] Mills, *The Sociological Imagination*, pp. 89–90.

[27] *Ibid.*, pp. 195–226. In a lengthy appendix, Mills sets forth a number of very sensible suggestions concerning intellectual craftsmanship. The list presented here is a highly modified summary of Mills' comments.

[28] The imagery employed here is not immoderate. The University of Kansas actually uses a factory whistle to call students to class. The same whistle tells professors when to go home in the evening. I gained the impression, during my pleasant years at this school, that one could tell the extent of a professor's intellectual commitment by the extent of his hostility toward that whistle.

Fifth, in the development of a system of notes, it is a good idea to lay out, at least in a sketchy manner, designs for research that would be relevant to interests stimulated by reading or by other experiences. In the course of this there is a constant rearranging of ideas and approaches. It is in the exercise of rearrangements that imagination is stimulated.

Sixth, there must be an attitude of playfulness toward phrases, words, and ideas. Along with this attitude of playfulness must go a fierce drive to make sense out of the world.

Seventh, the imagination is stimulated by assuming a willingness to view the world from the perspective of others. It is stimulating to the imagination of the sociologist to wonder how, for example, a political scientist or historian or even how a biologist might think about the topic which is concerning him.

Eighth, one should not be afraid, in the preliminary stages of a speculation, to think in terms of imaginative extremes.

Ninth, one should not hesitate to express his ideas in language which is as simple and as direct as he can make it. Ideas are affected by the manner of their expression. An imagination which is encased in deadening language will be a deadened imagination.

In this manner C. Wright Mills left behind a statement of his concerns and his mode of living with those concerns. His attempt to delineate the way to a brighter sociological "imagination" was, in a more serious sense than perhaps some of his colleagues would accept, an attempt to correct the excesses of an unimaginative empirical methodology.

Yet Mills was excessive in the other extreme. He seemed too involved. He was too much a part of the times. He was too clever in his writing. He showed too much interest in the well-turned phrase and possibly too little in the well-turned fact.[29]

If so, Mills was aware that this was his personal choice. Social thought, to Mills, was a matter of individual commitment—and it involved a sense of responsibility. The greater the commitment, the greater the responsibility. To Mills, social thought was the stuff of life. To live intensely was to think and to work intensely. Life, work, and thought were inseparable. This was what Mills meant when he said, a year or so before his death, "God, how I have lived." It was a fitting commentary on his work.

---

[29] Mills was candid. At one point he said, "Now I do not like to do empirical work if I can possibly avoid it . . . it is a great deal of trouble." *The Sociological Imagination*, p. 205. Mills was suggesting, however, that all other avenues of exploration should be exhausted before taking up the empirical one.

8 Abundance, Leisure, and Loneliness: An Introduction to David Riesman

A vexing dilemma confronting every social scientist is that involving the opposing demands of generalization and relevancy. On the one hand, the social scientist is expected to generate abstract descriptions of the way things work in the social order. A slavish dedication to this horn of the dilemma can result in formulations so general in character that they lose contact with the immediate concerns of everyday living. When a sociologist claims that a society must (1) control the environment, (2) gratify the system's goal, (3) maintain solidarity, and (4) reinforce the value system, he has formulated an abstraction so airy that its relevance to the more ordinary affairs of man and society becomes difficult to demonstrate.

On the other hand, the social scientist can, like the journalist, get caught in some fad which defines the relevancies of his time and discover, after a few years have passed, that his research and ideas are no longer of any value. I am reminded, as I write this, of a colleague of mine who was concerned with how to make advertisements in the ''yellow pages'' of the phone directory more effective. There is a relevancy to such research, but it can hardly, as my colleague tried to claim, be called ''basic research.''

Some social scientists are able to balance themselves between abstract formulations which aid our understanding and the significant aspects of modern living. In such cases we are offered ideas which are broad enough to provide general intellectual interest and yet specific enough to be relevant to events of the moment. These men produce books that endure. One such social scientist is David Riesman. Before taking up the central contributions of Riesman's thought, I would like to mention that it is necessary to be biased and selective in a review of his work as brief as this one is. It is possible to offer little more than a fragmented sample of his ideas. The reader is encouraged to browse through some of Riesman's better known works—it will prove a rewarding experience.[1]

The work which brought Riesman more notoriety than he ever anticipated[2] was a book entitled *The Lonely Crowd*, which he coauthored with Nathan Glazer and Reuel Denney. We shall now examine the central ideas in this work—recognizing, again, that it is impossible to do justice to the variety and imagination of Riesman's thought.

The relationship between the individual and his society

One of the most crucial concerns of the social scientist has been the nature of the relationship between the individual and the society of which he is a part. Some, like Leslie White, find the individual so dominated by his society or culture that there is little reason for the social scientist to keep the individual in the picture. Man is, as a social being, simply the neural expression of social forces. Others, like Peter Berger, see ways out for the individual, avenues of personal expression which are the creative act of the person and which offer him some freedom from the constraints of social bondage. This view sees personality existing in the interstices of the social fabric.

The relationship between society and the individual is the fulcrum upon which Riesman's thought is balanced. But his approach is different. First of all, Riesman is not especially concerned with resolving the problem of the priority of society *or* the individual. He is not concerned with proving that society dominates the individual. Nor is he interested in proving that society is a collective manifestation of individual instincts—an elaborately spread-out form of human nature. Instead, he takes the problem of the relationship between the individual and society as a point of departure for an investigation into national character. All we need to do is to presume that if there is some

---

[1] Much of Riesman's writing appears in the form of essays published in a great variety of journals. His major works are *Faces in the Crowd: Individual Studies in Character and Politics*, in collaboration with Nathan Glazer (New Haven: Yale University Press, 1952); *Individualism Reconsidered* (New York: Free Press of Glencoe, 1954); *Constraint and Variety in American Education* (Lincoln: University of Nebraska Press, 1958); *Thorstein Veblen, A Critical Interpretation* (New York: Charles Scribner's Sons, 1960); *The Lonely Crowd, A Study in the Changing American Character*, with Nathan Glazer and Reuel Denney (abr. ed. with new foreword; New Haven: Yale University Press, 1961); and *Abundance for What?* (Garden City, N.Y.: Doubleday & Company, Inc., 1964).

[2] Of the response to *The Lonely Crowd* Riesman says, "We did not anticipate such an audience, not only when the book was first published by a university press, but later when it was one of the first 'quality paperbacks,' for we and the publishers alike thought it might sell a few thousand copies as a reading in social science courses." *The Lonely Crowd*, p. xxix. Reaction to Riesman's work was so enthusiastically favorable that it led to the distinction of a cover story in TIME magazine (see TIME, Sept. 27, 1954). Riesman, so far as I know, is the only sociologist to have been so honored.

kind of relationship between society and the individual—and this seems apolo-
getically reasonable—then the historical experiences of our society may have
a bearing on what we, as individuals, have become today.

This is the simple motif. In this abstract form it is not especially enlightening nor is it subject to much in the way of critical comment. The premises
with which he begins are modestly qualified; it is when Riesman gets down
to the particulars of historical experience and their bearing on national character that he proves to be controversial and provocative. But what, specifically, does Riesman have to say about national social character?[3]

Three types of social character

We can begin by assuming that the different demands placed on the person
by different kinds of societies produce unique "social" characters. Thus,
Riesman suggests that societies which are relatively primitive, folk-oriented,
preindustrial, hunting or agricultural societies develop in their people a social
character typified by a tendency to follow tradition. Riesman refers to such
people as *tradition-directed* people and their society as one which is dependent
on tradition-direction.[4] The tradition-directed person possesses a social char-

---

[3] In his evaluation of national social character Riesman is often critical. He exudes the indig-
nant concern which any sensitive observer of the American scene must feel when he observes
practices which fall far beneath the potential of this culture. Perhaps the only difference between
the objective professional sociologist and the more free-swinging comments of Riesman is that
Riesman is willing to let you know exactly where he stands with respect to the object of his
observations. Consider, for example, the following comment on the typical American response
to problems of foreign policy: ". . . many Americans have no better utopia than a mad return
to the epoch of Theodore Roosevelt, imitating both the bravado of our own past and that of
the Soviet Union—as if it were possible to make a whole nation inner-directed again by internal-
izing the arms race under the label of 'national purpose.' If they win out, the fragile chance will
be lost that America might offer the rest of the world some clues to the uses of literacy and
abundance." *The Lonely Crowd,* p. xlvii.
   Such critical commentary, and the oversimplification that always goes with it, is a sure sign
of having fallen from the grace of objectivity; and it cost Riesman considerable loss of respect
from more scientifically oriented colleagues. At the same time, it won him a host of concerned
readers who were wrestling with the problem of what it means to be an American today. Even
so, Riesman should not be evaluated in terms of his occasional critical asides. What elevates
him to a very high intellectual status is his embracing interpretation of the development of
American character and his ability to express this development with striking lucidity.
   [4] The extent to which tradition is not only losing its utility in modern society but becoming
downright dangerous—a luxury only more primitive social systems can afford—is hinted at by
Norbert Wiener. Speaking of war games, he says, "It has been said that in every war, the good
generals fight the last war, the bad ones the war before the last. That is, the rules of the war
game never catch up with the facts of the real situation." In the context here, Wiener is pointing out that the traditionalist in war is the one who stands the greatest chance of losing. Omin-
ously enough, he adds, "Moreover, remember that in the game of atomic warfare, there are no
experts." The course of social movement today is one which provides less and less traditional
basis for decision making. These statements by Wiener appear in *God and Golem, Inc.* (Cambridge,
Mass.: The M.I.T. Press, 1964), p. 60 and p. 85.

acter which is uncritically accepting of tradition and resistant to innovation. The major problems of the society are resolved by the willingness of the individual to rely on tradition.

Tradition provides a place for the individual in society, and the individual responds by tenaciously endorsing tradition. In contrast to other societies, traditional societies incorporate all of their members. No one is "surplus."

> Indeed, the individual in some primitive societies is far more appreciated and respected than in some sectors of modern society. For the individual in a society dependent on tradition-direction has a well-defined functional relationship to other members of the group. If he is not killed off, he "belongs"—he is not "surplus," as the modern unemployed are surplus, nor is he expendable as the unskilled are expendable in modern society. But by very virtue of his "belonging," life goals that are *his* in terms of conscious choice appear to shape his destiny only to a very limited extent, just as only to a limited extent is there any concept of progress for the group.[5]

A small and relatively stable society may be able to maintain itself almost exclusively in terms of traditional definitions of roles and interpersonal behavior. Then, for reasons not well understood today, such societies may undergo a number of small but cumulative changes which tend to destroy the effectiveness of tradition as a basis of organization. With a decline in the effectiveness of tradition, the society enters a transitional stage of development and, during this stage, relies on a different form of social character— that of the "inner-directed" man. Riesman puts it this way:

> In western history the society that emerged with the Renaissance and Reformation and that is only now vanishing serves to illustrate the type of society in which inner-direction is the principal mode of securing conformity. Such a society is characterized by increased personal mobility, by a rapid accumulation of capital (teamed with devastating technological shifts), and by an almost constant *expansion:* intensive expansion in exploration, colonization, and imperialism. The greater choices this society gives—and the greater initiatives it demands in order to cope with its novel problems—are handled by character types who can manage to live socially without strict and self-evident tradition-direction. These are the inner-directed types.[6]

The inner-directed person is provided with the ambition to seek out generalized social goals. This may require novel solutions to problems which a traditionalistic approach would not have been able to resolve, or which, more likely, would not even have occurred. What Riesman is getting at here can be exemplified by the conduct of a Scotsman who was the grounds keeper

---

[5] David Riesman, with Nathan Glazer and Reuel Denney, *The Lonely Crowd; A Study in the Changing American Character* (abr. ed. with new foreword; New Haven, Yale University Press, 1961), pp. 11–12.
[6] *Ibid.,* p. 14.

at a small college where I spent a pleasant year after completing the nearly lethal requirements of graduate school. The Scotsman, an old but lively specimen from another generation, was determined that a sidewalk should be built across a particular section of the campus—despite the fact that the administration had given him orders not to build the walk. The old Scotsman adhered to the letter of the orders but not their spirit by digging a wide and shallow ditch down the line where he wanted the sidewalk. Once the ditch had been dug, the administration—not wanting to lose one of the best landscapers in the area—capitulated by allowing him to fill it in with concrete and the Scotsman got his sidewalk.

The behavior of the Scotsman was not traditionalistic, certainly. Traditionalistic behavior is, by definition, more highly conforming. We have, in this instance, a form of character which reveals itself willing to violate the canons of conformity in order to attain a more general and significant goal—in this case the esthetic improvement of the campus. Such inner-directed individuals are not completely lacking in a tradition-directed society; but, and this is Riesman's point, they will be more typical of a society which has need of them. They are more likely to be aberrant or unique in other forms of society.

After the expansive movements of a society have been completed, a new problem arises. During the expansive phase, the problem is to cope with novel situations and to pursue doggedly the task of exploiting a hostile environment; once this has been achieved, the problem becomes one of making peace with success. A period of entrenchment ensues. The land, the resources, the markets, the colonies have been successfully exploited. But the process of exploitation, of developing these resources, brings into being powerful agents of control—the most significant of these being large-scale organizational systems. Whereas before man found himself locked in dubious battle with nature, he now finds himself confronted with bureaucracies. The problem now is to adjust to others around him. Social adaptability rather than inner moral strength becomes the leading characteristic of the successful type in this new stage of social development.[7]

---

[7] Some people fear that Riesman is opposed to inner moral strength and that he is justifying more callow forms of opportunistic conformity. This would be unfair. Riesman is trying, as realistically as possible, to evaluate the impact of modern forms of social organization on character and he concludes that, for the most part, a common character of the hardheaded inner-directed type would prove extremely disruptive. Ayn Rand's plea for a return to older individualistic values is not so much right or wrong as it is unrealistic. A few men of the character of the hero of *The Fountainhead* can be absorbed by this society. But such willfulness would prove intolerable in great numbers. Riesman, incidentally, views Rand's work as a caricature of inner-directed values. In any event, we cannot avow the rightness or wrongness of strong moral character. We can, however, consider the possibility of its disruptive effects if practiced on a large scale in a society where the central problem confronting people is that of making their peace with other people.

Because relations with other people become so crucial and because the individual is so sensitive to the demands of others, Riesman calls a person having this form of social character "other-directed" man. He defines other-directed man and his society in the following way:

> Under these newer [other-directed] patterns the peer group (the group of one's associates of the same age and class) becomes much more important to the child, while the parents make him feel guilty not so much about violation of inner standards as about failure to be popular or otherwise to manage his relations with these other children . . . What is common to all the other-directed people is that their contemporaries are the source of direction for the individual—either those known to him or those with whom he is indirectly acquainted, through friends and through the mass media . . . This mode of keeping in touch with others permits a close behavior conformity, not through drill in behavior itself, as in the tradition-directed character, but rather through an exceptional sensitivity to the actions and wishes of others.[8]

This tripartite typification of societies and social character, relatively simple and straightforward, proves to have astonishing success in making sense out of a tremendous variety of social events ranging from changes in child-rearing practices to the problems of personnel management in modern industry. As we shall see, practices taking place in one sector of society are not always as removed from those taking place in another as it might first appear. Indeed, the hallmark of an outstanding social scientist is his capacity to reveal commonalities in events which have, in the past, seemed perfectly disparate.[9]

If vast changes in the social structure can be summarized in terms of pervasive effects on social character, then we should be able to find these effects at work in almost any setting. We should be able to see shifts from tradition- to inner- to other-directed man at work in the army, the school, the practice of medicine, the practice of law, in the treatment of criminals, the practice of business, leisure pursuits, literature, government, religion, and any other part of the social order. One social activity which occupies much of Riesman's thinking is education and he turns toward a consideration of the tradition-, inner-, and other-directed school.

---

[8] Riesman, *The Lonely Crowd*, pp. 21–22.

[9] John Kenneth Galbraith expresses this point better in his description of Marx as a social scientist. He refers to ". . . the breath-taking grandeur of Marx's achievement as an exercise in social theory. No one before, or for that matter since, had taken so many strands of human behavior and woven them together—social classes, economic behavior, the nature of the state, imperialism, and war were all here and on a great fresco which ran from deep in the past to far into the future." John Kenneth Galbraith, *The Affluent Society* (Mentor Books; New York: New American Library, Inc., 1958), p. 63.

Schooling in different societies

In the tradition-directed society the child is likely to have little encounter with schooling. The traditions which he comes to rely on are acquired through intimate observation and involvement with adults and peers. For example, a Navaho child whose parents belong to the Native American Church, a peyote-using religion, is taken to all-night peyote sessions and allowed to watch and participate to whatever extent he can. When he becomes sleepy, he is allowed to fall asleep. The child is allowed to experiment with peyote at any time he wishes—regardless of age.[10]

In the inner-directed society, the problems of education are more complicated. The child must be infused with general goals which he is willing to pursue even though it may exact a cost in terms of indifference and hostility on the part of others. The governess in Victorian England helped promote such a character. The relationship of the governess to the head of the household was such as to provide the child with a very realistic training in the disparities of power. A child reared under such conditions was less likely to be awed by the authority of his teachers. As Riesman puts it,

> When he goes off to boarding school or college he is likely to remain unimpressed by his teachers—like the upper class mother who told the school headmaster: "I don't see why the masters can't get along with Johnny; all the other servants do." Such a child is not going to be interested in allowing his teachers to counsel him in his peer-group relations or emotional life.[11]

The character of schooling in the inner-directed society can be summed up as follows: The task of the teacher is to train children in matters of decorum and intellectual subjects. The approach is impersonal. The sexes are segregated. The emphasis is on learning a curriculum, and whether or not one enjoys it is really beside the point. Standards are unequivocal—they are immutable. They cannot be challenged nor can they be seen in a relative manner—they apply to all. They are not held to be more appropriate for some students than for others. Thus, children are ranked in terms of their ability to conform to the standards, and the security they achieve from knowing where

---

[10] I am indebted to Professor Omer C. Stewart of the University of Colorado for this illustration. Reliance on tradition does not necessarily mean a stultified life-form for the tradition-oriented person. Part of the peyote ritual consists of singing hymns. These hymns are traditional, but they can be varied to a considerable degree within this limitation. Professor Stewart illustrates this nicely by singing a peyote hymn which he learned from a Navaho Indian. The Navaho learned the hymn, in turn, from the generator of his automobile as he was driving home one evening.

[11] Riesman, *The Lonely Crowd*, p. 56.

they stand in terms of these standards is balanced by the fact that little mercy is shown them by taking into account any psychological or social handicaps under which they might be straining.

George Orwell, describing his experiences at Crossgates, nicely underscores Riesman's main point:

> . . . That was the pattern of school life—a continuous triumph of the strong over the weak. Virtue consisted in winning: it consisted in being bigger, stronger, handsomer, richer, more popular, more elegant, more unscrupulous than other people—in dominating them, bullying them, making them suffer pain, making them look foolish, getting the better of them in every way. Life was hierarchical and whatever happened was right. There were the strong, who deserved to win and always did win, and there were the weak, who deserved to lose and always did lose, everlastingly.

> I did not question the prevailing standards, because so far as I could see there were no others. How could the rich, the strong, the elegant, the fashionable, the powerful, be in the wrong? It was their world, and the rules they made for it must be the right ones.[12]

But times and social character have changed—and these changes can be seen dramatically within the context of the school. Riesman describes schooling in an age of other-direction: Children go to school at earlier ages, and the two- to five-year-old school children come to associate school more with playing and with games than with forbidding adults and dreary subjects. Physical arrangements are altered. The sexes may be mixed, and alphabetic placement of students may give way to sociometric forms of seating—the child sits not where he is told to sit but where he finds his friends. Concern is focused increasingly on problems of group relations and decreasingly on problems of production. The teacher

> . . . conveys to the children that what matters is not their industry or learning as such but their adjustment to the group, their (carefully stylized and limited) initiative and leadership.[13]

In the other-directed school there is a deemphasis on the content of learning and an emphasis on democratization of social relationships. What a child learns is not too important—so long as he learns it in a way which shows a capacity to get along with others. The child is readied for his place in a so-

---

[12] Few reading experiences more dramatically reveal how education practices have changed than reading Orwell's description of his experiences as a boy in attendance at Crossgates. See George Orwell, "Such Such Were the Joys," in *A Collection of Essays by George Orwell* (Anchor Books; Garden City, N.Y.: Doubleday & Company, Inc., 1954), pp. 9–55. The quotation cited here appears on pages 43–44.

[13] Riesman, *The Lonely Crowd*, p. 63.

ciety which is moving increasingly from a dedication to morality to a promotion of morale.

The value of Riesman's inner- and other-directed classification of social character is, as I mentioned before, that it has the capacity to bring together a great variety of social threads and show them to be part of a common cloth. We have, at this point, briefly examined differences between schooling in the inner-directed and other-directed society. Now let us examine Riesman's treatment of sexual relations in the inner- and other-directed systems.

Sex in different societies

Sex for the inner-directed person had[14] a character different from what it has for the other-directed person. It played a less predominant role in the life of the inner-directed man. Sex was an integral element in the daily round of coping with problems of production—and sex, though enjoyed for its own sake, was never removed from the fact of its consequences. For the inner-directed man, preoccupation with the more serious concerns of struggle and control gave sex a smaller role to play in the scheme of life. Life and business could be and was, in many instances, a grim and gloomy confrontation with conflicting ambitions. Sex could be treated as gloomily. In inner-directed ideology, at least, masturbation was a peril to be avoided at any cost. The modest pleasures of onanism could not be permitted to appear to compete with the serious moral dedication necessary for bringing the material resources of nature to heel.

Relationships with women verged on the morbid. The wife of the inner-directed man was not to allow herself expressions of pleasure in sex. The emancipated woman with whom the inner-directed man might allow himself relations was socially inferior. The sexual conduct of the inner-directed man was supposed to be restrained and subordinated to the higher directives of social and economic exploitation of the frontier.

If in private practice sex was constrained and even dismal by modern standards, its presentation in literature and drama was often humorous. Sex was something you could poke fun at, but a serious scientific treatise on the subject was less tolerable. Sex, in an age of inner-direction, could also be used

---

[14] It is problematic whether one should use the past or present tense here. Riesman tends to use the past tense when talking about inner-directed man. However, Riesman is well aware that inner-directed men are still with us and that inner-directed characteristics are to be found even in highly developed other-directed types. So, we can also correctly say that sex *has* a different quality for inner-directed men.

as a means for self-advancement. Women, especially, could and did use sex as a means to status in spheres controlled by men. Even so, such practices were conducted in private and the ideal was to respect the secret nature of the relationship by maintaining confidences.

Sex apparently has a different meaning today. Furthermore, the difference is not simply attributable to greater knowledge about sex. Rather, it is a reflection of changes that have been taking place in various sectors of society— these in turn have had a bearing on sexual attitudes and conduct. Riesman argues that sex takes on greater importance for the other-directed man because he lacks the grand moral imperatives which give meaning and a sense of being to life. Sex is something which lies within and its imperatives still remain alive even when social imperatives have been reduced to the level of "Mickey-Mouse" playacting. Women are no longer objects in a gloomy exercise of power, but emancipated members of the peer group—sensitive and knowing consumers in the realm of sex.

As Riesman notes,

> While the inner-directed man, who could still patronize women, complained to his mistress that his wife did not understand him, the other-directed man in effect complains that his women understand him all too well.[15]

Sex, in an age of other-direction, has become a competitive and continuous quest for an experience or, more properly, a development of talent, which previously was encountered, if at all, in a visit to a brothel. Because sex remains an inner-compulsion in an age of other-direction, its demands must be met. At the same time, the private nature of sex[16] leaves the other-directed

---

[15] Riesman, *The Lonely Crowd*, p. 280.

[16] Riesman, a perceptive but tasteful observer of social events, would not have mentioned in his writing the possibility that sex might move in the direction of losing its privacy. It has become increasingly realistically portrayed in the movies—losing some of its mystery there and granting the other-directed observer the opportunity to match his experiences and capacities with those heroically depicted on the screen. For an interesting discussion of sex and the movies see Arthur Knight and Hollis Alpert, "The History of Sex in Cinema," *Playboy* magazine (April 1967), pp. 136–143 and 196–212. This is one of a series of articles on the subject.

More importantly, some young intellectuals are convinced that parties should be held in the nude with participants indulging privately or openly and without shame in whatever forms of conduct they feel moved to indulge in. (See also "The Sexual Freedom League" by Jack Lind in *Playboy* [November 1966].) Riesman would suggest that this is not only a revolt against the presumed prudery of Victorian times, it is an attempt to provide other-directed young people with the opportunity to see for themselves the levels of talent against which they are to measure themselves. This might appear, to a liberal person, like a healthy return to the direct observational learning of the tradition-directed child who observes his parents in coitus or indulges in direct sexual play with his friends. It differs, however, in the amount of importance that is given to sex and in the competitive attitudes which develop—attitudes directed by social responsiveness.

consumer in something of a quandary about how he matches up with others in this now significant realm of social action. Inner-directed man did not especially care how he compared with others and, even if he did, he could count on women to remain discrete about his talents or lack of talents—they could at least be counted on not to tell him if he was incompetent. But in an age of other-direction, as Riesman notes, men—and women as well—have to contend with the fact they may be understood all too well. Being told where one ranks in sexual consumership is not the problem[17] The problem comes from being ranked while, at the same time, being denied access to a direct observation of the performance of one's peers.

Literature and entertainment in different societies

Let us turn from education and the relation between the sexes to Riesman's comments on literature and entertainment and their relation to ideals of success. As we go from a period of inner-direction to one of other-direction . . .

> We can trace an edifying sequence that runs from the success biography of the Samuel Smiles or the Horatio Alger sort to the contemporary books and periodicals that deal with peace of mind. The earlier books were directly concerned with social and economic advance, dealt with as achievable by the virtues of thrift, hard work, and so on . . .

> From then on, inspiration literature becomes less and less exclusively concerned with social and economic mobility. Dale Carnegie's *How to Win Friends and Influence People*, written in 1937, recommends self-manipulative exercises for the sake not only of business success but of such vaguer, non-work goals as popularity.[18]

This brief reference to Carnegie is a little surprising because *How to Win Friends and Influence People*, perhaps more than any other written work, illustrates what Riesman is saying. It is worth spending a few moments to look further at this extraordinary book.

What Carnegie does, in effect, is lay down a set of rules or suggestions for transforming the individual into an other-directed form of man. Carnegie boasts,

> The rules we have set down here are not mere theories or guess work. They work like magic . . .

> To illustrate: Last season a man with 314 employees [applied these rules]. For years he had driven and criticized and condemned his employees without stint or

---

[17] In the movie *Georgy Girl* the heroine is told by her lover that her problem is not so much that she is ugly and heavy but that she tries too hard to save people. In an age of inner-direction the relation between the sexes was such that chivalrous attitudes toward the female were supposed to protect her from such blunt evaluations of her character. The women reciprocated by not telling men what they thought of them.

[18] Riesman, *The Lonely Crowd*, pp. 149–150.

discretion. Kindness, words of appreciation, and encouragement were alien to his lips. After studying the principles discussed in this book, this employer sharply altered his philosophy of life . . . Three hundred and fourteen enemies have been turned into three hundred and fourteen friends. As he proudly said . . . "When I used to walk through my establishment, no one greeted me. My employees actually looked the other way when they saw me approaching. But now they are all my friends and even the janitor calls me by my first name."[19]

It is difficult to imagine an earlier, inner-directed employer being concerned with getting someone to call him by his first name. He might, to the contrary, have found the whole idea worse than an affront; it would have made things messy.[20]

It is possible that other-directed man, at least as he appears in Carnegie's writing, loses a great deal of his individuality in his attempt to be delicately and sensitively responsive to the needs of others. Consider the implications, for example, of the following observation by Carnegie:

> I go fishing up in Maine every summer. Personally I am very fond of strawberries and cream; but I find that for some strange reason fish prefer worms. So when I go fishing, I don't think about what I want. I think about what they want. I don't bait the hook with strawberries and cream. Rather, I dangle a worm or a grasshopper in front of the fish and say: "Wouldn't you like to have that?"[21]

One sacrifices one's taste for "strawberries and cream" in order to gain access to the other fellow's preference for worms. Such a procedure, it seems, would strip both persons of the vigor of their own characters and identities. Evidently, in this scheme of things, the extent to which this would greatly facilitate social exchanges would make it worth the cost.

It is instructive to note further, in Carnegie's bible for the other-directed man, that he often dehumanizes his subject by making use of figures of speech that reduce men to animals. He does it in the above quotation by

---

[19] Dale Carnegie, *How to Win Friends and Influence People*, (New York: Simon and Schuster, Inc., 1937), p. 22. Copyright 1936 by Dale Carnegie. Copyright © renewed 1963 by Dorothy Carnegie. This book, published in 1937, is still selling. Few books provide a more blunt and open insight into the American ideal. Here is Willie Loman's bible, leading him to happiness on a shoeshine and a smile.

[20] We encounter a similar thing happening in Dicken's *A Christmas Carol*, but the effect is achieved through the power of Christmas. We are not as inclined to see the victory over inner-directed man in *A Christmas Carol* in the same way we see the victory over inner-directed man in a work like Carnegie's. Yet, Scrooge, before his transformation into a "nice guy" was a man who drove himself as hard as he drove his employees. If he was grim toward them, he was equally, if not more, grim toward himself. We tend to react negatively toward the Scrooge-like character which makes up a greater portion of the inner-directed man. For this reason it is quite enigmatic that students seem to romanticize the inner-directed man—finding in him a moral quality which they believe is lacking in the other-directed man.

[21] Carnegie, *How to Win Friends and Influence People*, p. 56.

talking about dangling "worms" in front of "fish." He does it again in the following suggestion:

> Many of the sweetest memories of my childhood cluster around a little yellow-haired dog with a stub tail. "Tippy" never read a book on psychology. He didn't need to . . . He had a perfect technique for making people like him . . .
>
> Do you want to make friends? Then take a tip from Tippy. Be friendly. Forget yourself. Think of others.[22]

Or, consider the following quotation,

> That is why dogs make such a hit. They are so glad to see us that they almost jump out of their skins. So, naturally, we are glad to see them.[23]

Finally, we should consider one last quotation from Carnegie. Here we come to possibly the ultimate reduction of the worth of the individual. While reading this quotation keep in mind that the individual is being subordinated to the greater goal of making him socially viable. It is supremely ironic that this book, which in my estimation is perhaps the most deviously anti-individualistic work ever written, has been magnanimously endorsed by the more conservative business elements in American culture—a group which likes to believe it stands behind the cause of individualism. Carnegie says,

> We ought to be modest, for neither you nor I amount to much. Both of us will pass on and be completely forgotten a century from now. Life is too short to bore other people with talk of our petty accomplishments. Let's encourage them to talk instead. Come to think about it, you haven't much to brag about anyhow. Do you know what keeps you from becoming an idiot? Not much. Only a nickel's worth of iodine in your thyroid glands. If a physician were to open the thyroid gland in your neck and take out a little iodine, you would become an idiot. A little iodine that can be bought at a corner drugstore for five cents is all that stands between you and an institution for the mentally ill. A nickel's worth of iodine! That isn't much to be boasting about, is it?[24]

What an astounding assertion! A man is worth a nickel . . . he must be modest . . . his accomplishments are petty . . . encourage the other fellow to talk . . . be responsive . . . avoid argument . . . watch what the other guy is doing so you will know how to match his performance . . . do not assert yourself.

---

[22] *Ibid.*, p. 83.

[23] *Ibid.*, p. 97.

[24] *Ibid.*, p. 205. This is one of the most peculiar pieces of humanistic reasoning in Western literature. The individual is evaluated in terms of his chemical make-up and its current price on the market. After being reduced to his physical nature, he is then, not surprisingly, found to be worth nothing! In his eagerness to create a friendly, outgoing, socially sensitive, other-directed kind of man, Carnegie loses sight almost completely of the broader implications of his arguments and his imagery.

In Carnegie's book we have a direct, if crude, delineation of the personal qualities of the other-directed man. Though Carnegie unwittingly makes the other-directed type of character look bad, it is not necessarily true that such a character is bad. The friendly, sociable, other-directed kind of person can be and is socially valuable. Carnegie was only gauche enough to make the social and individual costs of other-directed morality glaringly apparent.[25]

The literature of the other-directed society achieves an extreme form in the works of Dale Carnegie. But the other-directed theme appears diffusely throughout a great variety of novels, stories, movies, and dramas. The gangster, for example, is mentioned by Riesman as a case in point. The gangster is a tragic hero despite rather than because of his violation of the rules of the law-abiding community. If he is successful, he isolates himself not only from society at large but from his own gang as well. Success forces him into a cul-de-sac where he must wait, alone and frightened, for the miserable finish to his career.[26]

But there is more to other-directed and inner-directed literature and entertainment than its content. There is the way one is supposed to respond to it.

> Though popular culture on one level "fills in" between people so as to avoid any demand for conversational or sexual gambits, on another level the popular-culture performance is not simply a way of killing time: in the peer-group situation, it makes a demand that it be appraised. The other-directed girl who goes in company to the movies need not talk to the others during the picture but is sometimes faced with the problem: should she cry at the sad places or not? What is the proper reaction, the sophisticated line about what is going on? Observing movie audiences coming out of "little" or "art" theaters, it is sometimes apparent that people feel they ought to react, but how?

> In contrast to this, the inner-directed person, reading a book alone, is less aware of the others looking on; moreover, he has time to return at his own pace from being transported by his reading—to return and put on whatever mask he cares to.[27]

Riesman's approach to man, society, history, human character, and action is thematic. Like a composer from the romantic period, he takes a simple but expressive theme and then proceeds to create a series of variations. Eventually we are overwhelmed by the potential contained within what, at

---

[25] Riesman is very aware of the problem. At the beginning of the revised version of *The Lonely Crowd* he comments on the preferences of students for the inner-directed type. He goes on to point to the sensitivity and adaptiveness of the other-directed man—qualities which can be and are virtues. Evidently each social type has virtues which come at the cost of some other form of moral deprivation.

[26] Riesman, *The Lonely Crowd*, p. 155. Riesman refers here to Robert Warshow's article, "The Gangster as Tragic Hero," which appeared in *The Partisan Review*, XV (February 1948), 240–244.

[27] Riesman, *The Lonely Crowd*, p. 158.

first, seemed to be no more than a minor melody. This, incidentally, seems to be characteristic of many of the works on man and society which have gained great popularity in recent years.[28]

Riesman takes the rather simple theme, then, of three types of man: tradition-directed, inner-directed and other-directed. This theme is applied to various settings, ranging from sexual behavior to the realm of political action and, seemingly, it brings together what otherwise would remain greatly disparate areas of social behavior. But what is the final movement? Where do the variations lead? In music, despite pretensions to the contrary, it is not proper to ask such a question. A string quartet, after all, is a string quartet. It really is not supposed to lead us anywhere—it begins and ends with itself. However, people can and do ask more of the social scientist. It is not sufficient for science or the humanities to begin and end with themselves—though some scientists and humanists would insist that this is exactly what they should do. There is always some pressure to bring thought around to application—to orient science, whether physical or social, to some kind of utility. Does Riesman have utility? Or, is his work like a symphony by Mahler, something which induces a mood; something which depends on the artistic or humanistic sensitivity of the person responding to his work?

The adjusted, the anomic, and the autonomous man

In the final passages of *The Lonely Crowd* Riesman provides his readers with what amounts to a set of program notes telling his audience how to interpret

---

[28] Any number of examples come to mind. Arnold Toynbee's "challenge and response" theme was applied to the historical development of all of civilization. Pitirim Sorokin utilized the theme that cultures go through cycles of intense religious experience and then degenerate into "sensate" forms of experience from which they return to the religious state. Ruth Benedict used a simple dichotomous theme of Dionysian and Apollonian ways of living to bring together a variety of behaviors. Freud took the elementary theme of conflict between human animal nature and the demands of society and worked it into one of the most fully orchestrated and developed variations on a theme in the literature of psychology. Today Marshall McCluhan seems to have hit upon a responsive theme with the simple idea that the medium of a message is of as much importance as the message itself. A similar theme, developed in a slightly different way, is Goffman's elementary observation that how one says something is as important as what he says. In each case, the simplicity of the theme is shocking. The theme often boils down to a cliché or bit of folk wisdom that everyone has known for centuries. After all, the men in Caesar's armies probably joked about the relationship between sexual deprivation and nervous conditions several thousand years before Freud came along. The difference, of course, between the soldiers' superficial grasp of a truth and that of a perceptive intellectual is in the capacity to see that truth in thousands of different settings and applications—recognizing those where it has a validity and those where it does not. In this respect, when someone says that psychology or, more often, sociology, is an elaboration of the obvious they are many times quite correct. The point is, the process of elaboration is often worth the effort. Proper elaboration of the obvious can lead—and almost invariably does lead—to the not so obvious. If this is disputed, look to the humble origins of modern mathematics and physical science.

and respond to what he has had to say in the earlier segments of his work. The notes lean, interestingly enough, on another tripartite classification of people—the adjusted, the anomic, and the autonomous. The adjusted are those who conform to and at the same time make their peace with the demands of their culture—whether it is tradition-, inner-, or other-directed. The anomic are those who are, in some serious way, shattered or broken by the culture; they are those who cannot, for whatever reason, meet the demands of the culture; they are lost in their culture. The autonomous are those who neither become lost to the demands of the culture nor broken by them. They live within the culture, but they retain a strong and assertive sense of self. It is the autonomous type, the most difficult and yet the most engaging of the three, which receives most of Riesman's attention.

The attainment of autonomy for the tradition-directed person is extremely difficult, if not impossible. Riesman tells the story of the Lebanese farmers who, for centuries, suffered from invasions by Arab horsemen, and it never occurred to the farmers to become horsemen and it never occurred to the horsemen to become farmers. Through the centuries they remained locked in a pattern which had an almost animalistic inevitability about it. Then Riesman makes his point,

> If Arabs could imagine becoming cultivators, and vice versa, it would not neces-
> sarily follow that the symbiotic ecology of the two main groups would change.
> These tradition-directed types might still go on doing what they realized they need
> not do. Nevertheless, once people become aware, with the rise of inner-direction,
> that they as individuals with a private destiny are not tied to any given ecological
> pattern, something radically new happens in personal and social history. Then people
> can envisage adapting themselves not only within the narrow confines of the animal
> kingdom but within the wide range of alternative possibilities illustrated—but no
> more than illustrated—by human experience to date. *Perhaps this is the most im-*
> *portant meaning of the ever renewed discovery of the oneness of mankind as a*
> *species: that all human experience becomes relevant.*[29] [Italics mine, RPC.]

Relevant to what? Relevant to our own autonomy would be the reply. The practical consequence of social knowledge is that it provides the individual with the capacity to empathize with others and thereby gain two very broad but powerful extensions of choice. He can, on the one hand, empathize to the point where he becomes the other in actuality. He might, for example, gain sufficient understanding of the life of an executive to enable him to rise to that status—or decide not to take on that role. The second consequence of empathetic knowledge is the extent to which it can promote manipulation. If one does not elect to become an executive on the basis of his knowledge,

---

[29] Riesman, *The Lonely Crowd*, p. 246.

he may, nonetheless, find such knowledge helpful when it comes to managing those whose task it is to manage.

The fate of autonomy is different in inner- and other-directed societies. Riesman speculates that the attainment of autonomy—the maintenance of individuality in the midst of social control—is probably easier to achieve in an inner-directed society than in modern other-directed forms of society; though it is not easy to attain in any society. Society has a way of either inducing the individual to adjust to its demands or breaking him, leaving him in an anomic condition in the process.

In the inner-directed society a man's place in the social order was relatively definite and the boundaries of custom were sufficiently clear to enable the autonomous person to define his enemies; to define his cause; to assert himself as a unique force. It is no longer so simple. In an age of other-direction the individual seeking autonomy is confronted not only with the problem of determining who is, in fact, the enemy to serve as the background for his portrayal of self; he is also confronted with the problem of his own motivations. There always exists the possibility, in an age of social and psychological enlightenment, that the other fellow is not really the enemy after all but only a projection of some despised element of one's self.

In an age of inner-direction the autonomous man could assert himself against the tastes and insensitivities of the middle class. Today such an enemy is both difficult to find and, at the same time, too much on the defensive when discovered. This, in part, is why the quest for autonomy within Bohemia is probably more deceptive today than in the past. Bohemian conduct is simply too matter-of-fact to allow us to view it as a manifestation of autonomy. There are exceptions, Allen Ginsberg qualifies, but for many others it may be a different matter. As Riesman expresses it,

> . . . young people today can find, in the wide variety of people and places of metropolitan life, a peer-group, conformity to which costs little in the way of search for principle.[30]

The only road to autonomy, if this is a valued goal—and Riesman makes it apparent that it ought to be—is, paradoxically enough, through further self-consciousness. It is paradoxical because it has been self-consciousness which has made the acquisition of autonomy more difficult.

> This heightened self-consciousness, above all else, constitutes the insignia of the autonomous in an era dependent on other-direction. For, as the inner-directed man is more self-conscious than his tradition-directed predecessor and as the other-

---

[30] *Ibid.*, p. 258.

directed man is more self-conscious still, the autonomous man growing up under conditions that encourage self-consciousness can disentangle himself from the adjusted others only by a further move toward even greater self-consciousness. His autonomy depends not upon the ease with which he may deny or disguise his emotions but, on the contrary, upon the success of his effort to recognize and respect his own feelings, his own potentialities, his own limitations. This is . . . the problem of self-consciousness itself, an achievement of a higher order of abstraction.[31]

The consciousness of self, the ability to provide an identity for one's self in the midst of pressures to dissolve into the tastes and sensitivities, or insensitivities, of the other-directed society, is the only way, as Riesman sees it, one can achieve autonomy.

Riesman's contribution, in the final pages of this still powerful and relevant book,[32] is not only to bring together in a meaningful way the many practices of society—probing them with the concepts of inner- and other-direction. More importantly, Riesman tries to retain a sense of social values and relate his thought to such values. He is radical not in the selection of new values. He is quite conservative when he chooses freedom and autonomy and the dignity of the individual as his primary values. But he is radical in his comprehension of what is involved in the quest for such values and in his analysis of the relationship between the individual and society and the bearing of that relationship on the development of individual worth.

Small wonder, then, that Riesman has proved popular among many humanists and social scientists. He has shown, perhaps better than any other writer living today, the promise that modern social science holds for deepening further our comprehension of age-old humanistic concerns.

---

[31] *Ibid.*, p. 259.

[32] *The Lonely Crowd* stimulated considerable discussion and criticism. The interested reader is encouraged to examine Seymour M. Lipset and Leo Lowenthal, *Culture and Social Character* (New York: Free Press of Glencoe, 1961). In the last chapter of this work Riesman replies to his critics. See also Walter Williams, "Inner-Directedness and Other-Directedness in New Perspective," *Sociological Quarterly*, **5**, 3 (Summer 1964), 193–220; Carl N. Degler, "The Sociologist as Historian: Riesman's *The Lonely Crowd*," *American Quarterly*, **5**, 4 (Winter 1963), 483–497; and Cushing Strout, "A Note on Degler, Riesman and Tocqueville," *American Quarterly*, **16**, 1 (Spring 1964), 100–102.

9 Humanity as the Big Con: The Human Views of Erving Goffman

In the course of growing up we learn the language of the culture in which we live. It is a thorough and exact form of learning. We learn a language so precisely that phonetics experts, like the fabled Professor Higgins in Shaw's *Pygmalion*, can locate many people to within a few miles of their birthplace merely by listening to idiosyncracies of dialect. The learning is not only precise, so that we are instantly attuned to a slightly mispronounced word, but it is extensive: by this I simply mean that we learn a very complex and vast amount of material. The typical child entering school between the ages of five and six already has a vocabulary of some 2000 words at his command.[1] Moreover, mastery of the art of language is virtually universal within a culture; even persons with low intellectual endowments may acquire at least a working knowledge of the language of their culture. Though this mastery is an astonishing feat of memory and learning, it is so common we take it for granted. Only when we try to learn a foreign language do we begin to discover how much we learned of our mother tongue. And only when we cease taking language for granted do we become aware of its deep influence in our lives.

Learning language is obviously important in becoming "human," and it is also obviously necessary for maintaining the elaborate social and cultural sys-

---

[1] Fred J. Schonell, *The Psychology of Teaching and Reading* (4th ed.; New York: Philosophical Library, 1961), p. 36. The total vocabulary of twelfth-grade high school students ranges from 36,700 to 136,500 words. McCarthy, "Language Development in Children," in L. Carmichael (ed.), *Manual of Child Psychology* (New York: John Wiley & Sons, Inc., 1946), p. 59. Cited in the student manual on *Stereotypes* prepared by Sociological Resources for Secondary Schools, 1966, p. 7. Figures such as this are not very reliable. Even if they were, they would not give a good indication of the full complexity of speech and language. For example, the sentence *You know what I mean.* has five different words; but it can be given many different meanings by changing intonation and/or word order. Thus, we might say, "What *I mean*, you know." Or, "You mean I know *what?*" For a graciously written exposition of such complexities of language, see J. R. Firth, *The Tongues of Men* (London: Oxford University Press 1964), p. 34.

tems within which we operate today. But just what is it we learn when we learn a language? Certainly we learn more than spoken or written words. What symbols, words, or meanings are involved in human social exchanges? How does language work? What are the effects of language? We shall explore these questions throughout this chapter and arrive at some engaging conclusions and observations. The most general and most significant conclusion we shall come to might be stated in the following manner.

Man and symbols

Suppose we begin by accepting the fact that man is a symbol-using creature. (Walt Kelly, creator of the comic strip *Pogo*, once said he is "symbol minded.") If we recognize at the same time that symbols are, in a sense, "false" because they are never the same as the reality they represent, then man is, in a sense, "false." Unlike the nonsymbolic animals around him, man cannot merge with nature. He is, by benefit of his language, in a sense separated.[2] This separation is a product of the deceptive and imperfect nature of language. To begin to dwell on the implications of man as a symbol-using creature leads us, then, to view man as a being deceived by his own words. He deceives himself and he deceives others. There is no way out of this situation! To be human is to use and to be used by language.

 It is this feature of the human condition that receives the attention of Erving Goffman. Essentially all that Goffman does is make evident the fact that in the course of social action men influence each other by means of elaborate symbolic devices. In itself this is nothing new. It certainly does not seem, at least at first sight, to be especially shocking or penetrating. Nonetheless, Goffman's works[3] form the foundation for a view of mankind more disenchanting than that emanating from Darwin's theory of evolution or from

---

[2] I am again indebted to Professor Warriner of the University of Kansas for warning me against giving the impression of a false dichotomy. One can, for example, view symbols as enabling man to merge more consciously with nature. A debate on whether symbols enable us to merge with nature can quickly turn into a profitless metaphysical dispute. I am only trying to suggest, through this phrasing, that labeling an object or event has the capacity to separate us from other qualities which that object or event might possess.

[3] Possibly the most significant of Goffman's books is *The Presentation of Self in Everyday Life*, which was first published as a monograph at the Social Sciences Research Centre at the University of Edinburgh in 1956. This chapter is based on materials appearing in the Anchor Books version (Garden City, N.Y.: Doubleday & Company, Inc., 1959). Goffman's other major works include *Encounters* (Indianapolis: The Bobbs-Merrill Co., Inc., 1961); *Asylums* (Anchor Books; Garden City, N.Y.: Doubleday & Company, Inc., 1961); *Behavior in Public Places* (New York: Free Press of Glencoe, 1963); *Stigma: Notes on the Management of Spoiled Identity* (Englewood Cliffs, N.J.: Prentice-Hall, Inc., 1963); and *Interaction Ritual: Essays on Face-to-Face Behavior* (Chicago: Aldine Publishing Company, 1967).

Freud's conception of man as an impulsive animal held in an uneasy state of control by society.

Darwin leaves open the possibility that if man is an animal of low heritage, at least he is an intelligent one. If man is an animal, he is, nonetheless, an animal capable of building vast cultures. Above all, Darwin permits us to view man as a creature standing at the apex of an evolutionary process whose origins are lost in time. Darwin allows us to keep intact our view of man as something special and privileged in nature's realm. Freud, on the other hand, disenchantingly leaves us at the mercy of unconscious and devious impulses. Even so, the Freudian picture is a dramatic and, in a sense, thoroughly romantic one. Though Freudian man may be crushed by a repressive morality, he never admits defeat without a fight. The fight may take place within the unconscious, but it is always a fight. Freud sees man embroiled in combat with society throughout the entirety of life; it is an invigorating if not flattering conception of man.

But Goffman leaves us, at first glance anyway, with practically nothing. Goffman appears to divest us of our sanctity by suggesting that we are all incorrigible "con" artists—and that we have no choice. Moreover, the same tricks that make a con game work are basically the devices used in the act of being "human."

Goffman sees man as a manager of impressions. These impressions, grounded in the meanings we give to appearances, gestures, costumes, settings, and words, are all that man *is* as a social being. Strip these away and we have dehumanized man. Conversely, cloak man with those fragile devices that permit him to maintain an impression before others and we have given him the shaky essence of his humanity. This perspective reduces humanity to an act or performance; moreover, it is a performance based on dreadfully flimsy devices. At the same time, to become aware of the devices being used to sustain a performance causes us to respond to the performance with a different—and generally more negative—attitude than before. The child who discovers his uncle hiding behind Santa's false whiskers might continue to play the game, but he will do so more from choice than from a belief that he really is playing with Santa Claus.

It is in this sense, then, that Goffman appears to leave man more naked and alone than did Darwin or Freud. The distinctive feature of human activity resides ultimately in something which is little more than a Santa Claus outfit. To be human is to perform, like an actor, before audiences whom we "con" into accepting us as being what we are trying to appear to be. And our humanity is the costume we wear, the staging on which we perform, and the way we read whatever script we are handed.

Two aspects of language: content and style

When we try to impress others, two somewhat separate kinds of language are involved. We impress others by *what* we say; and, of course, we impress others by *how* we say it. Usually we do not think of *how* we say something as a form of language. We reserve the idea of language for the content of what we wish to express. *How* we express ourselves we generally think of as "style" or as "technique." Goffman suggests that what we commonly consider to be style is, in actuality, another manifestation of language. In fact, it is a form of language that serves the significant purpose of validating whatever it is we wish to express as content.

A simple illustration will quickly make clear what Goffman means when he refers to the validating properties of styles of expression. The difference between a performance of Hamlet by Laurence Olivier and one by a not particularly talented high school student is certainly not a difference of content. Both are expressing the same words or lines from identical scripts. However, the performance of Olivier is believable. It impresses us as authentic. It appears to be a valid characterization. That of the high school student may appear lifeless, dull, artificial, stilted, or unreal. We know the high school student is not "really" Hamlet, but Olivier can "con" us into accepting himself as really being Hamlet. The difference, of course, rests in the style of the performance. But if style can communicate a sense of validity, then it must be seen in itself as a form of language. Moreover, its importance must not be overlooked; lack of control of the language of style may mean the difference between having one's message or performance accepted by others or having it rejected.

Symptomatic behavior

Goffman uses the term "symptomatic" behavior[4] to refer to what I am calling the language of style. By this he means certain actions are symptomatic of a valid performance. For example, an erudite and competent professor who comes to his class on the first day with trembling hands may lose his audience because his students will see this as symptomatic of fear or nervousness; if

---

[4] *The Presentation of Self in Everyday Life*, p. 2. Goffman's emphasis on the symbolic nature of social interaction places him among those sociologists who refer to themselves as "symbolic interactionists." The foundations of symbolic interactionist thought were laid by George Herbert Mead and Charles Horton Cooley.

he is confident in his knowledge, then his hands should not reveal a nervous tremor. The fact that the professor suffers from an incurable nervous disorder does not prevent his trembling from symbolizing something quite different to his class. In this illustration, the nervous disorder is seen as symptomatic of a person who does not have completely valid claims to the performance he is about to stage. Conversely, a calm, poised, and steady bearing is symptomatic of a valid claim to the performance.

We have identified two classes of symbolic behavior so far. One of these is the content of the performance and the other is the symptomatic behavior which validates or lends "reality" to the performance. The relationship between these two classes of symbols can be summarized in the following scheme.

CONTENT	SYMPTOMATIC BEHAVIOR	AUDIENCE REACTION
1. positive	positive	A person possessing control over both levels of expression will be highly effective.
2. positive	negative	Despite content mastery, such a person may lose his audience because of incongruities in his performance.
3. negative	positive	This person may prove acceptable so long as he can conceal the existing incongruity.
4. negative	negative	This person will be highly ineffective.

The first and fourth cases in this scheme are self-evident. The second and third cases are the interesting ones. Consider the second case, where a man may have content but lack mastery over symptomatic behavior. Such a person, despite his control over content, may not be able to disguise his ineptness with regard to symptomatic behavior. The lecturer whose hands shake illustrates this condition. A specific and actual case in point was the platform conduct of Thorstein Veblen, the great American economist and social analyst. Although his brilliance was widely recognized, and although hundreds of students flocked to his classes, the end of the semester would find the classroom nearly empty.[5] Students would abandon his courses by the hundreds. Veblen's lack of concern for classroom oratorical devices eventually proved more than his audience could bear.

---

[5] A student of Veblen's is quoted as having said, "Why it was creepy. It might have been a dead man's voice slowly speaking on, and if the light had gone out behind those dropped eyelids, would it have made any difference? But we who listened day after day found the unusual manner nicely fitted to convey the detached and slightly sardonic intellect that was moving over the face of things." Even so, Veblen's classes dwindled, and one ended with only a single student. See Robert L. Heilbroner, *The Worldly Philosophers* (New York: Simon and Schuster, Inc., 1953), p. 214.

"Phony" behavior

The third case represents a type we usually refer to as a "phony." He is capable of manipulating appearances to make his performance look like the real McCoy. However, the performance is invalid because the performer does not possess content. I witnessed a case in point during an amateur performance of *The Merchant of Venice*, when an actor momentarily forgot his lines. His stage presence was impressive, however, and he continued talking and gesturing as though nothing were wrong—all the while spouting a pseudo form of Shakespearean dialogue which he invented as he went along. Eventually he recalled his lines and continued with his part. The attention of the audience was retained and it appeared, at least to me, that very few people were ever the wiser. In this instance, the performer was able to disguise the fact that he had momentarily lost mastery over the content of his performance. So long as the disguise was effective, the incongruity between loss of content and retention of symptomatic behavior never became apparent.

We cannot, of course, presume that the phony is superior to the person who lacks control over symptomatic behavior. Loss of either aspect of a performance is threatening to the maintenance of the performance. The phony is more likely to be effective simply because it is often easier to disguise lack of content. Students, for example, have been known to prefer a teacher who is a kindly appearing old phony over an ominous appearing recognized authority simply because they could not distinguish between the two on a professional basis.

It is apparent that a phony performance will be successful only to the extent to which the performer is capable of concealing from his audience the fact that he does not possess control over the legitimate content of the performance. But concealment in other forms is involved in situations where the performer is not a phony and not careless or incompetent.

Some of these matters for concealment may be suggested here.

First . . . the performer may be engaged in a profitable form of activity that is concealed from his audience and that is incompatible with the view of his activity which he hopes they will obtain . . .

Secondly, we find that errors and mistakes are often corrected before the performance takes place, while telltale signs that errors have been made and corrected are themselves concealed. In this way an impression of infallibility, so important in many presentations, is maintained . . .

Thirdly, in those interactions where the individual presents a product to others, he will tend to show them only the end product, and they will be led into judging him on the basis of something that has been finished, polished, and packaged. In some cases, if very little effort was actually required to complete the object, this fact will be concealed . . .

A fourth discrepancy between appearances and over-all reality may be cited. We find that there are many performances which could not have been given had not tasks been done which were physically unclean, semi-illegal, cruel, and degrading in other ways; but these disturbing facts are seldom expressed during a performance. . . . we tend to conceal from our audience all evidence of "dirty work," whether we do this work in private or allocate it to a servant . . .[6]

Concealment is a necessary element in practically all social performances, and it poses a rather trying dilemma for the actor. If he is honest and open, that is, if he refuses to engage in concealment, then he risks losing his audience. If he engages in concealment, then he is practicing deceit. All human social performances, from Goffman's perspective, involve a constant weighing of the costs of losing one's audience against the cost of losing one's integrity by behaving in a deceptive manner. The doctor may have to convince his patient that he, the doctor, is more certain of the effects of a given therapy than he may be in fact. A teacher may have to conceal from his students the doubt that plagues him as he presents a lecture. A salesman may have to conceal his contempt for his customer. So it is, then, that all social performances have a "phony" element about them. Not only does the fraudulent performer conceal his ignorance, but also the legitimate performer conceals items of information which would, if they became known, cause him to be rejected by his audience.

This human dilemma can be seen in an overly cynical manner. Such a view is depicted, for example, in J. D. Salinger's novel *The Catcher in the Rye* when Holden Caulfield discovers that people all around him are engaging in a variety of deceits. He concludes that people, especially adults, are phony. Caulfield's rejection of these "phonies" is based on his feeling that phony behavior betrays a great weakness in the character of the person. Goffman would suggest something different: "phony" behavior is a product of the relationship existing between the performer and those who observe him. If retention of the audience is important, then deceit may be necessary. Thus, the teacher who is committed to the ideal of educating youth can do so only by retaining the attention and the acceptance of the students who become his immediate concern. This can be achieved only through performances which convince the audience of the worth of the performer. Such performances will necessarily conceal errors, hidden pleasures, "dirty work," and tedium. On

---

[6] From *The Presentation of Self in Everyday Life* by Erving Goffman, pp. 43–44. Copyright © 1959 by Erving Goffman. Reprinted by permission of Doubleday & Company, Inc., and Penguin Books Ltd.

these occasions the performer often cannot escape the sense of deception that he is practicing.

Goffman locates phony behavior not within the actor but within the complex of social relationships containing the actor. Consider the following situation. If an organization in which a person is located demands adherence to several conflicting standards or ideals, the individual will probably hide unavoidable violations of one of the ideals. He will usually hide those violations that are easiest to hide. The act of hiding violations of the ideal, however, serves the purpose of keeping the ideal intact. Goffman gives the example of an attendant in an asylum for the mentally ill who must maintain order and must, at the same time, conform to the ideal of not physically injuring patients. Violations of the latter ideal are more easily disguised than those of the former. Therefore, the attendant may indulge in such practices as "necking" a patient, that is, forcing him to behave by throttling him with a wet towel—an act which leaves no marks.

We are inclined to criticize the behavior of the attendant. Goffman suggests, however, that behavior such as this is an attempt to maintain the ideals of the social organization. If keeping order and not physically injuring the patient are both legitimate ideals and, at the same time, are difficult ideals to achieve simultaneously, then the only way they can be kept intact is to hide the fact that one of them must be violated. The behavior of the attendant, when viewed in terms of conflicting legitimate ideals of the organization and his endeavor to preserve these ideals, becomes less susceptible to criticism. The point that Goffman makes is that critical response to the *individual* in a situation such as this is misdirected. Attention should be given instead to the ideals of the organization and the means made available to the individual for supporting those ideals.

Goffman shows us, perhaps more sympathetically than any other observer of human behavior, that there is a large element of "phoniness" in all human interaction. We pose, as it were, behind a variety of masks used to frighten, intimidate, implore, awe, beg, or otherwise elicit from others the kinds of reactions we seek. Sometimes we do this self-consciously; at other times we may be unaware of the extent to which we use these devices.

Cynical and sincere behavior

Goffman calls consciously manipulative behavior "cynical" behavior, while an unconscious use of manipulative devices produces behavior which is "sincere." It is worth noting that this places sincerity and cynicism within the subjective understanding of the actor. It is impossible to detect it from outside. For example, a cynical lover may consciously and knowingly behave ineptly in order to convince the woman he is trying to seduce that he is sincere. A sincere lover, unknowingly, may behave in a similar manner. The performances might be virtually identical; the difference is a subjective one. Goffman makes the difference subjective to highlight the significance of the performance itself. The cynical performer or the phony is a threat not because he performs less effectively; to the contrary, he is a threat or a concern because he performs so well! The effective cynic or phony demonstrates that it is not necessary to be friendly in order to act as a friend; it is not necessary to be in love in order to be a lover; it is not necessary to be respectable in order to appear respectable.

There is a real problem, then, in everyday behavior when it comes to evaluating the sincerity or value of a performance. If two performances are equal in the skill maintained by the performer, the only difference being that one is legitimate or sincere and the other not, then how is legitimacy to be established?

. This problem is solved by the institutionalization of "labels" that give the performer a legitimate claim to the performance he is conducting. We establish licensing agencies to perform the service of providing documentary evidence that an individual has the right to engage in certain types of performances. In effect, this is one of the major services provided by educational systems. It is well known that many people come out of such systems with little more knowledge and enthusiasm than when they went in. It is known, also, that people can acquire an education of considerable merit without attending school. Nonetheless, all college graduates get a certificate that legitimizes their level of learning; the self-made man does not. It is especially important to see that an effective fraudulent or phony performance conducted by an "illegitimate" performer threatens the legitimizing agency.

Consider, for example, the following instance:

A victim of his latest ruse calls "Dr." Arthur Osborne Phillips "one of the most remarkable medical phonies of all time."

And from his jail cell, "Dr." Phillips replies: "I'm a genius. I had to be a genius to do all that I did with no formal medical education."

"All" he did was hoodwink the federal government and authorities in 10 states during a 40-year career as a phony doctor.

The 70-year-old man's latest caper was working on delicate research into the surgical use of the laser light at the University of Colorado medical center in Denver. His associates there said he "did competent work."

According to prison records, Phillips' career began when he worked as an orderly during World War I for a Dr. James Herman Phillips of Doro, Ala. The real Phillips died in 1920 and the phony Phillips, according to the records, took over his name, medical shingle and license.

While working as a "surgeon" with the Civilian Conservation Corps in Wyoming, Montana and Idaho in the 1940's, Phillips performed 32 successful appendectomies.[7]

In cases such as this we are confronted by a person who, according to his colleagues, does "competent work." But if his performance is competent, even though he did not attend medical school, then what is the point of medical school? It is in this sense that the phony performance is threatening. Let me make explicit once again that the legitimacy of the performance is not determined by the adequacy of the performance. Legitimacy is external and is bestowed on an actor by an established legitimizing agency such as a school, military system, church, political party, or family heritage.

The phony or illegitimate performer is threatening only to the extent to which his performance is a competent one. After all, if the phony is incapable of performing competently, then the problem of identifying the illegitimate performer is simple, and the need for legitimizing agencies is reduced. This appears to be pretty much the case with professional athletics. In the athletic contest the claims of the performer are expressed in his performance, and the criteria for evaluating the performance are clear-cut. The only problem here is to assure that a performer is not lying when he claims he is lacking in skill. In situations where the performance is the criterion of adequacy, the phony may be a person who is pretending to be less skilled or experienced than he is in fact. An example of this is the "hustler" in golf or pool who makes a living by leading an unsuspecting "pigeon" into a wager that the "pigeon" cannot hope to win. Some kind of legitimizing device must exist, therefore, to assure that a person who claims to have a certain lower level of skill does not, in fact, possess a higher level. For this reason performances such as those given by the athlete are divided into amateur and professional categories, and elaborate means are taken to ensure that professionals do not pose as amateurs.

There is one other area where the problem of legitimizing a performance introduces some interesting problems. Where no professional legitimizing agency exists, and where the criteria of competency are not clear, other lines may be drawn for distinguishing between the "true" performer and the performer

---

[7] A United Press International news item that appeared in the Urbana, Illinois, *News-Gazette*, January 20, 1966, p. 12.

whose actions are suspect. This occurs in the theater where people who live by acting will make much of the distinction between themselves and actors who do not make a living by performing. Presumably the claims of the man who does not make any money by acting are' suspect, and this may be the case regardless of the quality of the performances given by the amateur.

The scheme we now have is sufficiently developed to let us see, along with Goffman, that social performances are rather fragile. The problem of making your audience believe you *really* are what you are trying to be involves several layers of symbol—the content and symptomatic actions—and it may involve legitimacy as well. To the extent a person has control over these elements, his performance is affected accordingly. But some social roles make it easier to control these elements than others. This is especially important to note because it forces us to recognize that human behavior is not a simple manifestation of personality or "inner" character. Rather, it is a very complex exchange of symbols and meanings between at least two people. Sometimes, in this exchange, a person is required to perform a routine that lacks dramatic quality. To recognize that such a performance is required implies that it is not a simple product of personality. At the same time, the fact that the performance is lacking in dramatic quality produces an interesting problem for the individual. Let's see how Goffman describes this problem.

Dramatic realization

Some performances are developed in such a manner as to make audiences easily and quickly convinced of the "reality" of the performance. That is, the person is seen as being what he is trying to appear to be. Moreover, he is able to do this easily. There are other kinds of performances which do not easily dramatize themselves. In such situations a person may, even though he is doing his work, have some difficulty impressing others that this is so. We can, therefore, talk about the extent to which a role permits "dramatic realization."

Goffman relies on the example of the medical nurse and the surgical nurse to illustrate what he means by this. The duties of the surgical nurse are such that her performance is quickly accepted. As she stands beside the surgeon, masked and attentive, no one is doubtful about the work performance. The case of the medical nurse is different. In this instance, the nurse may come to the door of a patient's room and casually converse with him. As she is conversing she may be observing changes in the patient's skin color, his breathing, his voice, and so on. Each of these observations may provide pertinent information about the progress of the patient's condition. Even so, the

nondramatic character of the nurse's actions may cause the patient to conclude that she is simply ''messing around,'' or ''goofing off.''

The medical nurse, to avoid this, may invent or develop routines that lend
dramatic quality to her performance. But some of these actions, because
they are added merely for this reason, may interfere with the task that has been
assigned. There develops, therefore, a ''dilemma of expression.'' The dilemma
rests on the following horns: (1) if the nondramatic task is adhered to exactly,
it may result in the actor being rejected by his audience; however, (2) if
dramatic elements are added to the task in order to retain the audience, they
may interfere with the proper conduct of the task. The performer is required
to balance himself between the horns of impressing people and getting the
job done. Goffman puts it this way:

> . . . a *Vogue* model, by her clothing, stance, and facial expression, is able ex-
> pressively to portray a cultivated understanding of the book she poses in her hand;
> but those who trouble to express themselves so appropriately will have very little
> time left over for reading . . . And so individuals often find themselves with the
> dilemma of expression *versus* action. Those who have the time and talent to per-
> form a task well may not, because of this, have the time or talent to make it ap-
> parent that they are performing well. It may be said that some organizations resolve
> this dilemma by officially delegating the dramatic function to a specialist who will
> spend his time expressing the meaning of the task and spend no time actually
> doing it.[8]

Role expectation

Any performance, whether on a theatrical stage or in everyday life, requires
some conception of what is expected of the performer. Sociologists refer to
this as ''role expectation.'' Goffman suggests that role expectations may be
realistic or idealized. The difference between a realistic and an idealized conception of a role seems to hinge on whether or not the conception derives from
the experience of an ''insider'' or the credulity of an ''outsider.'' Goffman
gives the following examples of what he means by ''idealization.''

> American college girls did, and no doubt do, play down their intelligence, skills,
> and determinativeness when in the presence of datable boys, thereby manifesting
> a profound psychic discipline in spite of their international reputation for flightiness.
> These performers are reported to allow their boy friends to explain things to them
> tediously that they already know; they conceal proficiency in mathematics from
> their less able consorts; they lose ping-pong games just before the ending . . .[9]

Goffman cites a girl who is concerned with how she impresses her boy friend:

---

[8] Goffman, *The Presentation of Self in Everyday Life*, pp. 32–33.
[9] *Ibid.*, p. 39.

"One of the nicest techniques is to spell long words incorrectly once in a while. My boy friend seems to get a great kick out of it and writes back, 'Honey, you certainly don't know how to spell.' "[10]

The realities of a woman's role are known best by women. In the instance cited above, however, the woman is not "being herself." She is putting on a performance. Moreover, it is a performance that plays upon the credulity of men. It is in this sense, then, that the woman is behaving in terms of an idealized conception of her role.

Girls who misspell words and Negroes who put on a dumb show for the benefit of whites and morally proper college boys who pretend to be rogues are all engaging in performances that involve idealization. In such instances the form that the idealization takes may be to play down certain attributes the actor possesses. The girl plays down her knowledge, the Negro plays down his abilities, and the college boy plays down his secret commitment to old-fashioned morality.

Idealization may work in the other direction. The college student who complicates his prose because he thinks intellectuals write in an incomprehensible manner is doing this. The housewife who usually prepares quite common meals for her family but presents guests with an elaborate feast is indulging in a form of role idealization. In such cases the performer expects to lead a credulous audience into an acceptance of the performer on the basis of the performer's conception of how the audience feels the role should be played. Moreover, the performer is playing up certain abilities which, in actuality, he may either lack or be less inclined to exercise.

Idealization and its relationship to performances is significant because it forces us to recognize that human social behavior involves (1) our own understanding of how our role should be played; (2) the conceptions others have of how the role should be played; and (3) the possibility of discrepancies between these conceptions. Severe discrepancies will result in performances that are bizarre and ineffective. A lower-class boy who thinks upper-class men are arrogant and tries to emulate this pattern as he strives to be upwardly mobile will, in all likelihood, simply wind up losing his friends.

There is an important difference between roles played on the stage and those played in everyday life. The former are well defined. A script is provided the actor and his performance is directed in a manner that reduces errors of which he may not be aware. In some instances everyday roles are also very

---

[10] Here Goffman quotes Mirra Komarovsky, "Cultural Contradictions and Sex Roles," *American Journal of Sociology*, LII, pp. 186–188, in *The Presentation of Self in Everyday Life*, p. 39.

well defined. Take, for example, the role expected of us when we are called upon to participate in certain rituals. A priest conducting a high mass goes through a set of role behaviors virtually as well defined as those in a play. On the other hand, the behavior expected of us when we have been introduced at a party is, within considerable limits, subject to a variety of possibilities. The actor is on his own. He may feel that he is supposed to be congenial and amusing; but how he elects to do this must come from his own background, abilities, and conceptions of the responses others will make to his actions.

In such circumstances the person has an opportunity to "ad lib" and to play his role creatively in terms of his interpretation of that role. This allows the performer to engage in role "idealization." He may attempt to upgrade or downgrade himself, but in doing so he conforms to a conception of how such downgrading or upgrading should take place. He has, in other words, a model of performance before him that he follows in order to achieve the particular effect he seeks. In this respect the person is never, in his performances before others, completely independent of social roles and the definitions that society has given to these roles.

This view of man as a performer before audiences whom he is trying to impress seems to be a cynical one. It suggests, as I said before, that much of what is human is really a kind of show. Humanity is a matter of putting people on. There is a deceptiveness and a phoniness about much of human conduct. Goffman gives us a picture of man that emphasizes this "artificial" quality in our behavior. However, it is necessary to be careful in this evaluation of Goffman. In the first place, although in much of his writing he views man as "phony," he does not judge this as "bad." To the contrary, Goffman forces us to see much of this behavior as an unavoidable consequence of our attempts to please others; such behavior usually facilitates those affairs of daily life necessary for survival and comfort.

A cynic is defined as a person who thinks any action is motivated by the worst of motives. Goffman is cynical insofar as the motivation he gives to human action is often that of the "con." But Goffman, unlike a thoroughgoing cynic, does not consider this to be the worst of motives; the "con" more often than not is altruistic. Con behavior or phoniness is certainly quite thoroughly universal, and we are on dangerous ground when we begin to criticize others for *their* phony conduct.

Above all, Goffman probes deeply enough to make us see that what we consider a "real" performance has elements identical to those involved in the phony performance. This requires us to think in new ways about the essential nature of humanity. When we see the larger conception of man which Goffman reveals, we find it will not permit us to define humanity simply in terms of the trappings men use to frighten and awe each other. In this sense Goffman is the most humanistic of the authors discussed in this book. He views sardonically the shows men put on before each other, and he views them as an outsider would. But throughout his work there can never be any doubt that his basic conception of humanity is one which cuts through to the inner experiences and understanding of the world which any individual human being has. He is concerned with how man's relation to others and to his society affects his understanding of himself and the world around him. In other words, Goffman relates society and man; but of the two, man is always the more important.

The problems of stigma

Goffman's humanism is brought out by the unique treatment he gives to the problems experienced by people suffering from stigma of different kinds.[11] Goffman defines what he means by stigma in the following way:

> While the stranger is present before us, evidence can arise of his possessing an attribute that makes him different from others in the category of persons available for him to be, and of a less desirable kind—in the extreme, a person who is quite thoroughly bad, or dangerous, or weak. He is thus reduced in our mind from a whole and usual person to a tainted, discounted one. Such an attribute is a stigma . . .[12]

It is very important at this point to see that stigmas are *not* purely physical defects, even when the manifestation of the stigma is, let us say, a scar that runs from the ear to the mouth of a man—giving him a twisted, leering expression. Stigma must be viewed always in terms of a language of relationships. What the scar, in this case, is defined as being (much as what a word is defined as being) determines whether or not the relationship between the person with the scar and those without it will take a certain form. If, for example, the scar is obtained by a German university student while a member of a *Schlagende Verbindung* or dueling society, he may define it in terms of virility, courage, and military values and wear it as a badge authorizing him

---

[11] *Stigma* traces some of the problems and involvements that arise when an individual is forced to play the social game while, at the same time, wearing a mask that is marred or reading a script that is flawed.

[12] From *Stigma: Notes on the Management of Spoiled Identity*, © 1963, pp. 2–3. Reprinted by permission of Prentice-Hall, Inc., Englewood Cliffs, N.J.

to assume an arrogant stance toward those without it. If, on the other hand, the scar is obtained in an automobile collision in the United States and the victim is a woman, the whole thing will be interpreted quite differently.

Our reactions to people possessing a stigma of some kind are influenced by the common theories we have regarding the nature of that stigma. Goffman points out

> By definition, of course, we believe the person with a stigma is not quite human. On this assumption we exercise varieties of discrimination, through which we effectively, if often unthinkingly, reduce his life chances. We construct a stigma-theory, an ideology to explain his inferiority and account for the danger he represents, sometimes rationalizing an animosity based on other differences, such as those of social class. We use specific stigma terms such as cripple, bastard, moron in our daily discourse as a source of metaphor and imagery, typically without giving thought to the original meaning. We tend to impute a wide range of imperfections on the basis of the original one, and at the same time to impute some desirable but undesired attributes, often of a supernatural cast, such as "sixth sense," or "understanding."[13]

Stigmas fall into three broad classes: gross physical defects, defects in character, and stigmas resulting from membership in a social class or group which is not acceptable. Stigmas may be acquired at birth or at any time during the life of the individual. Although there are some variations caused by the kind of stigma or the time of acquisition of the stigma, most stigmatized persons share a number of common problems and common strategies by which they meet these problems. Goffman sees stigmatized persons generally as humans who employ strategies designed to meet a particular difficulty—that of managing the "spoiled" identities they have acquired. But that identity is not inherent in the manifest form of the stigma. A stigma is, in Goffman's terms, a "perspective." He puts it this way:

> . . . may I repeat that stigma involves not so much a set of concrete individuals who can be separated into two piles, the stigmatized and the normal, as a pervasive two-role social process in which every individual participates in both roles, at least in some connections and in some phases of life. The normal and the stigmatized are not persons but rather perspectives.[14]

A stigma does not determine the type of performance that is required of the person having it, but it will help determine the extent to which a person will have to accept whatever role is given it. Goffman is saying that a stigma such as epilepsy, for example, does not in itself produce a particular way of life for the person having epilepsy. Nor, on the other hand, does it, in itself,

---

[13] *Ibid.*, p. 5.
[14] *Ibid.*, pp. 137–138.

establish the manner in which the epileptic is to be viewed by persons who do not have this condition. However, once a set of norms are generated that define how an epileptic is to relate himself to others, then the epileptic will have a greater likelihood of encountering these requirements. Thus, in cultures where an epileptic is believed to have divine powers, the likelihood of encountering this expectation is increased for the epileptic to the point that he is likely to conform and accept the role of shaman. On the other hand, in a society where epilepsy is degrading, the person having this condition is more likely to encounter perspectives that lead him to view himself in a self-derogating manner.

Goffman's treatment of the stigmatized person is concerned with the extent to which certain signs or manifestations of character increase the likelihood that a person will be coerced into a social performance that sets him at a disadvantage. The social relevance of the stigma is that it moves the individual into playing the social game with the cards stacked against him. The problem for the stigmatized person is to attempt to minimize the extent to which he will be injured or suffer loss by such circumstances. There are several things he can do. He can attempt to withdraw and not play the game. He can try to withhold information and thereby avoid getting himself into a position where he has to play against the stacked deck. Or, a third general stratagem is to develop ways of meeting the situation directly. It might be possible, for example, to take advantage of the fact that the other players feel a sense of guilt because they know the deck is stacked.

Withdrawal as a means of coping with the situation does not mean that the stigmatized person completely isolates himself. He might withdraw by encapsulating himself within a group which knows or is "wise to" his condition and will not use it against him. One such group may be those persons who share his stigma; another may be those who are normal but sympathetic.

The normal and sympathetic person is "wise to" the condition of the stigmatized person and, at the same time, behaves in a manner indicating that the stigma does not matter. In the company of the wise, the person with a fault need feel no shame nor exert any special form of self-control. Goffman cites an example from the world of prostitutes:

> Although she sneers at respectability, the prostitute, particularly the call girl, is super-sensitive in polite society, taking refuge in her off hours with Bohemian artists, writers, actors and would-be intellectuals. There she may be accepted as an off-beat personality, without being a curiosity.[15]

---

[15] Goffman quotes J. Stearn, *Sisters of the Night* (New York: Popular Library, Inc., 1961), p. 181, in *Stigma*, p. 28.

There are differences between the groups sharing the stigma and those composed of the wise. Perhaps the most significant is that the stigmatic group will dramatize the stigma through formalized organizations or journals devoted to a treatment of how to live with the stigma; stories are told of individuals who have achieved outstanding success despite possession of the stigma. Contrary to this, groups made up of the wise are more inclined to reinterpret the stigma in a way which minimizes its existence, for example, the call girl is seen as an "off-beat personality."

A second way in which the stigmatized person can avoid playing against the stacked deck is to attempt to control his identity so that the stigma will not be perceived by others. Thus, illiterates may wear the trapping of the literate. Goffman cites the following illustration:

> . . . when goal orientation is pronounced or imperative and there exists a high probability that definition as illiterate is a bar to the achievement of the goal, the illiterate is likely to try to "pass" as literate . . . The popularity in the group studied of window-pane lenses with heavy horn frames ("bop glasses") may be viewed as an attempt to emulate the stereotype of the businessman-teacher-young intellectual and especially the high status jazz musician.[16]

Identity control may or may not be effective, of course. If it is effective, the stigmatized person is able to "pass" for a while as a nonstigmatized person. But the matter is more complex than simply successfully disguising a stigma. Between people who can completely cover their stigma and pass without fear of discovery and those who can never cover their stigma lies a great range of cases.

> First, there are important stigmas, such as the ones that prostitutes, thieves, homosexuals, beggars, and drug addicts have, which require the individual to be carefully secret about his failing to one class of persons, the police, while systematically exposing himself to other classes of persons, namely clients, fellow-members, connections, fences, and the like . . . Secondly, even where an individual could keep an unapparent stigma secret, he will find that intimate relations with others, ratified in our society by mutual confession of invisible failings, cause him either to admit his situation to the intimate or to feel guilty for not doing so. In any case, nearly all matters which are very secret are still known to someone, and hence cast a shadow.[17]

Within this range stigmatized people have several alternative modes of information control. They may pass, as has been suggested, or they may attempt to convert the stigma into some lesser form. Some blind persons wear

---

[16] Goffman takes this example from H. Freeman and G. Kasenbaum, "The Illiterate in America," *Social Forces*, **XXXIV**, 4 (May 1956), 374. See *Stigma*, p. 44.

[17] *Stigma*, pp. 73–74.

dark glasses which immediately identify them as blind, but which may simultaneously diguise or hide facial disfigurements that accompanied being blinded.

Finally, the stigmatized person is confronted with unique problems in the realm of audience management. In these cases the stigmatized person has to play the game but he attempts to minimize his handicap by playing on the meanings that others give his condition. "Breaking the ice" exemplifies what is meant here. Initial contacts are important in determining how an interaction between two or more persons will continue. A stigmatized person can find himself either an object of pity—and thereby subject to those subtle forms of discrimination reserved for objects of pity, or he can establish his individuality and rights as a human, by how he handles his initial meeting with others. For example, a man who has lost both hands and is served by artificial limbs may, on a first encounter with others, take out a cigarette and light it regardless of whether or not he feels like smoking. This ostentatious display of skills within a stigmatic context is sufficient to warn the audience that there is no need to go beyond the normal set of social understandings.

Goffman as scientist and humanist

Whether it is a man with a stigma or a normal individual coping with a common problem in everyday life, Goffman concentrates on how people manage the impressions they try to convey to others. Goffman is not, in the usual meaning of the term, a "scientist." His work does not rely on elaborate measurements. His major works are not based on questionnaires or even structured interviews. He is not at all hesitant to make use of literary examples if they help illustrate a concept or an idea.

Yet it would be a mistake to discount Goffman as a scientist. There is in his writing a more dispassionate and unbiased reporting of human events than is to be found in many studies more heavily armored with quantitative data and statistical analysis. Goffman's methods, which consist largely of careful observation combined with extensive scholarship, flow from his general conception of human conduct. Human behavior, for Goffman, is not a series of discrete actions which result from biologically derived urges or drives. Nor is it a manifestation of some inner condition like "personality." Instead, human behavior is distinctively complex and consists for the most part of an elaborate progression of symbolic performances. This conception of humanity forces us to see our conduct as though it were a work of art. We are artists—"con" artists, Goffman might suggest, but nonetheless artists. If this is so, then the important thing is to see the total impression created by our behavior. But this cannot be done unless we try to evaluate or understand the complete performance. We would have a very limited understanding of a painting by Picasso if we were informed only of the percentage of the painting that is blue.

Goffman stands back and observes, through the perspectives of science, the artful behavior of man. The effect is powerful. The large following which Goffman enjoys today in both sociological and psychological circles is a result of the fact that he brings together the synthetic powers of the humanistic artist with the analytic and objective powers of the contemporary social scientist.

To read Goffman is to be brought directly and cleverly to a perception of man as a role player and manipulator of props, costumes, gestures, and words. Goffman is able to suggest, indirectly, the injustices that such role playing can produce as when, for example, we deny a woman status as a warm and intelligent human being because she is deformed and dwarflike. But if Goffman is able to penetrate into the most subtle irrationalities of human conduct, he simultaneously is generous in the extent to which his conception of humanity embraces all men. Goffman's writing asserts that no man is more human than another; only that one man might be able to give a certain kind of performance better than another. If so, then in human terms a beggar is the equal of a king. Goffman finds people caught up in myriad "con" games; at the same time the objective and cold vision of this social scientist upholds in a devious way one of the most sympathetic of human values—the fundamental equality of all men.

10 The Use of Sociology as Bad Faith: The Views of Peter L. Berger

One of the most expressive writers in modern sociological literature was, at one time, a professor at a seminary in Connecticut. Perhaps his research and writings in the field of religious institutions made him more receptive to humanistic issues than is common among sociologists. Possibly the fact that he came here from Europe in his late teens led him to acquire a humanistic bent before going into sociology. Whatever the reason, Peter L. Berger has produced several books graced by style and dramatic quality.[1] In the work to be discussed here, Berger achieves this dramatic effect by bringing several incompatible ideas together. The result is like that arising from the meeting of a very cold with a very warm front—there is a stormy period before the air is cleared again. In his most general work, *Invitation to Sociology*, two sets of incompatible ideas are brought together. First, Berger presents us with a heavily lined sketch of what might be called "classical" sociological thought. He pares away most of the academic issues which float about sociology and lets us take a look at its essence; thus we have sociology stripped of those qualifications which often hide its fundamental character. Then Berger confronts us with existentialist thought—the warm front which clashes with the colder views of sociology. Both positions have a legitimacy and both certainly have a large number of followers; yet the two seem to be in opposition. Sociology, for example, is analytical and deterministic; existentialism is personal and

---

[1] Peter Berger's major works include *Invitation to Sociology, A Humanistic Perspective* (Anchor Books; Garden City, N.Y.: Doubleday & Company, Inc., 1963); *The Human Shape of Work*, edited by Berger (New York: The Macmillan Co., 1964); *The Noise of Solemn Assemblies; Christian Commitment and the Religious Establishment in America* (Garden City, N.Y.: Doubleday & Company, Inc., 1961); *The Precarious Vision, A Sociologist Looks at Social Fictions and the Christian Faith* (Garden City, N.Y.: Doubleday & Company, Inc., 1961); *The Sacred Canopy; Elements of a Sociological Theory of Religion* (Garden City, N.Y.: Doubleday & Company, Inc., 1967); and *The Social Construction of Reality* (Garden City, N.Y.: Doubleday & Company, Inc., 1966).

volitional. Sociology is reliant on a scientific approach to man; existentialism is more subjective and humanistic. Let us see how Berger describes the conflict between these ways of thinking by beginning with his consideration of sociology.

Traditional sociological thought

The traditional sociological view of man comes very close to reducing him to the level of being a "victim" of his society.[2] Man is simply born into society and then is controlled by it. In a sense, as Berger nicely puts it, man is a "prisoner" of society. Society is the walls of our imprisonment in history.[3] And it guards us closely; even quite harmless acts, like growing a beard or mispronouncing a word, are apt to bring ridicule or some other form of social constraint.

Society is an external force, as coercive and as constraining as the physical and biological environments with which we have to cope. Moreover, society is internal as well as external. Not only is man within society; society is within man. The very ways a person comes to see himself, the daydreams he has, the aspirations and longings which come to dominate his thoughts, are not random or independent of society. They are subjective social actions which parallel the larger society. Thus, a person might daydream of military exploits as a jet pilot, or of intellectual attainments as a great writer, or of business successes as an industrialist—or he might dream of murder.[4] Even so, the form of the daydream—distorted by the individual's ignorance and desires— will conform generally to the model provided by the society. It is in this sense, then, that Berger makes his first point: the sociological view of man reveals him as a victim of his society. He is controlled by it from without and he is controlled by it from within.

Let us examine this matter of social control in a little more detail. We have to get a better sense of the extent to which the sociological "cold front" is in fact "cold."

A person is born into a social system and eventually is coerced, in various ways, into meeting its demands. Some idea of what is taking place might be

---

[2] An academic and well-developed criticism of this point of view can be found in the article "The Oversocialized Conception of Man in Modern Sociology" by Dennis H. Wrong which appeared in *The American Sociological Review*; **26**, 2 (April 1961), 183–193.

[3] Berger, *Invitation to Sociology*, p. 92. This is Berger's expression.

[4] It might seem, from one point of view, that dreams of murder are antisocial. Yet, in a sense, they follow a model provided by society. Consider, for example, the dreams that can be generated by the title of a recent movie—I am thinking of the film *Kiss the Girls and Make Them Die*. Though I disagree with many of his particulars, Dr. Frederic Wertham is correct in general as he develops this theme in both *Seduction of the Innocent* (New York: Holt, Rinehart and Winston, Inc., 1954) and *A Sign for Cain* (New York: The Macmillan Company, 1966).

obtained by imagining human bodies as a form of money which must be distributed and allocated throughout a "banking" system. Some money must go into certain kinds of activities and other money must go into yet other kinds of activities. But it is the banking system which does the allocation. In the case of actual money and banking systems we are dealing with an inanimate element, money, which goes wherever it is directed; the problems of allocation are not disturbed by any presumptions which might exist within the money itself.

But in society the problem is different. When we are allocating human beings to different activities, we find ourselves working with a more truculent and complex agent in the process of distribution. Yet, the problem of allocation is there and, if society is to retain its integrity as a system, the means of allocation must be efficient enough to ensure the system against disruption by the irritable qualities of human beings themselves. The problem, in brief, is to make certain, within limits, that men do what they are told.

Social control

In order to achieve reasonable certainty that men will, in fact, do what they are told, society has a variety of devices at hand. The range and character of these devices impress upon one the extent to which he is subject to control from others. Furthermore, as Berger notes, the control which comes from others has at the same time an effectiveness and yet a remoteness which can induce a feeling of helplessness on the part of an individual. For example, lower-class people often refer to having to do things the way an impersonal "they" wants them done. Or, Negroes refer to being exploited by "the man." One's history on this planet is not only narrowly circumscribed by the social milieu into which he is born, but most of that milieu is composed of strangers —people one has never met and never will. Even though the demands may come from distant (and usually long dead) strangers, the devices society uses for controlling man are generally sufficient to see that the demands are met. What are these devices?

First, the most common and the most fundamental device is a reliance on violence. People are kept in their place by either a threat of injury to their physical beings or an actual act of violence. No matter how sophisticated a society might be, it nonetheless shares in common with the most primitive a reliance on this form of social control. The police officials of a modern state are unique within the general population insofar as they have the legitimate right to engage in violence—to use physical force to bring order and stability into the community. The resort to violence to ensure control is simple and it is generally effective. But it is not, of itself, sufficient—it is not the only device upon which a society must rely.

The threat of violence is the demand that the individual conform or suffer. But there are times when the individual would rather suffer any form of physical injury than conform. For example, Sir Thomas More elected to have his head cut off before he would concede to the authority of his king. The Romans fed many a Christian to the lion, but they could not kill Christianity. Men have gone to the stake and the scaffold. They have stood smiling in front of firing squads. They have taken themselves and their families into confrontations with spitting mobs. They have been tortured with the thin edge of the razor. Yet, despite these physical horrors, they have kept their integrity. They have not conceded to the demand. They have not sold out when the ultimate pressure was brought to bear.

For this reason, violence is insufficient as a control device. There is yet another reason. Violence, for all of its dramatic simplicity, does not control the individual other than by the most outward manifestations. The individual who is forced to do something or else suffer a bash in the nose may do it, but his attitude toward the whole procedure will likely be one of scheming to find ways to escape. When the Union, through military power, defeated the Confederate States, it was able to dictate its terms. But a military defeat does not always mean a defeat of spirit. The South, even today, still manages to retain many of the sentiments and culturally prescribed ways of behaving that existed long before the Civil War.

Violence may be necessary, but it is extremely limited as a social control device. It produces a minimal outward conformity, but at the price of generating hatred toward the conformity-inducing agent. It would be better to achieve conformity and, at the same time, have the conforming individual love the coercion to which he is being subjected. If necessary, one can always physically threaten a potential nonconformist. However, it is better to win his loyalty. Then he conforms and, at the same time, brags about it.

Society can win a person's loyalty by means of a second device it has to achieve control. This device consists of controlling an individual's beliefs. At birth a person is perfectly vulnerable with respect to what he can believe. This fact provides the community with an opportunity to use belief as a means of controlling the individual and seeing to it that he fits into his place. Most significantly, he will fit into his place because he believes in it. For him it is a true and proper place.

A good example of the relationship between belief systems and social control appears in the autobiography of Malcolm X.[5] Malcolm X describes

---

[5] Malcolm X, with the assistance of Alex Haley, *The Autobiography of Malcolm X* (New York: Grove Press, Inc., 1964), p. 55.

his experience when he received his first "conk." "Conking" refers to a process whereby the kinky hair of a Negro is straightened to look more like the hair of a white person. What is important to note here is that the Negro who conks his hair believes straight hair is better than kinky hair. Conking is, then, just one way of acknowledging the natural superiority of the white man and "conking" is a concession to his demands. Malcolm X describes his experience,

> My first view in the mirror blotted out the hurting. I'd seen some pretty conks, but when it's the first time, on your *own* head, the transformation, after the life-time of kinks, is staggering.
>
> The mirror reflected Shorty behind me. We both were grinning and sweating. And on top of my head was this thick, smooth sheen of shining red hair—real red—as straight as any white man's.
>
> How ridiculous I was! Stupid enough to stand there simply lost in admiration of my hair now looking "white," reflected in the mirror in Shorty's room. I vowed that I'd never again be without a conk, and I never was for many years.
>
> This was my first really big step toward self-degradation: when I endured all of that pain, literally burning my flesh to have it look like a white man's hair. I had joined that multitude of Negro men and women in America who are brain-washed into believing that the black people are "inferior"—and white people "superior"—that they will even violate and mutilate their God-created bodies to try to look "pretty" by white standards.[6]

Malcolm X was influenced by belief. He later came to believe differently and, at this point, he became more truculent toward white domination. His description of "conking" reveals how far the white belief system was able, at one time in his life, to induce conformity to its ideals.

To the threat of violence and control by belief we can add a third device available to society—ridicule. Ridicule is essentially a veiled threat to with-draw affection. For example, one teen-ager might say to another, "If you don't take that turn at eighty-five, you're chicken." The threat of ridicule exists, then, if the taunted person does not respond. This is a common enough way to control the behavior of another person. The surprising thing is that such a taunt works. Logically, ridicule of this sort is saying, "If you don't take the turn at eighty-five, we will place you in the class 'chicken.' We do not like people who fall in the class 'chicken.' Therefore, if you don't take the turn, we won't like you any more." Ridicule is, therefore, an indirect as-sertion of possible dislike or disaffection—but the indirection of the statement seems to make it more effective. In any event, ridicule is an effective means for controlling behavior. We might add here that Japanese parents use it as

---

[6] *Ibid.*, p. 54.

a means of curbing their children by cautioning them with the admonition, "People will laugh at you."

A fourth, and very common, device is the use of fraud. If you cannot force or persuade or ridicule someone into conforming, you can sometimes trick him.[7] The following illustration of the effectiveness of fraud took place during World War II in North Africa. Allied interrogation officers were interested at the time in determining the identity of some new German divisions that had just entered the North African campaign. The use of force against captured German soldiers had not been effective. Finally, one interrogation officer suggested that the German prisoners be taken outside into a compound. He then had a variety of numbers put up on stands in an assembly building. After setting up the situation he told the guards to march the prisoners into the building on the double—with the order the prisoners were to line up by their division numbers. The prisoners were then rushed rapidly into the assembly hall and, as the interrogation officers watched, some prisoners ran over to and stood beside some new division numbers. What force had been unable to extract, cunning had.[8] Again, the point is that fraud exists as a device enabling control to be maintained over others. The German prisoners had tried not to give information to the enemy; nonetheless they were coerced into behavior which went contrary to their individual preference or choice.

A fifth device used by society to achieve compliance is the threat of ostracism. Ostracism has elements of physical violence or injury and elements of ridicule in it. Yet it is sufficiently different to warrant separate consideration. Ostracism says, in effect, that if you do not "shape up" and do what you are told, you will be asked to remove yourself from the group.[9] This social control device is very popular among universities. A student is not subjected to physical violence nor is he especially ridiculed or tricked into doing what

---

[7] The pervasive use of fraud in everyday life as a means of gaining control over others is the basis of much of Erving Goffman's approach to human social conduct. This was discussed at length in Chapter 9.

[8] I cannot vouch for the particulars of this illustrative anecdote. I heard the story from a naval intelligence officer several years ago. I like the story because it illustrates, as well as any I know, the place fraud can have in controlling behavior.

[9] In earlier times, ostracism could be an occasion for a ceremonious pronunciamento. An example is the excommunication order of Spinoza which read, in part, "We order that nobody should communicate with him orally, or show him any favor, or stay with him under the same roof, or within four ells of him, or read anything composed or written by him." This statement also demanded that Spinoza ". . . should be cursed by day and night, lying down and rising up, going out and coming in."

The above accounting of the excommunication statement appears in *Heroes and Heretics* by Barrows Dunham (New York: Alfred A. Knopf, Inc., 1964), p. 335. Spinoza was excommunicated for suggesting in the 17th century that the origins of religious doctrine were located in human historical processes rather than in divine miracles. When we ostracize people today we make less show of it, perhaps, but it is still an effective social control device.

is required of him by the school. The primary social control mechanism is ostracism—if you do not study and do what your teachers ask of you, you will be asked to leave the organization. As a matter of fact, you will be *required* to leave it. This threat is usually sufficient to maintain at least a semblance of order.

A sixth device for promoting conformity is occupational control. If an individual does not behave as he should, there are ways of seeing to it that the better jobs are somehow made unavailable to him. An interesting manifestation of this appears in the following quotation taken from the *Congressional Record*. In this quotation we witness an attempt to control religious belief by using occupational controls.

> Mr. Ashbrook (R.—Ohio): Mr. Chairman, I offer an amendment [to the Civil Rights Bill]: ". . . it shall not be an unlawful employment practice for an employer to refuse to hire and employ any person because of said person's atheistic practices and beliefs."
>
> Mr. Elliot (D.—Ala.): We leave the right of an atheist to believe, or not to believe, as may be his choice. All this amendment does is preserve for the American employer a freedom to insist that his employees be under God.
>
> Mr. Jones (D.—Mo.): It would be interesting to see how many people are going to stand up here and be counted, and say they feel an employer is compelled to give consideration to the hiring of an atheist, when he is trying to run a business that is based on good moral grounds.
>
> Mr. Wickersham (D.—Okla.): You might even require the churches and lodges, clubs and businessmen and Congressmen to hire atheists unless this amendment is accepted.
>
> The question was taken, and on a division demanded by Mr. Celler, there were —ayes 137, noes 98.[10]

It seems, from the above discussion, that religious freedom extends only so far as the right to believe in some religion or other—it does not extend all the way to having the freedom to believe atheistically. The amendment considered in this debate is interesting because it permits the discussants to feel they are permitting freedom (". . . the right to believe . . . as may be his choice . . .") while, at the same time, invoking a possible penalty if the individual is so naive as to tell a Christian or Jewish employer that he is an atheist. So, occupational control is another device available for inducing conformity and compliance from men who might otherwise behave "badly."

---

[10] A fuller treatment of this debate appears in the February 8, 1964, issue of *The Congressional Record*. Although much of *The Congressional Record* is not very exciting reading, there are more than occasional passages which surpass *Alice in Wonderland* when it comes to whimsy and fantasy. I am indebted to *The Realist*, a somewhat obscure but free-swinging paper, for bringing this debate to my attention.

A seventh device referred to by Berger in his discussion of the force that society can bring to bear on the individual is control coming from the "sphere-of-intimates." This is a subtle but effective form of control. Studies of soldiers in combat have revealed that the ordinary soldier is not motivated to fight by lofty political ideals and moral philosophy. He fights because his buddies are fighting. Or, another illustration of what Berger means by influence coming from the "sphere-of-intimates" is suggested in the following passage from Vance Packard's *The Hidden Persuaders*:

> A young New York ad man taking a marketing class . . . made the casual statement that, thanks to TV, most children were learning to sing beer and other commercials before they learned to sing the Star-Spangled Banner. Youth Research Institute, according to *The Nation*, boasted that even five-year-olds sing beer commercials "over and over again with gusto." It pointed out that moppets not only sing the merits of advertised products but do it with the vigor displayed by the most raptly enthusiastic announcers, and do it all day long "at no extra cost to the advertiser."[11]

Finally, there is an eighth way in which the behavior of the individual is directed and controlled by others, that is, through systems of mutual obligation. This is essentially a contractual variety of relationship which states, either explicitly or implicitly, "If you do such and such, then I shall do so and so." The point here is that once the contract is entered, the behavior of the individual becomes controlled by it. Even when a person may prefer a different course of action, he can still be coerced into conforming through the stipulations of reciprocal contractual agreements. For example, many of the letters addressed to "lonely hearts" columnists like Ann Landers and Dear Abby have to do with some problem arising from a reciprocal obligation that has gone sour. The following example is possibly too obvious a case in point,

> Dear Abby: Please help me. I'm in terrible trouble and I'm just sick about it. Yesterday a salesman came to my door, showed me his product and, before I knew it, I had signed a contract to buy it. I have two years to pay, but now I'm afraid to tell my husband about the monthly instalments.
>
> I don't know what got into me, Abby. I really don't need that product and we certainly can't afford it at this time.
>
> Is there any way I can get out of it now? I would appreciate any help you can give me.
>
> SIGNED WITHOUT THINKING[12]

---

[11] Vance Packard, *The Hidden Persuaders* (New York: David McKay Co., Inc., 1957), p. 159.

[12] As I wondered how I might illustrate what Berger is saying, I thought of the common problems so often brought to people like Ann Landers and Dear Abby. I picked up the previous day's local paper and was rewarded with the illustration used here. It was the first letter in the column. The quotation was taken from the *Boulder Daily Camera*, February 9, 1967, p. 29. Reprinted by permission of Abigail Van Buren.

Society has, then, at least these eight devices for assuring itself that any given individual will not step very far out of line. So, when Berger says man is the prisoner of society, he identifies the bars of the prison: threats of violence, belief systems, ridicule, fraud and deception, threat of ostracism, occupational controls, the influence of intimates, and reciprocal obligations. These are effective constraints and most people are kept in line by them. But they still do not exhaust the extent to which man is "held" by society. We must, says Berger, not only see man in society; we must become aware of the extent to which society is in man.

Social identity

Society enters man by providing him with an identity. Identity is related to the social class into which one is born, and identity is more specifically related to the social roles one is required to play as a member of the social system. Berger succinctly puts it as follows:

> This significance of role theory could be summarized by saying that, in a socio-logical perspective, identity is socially bestowed, socially sustained and socially transformed. The example of [a] man in process of becoming an officer may suffice to illustrate the way in which identities are bestowed in adult life. However, even roles that are much more fundamentally part of what psychologists would call our personality than those associated with a particular adult activity are bestowed in very similar manner through a social process. This has been demonstrated over and over again in studies of so-called socialization—the process by which a child learns to be a participant member of society.[13]

The belief system into which a child is born has, in addition to providing a person with ideas about the world around him, the special capacity of pro-viding the individual with certain notions about himself. It is in this sense that society can enter a person's character and thereby "victimize" him. Certain conceptions that one acquires concerning himself are relatively enduring. Beliefs related to major organizational elements of a society are especially connected to concepts of self. For example, in India caste has been a central organizational feature of Indian society. It is essential that people born into the different subcaste levels acquire beliefs about themselves that permit the caste system to operate relatively smoothly. In order that a member of a depressed caste will in fact feel inferior and unworthy, the caste system has imposed the following restraints on a lower-caste person:

---

[13] *From Invitation to Sociology* by Peter L. Berger, pp. 98–99. Copyright © 1963 by Peter L. Berger. Reprinted by permission of the author, Doubleday & Company, Inc., and Penguin Books Ltd.

1. Cannot be served by clean Brahmins.
2. Cannot be served by barbers, tailors, and the like who serve caste Hindus.
3. May pollute those with whom he comes in contact.
4. Cannot serve water to caste Hindus.
5. Cannot use public conveniences such as ferries, wells, or schools.
6. May not enter Hindu temples.
7. Must engage in a despised occupation.[14]

After being worked over in this fashion, it is not surprising that an individual, as he matures, takes on an identity which fits him into the caste system. He accepts the slot allocated to him—no matter how wretched that slot might be.

It is, however, an oversimplification to see society as a static structure with various positions to be filled and people placed in these slots to remain there throughout the remainder of their lives. Two complicating factors have to be taken into account. In the first place, positions that once were functional in a society may lose their meaning or value. Thus, with the advent of the automobile, a person trained as a blacksmith had to change his character. In the second place, it is generally necessary for a person, as he grows up, to make some modifications in his social position. After all, a man cannot be treated like a child all his life. These two simple qualifications require a consideration, then, of the problem of identity changes. Berger refers to more pervasive and durable forms of identity change as *alternation*. Thus, a student who comes to college with strong religious faith as an integral part of his identity and then becomes an atheist in his senior year has undergone alternation.

Alternation and lack of character

Alternation can be a relatively gentle process or an extremely violent one—depending on the extent to which the individual must be protected from further alternations. For example, if it is necessary to create a definite cleavage between a boy and his mother when the boy reaches adulthood, a society is likely to achieve this through very rigorous and painful tests of manliness. Any future alternation away from a very manly identity is made a less probable event by such tests. Where alternation is not as much a problem, initiation rites are less severe. Alternation suggests that social identity is subject to

---

[14] Kingsley Davis, *Human Society* (New York: The Macmillan Company, 1949), p. 380. I am aware, of course, that India is at present concerned with doing away with such caste constraints. But India, like the United States, finds the process of removing the inequities and inhumanities of caste a slow and troublesome one.

change. A person can be one thing at one time and something else at another. Berger is more descriptive—he uses the term ''lack of character'' to refer to this feature of human behavior.

Men lack character insofar as they are able to undergo changes in identity. The pacifistic civilian can be transformed into a bayonet-wielding marine. Or, in an example used by Berger,

> The Nazi concentration-camp commander who writes sentimental letters to his children is but an extreme case of something that occurs in society all the time.[15]

Or, one further example, consider the subtle lack of character described by W. B. Cameron, who observed jazz musicians engaging in jam sessions which had the purpose of purifying the musician after he had contaminated himself by playing ''good'' music before a square audience.[16]

For the sociologist, lack of character is not a cause for a diatribe on the hypocrisy of man. It is, rather, a cause for emphasizing more fully the social character of self. If lack of character is typical of man, and observation seems to support this view, then to whatever extent character exists, it is implanted there by the social performance required of the person. Identity, self, and character are sustained by social demands and cannot exist independently of such demands. Thus, the jazz musician who plays before ''square'' audiences feels himself possessed of a corrupt character which later must be washed away by a ritualistic musical performance. Or, we find the sadistic Nazi gauleiter being brutal in one context and gentle in another.

These are not insincere or hypocritical performances. When Berger says man suffers from a lack of character he does not mean he is entirely without character of any kind. He means, instead, that the character which man possesses is highly responsive to the social situation in which it finds itself. It can vary considerably from setting to setting and yet the individual can retain a sense of sincerity in his actions.

> That is why insincerity is rather a rare phenomenon. Most people are sincere, because this is the easiest course to take psychologically. That is, they believe in their own act, conveniently forget the act that preceded it, and happily go through life in the conviction of being responsible in all its demands. Sincerity is the consciousness of the man who is taken in by his own act. Or as it has been put by David Riesman, the sincere man is the one who believes in his own propaganda.[17]

---

[15] Berger, *Invitation to Sociology*, pp. 108–109.

[16] William Bruce Cameron, ''Sociological Notes on the Jam Session,'' *Social Forces*, **33**, 2 (December 1954), 178.

[17] Berger, *Invitation to Sociology*, p. 109.

The individual responds, then, to group opinions and can, within certain latitudes, adhere to contradictory identities and behave accordingly. What an individual "really" is amounts, in the final accounting, to an enumeration of the situations in which he is one thing and those in which he is another.[18]

The fact that man lacks character means he is susceptible to identities imposed on him by others. The illustrations just given were concerned with making the point that social identities do in fact have a social locus because they are subject to change. If, for example, the Nazi were cruel in all circumstances, we would have some reason to suspect his character might reflect some genetic or inborn quality. However, because he is gentle toward some and cruel toward others, submissive to his superiors and belligerently domineering toward his inferiors, we can conclude his character is actually quite variable—responding to the demands made by particular social occasions and relationships. We lack the ability to give meaning to ourselves in isolation from others. Others provide us with an identity and we have little recourse but to respond accordingly. This identity, furthermore, has a "real" quality. A woman who, as a result of an indiscreet love affair, finds others referring to her as a "slut" and a "tramp" might find the alternation being demanded of her impossible. She might react by becoming depressed or perhaps even going so far as to attempt suicide. Thus, the identity problem is sufficiently intense or real to produce behavior which can run contrary to the naturally grounded demands of biological survival.

The mechanical conception of man

Let us now pause for a moment and pull a few ideas together. Berger first attempts to overwhelm us with an extreme statement of what sociological determinism means. It means, in a metaphorical way, that we are the prisoners of society. Society has and uses a variety of devices to make certain we remain in line. The devices are generally successful because, by and large, people do conform. Look around you. In their public appearances, at least, people show a surprising "standardization." They talk alike, they dress much alike, and they generally keep out of trouble. Berger indicates why. Nonconformity is socially disruptive and will invoke controls over the individual. If he becomes too recalcitrant, he will be removed from the picture—sent either to an asylum or eternity.

So, man is a prisoner of his society. But this is not all—man is a willing prisoner. He comes to want what his society wants him to want. He is not

---

[18] The phrasing here is Berger's.

only controlled by external forms of coercion; he is controlled by internal coercion which takes the form of social identity. A person is granted a certain identity and he comes to view himself accordingly. Eventually he attempts to respond as he believes someone who has his character ought to respond.

We now have some idea of the extent to which sociology presents a cold and mechanical conception of man. Whatever man is, he is by virtue of the fact he exists within a greater social structure. His character, his fate, are determined by where he happens to be born within that structure. All else is irrelevant to the sociological quest.

A discussion of freedom

Overdrawn as this picture is, there is much truth in it. Still, it is a disturbing kind of truth, and we find ourselves longing for alternatives which might yet allow us to view man as a creature with heroic qualities. We want to think of man, and ourselves, as more than pawns or agents of social force. Berger examines a possible alternative by entering into a discussion of the nature of freedom. To what extent can man break free from the constraints of society and still survive as an individual? What means are available to men for finding freedom and individuality?

We can begin by considering a characteristic of the mechanical conception of sociology outlined in the previous pages: in at least one respect it bears a striking resemblance to instinct theory. Behavior in an ant is channeled by instincts; in man it is channeled by institutional directives. Both the ant and the man behave because of coercion. The only difference, it would seem, is that the coercion to which the ant is subjected comes from "inside"; that to which man is subjected comes from "outside." The ant responds to instincts; man responds according to his social character.

So, both the ant and the man, when asked why they behave as they do, might respond, "Because I must." However, such a reply is perfectly correct only in the ant's case. Man more often deceives himself when he says, "Because I must." We employ the phrase, "I must!" to hide from ourselves the fearful thought that it might be otherwise—the thought that we have elected to behave the way we are behaving. We may be only pretending something is necessary when, in fact, it is not. Jean-Paul Sartre refers to this as "bad faith." Berger describes it in the following way:

> To put it very simply, "bad faith" is to pretend something is necessary that in fact is voluntary. "Bad faith" is thus a flight from freedom, a dishonest evasion of the "agony of choice." "Bad faith" expresses itself in innumerable human situations from the most commonplace to the most catastrophic. The waiter shuffling through

his appointed rounds in a café is in "bad faith" insofar as he pretends to himself that the waiter role constitutes his real existence, that, if only for the hours he is hired, he *is* the waiter . . . The terrorist who kills and excuses himself by saying that he had no choice because the party ordered him to kill is in "bad faith," because he pretends that his existence is necessarily linked with the party, while in fact this linkage is the consequence of his own choice. It can easily be seen that "bad faith" covers society like a film of lies. The very possibility of "bad faith," however, shows us the reality of freedom. Man can be in "bad faith" only because he is free and does not wish to face his freedom. "Bad faith" is the shadow of human liberty. Its attempt to escape that liberty is doomed to defeat. For as Sartre has famously put it, we are "condemned to freedom."[19]

With this statement Berger has seemingly reversed himself and, by doing so, thrown everything into a state of confusion. Until now Berger has spent a great deal of effort confronting us with a sociological conception of humanity which finds man "locked" in society. Now he turns around and tells us that Sartre is correct when he says that we are "condemned to freedom." What is going on? If we stay with Berger a little longer, we will find he is not expressing ideas that conflict with each other as much as it may seem at first. The existentialist position of Sartre can, if we think about it more carefully, mesh with the arguments and perspectives of the sociologist. For the moment, let us return to a further consideration of the existentialist position.

> Sartre has given us a masterful vista of the operation of "bad faith" at its most malevolent in his portrayal of the anti-Semite as a human type. The anti-Semite is the man who frantically identifies himself with mythological entities ("nation," "race," "*Volk*") and in doing so seeks to divest himself of the knowledge of his own freedom. Anti-Semitism (or, we might add, any other form of racism or fanatical nationalism) is "bad faith" *par excellence* because it identifies men in their human totality with their social character. Humanity itself becomes a facticity devoid of freedom. One then loves, hates and kills within a mythological world in which all men *are* their social designation, as the SS man *is* what his insignia say and the Jew *is* the symbol of despicability sewn on his concentration camp uniform.[20]

Society can and has imprisoned men. But it has been able to do this only when men permitted the deceptions foisted on them by society to have the status of reality. What Berger is suggesting, as a sociologist, is that man is kept a prisoner by society only to the extent to which he permits himself to remain ignorant of its influence over him. With knowledge and understanding of the way in which society operates, man can begin to free himself of its controls. He can begin to comprehend the extent to which choice is available to him. We can play various social roles knowingly or blindly. When we play

---

[19] Berger, *Invitation to Sociology*, p. 143.
[20] *Ibid.*, p. 144.

them blindly, we are the victims of society. When we play them knowingly, society becomes the medium through which we express our volition.[21]

This conception of freedom suggests that social knowledgeability is a means toward attaining personal freedom. Social awareness prevents us from being "duped" or overwhelmed by the social fictions surrounding us. It would then seem reasonable to conclude that sociology—one way of obtaining a more sophisticated understanding of social reality—would be a certain route to the attainment of greater freedom. Unfortunately, it is not possible to make such claims for sociology. Sociology can be used as an academic justification for existing inhumanities or it can be an approach to a morally critical understanding of man's injuries to man. There is nothing within sociology itself which dictates the use to which it might be put. Berger states the problem as follows:

> . . . sociological understanding itself can become a vehicle of "bad faith." This occurs when such understanding becomes an alibi for responsibility . . . For example, a sociologist located in the South may start out with strong, personal values that repudiate the Southern racial system and he may seek to express these values by some form of social or political action. But then, after a while, he becomes an expert, *qua* sociologist, in racial matters. He now really feels that he understands the system. At this point, it may be observed in some cases, a different stance is adopted *vis-a-vis* the moral problems—that of the cooly scientific commentator. The sociologist now regards his act of understanding as constituting the sum total of his relationship to the phenomenon and as releasing him from any of those acts that would engage him personally.[22]

Berger is aware that the socially responsible use of sociology is not simple to describe. The cool and dispassionate scientist, described in the above paragraph, can be exemplifying bad faith or he can be acting on very sound moral principles. Whether it is bad faith or morally responsible action must rest, in the final analysis, on the sociologist's careful evaluation of whether, by maintaining a cooly analytical point of view, he is working toward the attainment of humanistic ends. There is always the possibility that the detached objectivity of the sociologist becomes a way of appearing to be interested, when in fact, objectivity and sociology have been allowed to operate *in lieu* of personal commitment.

---

[21] This idea appears in Richard Kim's taut novel *The Martyred*. Kim contrasts two Christian ministers. One believes in the validity of his God and, in the final moments before he is executed by a Communist firing squad, abandons his faith and his God. The second does not believe to begin with, but finds in his role as a minister a way of bringing aid and assistance to a suffering humanity. See Richard Kim, *The Martyred* (New York: George Braziller, Inc., 1964).

[22] Berger, *Invitation to Sociology*, pp. 153–154.

Sociology as a humanizing endeavor

In his final evaluation of sociology Berger finds it to be a humanizing endeavor; although, of course, it is not necessarily such—sociologists can promote inhuman or dehumanizing efforts as well as humanizing ones. It depends,
totally, on the manner in which sociology is to be used. As Berger puts it, it
is not easy to find a humanistic dimension in research which is trying to find
the optimum crew composition of a bomber or which is seeking ways to entice
a somnambulant housewife into buying a particular breakfast cereal.[23] Even
so, the typical or general effect of sociological sophistication is to bring about
a more humanistic sense. The kinds of understanding which sociologists have
brought to matters like the social meaning of race, sexual conduct, and capital
punishment have had liberating moral implications. Studies by criminologists,
for example, which have shown there is no relationship between capital punishment and indulgence in crime have torn at the fiction which stipulates
that capital punishment is necessary. If we retain capital punishment, we do so
now more from choice than from necessity.

The important thing which Berger gets at, however, is a recognition of the
fact that sociology is not *necessarily* morally liberating. A sociological understanding of the race problem can result in profound comprehension of why,
for example, the American Negro has been held in bondage for centuries.
Berger is well aware, as we have already seen, that such comprehensive understanding can produce a feeling of acceptance—it is simply the way things
are. The powerful and grinding interplay of vested interests, ingrained social
beliefs and fictions, the processes of intergroup conflict and struggle, social
differentiation, role demands, and the needs of a greater social system can,
as one begins to comprehend them, generate the attitude that it is only
natural some people must suffer in any social system.

If a sociologist or a student of human behavior gets no further than this,
then he is likely, in a very real sense, to employ sociology as a form of bad
faith. Existing inhumanities are justified in scientific terms and there is nothing
we can do to correct them. We can lecture about them, or we can research
them, or we can write books about them; but when it comes to improving
man's lot there is nothing to do but stand aside and assume the cool and
quite patronizing attitude of the dispassionate observer. Berger, of course,
does not endorse this attitude and he is willing to go considerably outside the

---

[23] *Ibid.*, p. 169.

limits of formal sociological scholarship to find a way of avoiding sociology as bad faith. It is for this reason he touches on existentialist philosophy. The sociologist must not become the apologist for the existing system. He must not be the Western equivalent of the articulate and educated Indian who says that the caste system is good because it permits the maximum amount of social differentiation with the minimum amount of friction.

Sociology and existentialism seem so fundamentally different in character that we need to attempt some kind of resolution of these differences before bringing this chapter to a close. A partial resolution, at least, can be achieved by comprehending the differences in what each approach seeks to achieve. Sociology is analytical. Essentially, it takes events after they have occurred and asks the question, "Why?" Once an event has occurred it is really quite foolish to rely on concepts like "choice" or "freedom" or "volition" as ways of bringing understanding to the matter. If a race riot has torn apart a Los Angeles Negro ghetto, then it gets us nowhere to say, "They did it because they chose to." After Adolph Eichmann has sent hundreds of thousands of people to their deaths in gas chambers, it is quite ridiculous to say he was expressing his volition. We now know that. He has done what he decided to do, and we know he decided to do it because he did it. This gets us nowhere at all. We still want to know why he chose this particular course of action over alternative courses of action that confronted him.

In response, historians and sociologists might point to such conditions or influences as the cultural reaction of Germany as a nation to the insulting demands of the Versailles Treaty, the charismatic qualities of Hitler, or the ability of the Nazis to dominate the military—but less brutal—Junker class. Psychologists might concentrate on the personal life of Eichmann, his relationship toward his Jewish friends, and his own fears and anxieties. So it continues, and out of the past comes at least a partial understanding of man's inhumanity to man.

If concepts like "choice" and "freedom" are useless within a sociological context, how do they acquire a validity within an existentialist context? Existentialism is able to maintain a validity of its own when it uses terms like "choice" and "freedom" because it is concerned with getting men to recognize that before an event occurs one does have choice. There is a place in the mental realm of man which cannot be touched by science or analysis—and this place is the subjective anticipation that occurs prior to taking a course of action.

The point is that prior to acting the individual is free to behave in a contrary fashion. There is still available to him the possibility of conducting himself in a fashion which a psychologist or sociologist would not have anticipated. Existentialist thought tries to make the individual face up to the possibility of choice in his life. Existentialism attempts to turn the individual toward the coming moment rather than the past determinant. Existentialism attempts to reconstruct a philosophy of individual responsibility. Above all, existentialism, as Berger is concerned with it, attempts to bring man to an awareness that inhumanity cannot be rationalized. When we impose suffering and misery on others, we do so through choice—not through necessity. After the fact, perhaps, we can explain away what has been done. But before the fact, we have chosen our course of action.

A trivial, but common enough, example may help clarify some aspects of this discussion. The teacher who isolates himself from his students, who curtly dismisses those in trouble as "stupid" and "worthless," and who prides himself on the high percentage of failures in his classes is behaving in an inhuman fashion. He may rationalize his behavior by pointing to the necessity to do research. The point is, however, that he has chosen from several alternatives the one which he finds self-gratifying. There was no necessity. The dehumanizing use of epithets like "stupid" and "worthless" may be a device protecting the teacher from the moral sense of conscience which his decision implies. "They" are stupid; "I" am wise. "They" are wrong; "I" am right. It is this kind of attitude which the existentialist fights, forcing the individual to see such conceptions of others as a matter of choice and personal responsibility. Sociology also fights such an attitude, but from another vantage point. The analysis of the past reveals, time after time, the social fictions which caught man up and led him into frightfully inhuman acts. And so, sociology and existentialism may have a meeting place after all.

Sociology, by emphasizing the "fictional" nature of much social behavior, provides the basis for seeing human behavior as a "construction." It is not something immutably determined by "human nature" or our genes. The hope exists that, with greater knowledge, man can create social systems which offer greater opportunity for the full expression of human life and consciousness. He can modify the set of fictions which surround him and bind him. But to do so, he must sense the possibility of escape. It is this sense of possibility which existentialist thought offers. Sociology provides the blueprints and plans that show the structure of the prison that contains us. Existentialism presents the possibility, indeed the moral necessity, of an escape into something better.

Sociologists like Peter Berger add a further dimension to sociology. In their hands it becomes not only an instrument for analysis; it takes its place between science and the humanities. It becomes a further means of developing a humanistic perspective. Peter Berger is not willing to let the sociologist say, ''Sociology for the sake of sociology.'' Unless sociology is used for humanity's sake, it is worse than an empty effort. Its use becomes an institutionalized and legitimized form of bad faith.

11 The Science of Culture: The Views of Leslie White

In the movie *Fail Safe* there is a scene in which two pilots for the Strategic Air Command talk about flying as they play billiards in the ready room. Both had flown in World War II and they nostalgically recall the pleasures of flying the old B-17 Fortresses and B-24 Liberators—they were great planes to fly. But modern planes are different, says one of the pilots; the thing about modern military aircraft is that you don't fly them—*they fly you*!

This is a fictional incident, to be sure, but it points to a real and very serious problem—a problem which concerns the humanist and the social scientist of our time. In its simplest form the problem can be stated as follows: To what extent is man becoming the agent rather than the master of his technology? Is technology a product of man's instinctive quest for improvement—a kind of epiphenomenon coming from some innate feeling expressed by the slogan *ad astra per aspera*? Is technology merely an extension of human nature? Or, is our technology, our ambition, our desire, something external to us with a coercive force of its own which drags us in its wake? Do we run our machines or do our machines run us?

This is not a new issue. Humanists have responded to it for years with ideas varying from delight over man's conquest of nature to brooding speculations about the triumph of matter over spirit.[1] Social scientists have also responded in varying ways. The most recent and faddish is to view complex and elaborate technological systems, along with their attendant demands on the social structure, as a sign of "modernization." "Modernization" is a goal which less fortunate countries should be encouraged to seek. Yet another way of

---

[1] Compare, for example, Sandburg's eulogies to Chicago, "Hog Butcher for the World," with E. E. Cummings' castigations of science.

looking at the rise of technology is to see it as something which has come into being despite intense resistance from mankind. It is, therefore, not an expression of man's nature but a force which, in a sense, creates man's nature.

It is in this latter fashion that the American anthropologist Leslie White examines the rise of technology and, more broadly, the entire evolution of human culture. We are wrong, says White, to think that human nature is the determinant of culture. It is quite the reverse; culture is the determinant of human nature. If we wish to understand man, we must understand his culture. To this reasonable—and not especially enlightening statement—he then appends another which seems less reasonable. We understand man by understanding his culture, but we cannot understand culture by studying man.

Culture, a self-generating force

White's work[2] is not distinguished by the novelty of the issues he discusses, nor is it especially distinguished by the conclusions he reaches. But between the statement of the problem and the assertion of an answer is contained one of the liveliest and engaging and, for some, irritating arguments in the literature of social science. These arguments, radically extreme in the opinion of many scholars, nonetheless serve the purpose of providing the student of social behavior with a well-delineated statement of the distinction between man's biological nature and man's cultural nature. What, more specifically, is White's position?

The singularly distinctive feature of White's thought is his constant reiteration of the importance of maintaining the distinction between what an individual is doing and what a culture is doing. We must, White asserts, be certain of our understanding of the difference between culturological and psychological interpretations of human behavior.[3] It has been popular in re-

---

[2] White has published a large number of monographs and articles, most of which are very technical in character. I have leaned heavily, in this chapter, on his two best-known works, *The Science of Culture* (New York: Farrar, Straus & Giroux, Inc., 1949), and *The Evolution of Culture* (New York: McGraw-Hill Book Company, 1959). Both books are attempts to reintroduce an evolutionary perspective into the thinking of the social scientist.

[3] Most, but unfortunately not all, social scientists are aware of the crucial nature of the distinction between social and psychological events. Developing this distinction is, for example, at the heart of Durkheim's thought (see Chapter 2). I have devoted this chapter to Leslie White because, in my estimation, no other writer is so single-mindedly concerned with making others aware of this distinction and its implications. After reading Leslie White, one finds it difficult to continue thinking that human behavior is subsumed by psychological theory and fact. This does not, incidentally, mean that psychology is in error or useless. It only means that psychology is, like any other field, limited in its application. Psychologists are not always easily convinced of this.

cent years to explain anything social or cultural in terms of the psychological make-up of individuals. Thus, war has been claimed to be a product of man's inner pugnacious character.[4] It has been argued that submission to dictatorial regimes is a result of man's deep inner craving for authority, certitude, and security. The institution of private property is merely an expression of natural acquisitive desires. Popular reliance on psychology for an explanation of social behavior has gone so far as to suggest that the prevalent use of Negroes as slaves indicates an instinct for submission among Negro people.[5] This kind of thinking, says White, is wrong and misleading. It is, in fact, dangerously close to being in perfect opposition to what is actually going on. Man does not have a competitive culture because he has a competitive psychological nature; he has a competitive psychological nature because he lives in a competitive culture.[6]

This seems like a circular kind of situation because we can still raise the question: Where did the competitive culture come from? White has a ready reply: It came from itself. The historical process which gave rise to the culture is the source to which we must turn in order to understand why the culture places tremendous emphasis on competition. We cannot understand such competitive spirit merely by saying that it is the nature of men to enjoy competition.

---

[4] White suggests that if man has an inner character relevant to his status as a pugnacious animal, it might be something more akin to cowardice. ". . . in modern nations pugnacity has been 'bred so weakly in our bones and marrow' that every nation has to resort to conscription. And despite such stinging epithets as 'draft dodger,' the number of men who prefer the degradation of prison to the glory of war is considerable. Thus it would appear that the lust for fighting and killing is not over-riding in primates in general or in man in particular." *The Science of Culture*, p. 131.

[5] White attributes this argument to the early 20th-century psychologist William McDougall (1871–1938), who attempted to devise a theory of human behavior based on the idea of instincts. This theory has been generally considered to be inadequate. In its stead psychologists, social psychologists, and other social scientists have relied on the idea of more diffused biological drives which may be satisfied in a variety of ways and which provide the basis for rewarded or "reinforced" behavior of tremendous complexity and variety. White's reference to McDougall appears in *The Science of Culture*, p. 127.

[6] A highly stimulating antidote to this kind of cultural determinism can be found in the writings of Konrad Lorenz. Lorenz argues that the highly aggressive and predatory animals have biologically determined inhibiting mechanisms which prevent them from killing each other. Wolves, even when fighting for mates, do not struggle to the death. The defeated animal will bare its throat to the victor, who makes some menacing gestures and noises but then withdraws to enjoy his conquest. Gentler animals, on the other hand, do not have such built-in inhibitions. When they strike at each other it is usually sufficient protection simply to run away. But, if flight is not available, the results may be more bloody than a fight between predators. Lorenz cites the case of two doves who were left together in a cage overnight. When Lorenz returned in the morning he found the female pecking and picking in the bloody skull of the male she had killed. See Konrad Lorenz, *King Solomon's Ring; New Light on Animal Ways* (New York: Thomas Y. Crowell Company, 1952); also see *On Aggression* (New York: Harcourt, Brace & World, Inc., 1966).

As an illustration of what White is saying, we can refer to football—an institution generally in favor on American campuses and now gaining popularity as a national sport with professional teams. Once one acquires the spirit of the game, it seems almost instinctive to react with excitement and enthusiasm as the quarterback fades to pass the ball to a receiver downfield. Yet, such behavior is quite obviously not instinctive. We have to learn enthusiasm—and it is a long and complicated learning process. Moreover, our enthusiasm is highly localized; we cheer our quarterback but groan with dismay when their quarterback shows signs of carrying the day. We turn out by the thousands to see a big championship play-off; while only a few hundred or so will sit and watch two freshmen teams play a hard-fought battle.

But most of all, the thing that is interesting about this game is the amount of publicity which must be given to it in order to get people excited about it. The game itself has many of the properties of a pagan rite.[7] Nubile young women dance before the crowds in the arena; batons are tossed high into the air; floats are paraded. Martial music is played. A very specialized group of performers attempts to solicit cheers from the fans in the stands.

Some people might suggest that all this is an expression of pent-up hostilities—a way of blowing off steam. But even a modest examination of what is going on raises the possibility that most of the steam being blown off is generated by the football game itself. This would be White's assertion. Football cannot be understood as a psychological event; it must be approached as a cultural event. There is no football instinct. There is, instead, only a socially and culturally supported pattern of behavior which retains its value and its meaning only so long as it has relevance within the greater cultural system.

The process of culture

Let us now look at how White expresses this in his own terms:

> If human behavior is to be explained in terms of culture, how are we to account for culture?
>
> Culture is an organization of phenomena—acts (patterns of behavior), objects (tools; things made with tools), ideas (belief, knowledge), and sentiments (attitudes, "values")—that is dependent upon the use of symbols. Culture began when man as an articulate, symbol-using primate, began. Because of its symbolic character, which has its most important expression in articulate speech, culture is easily and

---

[7] The young editors of an American high school newspaper recently had the temerity to suggest that there are close correspondences between the cheering at high school games and the slogans and chants once roared by Nazi youth groups.

readily transmitted from one human organism to another. Since its elements are readily transmitted culture becomes a continuum; it flows down through the ages from one generation to another and laterally from one people to another. The culture process is also cumulative; new elements enter the stream from time to time and swell the total. The culture process is progressive in the sense that it moves toward greater control over the forces of nature, toward greater security of life for man. Culture is, therefore, a symbolic, continuous, cumulative, and progressive process.[8]

The cultural elements which make up any given culture at a particular point in time are not independent of each other. They exist within a common culture and interact with one another. This suggests that culture has properties unique to it—it is a system *sui generis*.[9] It is a force unto itself.

Invention and innovation

White develops this argument by concentrating on the nature of invention. An invention is, after all, the introduction of something novel into the cultural system. We therefore have the problem of accounting for novelty. As Berger has already pointed out,[10] social and cultural systems tower above the individual and they are essentially conservative—they are resistant to change. How, then, does change come about within the system? The most naive approach to this problem is to claim that invention is a response to human need; to argue that necessity is the mother of invention. This is not sufficient for rather obvious reasons. In the first place, men may long have had a need for certain inventions which their limited cultural milieus prevented them from obtaining. Men could have used the farm tractor long before the 20th century, but their restricted cultural base prevented it from coming into being. More significant, however, is the fact that time after time men have proved to be resistant to innovation, even when later events proved the invention to be generally beneficial, or at least not especially harmful. We are told that

---

[8] Reprinted with the permission of Farrar, Straus & Giroux, Inc., from *The Science of Culture* by Leslie A. White. Copyright 1949 by Leslie A. White. Pp. 139–140. There may be some inconsistency in this statement. White is not certain that current cultural developments are necessarily progressive. Culture has tended to make life more secure for man, but the future course of this tendency is open to speculation.

[9] The term *sui generis* (of its own kind) is often used by White. We saw this same term being used in a slightly different setting in the works of Emile Durkheim (see Chapter 2). This is not an accident. White was very strongly influenced by Durkheim and thought of him more as an anthropologist than sociologist. Some idea of White's devotion to Durkheim can be gleaned from the fact that he introduced three of the fourteen chapters in *The Science of Culture* with lengthy quotations from Durkheim.

[10] See Chapter 10. It is interesting to contrast Berger's approach to social change with that of White. Berger emphasizes a breakdown in the mythology which supports the *status quo*, while White places emphasis on technology. The two points of view are not incompatible—they differ essentially in emphasis.

necessity is the mother of invention. However, men have so often been resistant to something new that it seems more appropriate to claim that invention is the mother of necessity. That is, once the invention has come into
being, people eventually make their peace with it.

This was certainly the case with Darwin's theory of the differentiation of the
species. The Victorian world did not immediately hail this as something wonderful which met the needs of the people.[11] There was a long and bitter fight
culminating in the American comedy of the Scope's Trial.[12] What seemed to
be happening in the case of evolutionary theory was that certain discoveries
and the growth of knowledge led to the point where one or two men became
the focal point for expressing a new concept. Once this concept was introduced into the culture, people had to take it into account and respond to it.
But it did not come into being because there was a general demand for it.
It came into being because the growth of culture had led to the point where
it was a necessary consequence of a cultural system which had reached that
particular level and form of development.

We can set forth two of White's most general principles at this point. The
first is that an invention or innovation will not come into being until the culture base is sufficiently developed to permit its occurrence. This is a self-
evident and not very interesting proposition. We can concede that early man
was not able to invent the rifle because of cultural limitations, even though
he was not lacking in intelligence. We can also presume he would have put
such an invention to good use—that is to say, he had a need for it. Nonetheless, he did not get it because his culture was too limited in scope—the
culture base itself did not permit the rifle to come into being.

The second proposition which White sets forth is much more interesting
and contentious. This proposition asserts that when the culture base has
reached the point where it is capable of supporting a particular invention,
that invention will come into being whether people want it or not. If this is
so, then culture is the force which generates culture. Before the invention of
of the gasoline engine, the possibility of powered, heavier-than-air flight was
impossible. This is in keeping with the first principle mentioned above. However, once the gasoline engine was invented, the development of the airplane
was assured. This is in keeping with the second principle.

Because the second principle is radical in its implications, White concen-

---

[11] See William Irving's *Apes, Angels and Victorians; the Story of Darwin, Huxley and Evolution*
(New York: McGraw-Hill Book Company, 1955) for an interesting account of how people reacted
to Darwinian thought. They did not, in general, take kindly to it.

[12] See J. T. Scopes and James Presley, *The Scopes Trial: Center of the Storm* (New York: Holt,
Rinehart and Winston, Inc., 1967).

trates on developing it. The central historical fact which he utilizes as evidence in support of this principle is the phenomenon of multiple-simultaneous-independent inventions. History is loaded with many surprises when it comes to discovery and invention. We learn in our textbooks that Samuel Morse invented the telegraph.[13] A more serious study reveals that several men share the honors here. The telegraph was invented by Henry, 1831; Morse, 1837; Cooke-Wheatstone, 1837; and Steinheil, 1837. The feud that arose between Newton and Leibnitz over who developed the calculus is a well-worn example of the multiple-simultaneous-independent invention.[14]

History is replete with independent and simultaneous discoveries and inventions. The fact that priority of invention precludes the recurrence of the invention restricts the number of multiple-simultaneous-independent inventions which might have been recorded in history. That is to say, once the Wright Brothers flew an airplane, the job was done. Something can be invented only once. Even in this case, however, it is still legitimate to wonder about who "really" invented the airplane. Langley's attempt, shortly before the successful efforts of the Wright Brothers, failed more from bad luck than bad design.

In any event, the multiple-simultaneous-independent invention is an historical fact. In case there is still some doubt remaining, the following list of such inventions and discoveries, prepared by William Fielding Ogburn, makes interesting reading.[15] The student is encouraged to scan this list and look for

---

[13] Morse was not unfamiliar with Henry's work on the telegraph. Henry seemed to be the more theoretical and basic inventor while Morse, who had also stumbled onto the same idea, moved in the direction of making it commercially feasible. See M. Blow, "Professor Henry and His Philosophical Toys," *American Heritage* (December 1963). The problem of independence of invention is a difficult one in listings of multiple-simultaneous-independent inventions, and the reader is cautioned to investigate in great detail the history of any invention which interests him before coming to some conclusions about who "really" invented it.

[14] Discussing this same topic, Stuart Chase says, "Thus when physics reached a certain point of development in the seventeenth century, a dynamic mathematics was needed to carry on. Whereupon both Leibnitz and Newton invented the calculus independently. If neither had lived, calculus would have been invented by somebody else. History is filled with scores of simultaneous inventions of this kind." Stuart Chase, *The Proper Study of Mankind* (New York: Harper & Row, Publishers, 1948), p. 119. Even so, Newton's name towers above that of Leibnitz. In a recent book on science Newton is mentioned eighteen times; Leibnitz is not mentioned at all. See Jacques Barzun, *Science: The Glorious Entertainment* (New York: Harper & Row, Publishers, 1964).

[15] From *Social Change with Respect to Culture and Original Nature* by William Fielding Ogburn. Copyright 1922 by W. B. Huebsch, Inc., 1950 by William Fielding Ogburn. Reprinted by permission of The Viking Press. The list given here is an abridged version of the one given by Ogburn. However, his original numbering has been retained to indicate the extent to which other multiple inventions have been skipped over. A careful review of this list or, better yet, the one by Ogburn can be an educational experience. The student is encouraged to do more than read these pages in a desultory manner. Both the variety and the extent of inventions which have been made by numerous individuals at the same time force upon the reader greater recognition of the degree to which invention is not a matter of personal idiosyncracy.

inventions like the phonograph and the steamboat—inventions which are often attributed to the inventive genius of a single person.

A LIST OF SOME INVENTIONS AND DISCOVERIES MADE
INDEPENDENTLY BY TWO OR MORE PERSONS

I

1. Solution of the problem of three bodies. By Clairaut (1747), Euler (1747), and D'Alembert (1747).
2. Theory of the figure of the earth. By Huygens (1690), and Newton (1680?).
5. Theory of planetary perturbations. By Lagrange (1808), and Laplace (1808).
8. Law of inverse squares. By Newton (1666), and Halley (1684).
9. Nebular hypothesis. By Laplace (1796), and Kant (1755).
14. First measurement of the parallax of a star. By Bessel (1838), Struve (1838), and Henderson (1838).
16. Certain motions of the moon. By Clairaut (1752), Euler (1752), and D'Alembert (1752).

II

17. Decimal fractions. By Stevinus (1585), Bürgi (1592), Beyer? (1603), and Rüdolff? (1530).
18. Introduction of decimal point. By Bürgi (1592), Pitiscus (1608–12), Kepler (1616), and Napier (1616–17).
20. Logarithms. By Bürgi (1620), and Napier-Briggs (1614).
22. Calculus. By Newton (1671), and Leibnitz (1676).
25. The principle of least squares. By Gauss (1809), and Legendre (1806).
28. Geometry with an axiom contradictory to Euclid's parallel axiom. By Lobatchevsky (1836–40?), Boylais (1826–33), and Gauss? (1829).
30. Method of algebraic elimination by use of determinants and by dialitic method. By Hesse (1842), and Sylvester (1840).
33. Logarithmic criteria for convergence of series. By Abel, De Morgan, Bertrand, Raabe, Duhamel, Bonnet, Paucker (all between 1832–51).
35. Circular slide rule. By Delamain (1630), and Oughtred (1632).
39. The law of quadratic reciprocity. By Gauss (1788–96), Euler (1737), and Legendre (1830).

III

45. Law of gases. By Boyle (1662), and Marriotte (1676).
46. Discovery of oxygen. By Scheele (1774), and Priestley (1774).
48. Method of liquefying gases. By Cailletet, Pictet, Wroblowski, and Olzewski (all between 1877–84).
54. The Periodic Law. First arrangement of atoms in ascending series. By De Chancourtois (1864), Newlands (1864), and Lothar Meyer (1864). Law of periodicity. By Lothar Meyer (1869), and Mendeleeff (1869).

55. Hypothesis as to arrangement of atoms in space. By Van't Hoff (1874), and Le Bel (1874).

59. Discovery of elements of phosphorus. By Brand (1669), Kunckel (1678), and Boyle (1680).

62. Process for reduction of aluminum. By Hall (1886), Héroult (1887), and Cowles (1885).

IV

66. Air gun. By Boyle-Hooke (prior to 1659), and von Guericke (1650).

67. Telescope. Claimed by Lippershey (1608), Della Porta (1558), Digges (1571), Johannides, Metius (1608), Drebbel, Fontana, Janssen (1608), and Galileo (1609).

68. Microscope. Claimed by Johannides, Drebble, and Galileo (1610?).

69. Acromatic lens. By Hall (1729), and Dolland (1758).

71. Spectrum analysis. By Draper (1860), Angstrom (1854), Kirchoff-Bunsen (1859), Miller (1843), and Stokes (1849).

72. Photography. By Daguerre-Niepce (1839), and Talbot (1839).

73. Color photography. By Cros (1869), and Du Hauron (1869).

75. Thermometer. Claimed by Galileo (1592–97?), Drebbel? (1608), Sanctorious (1612), Paul (1617), Fludd (1617), von Guericke, Porta (1606), De Caus (1615).

76. Pendulum clock. Claimed by Bürgi (1575), Galileo (1582), and Huygens (1656).

78. Ice calorimeter. By Lavoisier-Laplace (1780), and Black-Wilke.

81. Kinetic theory of gases. By Clausius (1850), and Rankine (1850).

84. Principle of dissipation of energy. By Carnot? (1824), Clausius (1850), and Thomson (1852).

87. Apparent concentration of cold by concave mirror. By Porta (1780–91?), and Pictet (1780–91?).

89. Parallelogram of forces. By Newton (1687), and Varignon (1725?).

93. Law of inertia. By Galileo, Huygens, and Newton (1687).

V

96. Leyden jar. By von Kleist (1745), and Cuneus (1746).

97. Discovery of animal electricity. By Sultzer (1768), Cotuguo (1786), Galvani (1791).

98. Telegraph. Henry (1831), Morse (1837), Cooke-Wheatstone (1837), and Steinheil (1837).

99. Electric motors. Claimed by Dal Negro (1830), Henry (1831), Bourbonze and McGawley (1835).

100. Electric railroad. Claimed by Davidson, Jacobi, Lilly-Colton (1847), Davenport (1835), Page (1850), and Hall (1850–01).

104. Method of converting lines engraved on copper into relief. By Jacobi (1839), Spencer (1839), and Jordan (1839).

106. Microphone. Hughes (1878), Edison (1877–78), Berliner (1877), and Blake (1878?).

107. The phonograph. By Edison (1877), Scott? and Cros (1877).

108. Self-exciting dynamo. Claimed by Hjorth (1866–67), Varley (1866–67),

Siemens (1866–67), Wheatstone (1866–67), Ladd (1866), and Wilde (1863–67).

109. Incandescent electric light. Claimed by Starr (1846), and Jobard-de Clangey (1838).

110. Telephone. By Bell (1876), and Gray (1876).

VI

114. Theory of infection of microörganisms. By Fracastoro (1546), and Kircher.

116. That the skull is made of modified vertebrae. By Goethe (1790), and Oken (1776).

121. Solution of the problem of respiration. By Priestley (1777), Scheele (1777), Lavoisier (1777), Spallanzani (1777), and Davy (1777).

123. Relation of microörganisms to fermentation and putrefaction. By Latour (1837), and Schwann (1837).

124. Pepsin as the active principle of gastric juice. By Latour (1834), and Schwann (1835).

125. Prevention of putrefaction of wounds by keeping germs from surface of wound. By Lister (1867), and Guerin (1871).

127. Invention of the laryngoscope. By Babington (1829), Liston (1837), and Garcia (1855).

128. Sulphuric ether as an anaesthetic. By Long (1842), Robinson (1846), Liston (1846), Morton (1846), and Jackson (1846).

129. That all appendages of a plant are modified leaves. By Goethe (1790), and Wolfe (1767).

VII

130. Theory of inheritance of acquired characteristics. By E. Darwin (1794), and Lamarck (1801).

131. Theory of natural selection and variation. By C. Darwin (1858), and Wallace (1858).

133. Theory of mutations. By Korschinsky (1899), and DeVries (1900).

135. Theory of color. By Young (1801), and Helmholz.

136. Sewing machine. By Thimmonier (1830), Howe (1846), and Hunt (1840).

137. Balloon. By Montgolfier (1783), Rittenhouse-Hopkins (1783).

138. Flying machine. Claimed by Wright (1895–1901), Langley (1893–97), and others.

139. Reapers. By Hussey (1833), and McCormick (1834).

140. Double-flanged rail. By Stephens and Vignolet.

141. Steamboat. Claimed by Fulton (1807), Jouffroy, Rumsey, Stevens, and Symmington (1802).

144. Typewriter. Claimed by Beach (1847–56), Sholes? (1875), and Wheatstone (1855–60).

146. Stereoscope. By Wheatstone (1839), and Elliott (1840).

147. Centrifugal pumps. By Appold (1850), Gwynne (1850), and Bessemer (1850).

148. Use of gasoline engines in automobiles. By Otto (1876), Daimler (1885), and Selden (1879?).

The role of the "great man"

White sees in this list the crucial documentation for his claim that culture is the cause of culture. We do not require great men to lead us upward toward progress. We require, rather, an extensive cultural base to turn the trick. If we have that base, inventions and discoveries will take place with such force that they will appear at various points in the culture and at the same time. When culture is ready for an invention, that invention will come into being, even though there is no general desire for it within the greater society.[16] This observation forms the foundation for White's position with respect to the role of the great man in the progress of history.

> Briefly stated, the problem is this: are epoch-making social and historical events to be explained in terms of men of genius, or are great men explainable in terms of social process and historical trends? Or, do both, the great man and his social matrix, combine to produce the event or trend, and if so in what proportions?

> Most of those who have wrestled with this problem have championed either the great man or society as the motive force, as the cause, the other being regarded as the effect; few have been willing to give equal, or even approximately equal, weight to each factor. Let it be said at once that we have no intention of being "impartial" and of taking the latter course. We are convinced that the great man is best understood as an effect or manifestation rather than as a prime mover.[17]

Oppin.o.
{ of
{ whi

White subordinates the man of genius to culture. In doing this he does not disparage the great men of the past. He recognizes that they have made con- tributions to progress and he concedes that they have behaved intelligently. He is, however, concerned with pulling us away from the diffused inclination to worship heroes in any field of endeavor—a cultural innovation that probably has its origins in the rise of individualism in the late 14th and early 15th cen-

---

[16] There is a problem here in determining what is meant when we say there is no desire or need for an invention or innovation. A vast majority of individuals probably had no desire for or even any conception of the possibility of Darwinian theories of evolution in the 1830s or 1840s. We are on rather firm ground, it would appear, when we claim in this case that there was no general need which brought the innovation into existence. On the other hand, the classic illustration of the atomic bomb is not so simple. No single individual had a need for such a device—and even its developers were appalled by the thought of it as they worked around the clock to bring it into being. But the bomb had an obvious utility for the waging of war; it was culturally necessary. Something can be needed by a culture and not be needed by most, or possibly all, of the people in that culture. This can extend to the point where the demands of a culture may prove lethal to the biological welfare of individuals. In reading White, at times one must pay close attention to the very specific and individualistic meaning he gives to the term "need."

[17] *The Science of Culture*, p. 190.

turies[18]—and he concentrates on the cultural context within which the great man was acting.[19]

The subordination of the man of genius to culture is achieved, in White's arguments, by his conception of invention. White defines an invention as a synthesis of existing cultural elements. For example, the invention of the steamboat was a matter of bringing together, or synthesizing, the boat and the steam engine. The invention of the airplane was a matter of synthesizing the glider and the gasoline engine. White is not always flattering in his comments on the inventive process. At one point he says,

> A consideration of many significant inventions and discoveries does not lead to the conclusion that great ability, native or acquired, is always necessary. On the contrary, many seem to need only mediocre talents at best. What intelligence was required to invent the steamboat? Is great intelligence required to put one and one—a boat and an engine—together? An ape can do this.[20]

When we have two traits existing in a culture, the possibility of their synthesis exists. If the synthesis is realized and if it proves useful in some fashion, then it is incorporated into the cultural stream and becomes itself a trait which may be synthesized with something else. For this reason, cultural growth has an exponential or geometric character about it. By this we mean that culture growth reveals a kind of snowballing effect—it is ever more rapid. This exponential growth of culture has taken place while men have remained essentially the same in biological character and intelligence. We cannot explain cultural change, then, in terms of something which has remained constant. Therefore, we must turn to something other than man. The only other thing left to turn to is culture itself.

---

[18] Hero worship has a long and general history, of course. I am referring here to the extension of such worship into fields such as art, intellectualism, etc.

[19] Herbert Muller has the following to say about Leslie White: "[The importance of the individual] was therefore most thoroughly discredited by anthropologists. He [the individual] served only to transmit the culture they studied, which was ready-made, intact, complete; they explicitly denied him any measure of independence, or of genuine individuality, by declaring that he was wholly a product of his culture. Even genius, according to Leslie White, is one 'in whose neuro-sensory-glandular-etc. system an important synthesis of cultural events has taken place'; culture somehow did all the work by itself (as one supposes it wrote the book to which White carelessly signed his own name)." Herbert J. Muller, *Freedom in the Modern World* (New York: Harper & Row, Publishers, 1966), p. 222. This is a clever, but unfair indictment of White. White is thoroughly aware of the effects of individual eccentricity and accident in shaping the course of history and he discusses it at length.

[20] *The Science of Culture*, p. 212. White, in his general works, writes with an unencumbered, blunt expressiveness. It makes for delightful reading, but it also calls for a willingness not to condemn him on minor points—after all, an ape could not invent a steamboat, despite White's claim to the contrary.

The exponential character of cultural growth

There is a property of culture, however, which forces us to qualify the exponential growth idea. Such growth will take place until certain limits are reached. After all, the mathematical properties of exponential growth systems are such that one can reach infinite quantities within a finite period of time—and this is certainly impractical as well as impossible in the real world. What constitutes the constraining force in the exponential development of culture? White suggests that the constraining limits are imposed by a theme which operates as the unifying premise of a culture. Once the culture has exhausted the potentialities of the theme on which it is based, it either reaches a static level or it establishes a new theme.

> . . . The development of geometry upon the basis of the axioms of Euclid had limits that were inherent in the system or pattern. A certain musical pattern reached its culmination or fulfillment apparently in the works of Bach, Mozart, and Beethoven. Gothic art as a pattern was inherently limited. Ptolemy carried the development of a certain type of astronomic system about as far as was possible. All cultural development takes place within organized forms, or patterns . . . when a pattern has reached the limits of its potentialities no further development is possible. The alternatives then are slavish repetition of old patterns or the revolutionary overthrow of the old and the formation of new patterns.[21]

White sees an interaction between culture patterns or themes and the great individual. Greatness is, in White's thinking, dependent to a large extent on the accident of timing. If one is born after a pattern has reached its apex and is in a state of decline, one's chances of distinction are slight. But, if fortune places one somewhere along a developing pattern, then the likelihood of achieving distinction is much greater. To be a genius requires more than brains and talent. As White puts it: "To become a genius it is necessary to be born at precisely the right time."[22]

Despite the limiting effects of patterns or themes in a culture, the development of culture when seen from a geological and world perspective has been essentially an exponential one. The reasoning here is relatively simple. Cultural accumulation is such that any item of absolute knowledge which comes into the culture becomes a factor promoting the further development of the

---

[21] *The Science of Culture*, pp. 215–216. The classical expression of this argument, in anthropological literature, is Ruth Benedict's *Patterns of Culture* (Boston: Houghton Mifflin Company, 1934). Benedict examined three primitive cultures and found that in each the various life-ways of the culture corresponded with a basic theme which permeated the culture. It should be mentioned here that there is considerable controversy among students of culture over the issue of whether or not cultures are "patterned."

[22] *The Science of Culture*, p. 218.

culture. More significantly, it increases the possible permutations and combinations available for further innovation. Suppose, for the moment, we have a culture in which inventions consist simply of bringing two traits together to form a third. Thus, $A + B = C$. If we have only two traits to begin with, we can produce only one invention. But if we have three, we can produce three new inventions: $A + B$, $A + C$, and $B + C$. If we have four traits, we can produce six new inventions: $A + B$, $A + C$, $A + D$, $B + C$, $B + D$, and $C + D$. As the number of traits increases, the possible number of new inventions increases more rapidly. This is expressed in the following formula for combinations taken two at a time where N represents the number of existing traits or elements in the culture.

$$\text{Number of possible new inventions} = \frac{N(N-1)}{2}$$

The following graph shows the possible number of inventions given an existing cultural base of N elements. This assumes, again, that the inventions consist of a simple combination of any two existing traits.

HYPOTHETICAL RELATIONSHIP OF POSSIBLE
INVENTIONS TO CULTURE BASE

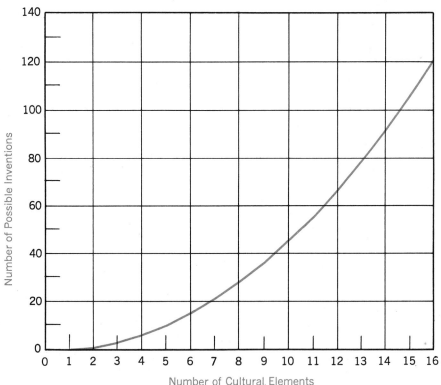

Number of Possible Inventions

Number of Cultural Elements

We have gone to the effort of developing this simple theme in order to bring home a more basic point—a point which is at the heart of White's argument and which is the motivating force behind it. A glance at the graph reveals a relationship between cultural innovation and the culture base *and excludes all other considerations!* Inventions or innovations are seen to be a function of the culture base. There is no need to include such biological or psychological concepts as drive, aspiration, genius, talent, ambition, altruism, greatness, or anything else. Culture is being used to explain or account for itself in terms that are extra-individualistic. White argues that we must not go down to the level of the individual to explain culture, but instead deal with culture in terms that are relevant to culture. This does not mean that culture exists without human beings; obviously it does not and cannot, at least at present. But we can understand culture without having to delve into psychology, just as we can understand the structure of language without having to take a course in cellular biology.

The formula and graph oversimplify the process, of course. They are merely devices for representing geometric progressions. In actual cultural systems we are confronted with the fact that many inventions are more than the synthesis or combination of two existing traits. We are also confronted with the fact that innumerable combinations of traits, while theoretically possible, are nonetheless meaningless or impractical. Only in our imagination will we combine a music stand with a mousetrap. Even so, some combinations, while seemingly silly, may nonetheless be given serious consideration. I am thinking, for example, of current serious efforts to combine the airplane with the submarine. Modern technology may permit a combination of elements which previously seemed out of the question.

The act of invention, once the mysterious realm of the Quixotic genius, has been reduced more and more to a commonplace event. The story, possibly apocryphal, is told about David Sarnoff who, on some occasion, brought his engineers together and informed them that television was an established fact—and so was the tape recorder. For his birthday he wanted to watch a tape-recorded television program. According to the story, Sarnoff watched a tape-recorded television program on his birthday. In this instance, the combination was apparent and was achieved in a more calculated fashion than has been the case in the past. Only since World War II have we very consciously and rationally invested heavy amounts of time and money in the act of promoting cultural progression. The question remains open, however, whether this investment will pay off. It might, as some intellectuals are beginning to wonder, bring about a degree of cultural development that will outstrip man's ability to adjust to his own creations.

So far we have concentrated on White's view that culture is a self-generating force which is evolutionary in character. White claims that culture should be understood in terms of its own dynamics—we must not resort to psychological explanations of cultural events.

"Come now," we can hear the humanist reply, "Do you mean to say that the Great Man does not affect the course of history and political events? How can we hope to understand a happening like the Civil War without resorting to judgments concerning the psychological and even moral character of the men who occupied positions of importance and authority?" This is a vexing question and White is well aware of its existence. He replies by suggesting that many social scientists are incapable of making the distinction between temporal processes and temporal-formal processes.

> The temporal process, or "history," is a chronological series of events each of which is unique. We separate these events, by conceptual analysis, from their matrix of the totality of events. The temporal-formal, or evolutionist, process is a series of events in which both time and form are equally significant: one form grows out of another in time.[23]

Temporal and temporal-formal processes

This distinction, which White has some difficulty making and maintaining,[24] really centers on the way in which we define our mode of cultural analysis. If we define it in a narrow microhistorical or temporal fashion, the role of accident as an influential factor is increased. If we take a macrohistorical approach—or evolutionist, as White would put it—the influence of accident grows smaller and smaller.

At the temporal level we must concede that Lee Harvey Oswald is a significant figure in history—even though he lacked the knowledge, power, and wealth of men who were far above him in social rank. Accidents and such unpredictable events, as genius, power, eccentricity, talent, and the like are intermeshed at the temporal level; to try to ascertain which is important and which is not becomes impossible. White states it nicely:

> But in the succession of chance occurrences that is history, the individual may be enormously significant. But it does not follow at all that he is therefore a "genius" or a person of exceptional ability. The goose who saved Rome was more significant historically than many an emperor who ruled it.[25]

---

[23] *Ibid.*, p. 229.

[24] It is worth noting that in illustrating the temporal process White resorts to an historical accident, Booth's assassination of Lincoln—an unpredictable event. But when he illustrates the temporal-formal process he turns to a physical example—the decomposition of a radioactive substance.

[25] *The Science of Culture*, p. 230.

When culture is viewed more generally as an evolutionary process, however, accidents seem to have balanced out or been reduced in their effects. The argument is purely hypothetical, but White would evidently be inclined to assert that space-age culture would have been achieved regardless of the vicissitudes of specific history. Not only would we have had the airplane had the Wright Brothers never lived; we would have passed through feudal into industrial and now welfare economies and societies if Europe had never existed.

It is in this sense that we must consider the formal properties of the cultural process without getting bogged down in the specific incidents which seem important but which, in fact, prevent us from obtaining a broader conception of human evolution. When we are able to view culture as a self-generating force and, moreover, as an evolutionary formal process, we are freed from the problem of determining what specific incident and what individual was "important" or "great."

The last question we will raise here is to ask where this temporal-formal process is leading. White does not have much to say about this. Culture could destroy man or carry him to greater heights. Technology will become more complex and great quantities of energy will be harnessed by the cultural process. Without making very specific predictions, White nonetheless argues that the study of culture, as he views it, is necessary for transcending the current limits of our ignorance about this force.

> If our ability to predict were greatly increased by the development and maturation of a science of culture the possibilities of a rational, effective, and humane adjustment between man and culture and between one cultural segment and another would be increased accordingly. If, for example, a science of culture could demonstrate that the trend of social evolution is toward larger political groupings, then the chances of making the futile attempt to restore or maintain the independence of small nations would be lessened. If the trend of cultural evolution is away from private property and free enterprise why strive to perpetuate them? If it could be shown that international wars will continue as long as independent, sovereign nations exist, then certain delusions now popular would find less nourishment and support. The fact is that culture has been evolving as an unconscious, blind, bloody, brutal, tropismatic process so far. It has not yet reached the point where intelligence, self-consciousness, and understanding are very conspicuous. Our ignorance is still deep-rooted and widespread. We do not understand even some of the most elementary things—the prohibition of polygamy for example. In short, we are so ignorant that we can still believe that it is we who make our culture and control its course.[26]

This is a strong plea for rationality in cultural affairs—a plea to recognize the importance and the true nature of cultural influences. It is a call to explore

---

[26] *The Science of Culture*, pp. 355–356.

the implications of the fact that man is a cultural being. It is also a very "iffy" statement. After pointing the way, White seems to tell us to continue in that direction and, with a great deal of luck, we might get to wherever it is we want to go. White provides us with a widespread view of the past—history is transformed into units of geological scope and we begin to recognize culture as a very real element in the evolutionary process. In the beginning was matter; then came that mysterious step that led to the long and enchanting process of the evolution of living forms. Then came the equally magical step that brought into being the arduous, tangled, and continuous process that has culminated in modern forms of culture.

Although White, and the field of anthropology generally, offer us a grand vision of the past, they hedge when it comes to the future. Yet the problem of predicting the future is important. Unless the examination of culture can help us in this effort, says White, it is a very pure science indeed—without any application of significance.

Cultural progression and the future

What does White's thought suggest with respect to the future of man? Here we shall extrapolate beyond the writings of White and sketch a possibility which his line of reasoning seems to suggest. White might disagree with the following paragraphs, but they are in keeping with the main themes of a radical cultural deterministic position.

The most extreme extension of White's thinking suggests a movement toward a transference of the evolution of culture from man to machine. The cultural process, which consists mainly of the synthesizing of existing elements, is even now gradually being removed from the minds and hands of men and transferred to modern thoughtful machines. Granted, these machines are not adept at the procedure as yet; and granted, we can still pull the plug on them if we are dissatisfied with their work. We can further grant that they work in a mechanical and unimaginative way—but then we have given them only ten or twelve years of practice and development.

There may yet come a time when we will look back on the past and reminisce about the days when man and his culture were organically related, and culture and man were only different sides of the same coin. The prospect for the future could be one in which men are mechanically related to culture and understand very little of it. The process of alienation, so significant in Marxian thought, may take a new form. Man may not only find himself removed from the product of his work and removed from much of what his culture has to offer—simply because the content of that culture has become so massive; he may also find himself removed from the containers of that culture. The time may be close at hand when the leading containers of culture will no longer be human intellectuals—narrowed by specialization and subject to the limitations of emotion and meager knowledge—but the thoughtful machine. The intellectual will be relegated to the status of a keeper of stored information whose nature and meaning will remain a mystery to him.[27]

This, admittedly, is a far-out though not especially novel speculation. Moreover, it is based on a theoretical position in anthropology which is, itself, a very radical argument. But perhaps the important thing is not to be concerned with the accuracy of such prognostications, but to be concerned with the form and the sentiment of this consideration of the future.

White views man as the neurological locus of culture—as the "lightning rod" through which the forces of culture conduct themselves. If the cultural process stands at the apex of evolutionary development,[28] and if the cultural process can be transformed to nonhuman agents, then what does the future hold in store for man? We do not know. We can only speculate. Even if we had every reason to conclude that such speculation was perfectly accurate, would we be able to alter the course of cultural progression and regain man's former place in nature—whatever it might have been? The answer is obvious and, at the same time, one which makes White's position appear more reasonable than we might, as humanists, wish it were.[29]

---

[27] A colleague of mine recently informed me that a computer programmer has been designated to act as the head of the research organization for which my colleague works. Perhaps a knowledge of content or meaning is becoming less significant than a knowledge of how to process data.

[28] Any evolutionist will dodge when one starts engaging in teleological arguments about the "purpose" of evolution. Neither White nor I would claim that human culture is the goal toward which evolution has been working for millions of years. However, it does stand, at this moment, at the end of the evolutionary process on this planet. We can, therefore, act *as if* culture were at the apex of evolutionary development for the purpose of speculating a little about the future.

[29] The matter has been interestingly expressed in a recent article in a popular magazine. "Eventually, Professor Minsky believes, the machines will be programed for self-improvement; they will get better and better of their own accord; then they will unquestionably display the traits we refer to as intelligence, intuition and consciousness, and the world will never again be the same. Will they be man's equal or even his superior? Dr. George Feeney of General Electric says, 'I think we'll get to the point where that question won't really matter. The humanists, if optimists, will say that the machine is an extension of man—and the realists, if pessimists, will say that man is an extension of the machine.' " From *Playboy* magazine (October 1967), p. 210.

There is still hope. I recently discussed this matter with a computer expert who told me about a little publicized feature of computers. It is well known that computers can handle increasingly heavy work loads; what is less well known is that the time it takes for the computer to break down has been declining. While earlier models did not reach the point of critical failure until after several days of operation, some modern computers fail to operate properly after being run for a few hours.

12 The Crisis of Our Age: The Views of Pitirim A. Sorokin

Professor Pitirim Sorokin is probably the most prolific and controversial of modern sociological writers. Few sociologists have been referred to with such a diversity of terms as "Old Testament prophet,"[1] "severe and sarcastic,"[2] "renowned,"[3] "bullheaded,"[4] "moderate,"[5] "unexcelled powers of penetration,"[6] and "philosophic."[7] Friendly or unfriendly, the readers and critics of the works of Sorokin[8] are forced to recognize the incredible energy, imagina-

---

[1] David R. Mace says, "The book [Sorokin's *The American Sex Revolution*] does, indeed, convey the atmosphere of grave concern and urgent warning that we find in the writings of some of the Old Testament prophets." See *Pitirim A. Sorokin in Review*, edited by Philip J. Allen (Durham, N.C.: Duke University Press, 1963), p. 141.

[2] Alexandre Vexliard in *Pitirim A. Sorokin in Review*, p. 179.

[3] Lucio Mendieta y Nuñez in *Pitirim A. Sorokin in Review*, p. 319.

[4] Sorokin cites some of his critics as claiming him to be idiosyncratic, bullheaded, and deviationist. See *Pitirim A. Sorokin in Review*, p. 35.

[5] Arnold J. Toynbee in *Pitirim A. Sorokin in Review*, p. 73.

[6] Othmar F. Anderle in *Pitirim A. Sorokin in Review*, p. 121.

[7] Joseph B. Ford in *Pitirim A. Sorokin in Review*, p. 39.

[8] An incomplete listing of Sorokin's works covers ten pages of printed material. We cannot list the nearly forty books and several hundred editorials and essays he has published. Among his more important works we can mention *Leaves from a Russian Diary* (New York: E. P. Dutton & Co., Inc., 1924); *Sociology of Revolution* (Philadelphia: J. B. Lippincott Company, 1925); *Social Mobility* (New York: Harper & Row, Publishers, 1927); *Contemporary Sociological Theories* (New York: Harper & Row, Publishers, 1928); *A Systematic Source Book in Rural Sociology*, with C. C. Zimmerman and C. J. Galpin, 3 vols. (Minneapolis: University of Minnesota Press, 1930–1932); *Social and Cultural Dynamics*, 4 vols. (New York: American Book Company, 1937–1941); *Crisis of Our Age* (New York: E. P. Dutton & Co., Inc., 1941); *Man and Society in Calamity* (New York: E. P. Dutton & Co., Inc., 1942); *Sociocultural Causality, Space, Time* (Durham, N.C.: Duke University Press, 1943); *Russia and the United States* (New York: E. P. Dutton & Co., Inc., 1944); *Society, Culture and Personality* (New York: Harper & Row, Publishers, 1947); *The Reconstruction of Humanity* (Boston: Beacon Press, 1948); *Altruistic Love: A Study of American Good Neighbors and Christian Saints* (Boston: Beacon Press, 1950); *Social Philosophies of an Age of Crisis* (Boston: Beacon Press, 1950); *S. O. S.: The Meaning of Our Crisis* (Boston: Beacon Press, 1951); *The Ways and Power of Love* (Boston: Beacon Press, 1954); *Fads and Foibles in Modern Sociology and Related Sciences* (Chicago: Henry Regnery Company, 1956); *The American Sex Revolution* (Boston: Porter Sargent, Publisher, 1957); *A Long Journey:*

tiveness, and involvement of the man who wrote them. Two colleagues paid Sorokin a tribute which, I believe, aptly sums up the quality and extent of his work. They wrote,

> We can, in fact, imagine that the sociologist of the future may well complain, much as a frustrated successor to Plato once did, "Whenever I go anywhere in my attempts, I meet Sorokin coming back."[9]

Sorokin's life career spanned nearly two-thirds of the 20th century. It was a career marked by adventure, controversy, astounding scholarly productivity, and laudatory recognition from professional societies and the general public. He was born in northern Russia in 1889.[10] In 1918, during the Bolshevist revolution, he was arrested and thrown into prison. Of this experience he commented, at the time,

> Well . . . I have been a prisoner of the Czar and now I am a prisoner of the Communists. From this varied experience I should emerge a practical as well as a theoretical criminologist.[11]

He was released, again imprisoned, and awaited execution. He was, however, released by order of Lenin.[12] In 1922 he left Russia, and in 1923 he arrived in America to begin life anew. He quickly attracted students and continued to write at a pace which, as he noted, enabled him to accomplish in three or four years an amount of publication which many sociologists would be happy to leave behind as a lifetime's effort.

Sorokin's view of cultural patterns

The fantastic richness and variety of his personal experiences, his Russian background and training, and his migration to another land and another academic setting made Sorokin a person ill inclined to accept provincial or narrow conceptions of humanity. The work for which he is most famous in this country is his four-volume investigation of cultural patterns entitled *Social and Cultural Dynamics*.[13] It is a work that attempts to take in the changing patterns of human societies and cultures across the globe and down the reaches of historical time. It is a work that has been held by some to be too vast in

---

An Autobiography (New Haven, Conn.: College & University Press, 1963). This is only a partial listing. The more complete list from which this partial listing was taken can be found in *Pitirim A. Sorokin in Review*, pp. 497–506. Even this partial listing makes one aware that to read the entire works of Sorokin would, in itself, constitute quite a sociological education.

[9] Matilda White Riley and Mary E. Moore in *Pitirim A. Sorokin in Review*, p. 224.

[10] Sorokin, *A Long Journey*, p. 11.

[11] Pitirim A. Sorokin, *A Long Journey: An Autobiography* (New Haven, Conn.: College & University Press, 1963), p. 142.

[12] *Ibid.*, p. 171.

[13] It is recommended that the student read *The Crisis of Our Age* before turning to the four-volume work.

scope to yield valid or worthwhile results. It has also been criticized because of its obvious contempt for the "sensate" character of modern civilization. Yet, granting its strengths and limitations, it is a powerful and intriguing work. It is, to use Sorokin's own term, one of his most fascinating "yarns."[14]

Sorokin makes use of the fact that if we examine in a comprehensive way the culture and society of any people at any time, we begin to acquire a sense, however vague, of a relationship between the disparate parts of the culture. Mythology, art, law, philosophy, morality, family structure, the conduct of war, architecture, music, religion, economics, sense of time, logic, science, mathematics, humor, and leisure pursuits seem to be associated with each other. For example, in a culture such as ours, where affairs of the market place appear to be dominant, a wide variety of cultural habits and practices are related in their mutual support of the business ethic.[15] The cultural practices of the Pueblo Indians, on the other hand, appear to be related to religious practices and concepts associated with the problem of bringing rain to an arid land.[16] Sorokin makes the problem very clear,

> Is every culture an integrated whole, where no essential part is incidental but each is organically connected with the rest? Or is it a mere spatial congeries of cultural objects, values, traits, which have drifted fortuitously together and are united only by their spatial adjacency, just by the fact that they are thrown together, and by nothing more? If it is the first, then what is the principle of integration, the axis around which all the essential characteristics are centered and which explains why these characteristics are what they are and why they live and pulsate as they do? If the second, then how did it happen that in a given area one kind of conglomeration of cultural objects and values took place, while in another area a different kind occurred? How and why did it happen that in the course of time one conglomeration moved in one direction while another changed in a way that was wholly diverse?[17]

Sorokin approaches this problem by presuming that a culture will be profoundly affected by the manner in which it defines the nature of reality. Such definitions are pervasive and may, as a consequence, influence a great variety of behavior ranging from art and leisure to law and science. As Sorokin views it, there are two approaches to reality. We may, on the one hand, think of that which we can sense through our bodily organs as illusory—the real reality

---

[14] In the conclusion of his autobiography Sorokin says, "Therefore I scarcely have reason to complain of being 'a forgotten man' or a 'has-been scholar.' If anything, the world seems to be paying my 'yarns' attention far beyond their merit." See A Long Journey, p. 319.

[15] Henry discusses this matter at some length. See the next chapter.

[16] Ruth Benedict, Patterns of Culture (Boston: Houghton Mifflin Company, 1934). Sorokin cites Benedict but disagrees with some of her conclusions.

[17] Pitirim A. Sorokin, Social and Cultural Dynamics (New York: American Book Company, 1937–1941), Vol. 1, p. 3. Extracts from this work are reprinted by permission of the estate of the late Pitirim A. Sorokin. (Reprinted by The Bedminster Press, Inc., Totowa, N.J., 1962.)

is held to be supersensory or spiritual.[18] The other approach to reality is to limit it as much as possible to that which is immediately apparent to the senses.

Ideational versus Sensate culture

To locate reality within the supersensory or spiritual realm is characteristic of what Sorokin calls the *Ideational mentality* or the *Ideational culture*. To locate reality within that which can be sensed directly through our organs of perception is characteristic of *Sensate mentality* or *Sensate culture*. The concepts of Ideational and Sensate cultures become the core terms whereby Sorokin is able to explore further the problem of the integrity of cultures. Ideational and Sensate culture mentalities are the axes around which various essential characteristics of the culture are centered. Sorokin states his case clearly in the preface to the second volume of *Social and Cultural Dynamics*:

> When a culture passes from, say, the Ideational to the Sensate type, or vice versa, all its art, philosophy, religion, science, ethics, and law undergo the same profound transformation. From this standpoint . . . what a given society regards as true or false, scientific or unscientific, right or wrong, lawful or unlawful, beautiful or ugly, is conditioned fundamentally by the nature of the dominant culture. In the Ideational culture, Ideational science, philosophy, religion, law, ethics, and art triumph, and their Sensate forms are rejected as false, wrong, unlawful, sinful, heretical, and blasphemous. Contrariwise, in a dominant Sensate culture—such as we are now living in—Sensate forms of science, philosophy, religion, ethics, law, and art become dominant; and their Ideational forms are branded as superstition, prejudice, ignorance and the like.[19]

Before applying the concepts of Sensate and Ideational culture mentalities to more specific features of society, we should expand them further. The following comparison, in brief, presents some of the significant differences between the two types of mentality.[20]

---

[18] A very dramatic insight into this kind of mentality is offered by Herman Melville. Captain Ahab says of Moby Dick, " 'Hark ye yet again,—the little lower layer. All visible objects, man, are but as pasteboard masks. But in each event—in the living act, the undoubted deed—there, some unknown but still reasoning thing puts forth the mouldings of its features from behind the unreasoning mask. If man will strike, strike through the mask! How can the prisoner reach outside except by thrusting through the wall? To me, the white whale is that wall, shoved near to me. Sometimes I think there's naught beyond. But 'tis enough. He tasks me; he heaps me; I see in him outrageous strength, with an inscrutable malice sinewing it. That inscrutable thing is chiefly what I hate; and be the white whale agent, or be the white whale principal, I will wreak that hate upon him.' . . . 'God keep me!—keep us all!' murmured Starbuck, lowly." From Herman Melville, *Moby Dick*.

[19] Sorokin, *Social and Cultural Dynamics*, Vol. 2, p. vii.

[20] Sorokin, *Social and Cultural Dynamics*, Vol. 1, pp. 97–99. The comparison presented here is a highly modified and very abbreviated version of the one presented by Sorokin. Sorokin includes in his discussion a cultural mentality type that is between the Ideational and the Sensate type. He calls this an "Idealistic" system. I have, in the interests of brevity, omitted this middle category.

IDEATIONAL CULTURE MENTALITY	SENSATE CULTURE MENTALITY
1. Reality is seen as eternal, spiritual, and transcendental to the senses.	Reality is seen as located in material "things." It is immediately apparent to the senses.
2. The main needs of the individual are spiritual. Physical desires are curbed.	The primary needs of man are physical. Sensory indulgence and gratification should be maximized.
3. "Progress" is achieved through self-control.	"Progress" is achieved through control of the external milieu.
4. There is belief in "Being," and an indifference to transient values.	There is belief in "Becoming." Values are transient. There is endless readjustment.
5. The sensual man and self are repressed.	People are dedicated to "self-expression" and to sensual fulfillment.
6. People are introvertive and subjective in character.	People are extrovertive and objective in character.
7. Truth is based on mystical inner experience. Intuition, faith, and revelation are used.	Truth is based on observation, measurement, and experimentation. Logic is used.
8. The moral code is imperative, everlasting, and unchangeable.	Morals are relativistic, changeable, and oriented toward the provision of pleasure and happiness.
9. Art is symbolic and directed toward religious values.	Art is directed toward entertainment.

Sorokin stacks the deck in his distinction between the two kinds of culture mentalities by including in his definition of the mentalities some of the characteristics he intends to explain with them. This is like defining a priestly mentality as one which abstains from marriage and then explaining priestly celibacy by saying it is a product of priestly mentality. But this is a criticism that dotes too much, perhaps, on the technical problems of explanation. If we grant the validity of this criticism, it still does not seriously detract from the vision Sorokin offers us. To comprehend this vision, let us take the culture mentalities and apply them to a specific concern—the ethical and moral structure of societies. It is in these applications that Sorokin displays best the orchestral nature of his scholarship.

Ethics under Ideationalism and Sensatism

A culture which is dominated by an Ideational mentality has a particular form of ethical system. In such a culture ethics cannot be placed in the service of promoting sensual happiness, comfort, pleasure, or utility. These conditions are imaginary or illusory and therefore cannot be the final concern of Ideational ethics. Medieval Christianity from the 5th to the 13th centuries typified a culture dominated by Ideational ethics. The summons of the monastery was a call to better things, and to all men the monastic life represented the highest goal on this earth.[21] Sorokin states,

> Seclusion from the world, holiness, devotion of the whole life to God, the vows of obedience, poverty, chastity; contempt, often torture, of the flesh; suppression of carnal needs—these were the traits of monastic Ideational ethics, whether for hermits or for monks living in monasteries . . . Monasticism and asceticism compose the main pattern of the medieval ethics even outside of the monks.[22]

Our first point, then, is that the Ideational system of ethics cannot promote happiness of an earthly kind. A second feature of such an ethical system is that its commands are absolute. The ethical system is geared toward bringing its adherents into unity with supreme and transcendental powers. It may not, therefore, be tampered with. It is binding on all and its moral imperatives are unchanging. Such a brief statement conjures up a static morality and a frozen world. This would be an error. We can get a more realistic understanding of the nature of an absolute morality from the following description of medieval European life by Herbert Muller:

> The famed unity of the Middle Ages is not a mere fiction. There was a practically universal agreement on the basic ideas by which men professed to live. Catholicism was not only the one Church but the primary inspiration of art, the main source of education, the accepted basis of all philosophy, science, political theory, and economic theory. Medieval men all knew the same absolute truth about the human drama, from the Creation to the Last Judgment. There was also an underlying similarity in social institutions. The world of chivalry was much the same everywhere, and everywhere rested on the hard work of villein or serf; the same literary and art forms were employed all over Europe, or even the same legends of Charlemagne, Alexander, and King Arthur; Latin was the Universal language of educated men. There were no strict nationalities, no fixed boundaries, no armed frontiers, no passports. Merchants, students, minstrels, buffoons, pilgrims, pedlars, friars, masons, scribes, pardoners, cheap-Jacks—all wandered freely from place to place, to give the medieval scene everywhere the same gaudy variety.[23]

Finally, the ethical commandments of an Ideational culture emanate from God or some other supersensory source. The point Sorokin is concerned with here is that the locus of the Ideational ethical system comes from a point outside man and, indeed, outside this world. It is, to use a term of Weber's, "other-worldly."

---

[21] The phrasing here is essentially that of F. J. Foakes Jackson, who is cited by Sorokin in *Social and Cultural Dynamics*, Vol. 2, p. 495.

[22] *Ibid.*, p. 495.

[23] From Herbert Muller, *The Uses of the Past: Profiles of Former Societies* (New York: Oxford University Press, 1953), p. 239.

In contrast to the Ideational ethical system, that of the Sensate culture reflects a radically different set of premises concerning reality and man's relationship to that reality. First of all, Sensate ethics are concerned with moral conduct geared to promote human happiness, comfort, and pleasure here on this earth during the person's lifetime. Compare, for example, the Ideational sexual codes of St. Paul with the Sensate sexual ethic of Hugh Hefner, editor of *Playboy* magazine. St. Paul, attempting to divine the nature of the divine, reached the point where he was concerned with whether or not a virgin girl commits a sin if she marries.[24] Hugh Hefner, on the other hand, promotes a sexual ethic which permits the widest latitude in sexual gratification—constrained primarily by the limitation that it should not be damaging to other people. The significant thing to note in Hefner's case is that ethical constraint has its locus in this world rather than in some supersensory realm.

A second characteristic of a Sensate ethical system is its relativism. It is subject to changing times and it changes along with them. Some contemporary intellectuals are of the opinion that the modern world may reach the point where morality will become largely a matter of style: Today one reads and discusses the sodomistic experiences of Genet and takes LSD; next month the style will be to read and discuss Ralph Waldo Emerson and drink hot chocolate. I ought to point out here that Sorokin is entirely in disagreement with such a point of view. As we shall see a little later, Sorokin argues that Sensate ethics, and Sensate culture more broadly conceived, have reached what he refers to as an "overripe" stage of development. The thrust of the future will be in the direction of a reestablishment of Ideational values.

Finally, Sorokin observes, Sensate ethics are patently man-made rules. If they serve the purpose of happiness, they are justified. A nearly perfect illustration of what Sorokin is saying appears in the writings of A. E. Taylor who, in 1899, wrote a dissertation, later published in 1901, which argued that the meaning of morality is to be found in the individual and not in the Absolute. Taylor wrote,

> The first law of moral action is, Know what you really want, and the second, like unto it, See that you are not misled into accepting a spurious substitute . . . Only before you embark on the profession of a harlot, it is your duty to find out all you can about the life to which you are committing yourself, and to make sure that a career of prostitution ending in a Lock Hospital will really give you what you want. If you decide that it will . . . you are morally on the same level as the missionary who chooses to end a career of self-devotion by dying alone and untended

---

[24] See First Corinthians, Chapter 7. Paul's famous statement reads, "Art thou bound unto a wife? seek not to be loosed. Art thou loosed from a wife? seek not a wife. But and if thou marry, thou hast not sinned; and if a virgin marry, she hath not sinned. Nevertheless such shall have trouble in the flesh: but I spare you."

in a leper-settlement; that the world in general does not recognize the resemblance is only another proof of the world's ample stupidity.[25]

The quotation from Taylor is all the more significant because Taylor was an Assistant Lecturer in Greek and Philosophy at Owens College, Manchester. It would be a trying task to find a medieval moralist who argued that an individualistic ethic could be used as the justification for entering harlotry as a career.

Economics under Ideationalism and Sensatism

The differences between an Ideational and Sensate system of ethics seem clear enough. What about some of the other characteristics of a sociocultural system? What about economic activities, for example? The differences between Ideational and Sensate cultures with regard to economic practices are as definite as they are with respect to ethics. Both economics and ethics, Sorokin claims, are enmeshed in the domination of the Ideational or Sensate point of view. In an Ideational culture the attempt to amass wealth and to concentrate on wealth-for-the-sake-of-wealth is considered a sin. Wealth is subordinated to greater ends. Business and economic conduct is a tolerated necessity and not an activity meriting the exclusion of an individual's other interests. For this reason, medieval society—a highly Ideational system according to Sorokin—punished those who sought wealth beyond what was necessary for a modest living. Moneylending for interest could and did result in expulsion, excommunication, and other severe measures.[26]

The role of wealth and the importance of the economic life are, of course, elevated considerably in the Sensate culture. Benjamin Franklin put it baldly and succinctly when he said, "Honesty is useful because it assures credit; so are punctuality, industry, frugality, and that is the reason they are virtues . . ."[27] Because it is of this world, because it can promote temporal physical pleasure, because it can augment worldly power, and because it is a visible and measurable sign of worth, wealth assumes greater importance in a Sensate culture than in an Ideational culture.

Art forms under Ideationalism and Sensatism

Ethics and economics share a common fate in the Ideational culture and in the Sensate culture. What of art?

---

[25] Quoted in Homer Smith, *Man and His Gods* (Boston: LIttle, Brown and Company, 1953), p. 423.
[26] Sorokin, *Social and Cultural Dynamics*, Vol. 2, p. 501.
[27] *Ibid.*, p. 506.

Art, whether it is in the form of paintings, sculpture, music, drama, or literature, is also enmeshed in either an Ideational or Sensate dominating culture. Ideational art forms exhibit a concern with spiritual or religious topics. The ambition of the artist is to "penetrate" the external characteristics of his subject and present a rendition of "eternal" or "absolute" qualities. Style tends to be more formal and symbolic. Medieval paintings of the Madonna, for example, pay careful attention to poses that, in themselves, have special meanings. Or, as a further example of such symbolism, a picture might show the Madonna with an egg, suspended from a string, hanging directly over her head. Ideational art is ascetic or, to use a current term, "dry." It has a nonerotic quality. Finally, the Ideational artist is directed toward God as his subject. His art is filled with saintly figures, superhumans, gods and demigods. There is pathos and tragedy, but there is always the triumph of the eternal, the spiritual, that which lies beyond the decay of the flesh and the dissolution of matter.

Sensate art—and modern art illustrates this form according to Sorokin—moves in the direction of worldly rather than spiritual topics. The ambition of the artist is to portray his subject dramatically, to catch a moment of sensual reality, to impress the viewer or reader with an art object that has "impact."[28] Style is neither formal nor "dry." The artist is concerned, whether in the graphic or literary arts, with achieving visual impressions. The subject is dealt with in terms of its "fleshly" character. In graphic art the Sensate movement means the development of nudism. In literature it means an increasing emphasis on the physical lusts of the writer's characters. As Sensate art forms develop, they increasingly take as their subjects nonheroic, everyday, commonplace people. Eventually, stage center of Sensate art is occupied by pathological individuals engaged in bizarre and pathological actions. In its "overripe" period, Sensate art produces works like Henry Miller's *Tropic of Cancer*, or William Burroughs' *Naked Lunch*. Painting moves toward dazzling the senses as is the case with the current "op" art.

Commenting on Sensate art forms Sorokin makes clear his attitudes toward them and leaves himself open, at the same time, to the objection raised by so many of his critics—his lack of objectivity and his "deck stacking" against modern views. Sorokin says of Visual or Sensate art,

> Criminals, prostitutes, courtesans, ladies of easy virtue, beggars, street urchins, ragamuffins, exotic Oriental personalities and scenes, "the poor," "the oppressed,"

---

[28] This Sensate art form has its ultimate current expression, perhaps, in advertising appeals to movies which inform the prospective viewer that the film will make him "blow his mind." I gather, from this expression, that the highest Sensate experience one can aspire to is having one's mind "blown." Since the actuality of a "blown" mind is almost incomprehensible, art forms exist which offer a safe and relatively limited version of this sought after Sensate excursion.

"the poverty-crushed persons," the social derelicts of all kinds, the socially and mentally maladjusted, the bloody, the greedy, the gluttons, the sick, the pathological—these and similar types of human beings become more and more favored topics of such an art and mentality. And the art of our days (just as we shall see, in its literature, its science, its politics, its ethics, its philosophy) is filled with such types and events. The "physio-dirty" stream of interpretation of man in the so-called science and philosophy of our days ("psychoanalytic," which reduces man to a bag filled with sex—and dirty sex—only; "the economic," which reduces him and his culture to a stomach only; the "behavioristic," which tells us that man is a mere combination of reflexes—conditional and unconditional; the biological and evolutionary, which makes of him a mere animal; the mechanistic, which assures us that man is merely a mechanism and so on) is the same phenomenon that we meet in our art.[29]

Statements such as this reveal Sorokin to be a vehement critic of modern culture. There is almost a quaintness about his revulsion. His claim that psychoanalysis reduces man to little more than a sex-filled bag—and dirty sex at that—is downright funny. If there were nothing more, we could consider such ranting only the harmless barbs of a 20th-century academic Don Quixote who has his head and heart somewhere back in the 9th century. But there is more to it than this. Sorokin is a critic, yet he is a critic who has the scholarship of more than fifteen volumes of his own effort as a basis from which to judge. If Sorokin is critical, we should not dismiss him with a simple-minded condemnation that he is not objective. We should, instead, look at the evidence on which he bases his thinking.

The evidence consists of four volumes of historical data. These volumes cover every kind of social and cultural activity and perspective from art forms to space-time concepts. In Volume 1 of *Social and Cultural Dynamics*, for example, over 100,000 paintings from Italy, France, Central Europe, Hungary, Poland, Czechoslovakia, Germany and Austria, the Netherlands, England, Spain, Russia, and Islam are evaluated in terms of Ideational and Sensate characteristics. The time span ranges across 3000 years.[30] Sorokin has, therefore, a wide perspective on which to draw as a critic. When Sorokin criticizes it is not, I believe, because he is caustic or because he is suffering from some kind of reactionary "hang-up." Rather, the historical view which he possesses makes him sensitively aware of the excesses to which we have gone in modern Sensate culture. It is not so much that Sensatism is "bad," but that the exhaustion of such an orthodoxy calls for someone to point it out.

We have, so far, established the distinction between the Ideational and Sensate forms of culture mentality. We have noted that ethics, economics, and

---

[29] Sorokin, *Social and Cultural Dynamics*, Vol. 1, pp. 499–501.
[30] Sorokin, *Social and Cultural Dynamics*, Vol. 1, p. 505.

art are some of the features of a culture that seem to conform to these dominant motifs. We have also noted the critical use to which Sorokin puts these concepts.

Cultural trends

Before going on to other features of Sorokin's work, we need to consider one further aspect of these two views of the world. If we grant that a culture can be defined as Ideational, how does it come about that a particular culture, such as our own, moves from the Ideational form to the Sensate? To put it crudely—how did we get from St. Paul to Hugh Hefner? If it is possible to answer this question, can we anticipate future cultural trends? Sorokin asserts that he has at least a general answer. In brief, a given cultural mentality—whether it is Ideational or Sensate—creates the conditions for its own downfall. If we are now in a Sensate period, the trend for the future will be in the direction of a new form of Ideational culture. And so the grand sweep of history consists of a constant ebb and flow across the centuries from Ideational cultures to Sensate cultures and back again. These historical tidal movements are measured in centuries.

The principal reason for this ebb and flow is that neither Ideational nor Sensate approaches to truth are perfectly correct. If the Sensate form, for example, were the final answer, then, once it came into being, it would remain dominant forever. But this cannot happen. By virtue of its weaknesses which become more apparent as the Sensate form assumes dominance, it is led into excesses. The corrective is to move in the Ideational direction. Similarly, the Ideational society is also fallible and also subject to excesses which are eventually corrected by a move in the direction of a Sensate form of culture.

Thirty years ago Sorokin cast his eye on modern Sensate culture and predicted its downfall—or, more correctly, its reform. From his vantage point in 1937, when the first volume of *Social and Cultural Dynamics* was copyrighted, Sorokin foresaw the necessary conditions for the fall of Sensate culture. He made thirteen forecasts.[31]

First, because of its materialism and its objectivity, Sensate culture will increasingly lose its sense of the distinction between right and wrong, beautiful and ugly, and the more abstract human values. As a consequence, moral, social, and esthetic anarchy will become predominant.

---

[31] Sorokin, *Social and Cultural Dynamics* (rev. and abr.; Boston: Porter Sargent, Publisher, 1957), pp. 699–701. The list presented here is a slightly reworded version of Sorokin's list.

Second, man will be debased. Man will be increasingly interpreted in mechanical and material terms. The spiritual—and lasting—basis of human worth will be lost sight of.

Third, with universal values lost, there will be a loss of binding and pervasive consensus. Instead, there will be a multitude of opposed opinions.

Fourth, in Sorokin's terms, ''Contracts and covenants will lose the remnants of their binding power. The magnificent contractual sociocultural house built by Western man during the preceding centuries will collapse.''

Fifth, force and fraud will be required to maintain moral order. Values will be ineffective as agents of control and we will be led into an age of ''might makes right.''

Sixth, freedom will be constrained and used as a myth of control by an unbridled dominant minority.

Seventh, governments will become more unstable and more inclined to resort to violence.

Eighth, the family will, under the decline of universal values and the intrusion of overripe Sensate values, continue to disintegrate.

Ninth, the Sensate culture will tend to become shapeless as undigested but sensually appealing cultural elements are dumped into the market.

Tenth, ''colossalism''—the idea that what is biggest is best—will replace the values given to quality. Men with ''gimmicks'' will be valued over men with genius, and the creativeness of the system will wane. Because valuable things are not, by any means, necessarily negotiable in our society, what is negotiable will win out while that which is valuable will tend to be ignored.

Eleventh, because of increasing anarchy and decreasing creativeness in the Sensate culture of today, depressions will grow worse and levels of living will deteriorate.

Twelfth, there will be declining security of life. Suicide, mental disease, and crime will grow. ''Weariness will spread over larger and larger numbers of the population.''

Thirteenth, the populace will divide into two parts. On the one hand will be the gluttonous hedonists who seek indulgence and pleasure. On the other will be those who withdraw and become antagonistic to Sensate values.

These forecasts form an engaging feature of Sorokin's work and thought. They indicate his concern for the future and his courage in being willing to attempt, at least in a general way, to fathom its possibilities. They stand at the conclusion of his major effort and, in a sense, leave to the future the vindication or rejection of his imposing argument. They also leave the reader to draw his own judgments.

From a vantage point of thirty years later, we can see that some of the forecasts missed the mark—at least in American culture. We have not, as yet, been subjected to lower levels of living. But then perhaps more time is needed. Or, possibly our levels of living are lower, but we are not aware of it. As we speculate in this fashion we begin to see some of the weaknesses as well as some of the strengths of Sorokin's vision. It is a grand and sweeping vision— of this there can be little doubt—but it is also a vision that is slightly out of focus. We know that we are seeing things on a breathtaking scale as we tour through history and humanity with Sorokin, but when we attempt to isolate a certain detail, we sometimes find it difficult.

For example, when Sorokin says the "creativeness" of the system will wane, we may be inclined to go along with him. But the term "creativeness" has so many varied meanings we can never be certain just what the forecast is referring to in specific terms—in concrete details. Sorokin can, in a sense, fit the present, or the future, to his prognostication merely by assigning to a term like "creativeness" meanings that will back up his predictions. Yet, even as I mention this criticism, I am loath to carry it very far. Despite a lack of focus, it is better to see vaguely than not to see at all. And, though every reader will interpret the thirteen forecasts somewhat differently, it seems, at least to me, they are more often right than wrong. Though Delphic in many places, Sorokin's probe into the future still provides a means of broadly interpreting a variety of modern events ranging from the subculture of the "Hippies" to the noisy wasteland of current American commercial television.

Fads, foibles, and faults

Sorokin's vast and roving scholarship is impressive. He directs it toward an understanding of broad patterns of historical change and development. He also, as we have seen, directs it toward a critical examination of modern Western civilization. Sorokin, like C. Wright Mills, expresses his love for humanity by poking—and not too gently—at its ugliness and shapelessness. If he cannot exorcise its faults, he can at least try to make others painfully aware of them. When Sorokin moves from a global examination of the entirety of humanity down to more specific and local events, his critical reflections become more pointed and devastating. Sorokin is not only concerned with humanity in general but with the specific means men have established for observing and thinking about themselves. Among these means is what we today refer to as "sociology." Sorokin takes a look at sociology—a field to which he has devoted a long and intelligent life—and appears to throw up his hands in horror.

Sociology, as Sorokin views it, is overrun with any number of faults.[32] It suffers from what he calls the "discoverers' complex." This consists of forgetting that others have already observed or commented on what the sociologist has observed—and often the earlier observer has done a better job. Having conveniently forgotten or overlooked that others have already covered the same terrain, the sociologist can then shout, "Eureka, we are onto something hitherto unheard of!" Sociology also suffers, says Sorokin—and he is not the first nor will he be the last to make this notice—from involuted language and "sham-scientific slang."

He then goes on to examine with an extremely critical eye a variety of other fads, foibles, and faults in the repertory of the sociologist, psychologist, economist, political scientist, or anyone else he happens to come across. He picks at nearly every weakness known to exist in psychological tests and he uses pungent language in the process.[33] He refers to our present "testomania" and to the 20th century as an age of "testocracy." The quest for quantification in the social sciences he dismisses as "quantophrenia."

Moreover, Sorokin does not hesitate to attack the very core of modern sociological belief—the idea that our knowledge of the social world should be grounded in "empirical" fact. This notion, suggests Sorokin, is both faulty and senile. Intuition plays a very important role in the development of scientific understanding and we cannot limit ourselves merely to the "empirical" realm of the senses. Indeed, social behavior is, when properly understood, beyond the direct observation of the senses. Furthermore, any number of fictions—in the strongest meaning of that word—play a most important role in scientific work, whether it is in physics or in sociology. The square root of minus one or the concept of infinity defies any empirical observation,[34] yet science would

---

[32] He lays out these faults in *Fads and Foibles in Modern Sociology and Related Sciences* (Chicago: Henry Regnery Company, 1956). In his biography he complains, at one point, that C. Wright Mills wrote to him and said that he had used much of Sorokin's critique as a basis for his own book *The Sociological Imagination*. Sorokin then wryly commented that nowhere in Mill's book is his effort cited.

[33] A later criticism of psychological testing which is more comprehensive and deals specifically and only with the problem of testing is Martin L. Gross's *The Brain Watchers* (New York: Random House, Inc., 1962). This book, published four years after Sorokin's, led to an investigation of psychological testing by Congress. According to the publishers of Gross's work, this investigation led the Civil Service Commission to withdraw, voluntarily, the use of psychological tests.

[34] For a very engaging discussion of the purely fictional qualities of a concept like "infinity" read *Mathematics and the Imagination* by James Newman and Edward Kasner (New York: Simon and Schuster, Inc., 1940). Visualize, if you will, a quantity which, when divided by 2 provides itself. That is infinity.

be seriously inconvenienced without them. The sociologist is fooling himself when he thinks that he can observe directly certain units of action or role behavior.

Worse yet, for all of his emphasis on empiricism, the sociologist, like the worst gossip monger, is too often willing to go along with "hearsay" evidence. Sorokin mentions the definition of marital happiness used by one sociologist as an illustration:

> Clifford Kirkpatrick operationally defines "marital maladjustment" as "that quality in marriage which causes one close friend to classify the couple as maladjusted." Thus if a scholar wants to give an "operational" definition of happiness or "adjustment" in marriage, all he has to do is, first, to ask a friend of the married couple whether the marriage is "adjusted" or "maladjusted"; second, without any verification, to accept this opinion as valid and scientific; and, third, to build upon it a huge statistical superstructure of measurements and predictions of success or failure in marriage.[35]

Sorokin then goes on to say,

> One can . . . sympathize with a physician who uses a thermometer to determine his patient's temperature or a cardiograph to diagnose his heart-activity, instead of adopting the much simpler and more infallible operation of just asking the patient or his friend whether the former's temperature and heart-activity are "normal" or "abnormal."[36]

These barbs, and others before them, have not endeared Sorokin to members of the sociological community. Sociologists have been inclined to ignore Sorokin (which is roughly akin to trying to ignore the Eiffel Tower while visiting Paris) or to dismiss him with a casual shrug.[37] Yet Sorokin has persisted and his writings, in many places, remain viable while those of his critics have receded into total obsolescence.

Sorokin's criticism of sociology is lengthy and negative with only a brief and general suggested remedy. He recommends that integralist sociology replace the atomistic, analytic, pseudo-operationalistic and empirical sociology of the present. As he develops his suggestion he also antagonizes deeply those sociologists of today who are committed to "factual" sociology. The reason is apparent. Sorokin suggests that it is necessary to transcend the observable in order to understand the reality around us in a fuller sense. Sorokin says,

---

[35] Pitirim A. Sorokin, *Fads and Foibles in Modern Sociology and Related Sciences* (Chicago: Henry Regnery Company, 1956), p. 37.

[36] *Ibid.*, p. 38.

[37] Cowell makes the following offhand comment concerning the response of the sociological community to Sorokin, "It has already been recorded that there was no discussion of Sorokin's views in the *Sociological Review.*" *Pitirim A. Sorokin in Review*, p. 284.

The integralist conception views psychosocial reality as a complex manifold in which we can distinguish at least three different aspects: sensory, rational, and supersensory-superrational. The sensory aspect is present in all psychosocial phenomena that can be perceived through our sense organs. The rational aspect is present in all the rational phenomena of the psychosocial universe: in logically and mathematically consistent systems of science, philosophy, religion, ethics, fine arts, up to the rationally motivated and executed activities of an individual or group. The supersensory-superrational aspect of psychosocial reality is manifested by the highest creative activities and created masterpieces of genius in all fields of cultural activity: by the great creative achievement of a genius-scientist, philosopher, founder of religion, great law-giver, great apostle of unselfish love, genius-writer, poet, painter, sculptor, composer, architect, and so on.[38]

What Sorokin is saying here (in terminology that lays him open to his own criticism of the sociologist's inclination for obtuse jargon) is that intuition and "spirit" are a part of the act of knowing. The present empirical psychosocial sciences have grown "tired" and "less creative." There is a need for a more daring integration of fact, reason, and intuition. Our awareness should not be subordinated to any single one of these three aspects of thought. In sum, Sorokin is saying that Sensate social science has exhausted itself as it passes into its "overripe" stage. The time has come to move back toward a more Ideational awareness of the nature of man.

Sorokin's criticism of the psychosocial sciences stands as a controversial statement, to say the least. It is written seriously, but not without humor. Sorokin indicates that he is shocked by what some of his colleagues are doing, but he is not so shocked as to divorce himself from the ranks of sociology. He depicts a situation which seems nearly hopeless, but he never goes to the extreme of claiming that it is. He grudgingly concedes that, when judged over-all, the social sciences have provided man with important knowledge about himself—but the time has come for reform. The wit and knowledge found in Sorokin's critique, *Fads and Foibles in Modern Sociology*, make it necessary tempering reading for anyone about to enter the miasmic swampland of a career in the modern psychosocial sciences.

Altruistic love

One phase of Sorokin's career must not be overlooked as we conclude this very brief introduction to his work. At the end of World War II Sorokin turned his attention toward a subject that other social scientists were inclined to ignore—the subject of altruistic love. One of the motivating factors behind Sorokin's interest in this subject was his growing awareness that democratic

---

[38] Sorokin, *Fads and Foibles in Modern Sociology and Related Sciences*, p. 316.

government, improved educational opportunities, or increased religious dedication were not, in themselves, sufficient to halt or even to slow down present levels and trends in intra- and international violence. He says,

> Having completed my *Society, Culture and Personality* [first published in 1947], I began to orient myself in the vast and almost entirely unexplored field of the phenomena of altruistic, creative love. An "inventory" of the existing knowledge in this field showed that this gigantic problem had been largely neglected by modern science. While many a modern sociologist and psychologist viewed the phenomena of hatred, crime, war, and mental disorders as legitimate objects for scientific study, they quite illogically stigmatized as theological preaching or non-scientific speculation any investigation of the phenomena of love, friendship, heroic deeds, and creative genius. This patently unscientific position of many of my colleagues is merely a manifestation of the prevalent concentration on the negative, pathological, and subhuman phenomena typical of the disintegrating phase of our sensate culture.[39]

In 1948 he published *The Reconstruction of Humanity*, a book concerned with the topic of altruistic love. This, along with other works on the same subject, reveals Sorokin's most serious intellectual involvement. The results, in terms of the extent to which they met support within the greater public domain, were extremely disappointing to Sorokin—a disappointment which he covers with the statement, ". . . the results are more modest than I might have wished."[40] It might be worthwhile to conclude our discussion of Sorokin by outlining some of his conclusions on the nature of altruistic love and creative genius, because, I believe, young people today appear to be more overtly concerned with the nature of love and the use of love than older generations seem to have been.

The Reconstruction of Humanity is an unusual work. Certainly this is true when it is viewed as the effort of a sociologist; it is also true even if we disregard this fact. *The Reconstruction of Humanity*, like most of Sorokin's efforts after 1937, contains reiterations of the main themes contained in *Social and Cultural Dynamics*. Sorokin criticizes Sensate values and sees in them the cause of the decline of altruistic sentiments. He lashes out at everything from decadent jazz music and demoralizing movies to the loss of creative genius in the arts. Nothing, as Sorokin sees it, will bring back altruistic morality short of a complete overhaul of the elemental cultural premises upon which our society rests. To find altruism we shall have to move away from Sensate values and toward Ideational values. We shall have to return to universal moral precepts and we shall not only have to envision these precepts but establish a state in which people live and act by them.

---

[39] Sorokin, *A Long Journey*, p. 277.
[40] *Ibid.*, p. 292.

Sorokin makes clear his position when he discusses what he considers to be the role of education in the improvement of society:

> As educational agencies the schools must establish a carefully elaborated system for developing altruism in their pupils. They must instill in them a set of universal values and norms, free from superstition and ignorance as well as from the degrading, cynical, nihilistic, and pseudoscientific theories of our time. This task should be deemed as important as intellectual training.[41]

But how is the foundation of the culture to be modified? How can we come to find the necessary "set of universal values and norms?" If it were found, how could people be made to endorse it and live by it? How could a self-indulgent, relativistic, and atomized society become unified in common expressions of the altruistic life? This question has probably concerned every man who has given serious thought to the nature of modern humanity. Each has tried, in various ways to answer it, and each, possibly leaving some small mark, has generally failed. Nonetheless, Sorokin suggests, it is from the models offered us by the great altruists of history that we might find some solution. So it is that Sorokin's solution to modern world problems is essentially a religious one and is cast in the form of an ill-disguised sermon. In substance, Sorokin says we must turn to the model offered by the great Yogis, the Christian mystics, and the teachings of the great world religions—Buddhism, Hinduism, Christianity, Judaism.

It is surprising, as Sorokin develops his plea, to note the correspondence between his ideas and those endorsed by the present "hippie" culture and, to a lesser extent, the "beat" culture that preceded it. Sorokin says,

> As a preliminary condition for obtaining control of the unconscious and conscious by the superconscious and for unlocking the forces of the superconscious, they unanimously demand the liberation of a person from all forms of egoism and the development of a love for the Absolute, for all living beings, for the whole universe, in its negative aspect of not causing pain to anybody by thought, word, or deed, and in its positive aspect of unselfish service, devotion, and help to and sacrifice for others.[42]

But the problem still remains: How do we achieve a general endorsement of such altruistic sentiments? How do we help precipitate the movement away from a Sensate system toward an Ideational one? Here Sorokin's platform falters on the steps of a series of "If only . . ." phrases. For example, he says at one point, "If most persons would even slightly improve themselves . . . the sum total of social life would be ameliorated . . ."[43] It is difficult to disagree with this statement, and it is also difficult to do much with it.

---

[41] Pitirim A. Sorokin, *The Reconstruction of Humanity* (Boston: Beacon Press, 1948), p. 153.
[42] *Ibid.*, p. 224.
[43] *Ibid.*, p. 233.

Sorokin's program for social change and reform has grand aspirations and a very naive and ill-developed sense of political strategy. Yet this may not be as bad or as common as it appears. Possibly Sorokin's is one of the early voices calling for a return to more religious concerns and understandings of ourselves and the mysteries in which we find ourselves enmeshed. We need to look at science, at commerce, at education and the other orthodoxies of our time, and concern ourselves with their excesses.

Our modern culture has produced a group of people, cryptic and awkward, who are attempting to express in their own purposely inarticulate way, the same criticism that Sorokin has stated academically and at great length. Moreover, they are attempting to act according to the precepts of what might be called modernized altruism. This group—the new left—might not be exactly what Sorokin had in mind when he called for a "well-planned modification of our culture and social institutions,"[44] but they come closer to moving us in the direction Sorokin claims is necessary than any other group extant.

The future

Like many of the other social observers considered in this book Sorokin is pessimistic about the future. He feels that unless humanity is able to reverse its present egoistic and Sensate trend, we shall have to resign ourselves to the inevitable end of creative culture. He sees hope, but it is small. He knows where man ought to direct his ambitions, but he is, in the final analysis, unable to tell him how to acquire such direction. Sorokin, like many other social scientists, reveals the frustration of having knowledge and vision and, at the same time, knowing as fully as it is possible to know, the frail capacity of a single man to act on the basis of that knowledge.

The humanistic nature of Sorokin's writing and involvement is so apparent we need only underscore it slightly to bring this chapter to a close. He is a man of broad and critical knowledge. He is open in his dislike and contempt for modern "Sensate" culture and he is strong in his enthusiasm for a "return" to more religious or "Ideational" forms of culture. His endorsement of "superconscious" approaches to the problems of life and the human social order has endeared him to numerous churchmen. At the same time, we should recall Durkheim's admonition that even a society of saints will have its sinners. The history of Ideational societies is also marked with grisly examples of man's inhumanity to man.

---

[44] Sorokin, *The Reconstruction of Humanity*, p. 234.

13 Cultural Dreams and Nightmares: Observations by Jules Henry

It is one thing to define a term and quite something else to use it in a way that furthers understanding. Man can be defined, for example, as a bipedal animal without feathers; but this does not greatly enhance our understanding of mankind or of ourselves. We encounter much the same problem with many of the concepts used by social scientists. A case in point is the concept of culture—one of the most profound concepts to come out of modern social science. This term is relatively simple to define, yet it is difficult to comprehend. Textbook definitions of culture are numerous[1] and the student, after going to the trouble of memorizing one of these definitions, believes that he has a sturdy grasp on the meaning of culture. However, if he remains in anthropology or sociology, he may begin to recognize—after several years of study have passed—that he is only on the threshhold of comprehending what an anthropologist is talking about when he uses the word "culture."

What culture *is*

At the simplest level we can say that culture is *everything* learned and shared by men. Culture is not simply a knowledge of the arts or the social graces. it is much more. It includes the profane as well as the sublime; the secular as well as the sacred. What we have learned from others and what we share

---

[1] Brace and Montagu define culture quite simply as ". . . the part of the environment that is learned, shared, and transmitted in society. The man-made part of the environment." C. L. Brace and M. F. Ashley Montagu, *Man's Evolution: An Introduction to Physical Anthropology* (New York: The Macmillan Company, 1965). Wissler, much earlier, defined it as, ". . . the aggregate of standardized beliefs and procedures followed by the tribe." Clark Wissler, *An Introduction to Social Anthropology* (New York: Holt, Rinehart and Winston, Inc., 1929). A number of slightly varied definitions of culture appear on pages 46 and 47 of M. F. Ashley Montagu's *Anthropology and Human Nature* (Boston: Porter Sargent, Publisher, 1957).

with them is the basis of our humanity. We learn and we share the language we use for communication—language is a part of culture. We learn and we share the attitudes which affect our behavior toward others—these attitudes are a part of culture. We learn and we share certain conceptions about how we should behave as a boy or a girl—sex roles are a part of culture. We learn and we share various ideas about the nature of God—religious beliefs are a part of culture. And so we might continue. But this is rather prosaic stuff. All we have said so far is that man learns many things and much of what he learns he holds in common with others who share and transmit his cultural background. What is so profound about this?

The profundity of the concept comes from the extent to which it can be applied to innumerable realms of human conduct. To the extent we can do this, we are able to ascertain that man is not ruled so much by biological or physiological demands as he is by different ways of perceiving the world; these modes of viewing the world are shaped by his cultural background. For example, I recall once hearing a physiologist refer to love as simply deoxyribonucleic acid calling out to itself. A student of culture is aware, by contrast, that for culture-bound creatures like man, love is considerably more. Culture can prescribe whether or not a man is more likely to fall in love with a fat girl or a thin girl. It can determine whether people will fall in love at all. It can determine whether husbands will respond jealously or happily to the attentions that other men give their wives. It can affect the extent to which men are aggressive or passive in making love. It can influence the extent to which people are aware or unaware of their sexual natures.[2] In a word, a comprehension of the nature of culture extends our understanding of the degree to which man is more than chemistry or physiology or a set of biological drives or animal instincts.

The concept of culture is broad and is similar, in at least one respect, to a physical concept like gravity. Both culture and gravity gain their value from the degree to which they are found to operate in the universes they deal with. Neither the concept of culture nor the concept of gravity is especially useful

---

[2] Morton M. Hunt refers to the case of a man who lived for ten years with a woman who accused him of being sexually inadequate because he could delay himself no more than half an hour during coitus. The husband had to be informed by a psychiatrist that he was extremely unusual and was, contrary to his wife's opinion, quite a man. (See *The New York Times Magazine*, January 1, 1967, p. 16.) The point is that the sexual conduct of this man and his response to it was a function of his understanding of sex and the meanings given it by others around him. Since, in our culture, one is generally kept ignorant of sexual functions and norms, it is not unusual to encounter people who are either confused, unhappy, or morbidly fascinated by this aspect of their lives.

or valuable as an explanatory concept in individual cases. If, for example, we say that a ball fell to the floor because of gravity we really have not said much. After all, how do we know gravity exists? We know it exists because the ball fell to the floor. So, when we say that something fell because of gravity, we are only saying something fell because something fell.[3] The significance of the concept of gravity, first grasped by the genius of Newton, comes from the fact that gravity was seen to reach out beyond the trees from which apples fall and farther still above the mountain heights and farther yet—continuing forever into the outermost reaches of the physical universe.

It is similar with the concept of culture. As we begin to comprehend man's cultural nature, we begin to see—in ever more subtle extensions—the intrusion of cultural influences. Emotions that may have their chemical origins in deoxyribonucleic acid will have the style and form of their expression dictated by culture.

How an anthropologist views culture

In modern times we have acquired so much cultural baggage that the problem of determining what is significant and what is not has become a central task of the intellectual. One kind of intellectual especially qualified to perform this service is the anthropologist; after all, an examination of culture, either primitive or modern, is the professional concern of the anthropologist. What does an anthropologist see when he examines a complex modern culture such as exists today in the United States? Numerous examinations of American character and culture can be found in anthropological and sociological libraries. However, we shall concentrate on one of the better examples of this kind of effort and examine what the anthropologist Jules Henry has to say about the American way of life.[4]

---

[3] This is called a tautologous or circular form of reasoning. It is surprisingly common and even more surprisingly satisfying—revealing the possibility that man is more willing to have his curiosity satisfied than aroused. In any event, we find this kind of thinking going on in all fields. In the next chapter, another tautology is discussed concerning explanations of criminal or delinquent behavior.

[4] Henry should be compared with C. Wright Mills, David Riesman, and Pitirim Sorokin among the writers discussed in this book. All these authors are concerned, ultimately, with the application of various social concepts to the American scene. They are interpreters of modern America. Riesman begins with an examination of social character. Mills was concerned with the distribution of power. Sorokin dealt with America as a form of Sensate society. Henry begins with America as a complex cultural system and then selects several aspects of this culture as critical ones—advertising, xenophobia, and child-rearing practices. That each of these authors despairs in his observations probably reflects more the critical nature of any intellectual than it does the possibility that all four are employing observational techniques that have high scientific reliability.

Henry's concerns are personal and therefore arbitrary. He is willing to indicate at times that there are things he does not like. Yet his point of view is never divorced from what might be called an anthropological perspective. This perspective can be summarized as follows: Very early in his development, perhaps as long as one million years ago, man gained the capacity to transmit to others and then to preserve those lessons which he had learned through hard experience. This capacity to "preserve" experience set in motion the development of culture. In its earliest stages this "preserved experience" served the purpose of enhancing man's possibilities for survival. Also, in its earliest stages culture was probably closely identified with human needs and survival demands. But the growth and development of preserved experience brought about a force which, in some ways, was unique to itself and which occasionally became alienated from primary human needs. Henry suggests that possibly we have today a situation in which culture is served as much by man as man is served by culture. Indeed, we may have reached the point where culture has turned against man.

Ours is a culture, says Henry, that imposes unessential and possibly degrading needs on us. We respond. But to the extent this is so, we have become the servants of culture rather than having culture serve us. Henry puts it the following way:

> It is the deliberate creation of needs that permits [American] culture to continue. This is the first phase of the psychic revolution of contemporary life.[5]

Henry, like Leslie White (discussed in Chapter 11), is concerned with the extent to which culture imposes rather than disposes itself. But whereas White's discussion was extremely general—an abstract formulation of cultural evolution—Henry comes in for a closer look. Henry asks, in effect, what are the *particular* consequences for us as members of a *particular* culture. Like Leslie White, Henry draws a gloomy picture for us.

The anthropologist has found mythology, folklore, stories, or culturally transmitted phantasy one vital way of entering into a comprehension of primitive culture. Henry, following his anthropological inclinations, does much the same thing with American culture. But what is the mythological locus of the American dream? What literature spells out most clearly the irrational nature of our

---

[5] From *Culture Against Man* by Jules Henry. © Copyright 1963 by Random House, Inc. The above passage and other quotations from the same book are reprinted by permission. This chapter is based, almost exclusively, on *Culture Against Man*, Henry's most widely known work. Henry has written a number of articles and monographs of a technical nature. His other work which might be of interest to the new student is *Jungle People* (Vintage Books; New York Random House, Inc., 1964). I understand, from a conversation with Henry, that a book entitled *Pathways to Madness* will be in print by the time this is ready for the press. *Pathways to Madness* will examine, in greater detail, some of the materials contained in *Culture Against Man*.

cultural commitments? Henry searches and finds in advertising the American analogue to the mythology of the primitive.

The place of advertising in American culture

Henry claims that the American dream is lodged within the para-poetic[6] exaggerations and claims of American advertising. It is here we glimpse the sex dreams of the American woman, the virility models of the American man. The pecuniary aspirations and urges of every American are reflected in and shaped by advertising. So, Henry begins with an examination of the advertising industry and the endless dream it manufactures. The essential character of the dream is infinite indulgence in a world capable of producing an infinite supply. Yet, for all of its indulgence, it is a troubled dream.

Dreams are violations of reality. We may, in the course of our individual dreams, violate physical reality as when we dream we are able to step from a high tower and sail out over the earth. Or, our dreams may violate social taboos or norms as when we dream we are naked before a large assembly. As our personal dreams usurp the traditional controls of society, so does advertising circumvent the higher values of the system—and it is this feature of advertising which is of greatest concern to Henry. Like the inner personal dream which steals upon us while we sleep, advertising bypasses the more rigorous established values of our culture. A dream may lead us to indulge in fantasies which violate our individual sense of decency, modesty, and shame. So does advertising. A dream may circumvent rationality and logic. So does advertising. Degradation of the sense of decency and reason is the result, and man becomes an object of contempt.

Advertising is forced to bypass the sternest values of our culture. It cannot, for example, rely on traditional logic and scientific modes of establishing truth about consumer goods. Advertising operates on the basis of a different logic— pecuniary logic. It is a logic never meant to be taken seriously, and yet it is a logic which "works," that is, it sells things. It is a logic which operates alongside the formal and demanding logic of science and is competitive with it for dominance within the culture. Henry puts it this way:

> . . . in order for our economy to continue in its present form people must learn to be fuzzy-minded and impulsive, for if they were clear-headed and deliberate they would rarely put their hands in their pockets; or, if they did, they would leave them there. If we were all logicians the economy could not survive, and herein lies a

---

[6] Henry never tells us quite what he means by this term. It could mean a disordered or abnormal kind of poetic expression or a form of poetry which only resembles true poetry.

terrifying paradox, for in order to exist economically as we are we must try by might and main to remain stupid.[7]

Examples of what Henry means by pecuniary logic are easy to find. Right in the middle of TIME magazine (December 9, 1966) appears the statement

'' 'BLACK & WHITE.'

SCOTCH FOR PEOPLE WHO KNOW THE DIFFERENCE.''

The logic is elementary, though slightly ambiguous, and the threat and insult are only slightly more subtle. The pecuniary logical implication is that if you are sophisticated enough to know the difference, you will first buy and then drink the Scotch whiskey pictured in the advertisement. If you are not drinking the Scotch shown in the advertisement, you presumably are gauche enough to drink pretty much anything. There is a logic here, but the important thing which Henry points to is that it is a logic not meant to be taken seriously. At the same time it is a logic which flows from a serious and highly competitive industry—the advertising industry. Though we are not supposed to take this logic seriously, it is nonetheless valid enough to warrant the expenditure, at the present time, of over ten billion dollars each year.

The producers of the dream, the advertising men, must live with the fact that they are the agents of mass produced hallucination and delusion. Their response is, on the one hand, an attempt to legitimize their work by referring to it as a ''profession'' and, on the other hand, the acquisition of a cynical contempt for the public. Henry mentions a sign hanging over the desk of a Hollywood press agent which reads, ''The Only Thing We Have to Fear Is the Truth.''[8]

The form of the dream is installed early in life. The child, like the adult, is exploited by the dream. Through the dream he acquires the motivation and the capacity to consume almost unthinkingly. Consumption becomes a way of life and the measure of what is good. The child is exploited by the dream and the parents are exploited by the child. The consequences are sometimes comic and pathetic. Henry cites the following instance:

---

[7] Henry, *Culture Against Man*, p. 48. A very glaring example of what Henry is talking about can be seen in the movie *Silk Stockings* with Cyd Charisse and Fred Astaire. This movie, based on the older film *Ninotchka*, tells the story of what happens to a puritanical revolutionary Russian woman after she meets an American man. At first she is all logical, self-denying, and altruistic. But she changes. The movie gleefully presents the history of her corruption and that of her aides. In the final scenes we find them succumbing to the delights of self-indulgence, consumption, and the American dream. This movie is daringly explicit in its endorsement of corruption.

[8] Henry, *Culture Against Man*, p. 91.

[A father is quoted as saying:] "My youngster is only 5. He cannot read. It's a helluva thing to spend $15 on a toy and then see my kid sit down and cry because it doesn't fly like the one he saw on television."[9]

Indulgence and permissiveness

Coming of age in America, as Henry views the process, involves learning the dream as it appears in advertising. There is more, of course, but the dream is central and shapes many other facets of the child's life. For example, one of the most critical features of the relationship between parent and child in America is the indulgence pattern that exists between them. Henry comes to this conclusion after examining the responses of several hundred children and teen-agers in St. Louis to a questionnaire which asked them simply to list what they liked most and least about their mothers and fathers. An example of the kind of response he received is the following from a twelve-year-old girl:

> I like my father because he is kind, good and funny, when he is with my brothers and sisters and I. When I bring my friends home with me, he is very nice to them and shows us a good time. He also lets me go to Plankville to see my grandparents, aunt and uncle and my two cousins every summer. This summer he talked Mother into letting me go to Bigtown, with my aunt, uncle, and cousins.

> I don't like my father because he doesn't believe in letting me go to the show at night, and he won't let me wear lipstick. Even if he knows that he is wrong, he won't admit it to anybody. He insists on wearing his hair in a crewcut, even though he is losing most of it.

> I like my mother because she lets me go to visit my friends often. She lets me invite them over whenever I please. If it was up to her, I would get a lot more allowance than I do. She lets me help her fix supper when I want to, and is very nice about it, when I make a mess (even though I have to clean it up). She also lets me do almost anything I want.

> I dislike my mother because she gets mad so easily. On Saturday morning she makes me clean the house, while she goes shopping. She won't let me wear lipstick, or go to the show at night. She makes me take care of my brothers and sisters (ugh).[10]

It is obvious that what the child likes about her parents is their permissiveness. Note the number of times the child refers to whether or not the parent ". . . lets me . . ." do something. The parent is not admired or respected or liked for what he or she is or for qualities he or she might possess. The parent is judged instead on the extent to which he permits self-indulgence. Rarely, Henry observes, does the child say he likes his parents because they are

---

[9] *Ibid.*, p. 75.
[10] *Ibid.*, pp. 133–134.

thoughtful or proud or dignified or intelligent or ambitious. To come of age in America is to become attuned, early in life, to a way of living which concentrates on permissiveness and self-indulgence.[11]

It is the adult who expresses the mature and full pattern of self-indulgence, and the child is expected to wait somewhat impatiently on the sidelines until he possesses the right to full expressions of self-indulgence. Henry observes that this culture of ours, probably more than any other, attempts a total division between impulse release patterns in children and adults. This is not so elsewhere. Henry comments,

> . . . Among my friends the Pilagá Indians of Argentina, children of all ages attempted or had intercourse with one another, played sexual games, listened to and told sexual stories, and smoked if the adults would let them have tobacco (which was very rarely, because there was so little). Older children did not go near the beer fiestas because this was for older men, not because it was "immoral." Thus, since the Pilagá have no impulse logic according to which children are excluded from the impulse release patterns of adults, when children engage in them they need not do it surreptitiously and are not made to feel immoral.[12]

Of course, our culture cannot, willy-nilly, adopt the ways of the Pilagá. The point is, however, that the culturally given forms of impulse release which we find in our culture virtually force the child into subterfuge, sham, and guilt.

The relationship between children and parents is complicated and tense. The self-indulgence of the child must be catered to and yet not allowed to go too far. The child must be readied for life in a society which subscribes to a metaphysic of fun and which subordinates everything to the attainment of a "high standard of living." Parents must provide a covert model of the pleasures awaiting the child and, at the same time, deny the child the overt practice of those activities which will specifically define his maturity for him. The parental model flowing out of this complicated system of impulse control is the parent who conducts himself as an "imp of fun."

The role of "Puck" or "fun-imp" is especially noticeable in the father. Because his work is abstract in nature and removed from the direct view of his children, and because he seeks the approval and recognition of his children, and because he competes for this approval with the mother whose value to the children is direct and obvious—the father compensates by entering the child's world as a fun figure. He becomes the Mary Poppins of the

---

[11] The theme of the indulgent parent is exploited by the movies. The strong character of the father in the film *Mary Poppins* is undermined by a magical nanny whose special magic is her capacity to play the role of imp in the mental world of the child. In the end it is the father's character that is finally forced to meet that of the child, and we leave daddy out in a field flying a kite in the last scene.

[12] Henry, *Culture Against Man*, p. 237.

family. Henry suggests that the mother may be sufficiently challenged by this response on the part of the father to feel impelled to take on some of the qualities of the ''fun-imp'' figure as well.

At the adolescent stage, the conflict between adult law which constrains impulse release and the informal cultural pressure to engage in impulse release, produces further complications. For girls, Henry expresses the problem simply:

> Girls fear they will not attract boys, and paradoxically, they fear the boys they attract too well. It is a difficult life to lead.[13]

Girls give away the conflict by wearing padded bras and provocative slacks and blouses while, at the same time, confessing that the boys in their high schools do not know they are so falsifying themselves. The implication is apparent. The girls do not permit the boys to uncover the deception. Moreover, the girls interviewed by Henry expressed contempt for boys who went out for ''what they could get.'' Part of the contempt stems from the fact that such boys are unwilling to accept the conventions of legitimate ambiguity and misrepresentation which the other adolescents consider binding.[14] These boys are not willing to accept being misled.

Henry suggests that maturity in Western culture is found in the capacity to misrepresent while being able, at the same time, to avoid being misled by the misrepresentations of others. Adolescence is a period during which the child begins to grasp the techniques of skilled misrepresentation. To be direct is to run the risk of being labeled a delinquent. The girl who, for example, is a real lover rather than a misrepresentation of a lover, is apt to find her status in jeopardy. The boy who is unwilling to accept the pseudo nature of the pseudo-nymph has no ''cool.'' Maturity, says Henry, is the capacity not to care if you are misled.[15]

The nightmare of failure

If unfettered consumption is the glowing dream of American culture, failure is its darkest nightmare. Without appearing to do so, American schools teach children how to hate. Very important here is the possibility that they teach children how to hate themselves when they fail. That is to say, the culturally induced response to failure is self-hatred. They also teach children to hate the successful person. Henry refers to the following observational notes to develop his point:

---

[13] *Ibid.*, p. 211.
[14] *Ibid.*, p. 211.
[15] *Ibid.*, p. 274.

Boris [a fifth grader] had trouble reducing ''12/16'' to the lowest terms, and could only get as far as ''6/8''. The teacher asked him quietly if that was as far as he could reduce it. She suggested he ''think.'' Much heaving up and down and waving of hands by the other children, all frantic to correct him. Boris pretty unhappy, probably mentally paralyzed. The teacher, quiet, patient, ignores the others and concentrates with look and voice on Boris. She says, ''Is there a bigger number than two you can divide into the two parts of the fraction?'' After a minute or two, she becomes more urgent, but there is no response from Boris. She then turns to the class and says, ''Well, who can tell Boris what the number is?'' A forest of hands appears and the teacher calls Peggy. Peggy says that four may be divided into the numerator and the denominator.[16]

This is such a common incident in our culture that one untrained in anthropology or sociology might find in it little cause for comment. To Henry, however, it is a small drama revealing a startling amount of unconscious cruelty. Henry goes on to point out that,

To a Zuni, Hopi, or Dakota Indian, Peggy's performance would seem cruel beyond belief, for competition, the wringing of success from somebody's failure, is a form of torture foreign to those noncompetitive redskins.[17]

The school is teaching this fifth-grader, but it is teaching him much more than exercises in the reduction of fractions. It is teaching him a lesson in self-control. Boris is expected to remain at the blackboard and live with the nightmare of his own public confrontation with self-inadequacy. It is putting it too mildly to say that Boris is being taught. Henry suggests culture goes further. It invades the mind. Its lessons become obsessions which dictate how the world is to be seen. Boris is learning the nightmare of failure and he is learning his vulnerability before a yapping and critical public. One consequence of this lesson is that Boris is very likely to become willing to believe anything which will spare him further painful confrontations. In order not to fail, Boris becomes willing to believe anything regardless of whether it is true or false, useful or useless. Paradoxically, then, only by remaining willing to be absurd can Boris feel free from the fear of being absurd.

The nightmare fear of the enemy

At the individual level the nightmare is the dream of failure. At the national level it is the recurring pathogenic fear of communism embodied in the form of the Soviet Union and Red China. We believe, regardless of whether the situation calls for it, that others should have and employ a democratic government operating hand-in-hand with a market economy based on private profit.

---

[16] *Ibid.*, p. 296.
[17] *Ibid.*, p. 296.

Like Boris, we are threatened if someone else does something differently and, at the same time, successfully. So it is that our newspapers dwell at great length on every failure experienced by Castro, Mao, Kosygin or any other threatening international figure. The best we can manage is to wish them the worst and then relish every setback. This culturally induced malice is another side of American culture—the nightmare side of the American dream.[18]

Very broadly, the American nightmare of the Soviet Union has produced (1) an economic reliance on the fear of war, (2) the commitment of our cultural elite to an attitude of "fun-and-games" in war, (3) total immersion in the struggle—with civilians included as warlike agents along with military men, (4) simple dichotomization of the world into friend and foe, (5) fear of trade and the extension of economic ties, (6) a reliance on the internal domestic economy to maintain production control, (7) an atmosphere of security and secrecy, (8) the development of a powerful and potentially uncontrollable industrial-military complex, (9) irrational negativism toward domestic public programs, and (10) obsessive concern with obtaining immediate relief from the problems of international struggle. Each of these points will be elaborated slightly.

1. An economic reliance on the fear of war by American industry is significant insofar as it narcotizes our sense of the consequences of conflict.[19] Henry puts it this way:

> The fact that the Soviets are in the opposite situation has helped to save us, for since their way of life is threatened by war, they lack the temptations we have. The reader need only imagine what his own attitude toward war would be if mere *preparation* for it meant that his clothes would become tattered, he would taste meat only once a week, he would have no butter or coffee, gasoline would be available only once a week and in two-gallon allotments and he would have to wait in line for it; that if his car needed repairs he would have to make them himself or wait weeks to get the job done, etc. In such a case even the most warlike statesmen would think a thousand times before announcing the possibility of war.[20]

2. The commitment, the degree of interest and reward, which our cultural maximizers (scientists, intellectuals, industrial administrators, and politicians) now have invested in war is, to Henry, more than alarming; it is morbid. It is an investment in death. Our cultural elite have become an elite of death.

---

[18] Henry is aware, of course, that Russia is not exactly inclined to cheer American successes. The point is not that Russia or the United States is "evil" in its malice but that the source of the malice is found within cultural rather than biological factors or something like "human nature."

[19] Henry, in a different way, is talking about the same thing Bronowski discusses in his treatment of science and human values (See Chapter 1, page 17). To put this in Bronowski's terms, Henry is concerned with the extent to which we are encapsulated from the consequences of our decisions by the immediate comforts of our economy.

[20] Henry, *Culture Against Man*, p. 102.

Moreover, death, once the final test of courage and gutty strength in individuals, is now the loser's trophy waiting for the elite and the nation whose computers and sense of strategy in gamesmanship are lacking. Death has become a game.[21] Henry quotes from an advertisement by the Rand Corporation to make his point. [Italics in the following quotation were supplied by Henry.]

> War *games* play an important part in RAND formulations. *Game* theories frequently evolve into doctrines of military strategy. *Playing games* simulating attack conditions provides answers to such problems as how to supply threatened fighter bases around the globe, and how to defend cities against bomber or missile strikes or even satellite bombings . . .[22]

3. Modern commitments to war as a form of conflict resolution have meant an increasing involvement of civilians. Civilians have become involved not only as casualties in the devastating air raids of World War II; they have, more importantly, become active participants in the war effort. The current personification of the culture hero in the folk-art media is not the soldier-killer-fighter, but the civilian-killer-fighter. A number of such civilian heroes come to mind— James Bond is the most outstanding. These heroes are often spoofed and are two-dimensional even when they are not. However, this does not make them any less significant. Whether we are confronted by an obviously bungling comic hero, or more "realistic" members of some saboteur team, the interesting thing about the hero is his civilian attire and his military mentality. Meanwhile, in the more down-to-earth activities of the Pentagon, there is concern over whether the military or the civilian strategist and tactician is going to have the final say about the disposal and utilization of today's instruments of war.

4. In a time which calls for an evaluation of world problems on the basis of extremely complex social and economic concerns, we have remained with the simpler position of evaluating people on the basis of whether we believe they are a friend or foe. The archaic and irrational posture this forces us to assume can be seen if we draw an analogy at the individual level. Suppose you were to go to a psychiatrist for help and he told you he would not be willing to treat your case unless he knew how friendly you were toward his

---

[21] More broadly, in a society which faces the problem of how to cope with leisure time on a scale never before confronted by a large cultural system, games become a way of dealing with many facets of life. Thus, love is a game, business is a game, social relations are a game, marriage is a game; indeed, life in general is an extended playing of a game. RAND theorists justify their actions on the ground that we should try to know as much about war as it is possible to know— we might, thereby, be able to control it. This is a most reasonable argument. The interesting thing is that RAND theorists seem to think they can know all there is to know about war by playing games like *Kriegspiel*.

[22] Henry, *Culture Against Man*, p. 108.

religious and personal beliefs. Such an attitude would probably be surprising and you would begin thinking of trying somewhere else. Yet such attitudes prevailed in our culture until recently—a person might be refused aid unless his religious and moral beliefs were in conformity with those offering it. Such attitudes still operate at international levels, even though our arsenal of atomic weapons makes us capable of destroying as much of this planet as we desire. Despite such military security—to attack us would be to commit suicide—we still think in terms of threat from the foe and we respond in terms of fear and retaliation. Henry finds this somewhat enigmatic. How can we account for it unless we concede that the culture, though not necessarily the individual, has something to gain in terms of solidarity and economic benefits from fear of the foe?

5. Our fear of the enemy has produced an obvious warlike posture. One element of this posture is the constraint of trade we have indulged in (and forced our allies to indulge in) with the hope that it would hurt the enemy. Henry has the following to say with regard to the consequences of the economic battle:

> High tariffs, economic isolation from the Communist countries, and the fact that much of the non-Communist world is too poor to buy from us, have made it necessary to consume at home most of what we produce. This is *relative consumption autarchy*. The growth of advertising is the institutional response to this, and the era of self-indulgence and fun is the emotional one.
>
> But consumption autarchy is not a viable form in an industrial nation, and billions of dollars have gone abroad looking for quicker and higher profits in countries where markets are expanding more rapidly than ours. The resulting loss of gold has become a constant headache because of the threat to the value of the dollar. When we cut ourselves off from Communist trade we open our own veins.
>
> Thus we come to one more delusion created by The Great Fear—the delusion of the effectiveness of economic warfare. It is delusive on two counts: first, it is not hurting the Russians; second, we are the only ones who think it important.[23]

6. Economic warfare has meant the internal economy must be relied on to attend to national needs and an internal market must be relied on to consume what is being produced by national industry. The economic consequences cannot be traced out in any detail here. But two central consequences of concern to Henry are the load placed on advertising to promote consumption and the role which war fear acquires as a means of stimulating a relatively self-contained economic system.

7. The atmosphere of security and secrecy which war fear breeds is so apparent that it almost seems unnecessary to comment on it. We cannot

---

[23] *Ibid.,* p. 114.

give our precious secrets to the enemy. But Henry observes that the fear and the secrecy go further than this. Obviously we cannot give precious secrets to the enemy, but in our state of fear we eventually find ourselves unwilling to declassify even mundane and useless, at least for war purposes, information.

> To the fear of leakage was now added the underlings' fear of releasing any information at all that might conceivably be interpreted as "embarassing" to the Department [of Defense] or as giving aid and comfort to the enemy. In these circumstances every employee ran the risk of a surprise reprimand for releasing even the most innocuous information, and it therefore became a regular practice for Department workers in all echelons to stamp as "secret" or "confidential" documents that could have no imaginable value to the enemy. It was repeatedly brought out in the hearings than any employee who had his head screwed on right would sooner withhold a document than release it to the public . . .[24]

It is not secrecy which gives away our fear; it is the extent to which secrecy is carried.

8. The alliance of industry and the military[25] has had the consequence of consolidating further the economic base from which this nation is thrust more solidly toward a warlike posture. Henry mentions the following result as only one of several:

> . . . since fear (i.e., defense) contracts are sound investments, banks lend more eagerly to companies having them than to others. The situation is made even more trying by the fact that domestic loans are more readily collectable than foreign ones; banks more easily lend to companies working for defense than to exporters shipping to troubled Latin America, Asia, and the Near East. Domestic fear is a better investment than foreign uncertainty. If anyone should ask me how to invest his money, I would say, "Invest in domestic fear. Fear and dollar grow together like root and branch."[26]

9. Although sociologists tend to emphasize the rational characteristics of administrative decisions in bureaucratically organized governments, Henry concentrates on the irrational. Fear produces more action than rational decision making. America, confronted by the nightmare of Russia, is more inclined to give in to this fear than it is to promote domestic programs. Domestic programs, now advancing under the country's aspiration to achieve the "Great Society," have been given their impetus by the fear of internal

---

[24] *Ibid.*, p. 119.

[25] This subject is covered in greater detail, though not without considerable bias and distortion, in Fred J. Cook's *The Warfare State*, (New York: The Macmillan Company, 1962). Despite the bias in this work, it is worthwhile reading. It at least provides one with some idea of the vastness of the military-industrial complex in America. When one considers the matching complexes found among our allies and enemies, it becomes difficult to face the future with much optimism.

[26] Henry, *Culture Against Man*, p. 104.

rioting and the fear that America will appear tyrannical toward her minority groups unless something is done to alleviate their condition.

Is fear a proper foundation for government? Henry, if he were a more cautious social scientist, would hesitate even to ask such a question and he certainly would not try to answer it. Yet Henry gives his opinion. He says,

A nation that will respond only to fear cannot govern itself wisely, for it has no destiny but fear, while its overshadowing goal is to defend itself.[27]

10. A last consequence of the nightmare is the desire for immediate relief from the problems imposed upon us and which we feel we, a good and just nation, do not deserve. Henry is suggesting that a realistic comprehension of international tensions is one which comprehends them in their full complexity and which recognizes, at the same time, that they cannot be resolved through any simple and immediate means. We cannot, for example, resolve our problems by going all out and winning the war with the Communists by total conquest and total military commitment. The reason, simple to an anthropologist, is that the problems which have brought on, let us say, the Viet Nam war, are not essentially military problems and cannot be resolved by military means.

We want an end to the nightmare, and we want it now. We can have an end to it, perhaps, suggests Henry, by responding not with fear but with comprehension. We must not allow our vision to become narrowed by terror.

The Great Fear resembles a true obsession: like all obsessions its perceptions and anxiety-reducing measures transgress the bounds of reality; fly in the face of the fact; have widely ramifying, unanticipated consequences; and, most important, are self-destructive over the long run. A person with an obsession takes steps that give him *immediate* relief from his anxiety, seizing upon what seems at the moment to be the element that immediately threatens his survival, only to discover later that he has chosen wrongly. A person in such a state is driven also to bizarre ways of protecting himself . . .

The American public has been so thoroughly educated to fear that statesmen think they would risk their political future by coming to an accommodation with the Russians on the only firm basis possible—the resumption of trade. But without it disarmament is only a dream, for we cannot continue economic *warfare* and expect that disarmament will bring military *peace*.[28]

So, our culture contains within it two opposed and yet reciprocal forces. There is the dream of indulgence on the one hand; and, on the other, the nightmare of "those" who would take from us our freedom to indulge. The nightmare encourages us to engage in ever more exotic and full-blown forms of self-indulgence. The more we indulge, the more frightening the nightmare

[27] *Ibid.*, p. 113.
[28] *Ibid.*, pp. 117–118.

becomes; the more we have to fear ''those'' who might interrupt our ''Midsummer Night's Dream.'' We remain, for all our technological and material development, still driven by fear.

The transmission of culture

Thus Henry provides us with an overall delineation of what he considers to be some of the major features of our culture. He is concerned, on the one hand, with the content of our culture—the ideas, beliefs, fears, aspirations, tools, and sustenance it provides. On the other hand, he is concerned with the process whereby, in daily human interactions, the content of culture is transferred to those who become transformed by it. As I mentioned earlier, culture does more than teach. As Henry put it, culture ''invades'' the mind. The lessons acquired from culture become obsessions. One finds himself ''welded'' to certain beliefs and attitudes and finds them as difficult to change as he finds it difficult to change his language.

Despite elaborate public systems designed to pass on cultural traditions, there is some possibility that we get less consistent transmission of culture from generation to generation than is the case in simpler cultures. Part of this is because it is impossible to pass on a cultural heritage so vast to each member of the culture. Another reason rests on the fact that one of our cultural traditions grants adults the right to bring their children up however they wish—so long as the child is not physically injured or so seriously damaged in character as to constitute a social menace. This means there has been a reduction in the extent to which others may correct faults implanted by the parents. The child, instead of acquiring beliefs and ways of relating to others which are culturally stable, may acquire very distorted and lethal ideas. He can be launched down a pathway to madness. Henry observes,

> In our culture babies are a private enterprise—everybody is in the baby business as soon as he gets married. He produces his own babies; they are his; only he has the right to a say-so in their management; they cannot be taken from him without due process of law; he has the sole responsibility for their maintenance and protection. He has the right to expand his production of babies indefinitely and curtail it whenever he wishes. As long as he takes care of his young children the outside world has no right to cross his threshhold, to say ''No'' or ''Yes'' about anything he does with his children. Pinched off alone in one's own house, shielded from critical eyes, one can be as irrational as one pleases with one's children as long as severe damage does not attract the attention of the police.

> In other words, there is minimal *social regulation* of parent-child relations in our culture; this is, above all, what makes lethal child-care practices possible. In a primitive culture, where many relatives are around to take an active interest in one's baby, where life is open, or in large households, where many people can see

what a mother is doing and where deviations from traditional practice quickly offend the eye and loosen critical, interested tongues, it is impossible for a parent to do as he or she pleases with his children. In a literal sense, a baby is often not even one's own in such societies, but belongs to a lineage, clan, or household— a community—having a real investment in the baby. It is not private enterprise. The almost total absence of the *social regulation* of parent-child relations in our private enterprise culture is a pivotal environmental factor . . .[29]

Within the home, then, removed from the eyes of neighbors, the child may receive an educational treatment from his parents long before he enters school—when social regulation begins to put in an appearance in the parent-child relation. This treatment can be socially damaging to the child. It can impress upon him the more self-destructive features of our economy. Most importantly, and what Henry is getting at here, this treatment is not—despite its sometimes bizarre and possibly lethal nature—removed from our culture. It comes out of it and appears in the form of exaggerated and distorted elements which already exist within the culture.

Henry comes to these conclusions after spending a number of weeks living in the homes of children considered sufficiently disturbed to require psychiatric care. Henry especially concerned himself with the relationship between the parents and the children in these homes. More significantly, he was concerned with the extent to which the parent misused a culturally sanctioned value and, as a consequence, damaged his child. A case in point is the relationship existing between Mr. Portman and his son Pete. The Portman home was one observed by Henry for some time. He says of the father-son relationship,

> Mr. Portman expresses his love for his son through throwing him around, punching him in the belly, and imitating a devouring animal. Pete cannot fail, therefore, to associate love with physical violence: to love a person is to throw him around, wallop him, and symbolically chew him up—in other words, to have fun. Pete tries a baby version of this on Elaine, his little playmate next door. Thus the toughness-love-violence combination, so common in our movies, is here built into the child's flesh and bone through the basic biological mammalian function of play.[30]

In a final summary of his observations of the Portman family, Henry makes the following statement:

---

[29] *Ibid.*, pp. 331–332. Unfortunately, examples of what Henry is talking about are common. As I was preparing this material I received a letter from a colleague informing me that a graduate student in counseling psychology had been shaken up by a recent experience. He had been working with a little girl who seemed to be unusually anally compulsive in her behavior. Then he learned that she is one of five children in her family, each of whom gets a daily enema from Mama. The mother is not malicious. She simply has taken too much to heart the adage that cleanliness is next to godliness. And, within the privacy of her home, she is determined to have clean kids—inside as well as outside.

[30] *Ibid.*, p. 347.

Coming together in *lethal* form in Mr. and Mrs. Portman, widespread American personality characteristics such as shallowness of involvement, confusion and vagueness, a tendency to read life off in terms of a dominance-submission struggle, a tendency to sacrifice tenderness to strength, and a tendency to humiliate others, have produced a dreadful, unplanned and unintended but nevertheless pathogenic entanglement of parents and children that has the quality of destiny and tragedy. In this state, isolated from public view, husband, wife, and children live out their secret misery. Babies are private enterprise in Western culture and so are misery and dissolution.[31]

So, from the perspective of the anthropologist, culture worms its way into our innermost beings. It is there when we are rationally calculating the orbital pattern of an artificial satellite. It is also there when we march down some seemingly lonely road to madness. It elaborates our fears and provides a platform for our vanities. It is the source of our knowledge and, at the same time, it determines those things of which we must remain ignorant. It can provide man with his most courageously human qualities and, paradoxically, it can be the source of his most wretched absurdities. It can dominate man to the point where he finds it difficult to tell where a culturally instilled desire begins and animal nature leaves off. Culture can extend man's vision in one direction and completely blind him in another.

The concept of culture is quite abstract and cultural forces themselves are extremely vast, powerful, and subtle. Yet, despite this, the anthropologist does not lose sight of the fact that the matter of culture is essentially a matter of what man does to himself. For after all, culture is simply what generations of men have passed on to those who follow. Culture is the hand of the dead on the shoulder of the living. It may be a very powerful hand, but it is still human and still fallible.

We can gain some idea of the extent to which the hand of the dead is still operative in American culture when we observe the extent to which we are motivated, in the midst of opulence, to pursue the ideal of a rising standard of living. How far must we go in this pursuit—the foundation of the older American dream—before we have exhausted it and ourselves? Perhaps, as Eric Hoffer suggests (and Henry, I think, would agree), we should now aspire to rising standards of intellect rather than rising standards of living. If this is a reasonable ideal, it helps make Henry's observations all the more poignant; for one of the most effective ways in which culture stands mobilized against man today is the extent to which it frustrates the pursuit of this ideal.

Though Henry's commentaries are depressing, they are not lacking in hope. Unlike the primitive or the members of societies ruled by tradition, modern

---

[31] *Ibid.*, p. 349.

man does not have to accept uncritically the dictates of a tyrannical culture. He has the opportunity to stand back and evaluate what his culture is doing to him. He can ask questions concerning his nature. Henry is not so presumptuous as to claim that he has answered these basic humanistic questions. However, he does tell those who are involved with them that many of the answers do not lie within a searching of the individual soul. Instead, we must consider the extent to which we, as cultural beings, have been helped or hindered by our culture. We must look around us as well as within ourselves. We must learn to recognize the lethal as well as the life-giving elements in our culture—for these appear ultimately within each of us.

14 The Formation of Delinquent Culture: Albert K. Cohen's Theory of the Gang

As a form of social behavior, crime poses many puzzles and contradictions for the modern sociologist and for the psychologist as well. There was a time when crime was seen as the simple product of mental deficiency.[1] Now we know that men who violate the law and are apprehended have mental abilities not significantly below normal levels.[2] There was also a time when criminals were considered to be more "primitive" biological types. A man who was likely to violate the laws could be identified by his "atavistic stigmata."[3] The idea here was that criminally inclined men were throwbacks, genetically, to an earlier form of man who was more savage in nature and, consequently, less inclined to adhere to modern laws and social regulations. The stigmas identifying such a type of man were those facial and bodily characteristics typical of early man. This theory, simple and appealing as it is, had to be abandoned. Psychologists found, for example, that when the pictures of known criminals were included among a group of noncriminals, even experts could not, to any significant degree, pick out the criminals. Although this idea has been abandoned by most criminologists, psychologists, and sociologists, it still has a surprising amount of popularity.[4]

---

[1] The early enthusiasm that came with the first employment of mental tests led to a heavy reliance on intelligence as a condition for all that is good while stupidity accounted for that which is bad. Caldwell makes the following comment: "In 1928 and 1929 Sutherland analyzed about 350 studies on intelligence and crime and showed that the proportion of delinquents and criminals diagnosed as feebleminded had decreased from more than 50 per cent in the average study made in the period 1910 to 1914 to 20 per cent in the period 1925 to 1928." Robert G. Caldwell, *Criminology* (New York: The Ronald Press Company, 1956), p. 208.

[2] One criminological authority, for example, completely ignores the question of mental ability. He makes no mention of mental deficiency in his book other than to say that today ". . . psychologists and psychiatrists seldom contend that mental deficiency is an important cause of delinquency and crime." Walter C. Reckless, *The Crime Problem*, (3d ed.; New York: Appleton-Century-Crofts, 1960), p. 270.

[3] This term is attributed to Cesare Lombroso, an Italian anthropologist of the 19th century.

[4] Dick Tracy, for example, hardly ever has a handsome adversary.

Popular ideas about the origins of crime

A simpler and more commonsense notion of crime is that the criminal is some-one looking for an "easy way out" of his problems. If he is poor, the "easy" way to get money is to steal it. If his wife is bothering him, the "easy" way out is murder rather than a divorce with its attendant alimony, publicity, and so on. Crime, according to this point of view, reveals a definite weakness of character. We have already seen how Merton used the distinction between institutional goals and means to characterize the criminal as one who seeks legitimate goals by illegitimate means. But this is a very abstract characterization. It still leaves hanging the question of why some people elect to employ illegitimate means while others do not. Common sense rushes in to fill the gap with an idea like "weakness of character." Sociologists and psychologists would also like to fill the gap, but they are not prone to accept a notion like this. It is very difficult to specify, for example, what exactly is meant by "weakness of character." One can argue most reasonably that it takes great strength of character to plan and execute a well-ordered robbery. Moreover, it is probably very easy to adhere to the laws when one is not desperate or driven by circumstances external to his character. The man who has many good friends, status, security, and bright prospects for the future will not be as likely to engage in violent criminal actions as the man whose situation is such that the most extreme measures seem necessary to save him from a bitter future. But, if this is the case, then the causes or factors that incline people toward leading criminal lives are external to character.

Finally, the only way we recognize weakness of character is by an individual's failings. Then, when we use weakness to explain the failings, we have engaged in a circular argument. So, why did Johnny steal? Because he has a weak character. How do we know he has a weak character? Because he stole. Really, all we are saying here is that Johnny stole because Johnny stole. This does not get us very far. We will have to abandon the idea of weakness of character because it cannot carry the burdens placed upon it.

Another idea popularly set forth has been to see criminal behavior as a rational calculation of benefits. According to this idea, the criminal is a fellow who considers the positive and negative consequences of breaking the law. If the positive consequences are greater than the negative, he will break the law. If they are not, he will continue to operate as a law-abiding citizen. This is the position of so-called "classical" criminology, which was based on Jeremy Bentham's notion of the "hedonistic calculus," that is, the calculation of pleasures. This idea, like the others, has not proved acceptable to critical social scientists. Nonetheless, it is still a central perspective underlying our legal system where it lives an active if somewhat senile life.

Our legal system implicitly endorses the idea that if punishments are made a little more painful than the pleasures to be derived from crime, then the criminal action will be averted. The fact that our jails and prisons are full does not seem to dampen the ardor of some men who, like the Mikado in Gilbert and Sullivan's operetta, exclaim,

> My object all sublime,
> I shall achieve in time,
> To let the punishment fit the crime,
> The punishment fit the crime.

While this idea remains active in our judicial-legal system, it is nearly dead everywhere else. The main reason is simply that too many crimes obviously violate the hedonistic calculus. A man is willing, quite often, to murder a hated enemy regardless of the costs. There are other occasions when crime seems to fill no personal or social needs. For example, there are occasions when youths engage in extensive destruction of property. They sometimes go down a suburban street and slash auto tires, break windshields, or cut convertible tops. Though such behavior is perhaps gratifying to the juvenile, it is not rational in the sense that theft, let us say, is rational. The malicious mischief of the juvenile does not show any purposeful utilization of property, while theft, on the other hand, does. For the moment, let us call crimes that seem to fill no apparent personal or social needs "irrational" and concede that they pose an interesting problem. Later, after we have considered the position taken by Cohen, such "irrational" crimes should be more understandable.[5] For the present, let us view them as a barrier in the way of accepting a rational theory of crime like the hedonistic calculus.

Another idea about crime which has been especially popular in modern times is the belief that crime is a product of association with criminals. An individual who hangs around with a bad crowd will himself become bad eventually. A criminologist named Edwin H. Sutherland developed this theory and documented it elaborately.[6] He used the term "differential association" and meant by it that differences in individuals with whom a person associates are influential in establishing the likelihood he will become criminal. This idea has

---

[5] Unfortunately, a lot of people believe that to make something understandable is to make it morally acceptable. Thus, if we understand why some people murder, then we are a step closer to condoning murder. I do not want to get involved with this issue and will dismiss it by suggesting that an understanding of the causes of lung cancer, for example, does not mean that we are obliged to contract one.

[6] Edwin H. Sutherland, *Principles of Criminology* (Philadelphia: J. B. Lippincott Co., 1939). The summary I have presented of Sutherland's ideas is a gross oversimplification.

some limitations, but it is generally acceptable to social scientists. Even so, as an explanation of crime it has one most glaring weakness—it presumes that crime already exists. That is to say, if we accept the idea that crime is a form of behavior learned from people who already practice it, then we are still left with the problem of where it came from to be learned in the first place. Perhaps Al acquired his criminal nature from Bill, and Bill acquired his from Charley, and Charley his from Don, but this can go on forever. Where did the pattern originate? How did it originate? It is in an attempt to solve this problem that we must turn to the works of Albert K. Cohen[7] because Cohen, perhaps more clearly and ingeniously than anyone else, has suggested a solution.

Lower-class male juvenile delinquency

Cohen's solution does not, we must point out at the very beginning, try to explain all kinds of crime. The following discussion will be restricted to an attempt to account for only a certain type of antisocial behavior: that of lower-class, male, juvenile, gang delinquents. With this restriction in mind we may begin. Later we shall see how Cohen's ideas may be extended to account for a wider variety of social actions.

Cohen opens his discussion of the lower-class male juvenile gang delinquent by warning us that we must not see gang delinquency in the same way that we look at adult crime—especially adult professional crime. Juvenile delinquency might not be professional crime on a smaller scale. Nor is it necessarily an introduction to or "schooling" for later professional crime.

> If we assume that "crime is crime," that child and adult criminals are practitioners of the same trade, and if our assumptions are false, then the road to error is wide and clear. Easily and unconsciously, we may impute a whole host of notions concerning the nature of crime and its causes, derived from our knowledge and fancies about adult crime, to a large realm of behavior to which these notions are irrelevant. It is better to make no such assumptions; it is better to look at juvenile delinquency with a fresh eye and try to explain what we see.[8]

Cohen examines juvenile delinquency with a fresh eye and finds it, in contrast to adult crime, to be nonutilitarian, malicious, versatile, hedonistic, and negativistic.

---

[7] Cohen's most influential work was *Delinquent Boys: The Culture of the Gang* (New York: Free Press of Glencoe, 1955), 202 pp. Cohen acknowledges his debt to Sutherland in this work. He also acknowledges it in a volume entitled *The Sutherland Papers*, edited by Cohen, Lindesmith, and Schuessler (Bloomington: Indiana University Press, 1956), 330 pp. A more recent and sophisticated volume by Cohen is *Deviance and Control* (Englewood Cliffs, N.J.: Prentice-Hall, Inc., 1966).

[8] From Albert K. Cohen, *Delinquent Boys: The Culture of the Gang* (New York: Free Press of Glencoe, 1955), p. 25. Copyright 1955 by The Free Press, a Corporation.

It is nonutilitarian in that it often serves no obvious use. It is irrational. Gang delinquency sometimes takes on the appearance of being a sport. When a professional criminal steals, we can usually understand his motives. He might need some money to take his girl friend out on the town; or he might need more cash to send his daughter to finishing school. The gang delinquent, on the other hand, will occasionally steal something from one store and then deposit his stolen goods in another store, where he also indulges in pilfering. Cohen concedes that such behavior is probably a kind of play activity or sport or recreation. But, at the same time, he raises the question of why this particular form of play can be so attractive to some and so unappealing to others. Before we can understand this kind of activity we must begin to under- stand why stealing, for example, can be a means to prestige and status in one group and, for some reason or other, be a degrading blot in a different group. This is a critical question and ultimately proves to be the fulcrum on which Cohen balances his conception of gang delinquency.

We have noted that gang delinquent behavior is nonutilitarian. It is also malicious; that is, the gang delinquent enjoys the discomfiture of others. The professional or adult criminal often discomfits others, but this is generally a by-product of his criminal action rather than an end in itself. In extortion, for example, it is occasionally necessary to "strong-arm" a reluctant victim. This is not preferred, however, to situations where the victim is more co- operative. The gang delinquent, on the other hand, will go to unusual extremes to provoke or torment or injure a victim. For example, one gang member gives the following account of the killing of a fifteen-year-old polio cripple who was in no way associated with the gang, either as a member or as an enemy:

> Magician stabbed him and the guy he . . . like hunched over. He's standin' up and I knock him down. Then he was down on the ground, everybody was kickin' him, stompin' him, punchin' him, stabbin' him so he tried to get back up and I knock him down again. Then the guy stabbed him in the back with a bread knife.[9]

Gang behavior is nonutilitarian, malicious, and it is versatile. Here Cohen means it is less specialized than adult professional crime. While an adult group might specialize in armed robbery, a delinquent gang will be engaged in a variety of criminal activities. These can range from malicious mischief to armed robbery and murder.

Cohen also claims that the gang behaves in a hedonistic fashion. By this he means the gang acts according to "spur of the moment" desires and

---

[9] Lewis Yablonsky, *The Violent Gang* (New York: The Macmillan Company, 1962), p. 19. © Lewis Yablonsky 1962.

interests. Gang members do not take kindly to rules and schedules. Their activities are seldom carefully planned and there is a characteristic lack of discipline. Although the gang member accepts the authority of the gang, this authority does not get him involved in a high degree of self-discipline.

The gang is also negativistic. Here Cohen means the gang is intolerant of any restraints except those coming from informal pressures within the group itself. There is a general rejection of commonly accepted ways of living and behaving toward others.

The delinquent code of conduct

Given these social and cultural characteristics of the gang, how do we come to understand them? What are the conditions leading toward a pattern of living which is so at variance with the general norms of society? This is an extremely basic question because sociologists are well aware that social forces are tremendously powerful and, in general, are quite successful in producing conformity on the part of most people. In Chapter 10, you may recall, we reviewed Berger's outline of the various devices that keep men "prisoners" of society. As described by Berger these devices seem overwhelming. Here, in the gang delinquent, we have someone who subscribes to a code of conduct not generally sanctioned by society. The problem now is to determine how the code came into being despite the massive contrary pressures of social control described by Berger.

Cohen answers this problem in the following manner. First, Cohen assumes that all human action involves an ongoing series of efforts to solve problems. He does not mean problems like an algebra examination or a crossword puzzle. He uses the term "problem" in a broad way to refer to tensions, disequilibria, or challenges that must be resolved.

Some problems have traditional modes of solution already available. Others may not be easily resolved. If the problem, let us say, is to become a successful man in the community, a traditional mode of solution is to go to school, get an education, establish a professional status, and advance from there. If, for any reason, this traditional mode of solution might not be available, the problem of achieving success will require a more novel solution.

So far it does not seem that Cohen has said very much. His notion of problem solving is similar to the pleasure-pain principle of the early hedonists, and it is much like the idea of drive or need satisfaction still popular today among many social psychologists. But there is more to Cohen's thinking.

There are two conditions affecting the nature of the problem confronting a human being and how he will resolve that problem. There is, first, the "situation." The situation involves the physical setting within which we operate, the time and energy we have to achieve our ends, and, most importantly, the social organization of the people around us. Second, there is the "frame of reference" through which the individual perceives the situation and evaluates it as a problem. The "frame of reference" involves the manner in which we perceive the situation. *It is possible, through varying frames of reference, to see the same situation in highly varied ways.* This is a fundamental conception in Cohen's thinking and it is also the basis for many other ideas currently endorsed by social and behavioral scientists.

Changing the frame of reference

Coming back, now, to the matter of solving problems, Cohen suggests that we can solve a problem in either of two ways. First, we can change the situation producing the problem. Second, we can change the frame of reference we bring to the problem. If we are hungry and the problem is to get some food, we might handle the problem by going out to the refrigerator, opening the door, taking out some rye bread, Swiss cheese, and beer. Then we can eat. In this simple situation we have solved the problem by changing the situation. The second way of solving problems does not sound as "real" as the first, and in a way it is not. It is, however, a thorough and effective solution in those instances where it may be applied. To continue with the hunger problem, the second way consists of becoming convinced that either we are not hungry or that hunger is a condition to be preferred over being satiated.

To illustrate how effective this second form of problem solving can be, consider the case of a boy who is taking a class in mathematics and is getting a failing grade. He has a problem. One way of solving it would be to work harder and earn a passing grade. This would require changing the situation. Another way of solving the problem would be to convince himself that passing a course in calculus is not worth the effort. This would involve changing his frame of reference—assuming he held a positive attitude toward the course originally. The crucial point here is to see that changing his frame of reference would be as complete a solution as getting a passing grade. In fact, if he can truly convince himself that mathematics is "bad" and that an interest in mathematics might have a dreadful effect on his character and mind, then a failing grade in the calculus course can be accepted more readily. Indeed, it might come to be seen as a positive benefit! When this is so, the problem has been solved. The previous possibility of discomfort because of a failing grade has now been changed to a sense of pleasure. Thus, the solution is a "real" one—it is effective. But what does all of this have to do with gang delinquency?

We must begin by seeing that people in different sectors of the social system may be affected differently by what appears externally to be the same kind of problem. Both a lower-class boy and a middle-class boy may be faced with the problem of becoming successful members of the community. But whereas success might simply mean getting a job for the lower-class boy, success for the middle-class boy might mean becoming a research physicist or a medical doctor. Not only will the two boys be affected differently by what externally appears to be the same problem, they will also rely on different actions available to them as a means of resolving the problem.

Cohen points out that the value given to democratic equality in America has meant denying the importance of such extraneous factors as family, race, and ethnic affiliation in the quest for success. This means, however, that the number of people against whom a child can measure himself, and against whom he is in fact measured, is extended tremendously. This is more clearly seen by pointing to undemocratic, feudal, or caste societies where it has been assumed that the society is permanently divided into "natural" social divisions. The child of a peasant family, for example, could not become "ego-involved" or competitive toward the son of a nobleman in the same way a lower-class boy of today might feel competitive toward a middle- or upper-class boy.[10] In the peasant society, the farmer's son and the nobleman's son lived in different status universes.

Today, in our society, the child of lower-class status is compared with all comers of his own age, regardless of background. At the same time, it should be apparent that family background is influential in determining the likelihood that an individual will rise within the society—or at least maintain an already established level of success. It is this situation which Cohen views as a basis for severe problems encountered by the lower-class boy—problems which lead him, ultimately, to resort to novel solutions.

---

[10] Compare this point of view with that suggested by the following quotation from Cervantes, who described a more fluid state of affairs in medieval feudal society. ". . . there are two kinds of classes in the world: those who draw and derive their descent from princes and monarchs, and whom time undoes bit by bit until they are totally ruined; and others who take their beginnings from the common people and rise from rank to rank until they become great lords; the difference being that some were what they are no longer, and others are what they once were not." Don Quixote, Book I, Chapter 21, cited in Henry Kamen, *The Spanish Inquisition* (New York: The New American Library, Inc., 1965), p. 8. The point here, of course, is that Cohen is possibly exaggerating the social immobility of feudal society.

Cohen suggests that the status aspirations of the lower-class boy are elevated by democratic ideals to the point where he is called on to compete on equal terms with others having many more advantages granted them in the race to get ahead. At the same time, the boy begins to see that his likelihood of success is limited. How can he cope with this problem? One way would be to try to change the situation. He could attempt either to change the larger social order, or he might try to extricate himself from the class conditions which lower his chances of success. For a single and powerless boy, changing the social order is obviously impossible. Coping with the situation by self-improvement or education is not impossible, but it could be extremely difficult. The educational system is an available way of extricating oneself from class conditions which frustrate the quest for success in our society. But what is to be done if the educational system will not accept you? You are then blocked. The educational system of this country is grounded in middle-class values, procedures, and customs—it is controlled and operated by people who subscribe to an American middle-class way of life. If a lower-class youngster is deviant enough with respect to his own background, he may be able to make the break and become acceptable to his teachers, and gradually become successful through the traditional climb up the educational ladder. But a lower-class boy whose background has "taken," as it were, may find himself unacceptable to his teachers and to the educational system which is dedicated to "middle-classing" him.

This, then, constitutes the problem encountered by many a lower-class male in this society. At a certain point he finds himself required to seek certain legitimate goals. These goals are strongly endorsed by the greater society. At the same time, for rather complex reasons, the means of achieving these goals may be denied. If we accept this evaluation of the position of the lower-class boy and presume, for the moment, that changing the situation is nearly impossible, then what is left? There is still one possibility—the lower-class boy might be able to cope with this problem by altering his frame of reference!

Essentially this means that the problem will be solved by rejecting the values society places on the goals of success and ambition. Cohen lists a number of goals strongly endorsed by the American middle class and then underscores the observation that delinquent behavior is characteristically a reversal of these. First we will list the values Cohen considers significant and then, second, we will want to consider how "reversing" them takes place. It is in the development of this reversal that we begin to gain a broader insight into how social differentiation takes place and how sometimes bizarre and generally unaccepted lifeways may be formed.

Middle-class values

The middle-class values mentioned by Cohen[11] are

1. AMBITION. Any good person is one who is ambitious for himself and who can appreciate ambition as a virtue when he sees it in others.

2. INDIVIDUAL RESPONSIBILITY. In the final accounting a person must accept responsibility for his actions. If he is successful or not, the outcome is a product of his decisions and actions and he must be willing to take credit or blame as the situation warrants.

3. CULTIVATION AND POSSESSION OF SKILLS. Skills ranging from the relatively practical, such as those acquired in the Boy Scouts, to the very impractical, such as baton twirling, are valued by the middle class. Any acceptable skill, regardless of its "practicality," is valued for the potential uses to which it may be put. Hopefully, the baton twirler finds popularity and the Boy Scout acquires manly habits.

4. DEFERRED GRATIFICATION. The middle-class youth is expected to acquire values that will enable him to refrain from immediate pleasures in order to attain long-range goals.

5. RATIONALITY. Thoughtful planning and consideration of the future is valued.

6. CULTIVATION OF MANNERS. The middle-class youth is expected to devote himself to the development of "mannerly" behavior. He should be aware not only of the form but also the spirit of mannerly conduct. The spirit of mannerly conduct consists of having a regard for others no matter what their station in life or their relationship to you.

7. PATIENCE AND SELF-CONTROL. The middle-class person should be capable of self-control and he should be willing to give his plans some time to develop.

8. CONTROL OF PHYSICAL AGGRESSION AND VIOLENCE. Middle-class values strongly underwrite gentleness in conduct. Behavior which is violent yet acceptable is usually carefully regulated. Football is an example of violent behavior which is still acceptable. Even here, middle-class values emphasize sportsmanship and maintaining respect for the opponent.

9. CONSTRUCTIVE USE OF LEISURE. In the middle-class set of values, time is money. Whether at work or at play, one should make constructive use of time. Golfing, for example, is not a waste of time if it can be seen as a

---

[11] Cohen, *Delinquent Boys*, pp. 88–91. The list presented here is very similar to that of Cohen. I have abbreviated it slightly and made "patience and self-control" a separate category.

means of "keeping fit," a way of learning self-control, and an opportunity for meeting business and professional associates.

10. RESPECT FOR PROPERTY. One is expected not only to take care of his own property and make good use of it; he is also expected to show respect for the property of others.

We will not elaborate on each of these values. If they are characteristic of the middle class, and this seems reasonable and generally accepted, then the gang delinquent lives by a quite different code. He appears to have reversed this value system. Rather than valuing ambition, he appears to subscribe to the idea that ambition is stupid. Instead of an ethic of individual responsibility, he conforms to the dictates of the gang. Where the middle-class youngster is motivated to acquire skills as diverse as football passing and techniques of qualitative analysis in chemistry, the gang delinquent is generally lacking in skills of almost any kind and he is not inclined to undergo the self-discipline such skills require. Rather than refraining from immediate pleasures, as does the middle-class youth, the gang delinquent is more inclined to behave in terms of immediate and short-run pleasures—the short-run hedonism referred to earlier. The middle-class youth is expected to exercise forethought and plan ahead—indeed, middle-class children of today may begin thinking about retirement before they enter college. The gang delinquent, on the other hand, is less given to planning. The boy who was stabbed to death in the example cited earlier was not the victim of a planned killing. As a matter of fact, he was not known to any of his assailants. His murder was an unplanned occurrence of the moment.

The lower-class delinquent gang cannot be described as seeking the cultivation of manners. If anything, gang delinquents appear at times to go out of their way to make others uncomfortable—to behave in ways that are obvious manifestations of their lack of respect for middle-class mannerliness. So we can continue through the other middle-class values. The delinquent does not cultivate patience or self-control; he is inclined to engage in physical aggression and violence; he is not concerned with the constructive use of leisure; and acts of vandalism exemplify his lack of respect or concern for property and property rights.

Theory of social differentiation

It seems, then, to Cohen, that somehow delinquency is the achievement of a way of living—a cultural scheme—which is an inversion of the generally accepted cultural scheme. How does the inversion take place? As we noted before, Cohen is not content merely with saying that it is learned. We must try to understand how such a pattern of behavior came into existence in the first place. Once it exists, it can then be learned. It is here that Cohen suggests the beginnings of a theory of social differentiation. His theory is based on a consideration of how changes in frames of reference occur under situations where the changed frame of reference will be socially unacceptable. Or, as Cohen phrases the question: "How is it possible for cultural innovations to emerge while each of the participants in the culture is so powerfully motivated to conform to what is already established?[12]

In order for cultural innovations such as we find in delinquent behavior to develop, it is necessary to bring together a number of people who have similar problems of adjustment. These people may have available a variety of conceivable solutions to their problems, some of which might not as yet be embodied in actions and which do not, therefore, exist as a cultural model. The blunt and direct introduction of such a model to the other members of the group could cause the person making the introduction to be ostracized.

Consider, for example, the problems faced by a group of new young faculty who are accustomed to having a few cocktails at parties but who are now members of a college which bans drinking among its faculty. Each member of the group may be willing to have a drink, but no member of the group is willing to blurt out an open invitation to indulge. To do so might jeopardize his or her acceptability to the group. There is, after all, the possibility that everyone else accepts and endorses the policy of the college toward drinking. In such circumstances there is apt to be a great deal of joking and teasing about drinking. In this way a serious problem can be approached in a nonserious fashion. If the teasing and joking references to drinking are met by others in a certain way, the conversation can develop to the point where the participants begin to become aware of the fact that all are actually in accord with the idea of having a drink. On the other hand, if the conversation goes in another direction, the person who initiated the joking references to drinking may discover that the group is highly critical of such behavior. He can then abandon his teasing without having been seriously in jeopardy at any time. A similar process is involved in the development of any socially unacceptable pattern of behavior or behavior which is believed to be socially unacceptable. The consideration important to note here is that the novel solution, or the socially disapproved solution, comes from a group process. The new solution does not appear full-fledged on the scene but is a result of group interaction taking place over some length of time. It is what sociologists call an "emergent"

---

[12] *Ibid.*, p. 59.

pattern of behavior. Because it has its locus within the group, it acquires a special strength as opposed to a solution which might be congenial to the individual but which is supported by no one else.

We have now begun to consider the importance of the group. When it was noted earlier that an individual may solve a problem by changing the situation confronting him or by changing the frame of reference through which he perceives the situation, we had not said all that needs to be said. We had not considered the necessity of group support for maintaining a novel frame of reference. Think, for a minute, of the little fable by Aesop concerning the fox and the grapes. When the fox tried to convince himself that the grapes he could not reach were sour, we had a case of an attempted solution of a problem by changing the frame of reference. The fox could not change the situation by grabbing the grapes, so he tried to change his attitude toward them and convince himself he was better off not to have been able to reach them. So, he walked off muttering to himself that the grapes would have been bad for him. The fable has a poignancy about it because we know that the fox was not actually able to fool himself. We feel equally sorry for some people when we observe them taking a "sour grapes" approach toward things we know they would like to have but cannot obtain. Our attitude comes from our awareness that they are not fully convinced of what they are saying. Such lack of conviction could be overcome, however, if the individual found a group which very strongly supported the "sour grapes" frame of reference.

If the fox, for example, had been told by another fox, or better yet by a gang of foxes who were his close buddies, that he was indeed lucky not to have been able to reach the grapes because they had been poisoned by the farmer, then the fable would be quite different in meaning and it would be less interesting. We would feel that the fox was now justified in his conviction. What before was self-deception now becomes a "fact." And when this happens, the fable moves from a character analysis to a straightforward report of events. However, we should continue to wonder whether the grapes were, in fact, poisoned. The gang could be as deluded as the fox alone.[13]

In order for the altered frame of reference to work, then, it is necessary for the individual to obtain external support for it. One way of doing this is to find a group that already exists and which is capable of reinforcing or rewarding and otherwise supporting the new attitude which will serve as a solution to a problem. This is what happens when, let us say, a college student

---

[13] Weston La Barre generalizes on this theme by saying, ". . . culture is also the immortality of dead men, a way in which their judgments and choices manage to coerce the living. Still, all men, including dead men, can be wrong." Weston La Barre, *The Human Animal* (Phoenix Edition; Chicago: University of Chicago Press, 1960), p. 221.

finds it difficult to meet the status competition coming from wealthier students on the campus. If he can find a group which subscribes to a Bohemian way of life and promotes poverty, nonconformity, and hostility toward organized student groups, then he may be able to solve his problem. Most importantly, he may begin to perceive his way of life as *the* way of life. He has solved the problem of poverty by making poverty an ideal way of living, a test of character, a symbol of independence, or an assertion of self. But in so doing, he must have the support of others who subscribe to the same ideals and frame of reference. If he is alone in his rejection of wealth, then we have a ''sour grapes'' approach; but if he is supported by an already existing organized set of beliefs, his attitudes take on a more ''realistic'' character.

But what if no already existing problem-solving frames of reference are around to be joined or used by the person?

In this event we may, if a number of people come together who share a similar problem, get the tentative collective movement toward an emergent solution illustrated earlier by the faculty in a school that prohibits drinking. Cohen suggests that this is what happens in some lower-class juvenile male gangs. Five or six boys come together and, at the same time, share a common problem with respect, let us say, to getting along in school. One way for a boy to solve the school problem would be to develop a negative frame of reference toward the school. But it might be the case that most of the other boys in the group happen to accept the school routine. So, at first tentative and relatively weak negative propositions will be introduced by the boy. If the others accept these, then each will begin to contribute toward the development of an antischool frame of reference. This frame of reference will ultimately emerge from the interaction of the boys and will be a group product—something which cannot be ascribed to any one of the participants in particular. It may also have the property of being more intensely negative than one that any individual boy might have been able to suggest. Thus, a group-developed norm of this type may lead toward greater violence and more intense expression of emotion than any individual in the group would have been willing to commit himself to alone.

The gang as a status system

The gang becomes important, then, because within it the boy may find support for a way of looking at things that helps him solve some of the problems confronting him. If, for example, he is having difficulty meeting the routines expected of him in an essentially middle-class school system, the gang can generate and then sustain a negative frame of reference toward the school. By so doing it enables the boy to acquire status and social rewards from the gang for behavior that would otherwise be punished by the greater society. This makes the gang an important social unit for the boy and it makes membership within the gang a gratifying experience.

But the fact that the gang represents a status system frowned on by the larger society produces a condition in which status within the gang will be accompanied by a loss of status outside the gang. The reaction to this problem is to devalue the goodwill and respect of those whose goodwill and respect would have to be forfeited anyway. So, the gang develops, as part of its way of perceiving the world around it, hostile and contemptuous images of any groups whose enmity it has earned. The repudiation of outsiders is necessary in order to avoid concern about what they think. Eventually nonconformity with the expectations of outsiders may be made a positive criterion of prestige within the group.

Cohen lends further insight to this process by referring to Redl's concept of "protective provocation."

> One curious but not uncommon accompaniment of this process is what Fritz Redl has called "protective provocation." Certain kinds of behavior to which we are strongly inclined may encounter strong resistances because this behavior would do injury to the interests or feelings of people we care about. These same kinds of behavior would, however, be unequivocally motivated without complicating guilt feelings if those people stood to us in the relation of enemies rather than friends. In such a situation we may be unconsciously motivated to act precisely in those ways calculated to stimulate others to expressions of anger and hostility, which we may then seize upon as evidences of their essential enmity and ill will. We are then absolved of our moral obligations toward those persons and freer to act without ambivalence. The hostility of the "out-group," thus engendered or aggravated, may serve to protect the "in-group" from mixed feelings about its way of life.[14]

Delinquent behavior becomes one means whereby youths may resolve the problem of defining their status. If their hostility toward the respectable elements of society is intense, the implication is that their dedication to their own group or subculture is equally intense. Cohen suggests this in the following comparison of the corner boy with the college boy:

> As long as the working-class corner boy clings to a version, however attenuated and adulterated, of the middle-class culture, he must recognize his inferiority to working-class and middle-class college boys. The delinquent subculture, on the other hand, permits no ambiguity of the status of the delinquent relative to that of any-

---

[14] Cohen, *Delinquent Boys*, p. 69.

body else. In terms of the norms of the delinquent subculture, defined by its negative polarity to the respectable status system, the delinquent's very nonconformity to middle-class standards sets him above the most exemplary college boy.[15]

Delinquent behavior becomes a means of resolving felt inferiority. It becomes a way of establishing meaning for one's life. It becomes a procedure for generating a particular standard of what is socially significant which may then be used for measuring the value of one's actions. In this respect delinquent behavior shares elements in common with many other forms of social activity. Whether a man is playing the role of father, or captain in the navy, or college student, or Ku Klux Klan member, one problem is to commit him to the significance of the social performance he is about to undertake.

Cohen is concerned with how delinquent behavior develops the particular standards that are uniquely characteristic of it and why these standards get such intense commitment from delinquent youths. He emphasizes the group nature of such standards, and this is an important emphasis. One cannot grasp Cohen's reasoning and continue, thereafter, to insist that delinquency is largely a product of psychological disturbances within the individual. Such an approach to crime and delinquency, so far as sociologists are concerned, gives too much importance to purely individual characteristics.

For Cohen, the social element in crime is critical in at least two places. The first of these is the massive social class structure which may impose heavy burdens on some members of the society and increase the likelihood that they will respond in defensive ways—some of which may prove to be criminal. The second of these is the social process within the delinquent gang which may ultimately provide the basis for the development and the support of intensely antimiddle-class lifeways.

The meaning of "good" and "evil"

The humanistic problem for which Cohen's writing is relevant is the problem of good and evil. Most sociologists, like Cohen, attempt to be objective in their study of human social behavior. This means they do not try to stipulate what people ought to do in order to be good or to avoid to keep from being bad. As a consequence the sociologist is sometimes viewed as a man who ignores the problem of evil. This is not so. Cohen, for example, does not ignore this problem. Instead, he takes evil out of human nature or some such metaphysical notion as "original sin" and places it within social processes. Most sociologists would support this perspective. In so doing they neither es-

---

[15] *Ibid.*, pp. 130–131.

pouse nor ignore evil behavior. Instead, they are concerned with understanding it as a human social condition.

Cohen goes further than Durkheim, who saw evil as a necessary condition for the definition of good; that is to say, what is good could not be established without the existence of contrary conditions which bring the good into clear relief. Durkheim put it this way:

> Crime, then, is necessary; it is bound up with the fundamental conditions of all social life and by that very fact it is useful, because these conditions of which it is a part are themselves indispensable to the normal evolution of morality and law.[16]

Cohen goes further than to say that evil is socially defined. Crime, delinquency, and other forms of antisocial behavior which, ultimately, come under humanistic considerations of evil, are natural products of the workings of a social system. Human society, unlike that of insects, is based on elaborately developed rules and regulations. The symbolic nature of these rules and their arbitrariness require devices for making people conform to them. These devices usually involve giving rewards to those who conform and punishing those who deviate. Once this situation exists, the basis is laid for the processes Cohen has described.

Those who are punished because they cannot, for various reasons, conform to the rules, may begin to reevaluate the rules. They may also reevaluate the system of rewards used to maintain these rules. The reevaluation takes the form of a reversal or a negative statement of the established system. Thus, in Cohen's scheme of things, and in the sociologist's scheme of things, evil is a recurring phenomenon in social structures. It is a "natural" condition within human societies and better understood as such. It can appear in extreme forms, such as we find in the behavior of the gang delinquent who may kill for reasons far beyond his own understanding; or it may appear in extremely attenuated forms, as when we try to depreciate the value of a college course because we have discovered that we cannot do well in it. In any event, the term "evil" is one which, though it appears in humanistic writing, appears seldom, if at all, in sociological writing. Cohen, for example, so far as I recall, does not use the term once in his entire book, nor does Yablonsky in a book dealing with the same phenomenon.[17] Sociological writing is relatively barren of such terms as evil, wicked, vile, dirty, filthy, beastly, perverted,

---

[16] Emile Durkheim quoted in Talcott Parsons, Edward Shils, Kaspar D. Naegele, and Jesse R. Pitts, *Theories of Society; Foundations of Modern Sociological Theory* (New York: Free Press of Glencoe, 1961), p. 873. Copyright © 1961 by The Free Press of Glencoe, Inc.

[17] Compare this with the writings of Hannah Arendt, who, in her extremely intelligent coverage of the issues raised by the Eichmann trial, did not hesitate to use the word "evil" in the title of her book. See Hannah Arendt, *Eichmann in Jerusalem; a Report on the Banality of Evil* (New York: The Viking Press, Inc., 1963).

disgusting, or similar adjectives often used to refer to behavior not officially sanctioned by the greater society. As a consequence, sociological literature has acquired a certain "coldness" and, as a TIME reporter once put it, a "bread-pudding" prose style as its form of expression.

To grasp the sociological perspective in its broader conception makes it difficult to resort to pejorative words or invectives. The sociologist is concerned with understanding the nature of various significant forms of human social conduct. The significance of human social conduct does not rest in ethical schemes, religious practices, or existential agonies when viewed from the sociological perspective. The significant forms of human behavior for the sociologist are those which raise critical problems concerning the nature of social structure. Thus, Cohen and other sociologists are interested in delinquency because it raises the issue of how nonconformist reactions to the massive agents of social control come about. In the course of examining this matter they may shed light on what have been traditionally humanistic concerns, such as the problem of evil. But this is a side effect.

The sociologist is more concerned with seeing the common processes operating within the juvenile gang and within, say, the following group of girls in a sorority as described by an undergraduate observer:

> As eight or ten girls were standing in front of the chart immediately after the weekly black marks had been put up, the second girl in terms of the most marks received said, "We ought to start a 'Black Mark Club.' " This suggestion received such enthusiasm from others who had more than three or four marks, that then and there they made up this song to the tune of "Pepsi-Cola Hits the Spot":
>
> > "Good ole black marks hit the spot,
> > One or two, that ain't a lot,
> > Noise and culture, pledge duty makes three,
> > Gotta get more to be cool like me."[18]

The novelist or humanist would, I presume, view this as a trivial scene. It lacks dramatic interest; it has no moral profundity. For the sociologist, however, it is a revealing account. If we understand Cohen and the perspective he attempts to bring to delinquent behavior, we begin to perceive the dynamics underlying the development of an attenuated delinquent subculture among the girls.

The power of the sociological perspective rests in its ability to bring greater order and commonality into what previously had been viewed as separate and

---

[18] Janet Graham, "Black Marks as Indicators of Subgroups in a Sorority," an unpublished paper prepared for an introductory Sociology course at the University of Kansas, Lawrence, Kansas, 1963.

disparate events. Cohen specifically is concerned with the problem of delinquency. But, in the course of his thought and writing, he has developed a scheme which applies more generally and which can be used to bring understanding to collective forms of nonconformistic behavior ranging from that of "beatniks" to the behavior of members of the American Nazi Party. This makes his ideas relevant to our times because today, perhaps more than ever before, we live in a society that generates pressures while, at the same time, it provides opportunities necessary for redefining situations and thereby evading the pressures.

Modern humanity is characterized, above all else, by variety and diversity. Cohen helps to account, in part, for this variety. Like Durkheim, he claims that social processes of differentiation are the basis of our diversity as much, if not more, than are biological or psychological processes. He moves beyond Durkheim by probing into the dynamics that bring variety about. The result is a work that extends in meaning and applicability much further than the problem of lower-class juvenile male delinquent gangs that gave rise to it.

15 How To Lose at Games: The Coalition Theories of Theodore Caplow

Up to this point we have examined a variety of ideas that direct us toward some of the broad implications of a sociological perspective. We have not, at any time, been deeply involved with the problem of proof. We have not considered the manner whereby the sociologist attempts to increase the amount of confidence that can be placed in some of his assertions. It is necessary to correct this deficit before bringing this book to a close.

In this chapter we shall examine in considerable detail the procedures whereby the sociologist begins to conclude that one theory about some aspect of human relations might have greater validity than another. We will approach this discussion of sociological methods by examining a typical case of sociological research. In particular, we will concentrate on the relationship that exists between theory and research. Facts obtained through research are important only if they have some bearing on a theory which is considered important. Theories are important not so much in terms of the facts they generate[1] as in terms of the extent to which they influence the distribution of power among men. Therefore, a discussion of the significance of research and the methods underlying it must begin with a consideration of the place of that research within the larger cultural and social milieu. Method is significant only when it serves to test significant theories.

---

[1] Facts can be generated by minimal theories. It was this feature of "dust-bowl empiricism" that made it extremely vulnerable to criticism. Early sociologists were justly criticized for their belief that counting any and everything—from outhouses to status symbols—would produce a science of man. It could not, of course. All it produced was more facts. Such reliance on the counted fact came, at least in part, from the desire of the sociologist to find scientific security.

The development of powerful theories is more difficult than the compiling of facts. Fortunately, even in an age of empiricism, sociologists—like men in other fields—continue to recognize the worth of the good theorist.

Life as a grand "game"

We will begin, then, with a consideration that seems, at first, to be far afield. It might even appear downright irrelevant. We will begin our investigation of sociological methodology by examining a point of view which has extensive popularity in our culture—a point of view which is now part of what might be called the American *weltanschauung*. I am referring here to our tendency to view many aspects of life as part of a grand "game." According to this perspective almost any kind of activity can be interpreted as a game. Love is a game, marriage is a game, war is a game, business is a game, graduate school is a game, politics or practically anything else is or can become a game.

When life is looked upon as a game, it is seen essentially in terms of the competitive employment of strategies. After all, a game is a demonstration of one's skill in the employment of strategy.[2] One presumes that he is confronted by an opponent (lover, husband or wife, enemy, business competitor, professor, or opposing candidate for office) and his task is to counter the strategies of his opposition. In a game situation—as opposed to a fight—the idea is not so much that of destroying your opponent as it is to demonstrate superior technique. When love is transformed into fun and games, the idea behind the interaction between boy and girl will be to see who is the master of technique.

So it is that when opponents face each other in a game situation—or when they think of themselves as being in a game situation—they attempt to maximize their advantages by the application of superior strategies. This is simple enough. The businessman who comes upon a good strategy uses it to achieve personal advantage. There is a similarity, at the national level, with war. So generally acceptable has the idea of game theory become that businessmen now play computerized games to maximize their sensitivity to winning strategies. Such computerized games also are viewed as a means of identifying those who lack talent as gamesmen.

The extent to which the idea of life as a game has permeated American thought can be revealed by a brief reference to Eric Berne's book *Games*

---

[2] This characterization of a game is made by Anatol Rapoport in his book *Fights, Games and Debates* (Ann Arbor: The University of Michigan Press, 1960). A fight, according to Rapoport, consists of an attempt to destroy an enemy. In such a situation, the weaker the enemy, the better the fight, that is, the more easily one accomplishes his goal. In a game, the objective is to test competitive strategies. In this circumstance one seeks a strong and properly matched opponent. In a debate the objective, as Rapoport defines a debate, is to come to an understanding. This calls for a sympathetic exchange of points of view.

People Play.[3] This book remained on best-seller lists in the United States for two years—a fact providing us with some measure of the popularity of the game perspective. According to Berne, games can be played to win psychological points for an emotionally disturbed person or one who lacks insight into his nature. For example, a frightened woman can simultaneously assert her femininity and preserve her virtue by playing the game of "Rapo." In this game, the woman makes herself attractive and then, if her strategy is successful, protests violently when some man who is attracted to her makes his interest known. It is worth mentioning here that Berne was concerned with the extent to which an attitude of game playing—whether consciously or unconsciously held—could be symptomatic of pathological forms of human interaction.

The main point I am developing, however, is that the importance of the idea of games in our culture cannot easily be denied. Americans, who now possess greater leisure and security than ever before known in the past, have come to think of life as a game.[4] We think in terms of the odds. We seek to gain the "edge." We are constantly hoping for the strategy that will give us the advantage. Whether we are pressing through traffic in our cars or shopping in a supermarket, we are conditioned by the concept of life as a game.[5]

Von Neumann and Morgenstern's theory

It is not surprising that a culture which views life as a game would, eventually, produce a highly formalized and academic statement of this idea. In 1944 two men performed this task. John von Neumann and Oskar Morgenstern carefully developed a formal theory of how men would have to conduct themselves if they were playing games in such a manner as to maximize the utility of the strategies available to them.[6] Shortly afterward sociologists began to

---

[3] Eric Berne, *Games People Play* (New York: Grove Press, Inc., 1964).

[4] Orin E. Klapp points out that the game perspective has very strong elements of anomie in it. He comments, "Another form of *anomie* would be viewing life as a game where one need not obey the rules but can manipulate them and 'con' his way, using legalism to cheat, press, or intimidate others. In such an unethical situation—closely approaching *anomie* though outwardly formal—the person abusing the law the most might seem like a stickler—a superconformer—who knows every cranny and loophole, and speaks loudly in favor of law, namely of a game in which he has the aces." From Orin E. Klapp, *Heroes, Villains, and Fools: The Changing American Character* (Spectrum Books; Englewood Cliffs, N. J.: Prentice-Hall, Inc., 1962), p. 87.

[5] Supermarkets across the country have been heavily criticized by women's organizations for wasting money on promotional games. The supermarkets claim they do not like such stunts any better than the housewife, but competitive circumstances require that they continue the use of such games.

[6] John von Neumann and Oskar Morgenstern, *Theory of Games and Economic Behavior* (Princeton, N.J.: Princeton University Press, 1944).

consider the extent to which theories of games could be used more generally to account for the actions of people.

In the game world of Von Neumann and Morgenstern men are viewed as rational beings concerned with maximizing their personal advantage. The game world is a competitive world. There is no place for sentiment of an altruistic sort; this interferes with the conduct of the game. If there is altruism, it is limited to an agreement between players that they will respect the rules. Otherwise, altruism has the capacity to interfere with the rational evaluation of a given strategy. When one's opponent assumes an altruistic stance, the best reaction, assuming the context of a game, is to conclude that he is attempting to "fake" you out. The game setting requires that expressions of goodwill, altruism, and concern on the part of one's opponent be met with great suspicion.[7]

One should not involve himself with a strategy because it has tradition in its favor or because it has sentimental value. A strategy must be evaluated strictly in terms of whether or not it will produce one effect—winning the game. In this sense, game theory brings social interaction within the rationalistic determination of interests which Weber saw as the major change in the moral character of modern man. The game world of Von Neumann and Morgenstern offers us a view of humanity as slit-eyed, externally emotionless men sitting around a very quiet table playing hands of poker into the stretches of mathematical infinity. Now and then a voice says, "I raise." Now and then one says, "I'm out."

So far we have been approaching the research that we are going to discuss in what must seem to be a roundabout manner. Yet, the matter of setting is important. We have indicated that our culture, for various reasons, subscribes heavily to the idea that life is a game. This has led, in turn, to a formalized development of theory using this approach to human behavior.

Let us now consider some of the implications of game theory by turning to a more specific illustrative case. Suppose that we have three people behaving in a competitive fashion. The three of them are struggling for some reward

---

[7] To the extent that a game perspective dominates world affairs, we are committed to a kind of institutionalized paranoia. Surprisingly enough, the strategy sometimes dictated by a game perspective is actually a losing strategy. That is to say, the rewards coming to the players in a competitive situation can often be maximized by destroying the pure game nature of the relationship. Industrial concerns, for example, do this when they practice price fixing. A very interesting discussion of the paradoxes and problems involved in the use of altruism in game settings appears in Kenneth Boulding's *Conflict and Defense* (New York: Harper & Row, Publishers, 1962.) See also Anatol Rapoport, *Fights, Games and Debates*, mentioned in footnote 2.

which cannot be shared by all. Someone will have to lose. Let us also suppose that any of these three people may, if he wishes, form a partnership with some other member of the group. We shall finally assume that forming a partnership with another person can be part of the strategy of winning.

If the players are equally competent gamesmen, game theory would predict that they would be equally inclined to form partnerships.[8] Not to form a partnership, and thereby face the combined powers of those who had, would mean certain loss. Game theory, then, predicts the necessity of immediate formations of partnerships. Let me illustrate this further. Suppose that three men sat down to play a game of poker. The rules of this particular game are such that two of the men may connive to cheat against the third. It would be to each player's advantage to become one of the two cheaters as quickly as possible; otherwise he would be placed at such a disadvantage that he would necessarily lose. It seems obvious, granting such a situation, that in any "game" men would act immediately to get in with the connivers. However, we have both theory and proof which indicate that men often behave in a game situation in irrational ways. Their behavior is irrational in the sense that they lose when they could win. They do not evaluate the situation purely in terms of the elements of the game. Instead, they respond erroneously in terms of perceptions of the distribution of power and status. These perceptions work to their disadvantage. What is going on?

Caplow's "coalitions in three-person groups"

In 1957, responding in part to the popularity of the theory of games, a University of Minnesota sociologist named Caplow[9] published a brief paper on the formation of coalitions in three-person groups. Caplow argued that people in three person groups would form partnerships on the basis of how they perceived the distribution of power rather than in terms of how they perceived the purely strategic utility of partnerships. Men will form partner-

---

[8] This assertion is a gross oversimplification of Von Neumann and Morgenstern's position. Game theory has been primarily concerned with how men *should* behave if they wish to act rationally. This is different from claiming that men do, in fact, act rationally. Yet there is a strong element of rationality in the game theory approach to human behavior. Economists and mathematicians, perhaps, are inclined to project the rationality of their fields onto the whole of humanity.

[9] Professor Theodore Caplow is now at Columbia University. In addition to the work presented here, he has published a number of articles and several significant books. His major works are *The Sociology of Work* (Minneapolis: University of Minnesota Press, 1954); *The Academic Marketplace*, with Reece J. McGee (New York: Basic Books, Inc., 1958); and *Principles of Organization* (New York: Harcourt, Brace & World, Inc., 1964).

ships in terms of the "prestige" or the sense of "propriety" which they think is involved.[10]

Caplow speculated, on the basis of this presumption, that if power were arranged in different ways within three-person groups, then the pattern of partnerships would be affected accordingly. (Incidentally, for the purpose of convenience, we shall henceforth call three-person groups "triads.") In the diagram below, Caplow provides us with six different power distributions within triads. He also indicates, by means of the arrows, who would be most likely to form coalitions. The nature of his reasoning will be indicated by a consideration of the third case in the diagram.

In what Caplow calls a "Type 3 Triad," power is perceived as being distributed so that two members of the group are equal and the third is weaker than the other two. In this case, Caplow predicts that it will be the weaker member who will be most likely to be included within a coalition. Both of the stronger members feel that they will be able to dominate the weaker member and each attempts to form a coalition with him rather than between themselves. In the second case (Type 2 Triad), the two weaker members will form a coalition to protect themselves from the stronger member. It is important to keep in mind that Caplow believes the actual distribution of power is not as important as the manner in which the distribution of power is perceived. It is also interesting to note, in these speculations, that the weaker member of the triad usually comes out a member of the winning coalition.

Caplow's reasoning has introduced a new twist. Game theory, as it was advanced by Von Neumann and Morgenstern, was based on a mathematical consideration of what constitutes rational game playing. The conduct of a game, they held, should be fitted into a purely rational and logical system. But are men logical when they play games? Caplow suggests that they are not. At least, he says, there are times when men, in playing games, are more concerned with maintaining social postures of various kinds than they are with the game itself. They are led by status considerations into behavior which causes them to lose.

---

[10] The "shock" value of much sociological research comes from its capacity to demonstrate the irrational nature of human conduct. Men say one thing and do another. Sociologists are endlessly fascinated by the extent to which humanity walks on feet of clay. For example, a recent study of sick doctors revealed that doctors, like everybody else, tend to select as their own physicians men they like in a personal rather than a professional sense. We would expect doctors—because of their particular professional knowledge and concern—to select the most competent men for their personal physicians. We are surprised when they reveal a different basis for selection. This observation came from the research of Professor Herbert Bynder of the University of Colorado.

DIAGRAM.—EXPECTED COALITIONS IN TRIADS ON THE BASIS
OF PERCEIVED DISTRIBUTIONS OF POWER. 11

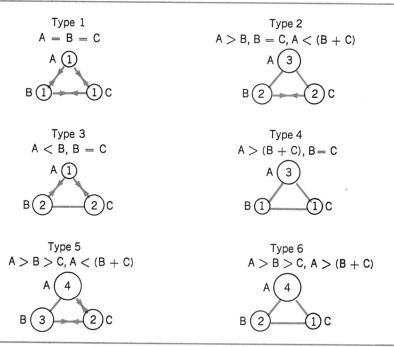

Type 1
A = B = C

Type 2
A > B, B = C, A < (B + C)

Type 3
A < B, B = C

Type 4
A > (B + C), B = C

Type 5
A > B > C, A < (B + C)

Type 6
A > B > C, A > (B + C)

Legend: A>B means A is perceived as greater in power than B. A<B means A is
perceived as having less power than B. The numbers in the circles illustrate
units of perceived power. The arrows indicate expected coalitions according
to Caplow's speculations.

Two theories

At this point we have reached an ideal situation in the scientific exploration
of human behavior. First of all, we have two clearly defined theories. One
theory postulates rational conduct; the other postulates irrational conduct.
Moreover, both of these theories are related to a perspective that is a general
and influential part of the culture. That is to say, the theories are significant.
Finally, these theories stand in opposition to each other. That is to say, when
applied to simple and readily observed forms of action, they predict different

---

[11] This is a modified version of a diagram reprinted from Theodore Caplow, "Further Development of a Theory of Coalitions in the Triad," *American Journal of Sociology*, **LXIV** (March 1959),
by permission of The University of Chicago Press. Copyright 1959 by the University of Chicago.
There were eight expected coalitions in the original article.

outcomes. In this instance, the simple form of action consists of the formation of partnerships in triads. Von Neumann and Morgenstern would claim that if the game is played rationally, then any partnership is a winning one and ought to be formed. The exception would be the two cases in our diagram where one player has so much power that a partnership would not have any value for him or the others. Caplow argues, on the contrary, that extraneous social considerations are usually involved in game playing. On the basis of these, we should predict the formation of particular partnerships.

Now that we have two theories—one based on a postulate of rational conduct, the other on the postulate of values assigned to social perceptions—the task is to determine which position can be given greater credibility in terms of how people do in fact behave. This task was accomplished by two social scientists at the University of Hawaii—W. Edgar Vinacke and Abe Arkoff.[12]

The device employed by Vinacke and Arkoff for a factual evaluation of these theories consisted of an extremely simple three-person game. Each player in the game moved a marker around the edge of a Parcheesi board on the basis of the toss of a die. All three persons moved with each toss. In addition, each player was assigned a number. This number gave him the right to increase his moves by that multiple. For example, if a player had the number "2," he could move twice as far with each toss of the die. If he had the number "3," he could move three times as far. If two players had the numbers "2" and "3," they could combine forces and move five times as far.

Having set up this situation, Vinacke and Arkoff then observed how the players combined forces as they played the game. The game was so simple that once certain coalitions were formed, the game was conceded by the loser. Thus, the advantage of a coalition was made about as obvious as it could be made. This is important because it means that every opportunity is being provided for the rational mode of play. Vinacke and Arkoff bent over backwards to avoid stacking the deck against Von Neumann and Morgenstern.

The findings of Vinacke and Arkoff

The findings of Vinacke and Arkoff appear in Table I. They found basically that the data supported the conclusions of Caplow. Coalitions were formed on the basis of perceived distributions of power. A person with a "power" of "3," for example, would hesitate to combine forces with the other persons

---

[12] See W. Edgar Vinacke and Abe Arkoff, "An Experimental Study of Coalitions in the Triad," *American Sociological Review*, 22 (August 1957).

in his groups, each of whom had powers of "2." (See the data for the Type 2 Triad in Table I. The reader is enjoined to examine the findings somewhat carefully, paying especial attention to the extent to which they conform to and deviate from theoretical expectations.)

TABLE I
COALITIONS FORMED IN THE SIX TYPES OF POWER PATTERNS IN TRIADS

Allies	Type 1	Type 2	Type 3	Type 4	Type 5	Type 6
	(1-1-1)	(3-2-2)	(1-2-2)	(3-1-1)	(4-3-2)	(4-2-1)
AB	33*	13	24*	11	9	9
AC	17*	12	40*	10	20*	13
BC	30*	64*	15	7	59*	8
No coalition	10	1	11	62*	2	60*
Number of games	90	90	90	90	90	90

The figures in parentheses show the power of the three members; for example, in Type 1, A = 1, B = 1, and C = 1. The asterisks indicate those coalitions that would be expected according to Caplow's predictions.

Source: W. Edgar Vinacke and Abe Arkoff, "An Experimental Study of Coalitions in the Triad," *American Sociological Review*, 22 (August 1957), 409. [This table is slightly modified.] Reprinted by permission of the authors and the American Sociological Association.

Sociologists are often made objects of satire because of their fondness for tables and statistics.[13] But there is good reason for this concern with statistics. Ordered data, such as those appearing in Table I, are the best means sociologists have, as yet, of gaining clearer visions of human social nature. It is possible to appreciate both the awesome mysteries of human nature and the more pedestrian content of statistical tables if a proper perspective is maintained. The statistics we find in Table I are relevant only to theoretical formulations that clash with each other. The sociologist does not try to reduce all of mankind and the miracles of living to a few numbers in a statistical table. The finest function of statistical analysis is to examine the competing claims of rival theories.

To comprehend statistical analysis and make use of it, we must know those theories toward which such analysis is directed. Statistics can never stand alone. Statistics are related to theory in much the same manner that the military is related to political policy. That theory will win over others which has the best statistical evidence to bring to its support. Statistics and theory go

---

[13] Disraeli is reputed to have said there are lies, damned lies, and statistics. For an interesting and still up-to-date book on the misuse of statistics, see Darrell Huff, *How to Lie with Statistics* (New York: W. W. Norton and Company, Inc., 1954). Statistics, quite obviously, can be misused. However, without statistics, properly and carefully evaluated, we have no means for testing adequately a large number of theories concerning human social behavior.

hand in hand. They are complementary features of a larger endeavor—the development of confidence in our conceptions of man can take place only through organizing our observations of some features of human conduct. We must master both theory and methods of validating theory if we are to move beyond the level of mythology.

At this point we have considered the development of contrary theories and we have examined some evidence which suggests that in real game playing people are not motivated by purely rational considerations of the mechanics of the game. How can we have any faith in the evidence? Perhaps Vinacke and Arkoff distorted their data or altered it—this distortion could have occurred quite unconsciously—so that it would make Caplow's position look better. Perhaps they were using subjects who were not very bright. Possibly a different setting, using different people, would produce different results.

The value of replication

This kind of criticism leads us very quickly to one of the most important features of a scientific approach to human social action. If our theory and our data are good, then we should keep getting the same results time after time after time. We can test the findings of another scientist simply by repeating or replicating his work. If we get results that are drastically different, then further reevaluation of the whole relationship between fact and theory is required.

The findings of Vinacke and Arkoff were subjected to reexamination by Edgar I. Patterson.[14] Using the same procedure, but different subjects, Patterson obtained results much the same as those of Vinacke and Arkoff. Table II presents Patterson's findings. These should be compared with the original findings of Vinacke and Arkoff in Table I.

This kind of replication enables us to have greater confidence in the findings. Replication in the social sciences does not have the precision that we find in the exact sciences. Though there is a great deal of correspondence between the findings of Vinacke on the one hand and Patterson on the other, there is still some variation. If the researcher makes clear the procedures whereby he obtained his facts, this variation is often reduced. It is, therefore, a very important part of research to make explicit the procedures used to obtain facts. This aspect of writing up a piece of research tends to make for dull reading; at the same time, it is a part of research that simply cannot be ignored.

---

[14] Edgar I. Patterson, *The Hypotheses of Theodore Caplow Concerning the Triad: A Restudy.* Unpublished M.A. Thesis, University of Kansas, Lawrence, Kansas, 1961.

TABLE II
COALITIONS FORMED IN THE SIX TYPES OF POWER PATTERNS IN TRIADS IN
THE RESTUDY

Allies	Type 1 (1-1-1)	Type 2 (3-2-2)	Type 3 (1-2-2)	Type 4 (3-1-1)	Type 5 (4-3-2)	Type 6 (4-2-1)
AB	28*	12	31*	9	11	3
AC	35*	22	28*	7	20*	10
BC	20*	54*	29	5	53*	9
No coalition	7	2	2	69*	6	68*
Total	90	90	90	90	90	90

The figures in parentheses show the power of the three members; for example, in Type 1, A = 1, B = 1, and C = 1. The asterisks indicate those coalitions that would be expected according to Caplow's predictions.

Source: Edgar I. Patterson, *The Hypotheses of Theodore Caplow Concerning the Triad: A Restudy.* Unpublished M.A. Thesis, University of Kansas, Lawrence, Kansas, 1961.

Table II should be carefully compared with Table I. Remember, subjects were placed in much the same kind of situation and the observer recorded his information in much the same manner. The tables are not identical. Note, for example, the anomaly in the Type 3 triad. It is surprising, however, that they are as similar as they are. Once again, the data support, in a general way, the speculations of Professor Caplow. People do not, even under extremely simple and self-evident conditions, play games in a very rational manner.

It would seem, at this point, that the matter is pretty well sewed up. We presented two theories. Each theory predicted something different concerning the formation of coalitions in triads. Caplow's predictions were more in keeping with the data. Furthermore, the collection of further data produced the same results. We can now place greater confidence in Caplow's speculations.

The interpretation of data

Unfortunately, we cannot say that the data prove that Caplow is perfectly correct. All we can say is that the data do not disprove his contention. This is a puzzling feature of scientific proof that often causes trouble for the beginning—and even the advanced—student. We should examine what we have done a little further, or we will come away too optimistic about research findings.

We have examined two different theories which make different predictions concerning a simple pattern of behavior—the formation of coalitions in three-person groups. The facts reveal that in actual competitive situations the predictions of one of the theories are supported and those of the other are not. It would seem, from this, that the facts prove the first theory is correct.

However, it is necessary to be very careful in this matter of determining the "truth" of a theory. All the facts do in this instance is suggest that the theory is not *necessarily* wrong. The possibility always remains, however, that another theory will come along and lead to the same predictions on a different basis. Let us make this point by coming back to Caplow's argument.

Caplow said that perceived differences in power among the three people in the group determined the way in which coalitions would be formed. The use of the concept of power suggests that persons are motivated by a search for higher status or more recognition. However, when persons playing the Vinacke-Arkoff "game" were questioned about their motives in forming partnerships, they tended to reply that they sought a particular partner because he would share the rewards from winning more equitably. There is the possibility that the motivation underlying the selection of partners is essentially an economic rather than a status matter. Partnerships are sought with the idea of maximizing individual economic gains rather than social ones.

So it is that research is never conclusive. Even academicians sometimes poke fun at the extent to which researchers are inclined to conclude their articles with a statement to the effect that further research is necessary. The pursuit of reliable knowledge is an exasperating and endless task and, because of this, no social scientist can afford to be arrogant.

In this chapter we have been concerned with an elementary illustrative presentation of the procedure whereby the social scientist attempts to attain reliable knowledge. I have used as an example what I consider to be a fairly representative case of empirical research. Though much more could be said about purely methodological problems in social research, I shall resist the temptation to say more. Numerous works on sociological methods are available to the student.

The student should keep in mind that the principal purpose of good research method is to make a particular argument convincing. An argument is all the more convincing when the issues involved are clear-cut and the evidence supporting one side or the other is well established and simply presented. This does not mean research cannot be complex. It means, instead, that even when research is complex, the researcher is obligated to present his case in the simplest manner possible. Good methodology serves the purpose of simplifying matters.

Once more, in conclusion, I want to emphasize that good methodology is related to theoretical issues. Just as good theory will suggest a means whereby it might be tested, so good method will promote the further development of theory. This introduction to social research methods has tried to correct the present tendency of methodological texts to deal with research methods as though they existed independently of more metaphysical theoretical involvements. But even the most high-powered method, in the service of a minimal theory, can generate only pedestrian information. We have, in such an instance, a situation somewhat like having the world's finest defense lawyer expending his energies in court on a case involving a petty misdemeanor. Methodology and theory are not independent concerns.

16 The Uses of Sociological Thought: A Summary

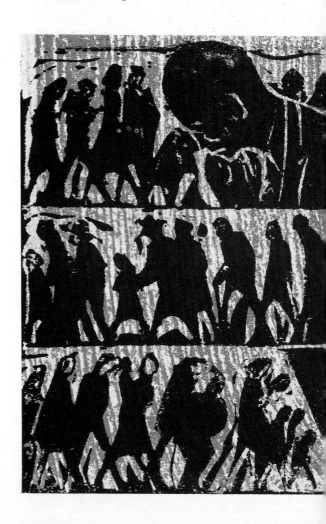

We have now surveyed the ideas of a variety of sociological thinkers and, at this point, the student might reasonably ask, "Where do we go from here?" The pragmatic applications of other fields are often apparent. But what does one do with sociology? Where do we go now? I find it difficult to reply to this question because there are many different possibilities.

Applications of sociological training

One possibility, of course, is to go nowhere. The student can, if he so desires, permit himself to rest secure in the feeling that he now has sufficient socio- logical sophistication to care for his needs. He might argue that while Durkheim, Weber, Goffman, Henry, and the others are decent enough fellows—possibly even interesting—what they have to say is, after all, rather academic. The central value of their work is to provide the student with information for passing examinations. When the final examination is over—when the semester ends— possibilities for the future are closed. I presume that students who look upon education as an empty ritual will find this alternative attractive.

But is there something else one can do with sociology? In this closing chapter I would like to discuss several other possibilities. Let me say now that these modes of utilizing sociological sophistication are not mutually exclusive. One might work toward all of them or perhaps only one or another. However, each suggests various ways in which sociology can be of value to the individual.

One possibility to be considered is that of becoming a professional sociologist. Today sociology can provide both good work and good incomes. Although there may be some tendency to view an interest in future income as crass materialism,[1] I do not think it is unreasonable to make inquiries of this nature when looking into different career possibilities. At the moment, as this is being written, a good sociologist can reasonably expect to make an income of between $15,000 and $20,000 for a nine-month academic year.

A very good sociologist, like a good businessman or professional, will make a large enough income to live comfortably. Royalties from publications, in addition to incomes from academic salaries or research institute salaries, can bring about gross incomes well in excess of $50,000 per year. This is the equivalent of many junior-level executive incomes and, in all save the largest corporations, is the equivalent of top-management incomes. In a report on the prosperity and success of the sociologist in recent years, TIME magazine made the following comment,

> The Berkeley campus of the University of California—where some people would say a need has been demonstrated—has offered more than $25,000 a year to a few renowned sociologists, $20,000 to others less well known. The University of Southern California will pay $20,000 for a top professor, as will New York University. A big name can try for $25,000 at Harvard and probably get it. A sociologist at Tulane who only five years ago was drawing $10,000 now gets $21,000. And average pay is also rising. Median salary at the universities is $10,000 only slightly below economists'.[2]

This comment appeared in a 1965 publication. Both the demand for sociologists and the incomes they can look forward to have since increased. The policy of inducting graduate students into the military, introduced at the time this was being written, will, if put into effect, make the demand even more severe.

The kinds of work a sociologist can expect to go into vary considerably. Most formally trained sociologists still go into college teaching. Students interested in college teaching as a career will, as a matter of course, be expected to continue their training in graduate school. Those who wish to progress into the higher ranks of the profession will be called upon to acquire a Ph.D. degree. A doctorate from a prestigious graduate school will enhance career chances more than one from an "out-of-the-way" graduate school. However, to a surprising extent, a sociologist's career depends on what he does after graduate school. A doctoral degree from a relatively small or weak graduate department does not necessarily mean that some irrevocable limit

---

[1] When one considers how much space the *Bulletin of the American Association of University Professors* gives to salary levels, such a concern on the part of the student should not be viewed as an abandonment of intellectual idealism. Or, if it is, it certainly will not cripple the student for work as an intellectual in academe.

[2] From TIME magazine, October 29, 1965.

has been imposed on the extent to which one can advance within the profession.

Once the student has received his bachelor's degree, the time involved in obtaining a doctorate will vary. Four more years of graduate training is common. It is not unusual, in some instances, for students to spend seven or eight years in study before obtaining their final degree. Even after he has obtained his degree, it is not remarkable for an established Ph.D. to take still further postdoctoral work.

I would advise the student who is thinking of extending a sociology major into graduate school to discuss the matter with anyone and everyone he knows. He should especially discuss the matter with his instructors and others who have had training in graduate school and who may, therefore, be able to counsel him concerning problems he might reasonably expect to encounter. Too often students hesitate to do this for fear they will be imposing on their teachers. As a matter of fact, this is an integral part of the instructor's duties as a teacher, and the student should not hesitate to seek and make use of such counsel.

Sociologists function in other capacities than as college teachers. There is an increasing need for social information upon which administrative officials can rely for more effective formulation of their policies. Administering modern large-scale organizations and communities can no longer be trusted to a "wet-thumb-in-the-breeze" philosophy. Social facts need to be compiled. Organizations such as Community Studies, Inc., of Kansas City, Missouri, depend on the constant efforts of a staff of research sociologists to produce information on such matters as how to improve conditions for the aged population in the city, the problems facing the nonwhite population, and other conditions relevant to the welfare of the city and its citizens.

A sociologist going into a research agency such as Community Studies, Inc., has to be sophisticated in techniques of interviewing, designing research which will provide valuable information at a reasonable cost, analyzing social data, preparing reports which are readable and useful to men in positions of authority, and he has to possess a broad background of theoretical understanding which enables him not only to select critical problems but interpret them in a comprehensive and sophisticated manner.

Sociologists also work as writers, consultants, administrative officials, industrial analysts, and as independent operators of research organizations. Sociology majors are also going into high school teaching in increasing numbers. More and more high schools are offering courses in sociology—giving recognition to the fact that the older program of civics training in high school is not adequate for an understanding of today's social systems.[3] Students with undergraduate majors in sociology might also wish to consider social work as a career. The Council for Social Work reported that 15,000 jobs for social workers were going begging in 1965. The demand is great. For people with an interest in social problems and their alleviation, this is one career possibility that ought to be seriously considered.

Value of sociological knowledge in other fields

So, one can definitely find a career in sociology. If, as is true with all other fields of endeavor, an individual works hard and has a bit of luck, he can find it a very lucrative and very exciting career. But what about the student who has no intention of going on in sociology? Where does all of this leave him? Does sociology have any real value for the student of literature, the mathematician, the physical scientist, or the student who is going into athletics? I like to think it has. A person who is sociologically sophisticated will be more knowledgeable about his craft—regardless of what it might be—than will one who is not.

Space does not permit even a cursory examination of how this might apply to all career fields. Instead, I will pick a single specialty as a case in point. The student going into mathematics, for example, will find sociology offering him additional understandings of the nature of mathematics that he could not acquire simply on the basis of a specialized technical training. Any mathematician, I believe, would do well to read a sociological work like Professor Warren Hagstrom's *The Scientific Community*.[4] The student of mathematics should, I think, find it worth his time to discover the extent to which the mathematician is evaluated in nonmathematical as well as purely mathematical terms. He might, if he is like some mathematicians I have known, be surprised to discover that fad and fashion operate within the interplay of abstract equations just as they do in less "logical" realms of conduct.

There are any number of questions which a sociological consideration of mathematics can give rise to. What kinds of men gain prominence and power within the mathematical profession? How are status differences maintained between mathematicians? What kinds of differences in status are important

---

[3] The past several years have seen the development of more intensive attempts to revise the social science offerings of high schools. A case in point is the work of Sociological Resources for Secondary Schools, an organization of sociologists concerned with modernizing high school sociological offerings.

[4] Warren Hagstrom, *The Scientific Community* (New York: Basic Books, Inc., 1965).

and why? Why, for example, does the "pure" mathematician often feel he has the right to be condescending toward the "applied" mathematician?

What about the folklore of mathematics? A common story told about mathematicians is that which says the creative talent of the mathematical wizard flares up at an early age and quickly burns out. According to Hagstrom, however, this is not true. It seems, instead, that a young mathematician can find himself "benched" because his specialty has lost its faddishness.

Can a mathematician be truly sophisticated without understanding the social functions of mathematical thought? I would submit that without such sophistication a student of mathematics only dimly conceives the character of his discipline. The most he can attain is technical mastery—but this extension of his capacities will leave him little better informed than a mechanical computer. I think this is true for any other career as well.

So far we have considered the uses of sociology in relation to the career interests of the student. But sociology also has values which transcend matters of career, employment, and economic security. Sociology, I believe, can have a very personal value and meaning. This, I would argue, is its greatest value; and, at the same time, it impresses me as being the most difficult to describe. The person for whom sociology has come to have a personal value will have both a more sympathetic and a more inquiring attitude toward human actions. He will be interested in human social conduct in its various forms and he will have the capacity to interpret it in a greater variety of ways. He will be skeptical and he will be curious. He will not be as likely to be frightened by stories told about people who live outside the confines of the "in-group." He will be well aware of the extent to which people denigrate those whom they consider unacceptable. He will be highly sensitive to the arbitrary nature of much that is given social importance. He will, in his own way, be as humanistic in his sympathies and understanding as is the poet or artist. That has been, in part, the argument of this book.

I must express a word of caution at this point. The acceptance of a sociological point of view does not mean the student has to assume the stance of a cold-blooded scientist in any and all social settings. It does not mean, for example, that he is required to divide his friends into control and experimental groups and take notes on their behavior. A sociological involvement does not give anyone the right to hide tape recorders in bedrooms on the pretext that he is gathering scientific data. To be a sociologist, of either a professional or an amateur variety, does not justify, at any time, taking the attitude that people are only things to be observed and manipulated for the greater glory of science.

As I see it, to personalize a sociological perspective calls for acquiring greater versatility in interpreting human actions. The sociologically sensitive person will, as he listens to a sermon in church, be reminded of Durkheim or maybe Weber. When he looks at the offerings on a modern drugstore magazine rack he will recall, possibly with faint amusement, the harangues against Sensatism of Sorokin. When he goes to a cocktail party he will again think of the wry and cynical observations of Goffman. This, in part, is what personalization of a sociological perspective involves.

The questioning attitude

Above all, a sociological perspective requires the ability to retain a continuously questioning attitude about human activities. The following episode exemplifies what I am talking about here. A few years ago a student came to my office to discuss an examination. We talked for a while and he was satisfied with everything except a term that he claimed had caused him to miss one particular question. The question had to do with puberty rites among the Bantu of the Ituri Rain Forest; the particular word that gave him trouble was "circumcision." He had no idea of the meaning of the word and I did not trust myself to tell him. So I casually handed him a dictionary and asked him to look up the word for himself. He quickly found it and read the definition. There was an unusual expression on his face. Finally, he handed back the dictionary and exclaimed in a shocked voice, "Good God, why'd they ever want to do something like *that* for?"

Why would they ever want to do something like *that?* Here we have expressed, in ten words, the driving force behind sociology and all other behavioral sciences. It summarizes the fundamental concern of many humanists as well. My puzzled student had met—perhaps for the first time in his life—social conduct on the part of others which left him totally baffled. He was forced to reveal his bewilderment and shock. He was on the threshhold of sociological interest.

The sophisticated reader is probably thinking that any college-age boy so naive as to lack an awareness of the practice of circumcision deserves to be bewildered. However, such an attitude would be the antithesis of a sociological perspective. One cannot allow himself to become satisfied with what stands as established sophistication. The knowledgeable as well as the naive person must be willing to ask: Why would they do a thing like *that?* The personalization of a sociological point of view is the personalization of a continuous mild bewilderment over the actions of one's fellow men.

If the personalization of sociology means living in a constant state of mild bewilderment, it should be emphasized that one is not called upon to be completely and overwhelmingly bewildered. This would be too disorganizing and incapacitating. To avoid complete bewilderment and confusion a person needs some tentative answers to the "why" of human actions. A sociological perspective, however, calls on us to recognize two things about such answers. First of all, it calls on us to accept their tentativeness—we must accept no interpretation of *any* behavior as the final and incontrovertible word. Secondly, it calls on us to accept the fact that there are often many different interpretations of human behavior and each may have its own strengths and weaknesses.

If the various interpretations of social behavior presented in this book have made any impression on the student at all, he should be able to use them to enhance his own understanding of what is going on around him. This calls for the student to develop a facility for playing with ideas—and I use the word "playing" in its most literal sense. A theory, in many ways, is an intellectual toy; it is designed to be played with. Understanding does not begin with the reading of a book. It begins, if it begins at all, when the book is put down. It begins with playful thinking.

An example: Notes on the "sociology of horror"

To give the reader a better picture of what I am trying to describe, let me close this book with an example of an application of some of the ideas contained in the previous pages. This illustration is not systematic or formal. Rather, it is an extremely playful usage of some of Durkheim's, Goffman's, and others' ideas. I am trying here to exemplify the personalization of sociological forms of thought. No claim is made that what follows is some kind of final truth or the "officially" accepted position of modern sociologists. It is, instead, merely an initial engagement in an attempt to understand a very commonplace happening of the moment. The account is personal. I want the student to see, through this illustration, a case in point of the informal and immediate application of several sociological theories. More formal examples will be provided the student by advanced study in the field.

The commonplace event that begins this illustration was a dream I had a few months ago. Almost without exception my sleep is serene and untroubled. On this particular occasion, however, I was awakened by a nightmare that horrified me. It was about six o'clock in the morning when this happened and I decided to get up and make myself ready for the day's tasks. But the dream, and my sense of horror over the dream, kept returning to my thoughts. I became intrigued and puzzled.

Had I wished, I could have dismissed the matter by shrugging my shoulders and accepting a commonplace evaluation of a commonplace event. After all, a nightmare is not that unusual—nearly everyone has such experiences. One has a frightening dream and that is that. Some things are frightening and some are not. Being frightened is a part of human nature—people are fearful of the same things. Or are they? I thought about it some more.

A number of questions concerning the character of horror began to suggest themselves. To what extent is horror a universal psychological phenomenon? Is it natural—something virtually instinctive? Or is it essentially social in character? If it is the latter, then we might expect the nature of horror to vary with different social settings. Does it? Do particular kinds of role obligations intensify some kinds of horrific events? Is it not so, for example, that people have the capacity to enjoy witnessing the torture of a person to whom they feel related in one way; while, on the other hand, they are revolted and horrified by the same spectacle when the object of horror stands in a different relation to them?

Such speculations led me to wonder whether it might not be possible to develop a kind of sociology of horror. If this were possible, what would it be like? I tried to imagine how various sociological thinkers might approach the problem and develop it. How, for example, would Durkheim think about such a subject?

One of the central themes in Durkheim's work is that an event acquires meaning through the social or collective definitions given that event. Durkheim claimed, for example, that an incredible variety of objects share the distinction of having been held to be sacred objects by different groups of people at different times. The reason, Durkheim held, was because sacredness essentially rests in commonly shared meanings given to the objects. Sacredness is not inherent within the object itself. Can we look at the horrible event or object in the same manner? If so, then for something to be horrible, it would have to acquire its horror from outside itself. Horror could not, according to such a sociological perspective, be considered a quality inherent within the horrific object. I then wondered if I could at least exemplify such a position.

One case that came to mind, and which I had personally observed, was the reaction of a movie audience to two films. The first film was a newscast and the second was the main feature which followed the newscast. Each film presented a horrific happening. The newscast showed, in detail, the assassination of a Japanese official. The man was stabbed to death by a youth wielding a large knife. The assassin plunged the knife into his victim's side and, with a look of shock on his face, the dying man fell before cameras that had come to record a speech not a murder. I noted, at the time, the casual nature of the movie audience—even as they witnessed, on film, an actual killing. People went on munching popcorn; there was some restiveness; and there appeared, to me, to be an attitude of impatience as everyone waited for the main feature.[5] The main attraction, that evening, was Alfred Hitchcock's movie *Psycho*. The murder, completely fraudulent and faked, which took place in *Psycho* elicited a different—more highly emotional—reaction from the audience. There were shrieks and signs of intense fright and shock.

I recalled this event later as I mused over the possibility of a "sociology of horror." If my observations of the audience had some validity, then what might account for the different reactions? Several possibilities suggested themselves. The more casual reaction to the actual killing might have come about because the victim was a man. In the enacted murder the victim was a woman. In our society people are culturally prepared to tolerate cruelty directed against men to a greater extent than cruelty directed against women.

It also occurred to me that the assassinated official was a foreigner, the girl who portrayed the murder victim in *Psycho* was not. Perhaps we are more tolerant of the horrible event when it happens to someone who is ethnically remote.

Another observation that came to mind had to do with the social status of the two people in the films. In the actual killing the victim was a person in authority. In the staged killing in *Psycho* the victim was more on a peer relation with members of the audience. The risk of being assassinated is one of the costs of occupying a position of power. If one is assassinated, it is unfortunate, perhaps, but not especially horrifying. There may be a poignant sense of tragedy in the wanton killing of someone who has not, through ambition or aggression, exercised power over others. I thought of the revulsion and horror which followed the killing of the Clutter family in Kansas.

Finally, and most significantly, the factor which seemed most to account for the different reactions of the audience to these two films was the manner in which each film had staged the horrific event that it presented. The symbolic staging of the assassination of the Japanese official was minimal. The victim was shown in a hall that had been prepared for a few hours of political oration. Suddenly, from the front rows, came the assassin. He quickly leaped

---

[5] My interest in the reactions of the audience to these films was stimulated by the observations of a former student of mine. Mr. Robert Remple, now completing his doctoral work in mathematics at Stanford, wrote down his observations of the differential reactions of a movie audience to two horrific films as part of a course assignment. His observations were interesting enough to lead me to go to the same film, where I observed these responses.

onto the speaker's platform, plunged his knife into the side of the speaker, and then was attacked and carried off by police and guards. The horrific happening took only a few minutes. The audience was not prepared to be horrified; the meaning of the event was not symbolically established for them; and they interpreted it as nonchalantly as they might react to a Sunday School lesson on the brotherhood of mankind.

The symbolic staging of the murder in *Psycho*, by way of contrast, was elaborate, continuous, and cumulative—culminating in the murder itself. The audience was "set up" for a horrific experience. The use, for example, of such an old and reliable device as a stormy night for setting the mood was part of the staging. The cumulative effect of such devices was sufficient to produce a horrified reaction on the part of the audience.

If horror is a form of symbolic behavior, then, I thought, some of Goffman's ideas should be relevant. Goffman spent much time considering various aspects of the relationship between symptomatic behavior and the content of an act. As I wondered how Goffman might deal with the nature of horror, I mentally considered the possibilities that might result from incongruities in what might be called the horror performance. How might a horrific dramatization be spoiled? For example, what happens when horrible actions are carried out by people who are outwardly nice, gentle, and sweet souls? Surprisingly, the result is often amusing rather than horrifying. A case in point was audience reaction to the play *Arsenic and Old Lace*. The spectacle of two sweet old spinsters putting arsenic in the dandelion wine of visitors was hilarious. The content, when viewed objectively, was horrific—after all, the old women apparently were committing murder. If they had had the symptomatic qualities of murderers, the horrific qualities of the play would have been intensified. But the little old ladies did not have the symptomatic features of murderers. They were old, feeble, sweet, and scatterbrained. The incongruity produced a comic effect rather than one of horror.

There are other forms of incongruity in the horrific performance. What happens, for example, when the performer looks like a monster—is horrible in appearance—but his actions do not conform to his appearance? After all, a monster is supposed to behave like a monster. This is what we expect under ideal conditions and it helps maintain the predictability of behavior. A monstrous-looking person simply ought to behave in a monstrous manner—just as a stupid-looking person ought to behave stupidly. We might be horrified by his actions, but at the same time they would seem reasonable in terms of our understanding of the meaning of the person's appearance. But what if the monstrous person violates our understanding of the symbolic meaning of his appearance? The reaction can again be one of comic relief. This device was used several years ago in two television situation comedies. For example, many people thought it was funny to watch a man who was shaped like a hulking Frankensteinian monster worry about having to give a talk before the local PTA. People found humor in the idea of monster-like characters living in suburbia and living with middle-class aspirations and middle-class frustrations.

At this point in my musings over the nature of horror I made a mental note about the character of humor—much humor can be seen as a presentation of inconsistencies in role performance. Humor itself then becomes a social control device. Even more interestingly, considerations of the nature of humor might not be irrelevant to considerations of the nature of horror. Some forms of horror are actually funny. This is very obvious with respect to the kind of humor which is employed in American cartoon film features. It also appears in more realistic forms in some of the humor acted out by soldiers during warfare. I was informed, for example, by an officer who participated in the Korean war, that snipers were often delighted and thrown into fits of laughter when they had an opportunity to shoot an enemy soldier in the crotch.

Certainly horror is not simply something which is inevitably evoked by a particular action. It more and more appeared to me, as I thought about the matter, that horror was a complex interplay between the horrifying act and the person interpreting the act as horrifying. Social settings and social meanings struck me as being crucial.

The use of "horror" props for situation comedy also led me to think about cultural change. Symbols which were horrifying and frightening only a generation ago are now tolerated with amusement. They are "camp." People no longer respond in the appropriate manner to simple registrations of horrific symbols. If a sense of horror is to be invoked, it requires a more systematic and complex development of an idea. People do not shriek or feel horrified by seeing a monstrous mask. As our society has become more complex, it has become more sophisticated. This sophistication has had pervasive effects. Not only have our machines become more complex, so has our symbolic system. Because our sense of the horrific is a part of this system, it has also become more complex in character.

I played with this thought for a while, but it remained uncertain. I had the feeling that it would require intensive investigation and effort if it were to be sustained. It would require a more careful definition of what is meant by horror; and it would require a considerable examination of the extent to which other cultures have employed elaborate horror manufacturing devices.

Second thoughts about the matter led me to entertain the possibility that more simple cultures than our own might possess fright techniques as complicated as any used by Hitchcock. Still, it did not seem unreasonable to conclude the conceptions of what is horrifying change with time. If this is so, then we are not being unreasonable to stay with the proposition that much of what falls within the domain of the horrific is a manifestation of social forces or meanings.

I turned to another aspect of horror. Often the horrible object or the horrible act involves some kind of byplay with functional physiological aspects of living. Examples are common. The burn victim is horrifying because he might have his nose and lips burned away. In such cases we have an opportunity to see before us a person who reveals portions of his functioning physiological structure; we might be able to see his gums and inner nostrils, for example. But why should this be horrifying? We all have gums and nostrils and entrails and numerous other biological and physiological accoutrement. Why should it be upsetting to see them? It is not simply a matter of not being used to it. After all, we are not horrified by everything we are not used to.

This struck me as being a particularly interesting feature of the problem. Goffman had brought up similar considerations in his work *Stigma*. Goffman argued, both effectively and reasonably, that such appearances stigmatize the person because they symbolize the possibility of an incapacity to perform his role properly. I could not deny this. However, I thought there might be some further possibilities to consider.

I began thinking about this by conceding that the sight of functional organic aspects of the person does have the capacity to disrupt normal social interaction. The commonsense reaction to this would be to claim that such sights are disruptive because they are horrible. However, it might be as reasonable—if not more so—to claim that such sights are horrible because they are disruptive. My reasoning here was somewhat similar to Durkheim's reasoning concerning crime. I recalled Durkheim's statement that we do not reprove something because it is a crime; rather, it is a crime because we reprove it. So it is with the horrible object. It is horrible because it is disruptive. But why should functional aspects of one's organic nature have a disruptive quality?

I was led to entertain the possibility that a ''normal'' appearance in most public social interactions tends to minimize biological aspects of being. By so doing, the interaction can occur at a social rather than at a biological level. The interplay of symbolic relations is not distorted or interrupted by biological considerations. The biological level—upon which the interaction is dependent, of course—is subordinated or disguised or hidden. In some circumstances, in fact most of the time, we are kept unaware of the fact that we are biological beings. We help others and they help us to maintain this illusion.

For this reason, perhaps, sexual functions in Christian society have been looked on with something akin to horror. The intrusion of sex into social affairs can be disruptive. When we are fully "socialized" we hide our sexual and animal natures from others. To let them show would be disruptive. For this reason, then, the functional aspects of our physiology must not show. We should not display our sex organs in polite society. Nor should we display a bloody carcinoma that is growing on our ear. It is socially disruptive.

Something is not disruptive because it is horrible; it is horrible because it is disruptive. I played around with this notion for a while, and the more I thought about it, the more I was impressed by it. This basic Durkheimian proposition appeared to provide considerable understanding into the nature of the horrific experience.

If this argument is reasonable, we would expect to find that something considered horrible in a setting where it is disruptive will not be considered horrible in a setting where it is not disruptive. A number of illustrations suggest that at least this possibility is not completely implausible. Consider, for example, the following three cases. In the first case we have the observation of a machine gunner from a Huey helicopter involved in the Vietnam war. The machine gunner comments on his reaction to witnessing the death of a man. He says,

> I shot up a Charlie in the paddies today . . . I ran that little mother all over the place hosing him with guns but somehow or other we just didn't hit him. Finally he turned on us and stood there facing us with his rifle. We really busted his ass then. Blew him up like a toy balloon.[6]

In the second case I recall a conversation with a neighbor of mine in Lawrence, Kansas. He was a physiologist. He had, with another colleague, done a study on the physiological effects of hanging. I found the manner in which he acquired his data interesting. He told me that he had, along with a colleague, obtained the permission of a prisoner awaiting execution to use his body after death. The scientists then waited as the execution took place. They examined the suspended body as it hung, still warm, from the noose. As soon as death was certain they cut down the cadaver and severed the head. An inspection was made, on the spot, to evaluate the physiological aspects of the body. Later they wrote up their reports and published them.[7]

---

[6] From Frank Harvey, *Air War—Vietnam* (New York: Bantam Books, Inc., 1967). The imagery used in this description is not horrific but playful.

[7] I also recall, in a similar vein, the story that a well-known physicist, while dying, asked doctors to cut off his head and perform experiments with it. He would attempt to relay information back to them to indicate whether or not he was subjectively aware of what they were doing with his dismembered head. Unfortunately, I have lost the source of this story and have not been able to track it down. In any event, both this and the conversation with the physiologist reveal the extent to which normally horrifying experiences can be modified by the development of deep commitment to scientific norms.

Or, in the third instance, we can consider the following statement concerning lynching:

> Among marginal and uneducated men of certain localities there has existed the tradition of a man hunt (not unlike the tradition of the coon hunt). To "get your nigger" has been a permissible sport, virtually a duty. Toward this tradition law-enforcement authorities, as we have said, sometimes show a lenient or permissive attitude. When excitement grows high in the course of a lynching it is taken for granted that there will be looting and destruction of Negro homes and businesses. Not infrequently furniture from Negro homes is used as firewood for burning the victim's body.[8]

In each of these instances, normally horrific events are viewed by people in either a casual, experimental, or boastful manner. The typical person, I presume, would be revolted by the sight of a man being blown to pieces by 50-caliber machine-gun slugs. In a military context this is not looked upon as a disruptive event—indeed, it expresses the military role. In so doing, it is no longer horrible but playful. A corpse may be seen as a trophy—a way of measuring the extent to which one has fulfilled his socially assigned duties. The physiologist cutting down a freshly hung man and slicing off his head feels curiosity more than horror. His action is not disrupted but sustained by the corpse he examines. The lynch mob may not experience horror but rather elation as they cut off finger joints of the victim to carry home as souvenirs. When an action is essential to the social process, when it is not disruptive, it no longer horrifies.

Nor are we generally horrified by the sight of the bloody segment of some animal's corpse lying on a plate in front of us as part of our evening meal. This piece of partly raw or cooked flesh is an integral part of the social drama being enacted at meal time. As it becomes necessary to the drama, it becomes less horrific.

These elementary considerations led me to think about the employment of horror as a means of achieving social ends. When do men find horror or terror a good means of attaining social goals? What motivates men to use horror as a social device? Why would men seek to impose horror on others? In the light of my earlier considerations, I concluded that conscious use of horror would occur where the possibility of efficient organization in a competitive group was seen as threatening to the organization of the group employing horror. Horror becomes an instrument of social action when men begin to anticipate the disruption of their own organization by the challenge

---

[8] From Gordon W. Allport, *The Nature of Prejudice* (Garden City, N.Y.: Doubleday & Company, Inc., 1958), p. 61.

of another organization. A latent sense of horror generates a capacity to indulge in concrete forms of horror. The latent sense of horror, however, has its locus in how people respond to the integrity of their own social organizations. In a sense, people seem to be willing to rely on horror as a means of influencing others when they begin to lose faith in the integrity of their own system. The Ku Klux Klansman uses horror as an instrument against the Negro because he believes the Negro is a real threat to his organized way of life.

By this time my thinking on the nature of nightmares had moved off into other realms. There seemed to be no end to the possible interpretations that could be made. But I did not think much more about the matter. It was sufficient, at the time, to conclude that possibly the nightmare, in order to have the effect it has, requires a socially bestowed interpretation of the dream sequence as potentially disruptive. Furthermore, that which is being disrupted must be of high social value to the person experiencing the dream. I made a note of these speculations and then laid the problem aside. I did not go further into the matter and conduct a systematic investigation. Later, perhaps, I might return to this topic and develop it more systematically. At the moment, however, this seemed sufficient.

This playful analysis of a commonplace happening is intended to serve as an illustration of what I mean by the "personalization" of a sociological point of view. It is not intended as an example of systematic sociological investigation of a professional character. However, even the most systematic and rigorous sociological studies often have their origins in such "playful" considerations of a problem. Unless the student has the capacity to employ sociology in this manner, he will probably not make a very good professional. On the other hand, if he possesses this capacity, he will not have to become a professional to gain great value from sociological thought. Sociology can also be enjoyed by the amateur.

Summary of the uses of sociological knowledge

This chapter has concerned itself with the uses to which sociology may be put. I have suggested four possibilities.

First of all, it may be put to no use whatsoever—existing sociological sophistication, like that in any other field, can be ignored. However, I do not think people benefit by taking such an attitude.

Second, one can put sociology to use by becoming a professional sociologist —sociology offers both an interesting and a secure career. The demand, at present, is very high for people who are knowledgeable in sociological theory and sociological research methods.

Third, sociology can broaden one's understanding of any specific career field he might enter. Only the most naive person would claim that development within some career specialty is determined solely by technical competence in that field—innumerable socially significant factors almost invariably play a large role in shaping advancement and attitudes toward advancement.

Fourth, and finally, I suggested that sociology can have value in a "personal" sense. By this I meant that a thorough and sensible understanding of what sociologists are talking about can be used in the interpretation of many commonplace events. To the extent that we can understand the influence of social forces, we are more likely to use than be used by society.

Glossary

The following terms, and their definitions, include those with which I thought the typical undergraduate might not be familiar. Moreover, they are often words or concepts not likely, in the meaning they have within this text, to be found in the ordinary desk dictionary.

abstracted empiricism: A term used by C. Wright Mills to refer to factual studies that concentrate on some part of a process and, as a result, lose their grasp of the whole. For example, voting studies have demonstrated that wealthy Americans tend to vote Republican. These studies are empirically or factually sound. At the same time, the abstracted nature of such data leads us away from a consideration of the more complex political machinery that makes such facts significant. Mills used this term to criticize what he thought was one of the central limitations of empiricism as it exists in sociology—its tendency to destroy a comprehension of the complex unity of human social action.

altruism: Behavior revealing a concern with the welfare of others, unselfish conduct, subordination of one's interests to those of another. See "altruistic suicide."

altruistic suicide: Suicide resulting from altruistic motives. Durkheim saw in altruistic forms of suicide a means of indirectly assessing the nature of the social bond. Collective sentiments have the capacity to enable the individual to overcome his own fears of death. Altruistic suicide is self-destruction in the interest of socially established goals. An example of such conduct would be the recent instances of the self-immolation of Buddhist monks in Vietnam.

ambivalence: Having feelings or reactions of both a positive and negative kind toward some object, event, or condition. For example, the intellectual in America is probably viewed ambivalently by many people. On the one hand his knowledge is admired and recognized as the source of many cultural accomplishments. On the other hand, the intellectual is also viewed with some suspicion and hostility as a threat to established values and tradition.

analogue: A condition or event that is similar to some matter which one wishes to understand and, because of the similarity, can promote such understanding. For example, some people believe the electronic computer is, in many ways, analogous to the human brain. We can, therefore, come to understand some aspects of human thought by turning to the computer, which functions as an analogue for the brain. Most social theories rest, ultimately, on some kind of analogous reasoning. For example, in some theories the biological organism is implicitly taken as an analogue for society; society is then seen as having a "circulatory system," "intelligence centers," "digestive mechanisms," and so on. In other theories the analogue is the poker game, or it might be the tossing of many dice.

anomic suicide: (See "anomie.") Suicide resulting from being placed in a situation where the regulative controls of the social order have been weakened or removed. Durkheim saw in the higher suicide rates found among divorced people evidence supporting the proposition that anomie is conducive to self-destruction. The divorced person, he argued, finds intolerable the anomic conditions existing after being freed from domestic regulations.

anomie: Literally, without name or identity; to be placed in a position of not knowing what one's social character is supposed to be. The subjective character of anomie is similar to the feeling that comes when one is supposed to go someplace but has no map to tell him how to get there. This term was coined by Durkheim to identify those situations in which the individual is, or feels he is, loosely united with the community or social order.

asceticism: A philosophical point of view which claims that the individual can improve himself spiritually by denying his physical nature; a philosophy of self-denial and discipline of the flesh. According to Sorokin, asceticism is one of the distinguishing features of an Ideational society. Ascetic philosophy is virtually nonexistent in the overripe Sensate society. Ascetic conduct often involves such acts as fasting, self-flagellation or whipping, exposure to temperature extremes, self-mutiliation, self-degradation and humiliation. It is difficult to determine, however, whether, in its subjective state, such ascetic exercise serves to mute the senses or to excite them.

atavistic stigma or stigmata: The idea that some people carry marks (stigmas) that identify them as reversions (atavisms) to more primitive physical types. Lombroso thought that many criminals had a more primitive physical appearance. American white racists believe that the American Negro can never really be civilized because he is physically a primitive type; moreover, that this is proved by the Negro's physical appearance—his atavistic stigmata. Physical anthropologists, it should be noted here, have convincingly demonstrated that Caucasians share as many physical traits in common with the gorilla as do the members of any other race.

autarchy: Self-sufficiency, independence. Henry uses the term "consumption autarchy" to refer to the capacity of an economy to consume all the goods it produces.

biologism: As used in this text, the belief that the social nature of man is inherent within and explainable in terms of his biological nature. In its crude form, biologism argued that the major institutions of man are a reflection of biologically endowed instincts. The Bank of America, if we followed this line of reasoning, would have to be seen as a genetic phenomenon arising from an acquisitive instinct found in all men. Another naive form of biologism is the argument that a superior society can be created by producing a biologically superior form of man. In a more sophisticated form the modern biologist argues, quite reasonably, that we must not ignore man's animal nature. This form of biologism concedes that some aspects of the social order are not simple manifestations of biological urges or drives. Social and biological forces interact with each other. Thus, Konrad Lorenz, after exploring the biological nature of aggression in subhuman animals, very tentatively explores the possibility that the lessons learned at such a level might be applied to the aggressive nature of human beings. Note, however, his use, in the following quotation, of both biological and sociological or anthropological concepts.

> The ganging up on an individual diverging from the social norms characteristic of a group and the group's enthusiastic readiness to defend these social norms and rites are both good illustrations of the way in which culturally determined conditioned-stimulus situations release activities which are fundamentally instinctive. —From *On Aggression*, translated by Marjorie Kerr Wilson (New York: Harcourt, Brace & World, Inc., 1966), p. 259.

Sociologists for the most part have eschewed biological approaches to human behavior.

bureaucracy: A large-scale organization, hierarchically structured, dedicated to efficiency in the pursuit of its goals, with duties prescribed by a written set of regulations, personnel selected on the basis of examinations, and power resting within the concept of an "office" rather than in the individual. A modern bureaucracy can be almost incomprehensibly large. Seymour Melman, for example, says,

> The Department of Defense of the United States employs 3.7 million people, of whom 2,680,000 are in the uniformed forces. . . . The armed services use 340,000 buildings. The total property value of the installations and equipment exceeds $171 billion. —From *Our Depleted Society* (New York: Holt, Rinehart and Winston, Inc., 1965), p. 15.

Bureaucracies, because of their reliance on codified rules, are highly legalistic in nature. Bureaucratic modes of organization tend, in modern societies, to diminish the influence of traditionalistic and kinship systems of organization.

celibacy: For an adult, the state of living without a sexual partner. Dictionaries define celibacy as being single or unmarried. Celibacy, however, appears to be declining among the unmarried of our time. Vows of celibacy refer to the intention to lead a life devoid of sexual experiences involving a partner.

charisma: A greek word meaning divine gift. As used by Weber, this term referred to the dramatic or exciting personal characteristics of the prophetic leader or demagogue which enables him to retain power over his following. Charismatic power is located in the unique personal attraction of the leader. Because such power is neither long lasting—dying when the leader dies—nor dependable, one of the problems faced by any social organization is the need to achieve more stable modes of allocating power. Bureaucracy achieves greater stability in its power structure by placing power within an office or position rather than in the individual. Thus, men of power within a bureaucracy are often men having very little personal attraction or ''charismatic'' quality.

continuum: A condition which we can, in our imagination, assign any value as we move from its lowest to its highest extremes. A continuous variable differs from a discrete variable. The latter permits only particular values as one moves from its lowest to highest extremes. For example, wealth is a discrete variable. Along the tremendous range from no wealth to the billion-dollar worth of a Howard Hughes, one must move by a series of discrete steps resulting from the fact that wealth is an accumulation of pennies. One must go from $25.00 to $25.01—there is no stage in between. Time, on the other hand, is continuous. No matter how finely we divide a second, we can think of a still finer division.

cultural lag: The idea that the material aspects of culture progress more rapidly than the nonmaterial or symbolic aspects of culture. The adherents of this point of view claim that many social problems of our time arise from the inability of our moral concepts to keep pace with our technological development. Thus, while we are surrounded by atomic technology and super computers, we still depend upon a legal and moral philosophy which met the needs of a pastoral people who lived two thousand years ago. Opponents of the culture lag theory argue that all aspects of culture, including the technological, are essentially symbolic in nature and that the distinction between material and nonmaterial features of culture is spurious.

dehumanize: According to Goffman, the act of divesting any person of the right to employ those props, symbols, costumes, or fronts which enable him to impress others favorably. A subtle example of dehumanization was offered me by a woman who told me that during the 1930s, when she was employed as a clerk in a department store, she was instructed by her superiors to outfit

Negro customers with clothes that fitted poorly or were in bad taste. Our conception of humanity, however we define it, is associated with group membership. A particular action which might be seen as human when carried out by a group member can be viewed as less human when performed by someone outside the group. Sociologists have summarized this phenomenon with the phrase, "In-group virtues are out-group vices." So it happens that *we* are "ambitious," but *they* are "pushy." *We* are "intelligent," but *they* are "too smart for their own good." Dehumanization is a complex form of behavior, operating at a symbolic level, which requires first of all a set of devices for depriving some class of persons of their right to use positive forms of impression management. Second, it requires a justificatory scheme for the enactment of such deprivation.

demography: The study of the numbers of humans living at any time as affected by fertility, mortality, and migration. Because mortality rates have been dramatically reduced in recent years, fertility has been the major factor accounting for variable rates of population increase in different nations. Demographers have, in recent years, become especially concerned with factors influencing human fertility.

determinism: The philosophy that, in principle at least, all actions, including those of people, are the result of causes over which the acting agent has no control. Thus, a rock falls because of the determining influences of gravitational force. A human being does something because of the numerous determining forces of the situation. If a person engaging in some action were placed in the same situation again, he would respond in the same manner. Advocates of this point of view claim that the idea of choice or volition is entirely a matter of illusion—that in actuality we have no choice. Just as we physiologically mature and enter senility because of biological processes over which we can exercise no control, so we behave in response to the very complex conditions in which we find ourselves and which are, in their entirety, fortuitous circumstances. Even whether or not we believe we have a choice is a matter of cultural and ideological determinants into which we are thrust by the accident of birth. Critics of a deterministic position argue that determinism requires the capacity to assign causes to events. Where such causes cannot be assigned, an indeterminant situation exists. When a situation is indeterminant, the future is uncertain. The uncertainty of the future offers man the opportunity to assign, in the present, the priorities he will give to future actions. This assignment of priorities is a decision-making effort and involves thoughtful choices. Thus, man can choose. The fact that a determinist cannot predict the choices that will be made is a limitation of deterministic philosophy. In summary, determinism is a conceit that arises from the feeling that man will someday understand the workings of the entire universe. Meanwhile, we must live with the fact that our understanding is not sufficient to tell us whether we will survive the present century.

dichotomy: A twofold classification of some condition. For example, we can dichotomize people as rich or poor, strong or weak, bright or stupid, good or bad, and so on. The most famous dichotomy I can think of is that pertaining to the sexes.

dust-bowl empiricism: A term coined during the thirties, when the southwestern areas of the United States had suffered monstrous dust storms. The term refers to arid factual studies which have had the top soil of thoughtful interpretation blown away, leaving behind the bedrock of numerous statistical or descriptive observations.

dysfunctional: Any social action which disrupts the well-being of the greater social system. The prefix "dys" means bad; therefore, we are talking about a "bad" function. In medical terminology dysfunction refers to the incapacity of an impaired organ to maintain the welfare of the whole organism. The idea of dysfunction in social analysis implies that its user has a very good concept of what a healthy social system is. However, this would imply an ethical judgment because social structures are, as Durkheim pointed out, moral structures. But, social scientists are hesitant to make ethical judgments. Thus, the concept of dysfunction places sociologists in a bind. If they exorcise it from their terminology, then they become apologists for the status quo. If they include it, they can be accused of making hidden ethical judgments—which would contradict their commitment to ethical neutrality. It is difficult to find examples of dysfunctional features of a social structure with which all sociologists would agree. Rioting, for example, would seem to be dysfunctional. However, one might reasonably claim, as would Simmel, that such behavior is functional in nature.

ecological: A perspective that concerns itself with the interaction between organic systems and their environments. Ecology concentrates on life systems as complex interactions producing delicate mutually sustaining living patterns for a great variety of organisms. If this ecological system is disturbed at any point within its structure, the established equilibrium is destroyed and the whole structure will be affected. This can be illustrated by a story attributed to Charles Darwin having to do with the number of old maids in an area and the abundance of the clover crop in the vicinity. The old maids keep cats. The cats reduce the mice in the fields. Mice feed on bees. The reduction in mice increases the bee population. The greater number of bees improves the pollination of the clover crop. Thus, there is a connection between old maids and clover crops. One of the critical limitations of contemporary science is that it cannot tell us, at the moment, what the ecological consequences of man's present technology will be. Some ecologists are coming to the conclusion that we might see, in the near future, catastrophic changes in the earth's biosphere. These changes could be very abrupt.

egoism: Having a concern with one's own interests rather than those of others; a concern with self to the exclusion of a concern with others. Egoism should be contrasted with altruism. See "egoistic suicide."

egoistic suicide: Suicide resulting from egoistic motives; suicide in which self-destruction is seen as serving the interests of the person who kills himself. Such suicide may take quite elaborate forms and the individual often shows a curiousness and interest in the fact of his own death. Durkheim relates,

> A calm melancholy, sometimes not unpleasant, marks his last moments. He analyses himself to the last. Such is the case of the business man mentioned by Falret who goes to an isolated forest to die of hunger. During an agony of almost three weeks he had regularly kept a journal of his impressions. . . . —From *Suicide* (New York: The Free Press of Glencoe, 1951), p. 281.

empathy: The ability to feel or experience the subjective state of others; the capacity to enter the experience of another person. Social psychological studies have shown that students who can easily empathize with their teachers tend to make better grades than those students who cannot empathize.

empirical: Having a factual quality, based on facts and observations as opposed to being based on logical or rational considerations. According to the well-known story, purely rational considerations led to the conclusion that the bumblebee is aerodynamically incapable of flying. Empirical considerations force us to conclude, to the contrary, that bumblebees do a very reasonable job of flying. Sociologists argue that much of what is wrong with our understanding of human social conduct arises from the fact that we have dealt with this subject on the basis of reasoning rather than observation. Sociology owes its distinction as a field pretty much to the commitment it has made to finding ways of factually determining the nature of human social behavior. However, because social conduct is both very complex and generally symbolic in character, the application of purely empirical modes of investigation is an ideal difficult to meet. The sociologist, when functioning at his empirical best, generally relies on official records of various events, which are then submitted to statistical analysis. Demography, usually conceded to be the most empirical wing of the sociological enterprise, is of this character.

epistemology: The study and examination of the means whereby one can establish true or valid statements. The epistemologist is concerned with establishing the limits that hold for human knowledge. The epistemologist keeps raising the question: But how can you be *certain* that what you say is true?

esthetic: Having the quality of beauty, considered pleasing to the senses, meeting cultural definitions of what is thought to be symmetrical, well formed, and artistically appealing. Until recently, at least, one could give the example of a junkyard as a place lacking esthetic qualities.

ethical: According to the sociologist, behavior which conforms to the normative structure of the society in which the individual lives. Because sociology strives to be a science, and because science is ethically neutral, the sociologist tries to assume an ethically neutral stance. Professional ethics, thus, place the sociologist in the unusual position of being unethical when he writes or lectures with an ethical bias.

existentialism: A philosophical position of a highly varied nature grounded in the observation that mortal man is contained and must exist within a universe that appears to be neither for nor against him. Faced with the fact of existence in an unconcerned world, the individual must elect the meaning he will give his life. Existentialism, as employed in this book, refers to a philosophy of choice—that man has the possibility of making what he will of his life.

exponent or exponential: Referring to a figure indicating how often a number is to be multiplied by itself. The exponent 3 in 2^3 means that 2 is to be multiplied by itself three times, or, (2) (2) (2). Reference to exponential forms of growth has to do with the extremely rapid increases in values that come from repeated raising of a value by a factor contained in an exponent. Thus, if the factor in the exponent is 2, we would rapidly get very large terms by repeatedly squaring any real number greater than 1 or less than -1. For example, beginning with 2, we would have $2^2 = 4$; $4^2 = 16$; $16^2 = 256$; $256^2 = 65,536$; and so on.

Gauleiter: A Nazi administrative official, having charge of a province or district.

hedonistic: Subscribing to a philosophy of the pursuit of pleasure. The hedonistic calculus, a concept used to explain preference for criminal behavior, argues that if such behavior gives more pleasure than pain, it will be engaged in. A modern revival of hedonistic theory has appeared in the works of Skinner, a behavioristic psychologist at Harvard. According to Skinner, any organism will reveal a greater predisposition to repeat behavior which it has found rewarding. We can employ this knowledge to make an organism behave as we would like it to by rewarding it each time it performs according to our preference. Thus, we can get a dog to roll over by rewarding it quickly on that occasion when it rolls over by chance or even begins to look as if it might roll over. One of the difficulties in applying such theory to human behavior is that we cannot always be certain just what it is we want to reward. If we give a novelist a great reward (reinforcement) for writing a wonderful novel, this does not mean he is supposed to sit down and write the same novel again. Sociological theory, concerned as it is with the structural relations between statuses or roles, is surprisingly devoid of a reliance on hedonistic principles in its approach to human conduct. Sociological man often appears to go about his role performances in a cheerless and conformistic fashion. If he experiences pleasure, it is because the role he is playing tells him to; he does not experience the role because of his desire for pleasure.

heuristic: A device or concept which, though perhaps meaningless in itself, nonetheless has the capacity to promote, advance, or stimulate understanding. I believe I would label Riesman's concept of ''other-direction'' a heuristic concept. Though it is difficult to find its counterpart in the real world, the term sensitizes us to many aspects of institutional living as it takes place in modern society. Many mathematical models have heuristic qualities. Boulding tells his students that mathematical models are wonderful, so long as you do not believe them. He means that one should use the model to comprehend the nature of the real world, while at the same time remaining acutely aware of the constricted and artificial nature of the model itself. Boulding is saying the mathematical model is best seen as a heuristic device.

hierarchy or hierarchical: Being arranged in a series of ascending orders of power or control, with each stage having greater power than those falling beneath it. The military is the typical example of a hierarchically arranged set of statuses with each level having authority over those beneath it.

humanistic: Being concerned with humanism; revealing a strong interest in human thought and ideals as opposed to an interest in nature or religion.

inner-directed: Having the ability to retain a strong and contrary sense of moral purpose when placed in circumstances where it would appear reasonable to succumb to the norms of the natives. As Riesman noted, the inner-directed nature of the British colonial administrator in the tropics was exemplified in his habit of dressing in Western clothing for dinner.

internecine: Referring to conflict which is mutually destructive; deadly rivalry; struggle which avails little to either side of the battle.

latent function: A consequence that was not anticipated or planned in the course of a social development. For example, if it is true that the institution of prostitution during the Victorian period helped hold the Victorian family together, then one of the latent functions of prostitution would be that it helps maintain the integrity of the family. Latent functions are the implicit, indirect, and "unofficial" reasons for the existence of some agency, corporation, institution, status, or position. Latent functions are contrasted with manifest functions.

mana: A Polynesian term used generally by anthropologists to refer to an impersonal and diffused supernatural force which has magical powers. Thus, a tree that is very fruitful might be claimed to possess mana. A successful and healthy man might be said to have mana. According to Swanson, a belief in mana exists only in societies with a particular form of social structure.

manifest function: A consequence that was planned or anticipated in the course of a social development. The manifest function of an aircraft plant, for example, is simply to provide a safe and rapid means of transportation for the people in a society. Manifest functions are the simple, direct, and "official" reasons for the existence of some agency, corporation, institution, status, or position. Manifest functions should be contrasted with latent functions.

metaphysical: Literally, after physics; speculative thought which attempts to move beyond the directly observable nature of the physical world. To be interested in the accelerative dynamics of falling bodies is a physical interest. To be interested in the question of whether or not God exists in the form of a perfectly symmetrical cube is a metaphysical interest. Science has abandoned metaphysical concerns on the grounds they cannot be responded to in a manner which produces consistent and reliable results.

methodology: The study of method. Sociologists, because of the problems they encounter in trying to establish reliable knowledge about the social order, have shown an especially sensitive concern with the methods they employ. Most sociology departments of any size in American universities have at least one man, and sometimes several men, whose special training is in the area of methodology. Sociologists subscribe to the belief that if their methods are sound, their conclusions will be acceptable. While concentrating on the means to be employed to establish factual results, the sociologist sometimes loses sight of the ends to be accomplished by his findings. The fact that the study of method is a separate and specialized area of concern to sociologists suggests there is such a thing as *a* sociological method of research. In practice there are any number of procedures which, depending on the effect being sought by the particular writer, can equally well serve as means of setting forth convincing arguments. Because sociologists subscribe to the belief that only scientific results are acceptable to the field, the study of method has concentrated almost exclusively on the application of scientific procedures which have produced valid results in other fields. A uniquely sociological method or set of methods has yet to be found.

milieu: A French term for environment or surroundings; a more elegant way of referring to environmental influences.

monasticism: Preference for solitary living; a form of institutionalization of solitary existence by taking up residence in a monastery where one lives a quiet, relatively solitary, and meditative life; a belief in the monastery as a way of life.

monotheistic: A belief in the existence of one God. We often hear Christian religious beliefs described as monotheistic. This is not correct. Christian theology contains a number of gods and godlike spirits. It is, therefore, a polytheistic religion. According to Swanson, there are relatively few cultures which contain purely monotheistic religions.

motifs: As used in this text, themes or central ideas around which the different elements of a culture are organized; the unifying concepts of a culture. Henry, for example, sees our emphasis on self-indulgence and consumption as one of the dominant motifs in modern American culture. This motif becomes the central figure around which are formed our industrial interests, courtship patterns, educational practices, child-rearing habits, the character of our youth, and other features of our culture.

national character: An elusive concept based on the idea that there is a correspondence between a cultural milieu and the personalities of the people brought up in that culture. The idea of a national character is a refinement of the folk awareness that people from different nationalities have different qualities—in addition to the obvious ones of language differences. In the more crude stereotypical forms which appear in common thought, German national character for example is viewed as militaristic, authoritarian, bureaucratic, romantically sentimental, and given to the enjoyment of heavy and fattening foods. The attempt to provide more factual bases for such thinking has proved difficult. Anthropological and sociological research has shown there is considerable variety in personality types within any cultural system. Such variety should be kept in mind when dealing with the concept of national character.

naturalism: The philosophical position that whatever is experienced in nature is to be explained, accounted for, or understood in terms of nature; the philosophical position that supernaturalistic or extranaturalistic explanations are mythical, fictional, or silly. The natural sciences lean exclusively on this position —as their name suggests. One physicist put it rather baldly by arguing that there is no place for God in the laboratory. Another scientist is reputed to have claimed that God is a redundancy in any mathematical equation because He would have to appear on both sides of the equal sign. An extreme naturalistic position is less attractive in the human realm. However, sociology, to the extent it assumes a scientific perspective, is grounded in the belief that *any* human institution—*any* human social action—ultimately has its origins in purely natural phenomena. Despite occasional demurrers to the contrary, such a position is logically and practically antithetical to a religious explanation of human conduct.

Oedipus complex: A term coined by Freud to refer to the tendency of the maturing male to find his mother an attractive sexual object. The son is biologically impelled to commit incest. Society, of course, is opposed to such practice. The maturing child thus finds himself biologically set against the demands of a constraining social order. A further feature of the Oedipus complex is the feeling of hostility developed for the father as the child becomes aware of his father as a block between himself and his mother. Thus, the son is led into a situation where he wishes to murder his father and make physical love to his mother. How the sexually maturing child resolves these horrifying desires has an impact, according to Freud, on the course of his adult life.

ostracize: To ban, to make someone an outcast, to shut out from the group, to set up barriers that make normal interaction with members of the group impossible. Ostracism often implies that a person being ostracized has been a member of the group and is then found unacceptable and banned from further participation in the group's activities. Ostracism is highly varied, however, and may take many forms, including the exclusion of persons who were never a part of the group. Ostracism can also be partial in character. I once was a member of a country club and asked the golf pro if I could invite a friend of mine to play a round of golf with me. When I informed the club pro that my friend was a Negro professor I was told the game of golf would be all right; however, my professional friend was not to go near the swimming pool.

paranoia: A psychiatric term referring to systematic delusions of persecution which have reached the point where the individual is incapacitated in the performance of his normal life routines. The paranoid individual lives according to the assumption that everyone is against him. If people are friendly, it is because they want to get close enough to take advantage. The paranoid person is often quite dangerous insofar as he comes to believe he has good justification for inflicting damage on those near to him—he must in order to protect himself. At a national level such systematic delusions of persecution and misanthropy result in internecine struggles in which no one benefits and many suffer.

para-poetic: A term used by Henry to refer to the literary qualities of modern advertising. The term has two possible meanings. It might mean, on the one hand, literary expression which is similar to poetry. It might also mean abnormal or crippled poetic expression. Henry probably had the latter meaning in mind. It is likely that Henry left the term open to allow the reader his own interpretation. It is difficult to classify the literary nature of modern advertising, and possibly the term para-poetic achieves such classification while, at the same time, keeping us aware of the difficulty. How does one handle the literary quality of advertising jingles that are known by virtually every citizen of an entire nation? Certainly they cannot be claimed to lack literary impact. On the other hand, the motives which give them form are not literary in nature. It is poetry which is not poetry. It is literature which is not literature. It is an influential rhetoric which serves the most banal of human aspirations. It is, to use Henry's term, para-poetic.

pathogenic: A medical term referring to anything which produces a disease or organic abnormality; in the context of this book, any event which leads to socially destructive behavior. In this sense, the term pathogenic is quite similar to the idea of dysfunction and has the same problems involved in its usage. Usually whether we consider something as pathogenic in a social sense involves a personal normative judgment.

pathological: Of a diseased nature; organically dysfunctional. Sociologists, often fond of organic metaphors, sometimes refer to crime, marital discord, rioting, conflict, or other violations of humanistic ideals as "pathologies." Such metaphors should be treated with caution. They are invariably disguised value judgments. They permit the sociologist to retain a cloak of objectivity while using a term which is the equivalent of an epithet.

pecuniary: As used here, showing an interest in money; relating events and people in terms of their monetary values.

peer group: Literally, a group of one's equals. Sociologists generally use the term to refer to equals in the sense of similar age levels. Thus, an eight-year-old's peer group would consist of other children of a similar age. However, the peer group of a college professor would consist of other professors who share similar levels of sophistication and prestige—regardless of differences in age.

peyote: A mescal cactus of the southwestern United States and Mexico which yields a drug capable of inducing unusual subjective and introspective states of mind.

pluralism: In its most general meaning, pluralism simply refers to the fact that something can exist in several forms. The term "pluralistic society" has become popular in recent years and has been applied especially to the American system in which a variety of ethnic cultures have been able to share in the common expression of American ideals. I employed the term "industrial pluralism" in the text to refer to the American industrial system in which a variety of industries are allowed to produce a common product. These products are supposed to be different because they come from different plants. Everyone is aware, however, that the differences which appear to exist come more from the office of an advertising agency than from the factory.

polygamy: Literally, marriages in which one may have several spouses. In common expression this term is often used to refer to that situation in which a husband has multiple wives. This is more correctly called *polygyny*. The situation in which a woman has several husbands is referred to as *polyandry*.

postulate: As used throughout this book, the assumption of a proposition without need of proof in order to further an argument; a statement regarded as self-evident and not in need of further verification. One of the postulates of structural-functional theory, for example, is that any social action must have social consequences and must, therefore, be capable of being interpreted in terms of its social functions. A basic postulate of naturalistic philosophy is that all natural events can be understood in terms of what we perceive in nature.

pragmatic: Subscribing to the philosophy that knowledge should be evaluated in terms of its practical values; the idea that the world exists to be manipulated; the conviction that knowledge which promotes manipulation is good—the rest, being useless, is worthless; dedication to the belief that events and people should be related in terms of their usefulness.

prognostication: An attempt to divine the future; a forecast; an estimate of the outcome of some course of action.

psychic: Having the capacity to go beyond natural constraints; transcending the boundaries of normal and natural mental processes. Persons who are psychic are said to be able to foretell the future; move objects by application of will; and have an awareness of what other people are thinking without having to resort to questioning and natural forms of communication.

quantophrenia: A term coined by Sorokin referring to the fanatic desire we have today to measure anything and everything. It was Kelvin who said, in effect, that if something could not be measured, then it could not be known. Sorokin felt such a position was excessive to the point of madness.

replication: The act of repeating. As used here, this term refers to the practice of repeating investigations over and over in order to check the validity of initial results. The fact that a sociological study often can be replicated and maintain a consistency of results is, in itself, a strong argument for the possibility of a science of human relations.

retreatist: As used by Merton, any individual who abandons both the goals and the means endorsed by a society as legitimate and worthwhile. The dropout is a retreatist.

ritualist: As used by Merton, any individual who becomes involved in a socially sanctioned means activity to the detriment of attaining socially valued goals. Ritualism implies a ''blind'' reliance on established modes of attaining goals even after these have ceased being effective. The court martial of Billy Mitchell offers an historical case in point. Traditionalistic officers were scornful of aircraft as an implement of war. Their desire to continue in the use of older and outdated methods moved them in the direction of being military ritualists.

Sensate: A term coined by Sorokin to refer to cultures in which emphasis is given to knowledge derived through the senses. Such cultures, according to Sorokin, have a number of common characteristics, such as sensual art forms, pragmatic philosophies, positivistic science, relative moral systems, situational ethics, and prestige systems based on external signs of worth.

shaman: A term broadly used to refer to men who believe they can interfere directly in the workings of good and evil spirits; a medicine man.

social goals: Objectives which achieve a special significance because they are collectively held. When, for example, acting was considered a rather common way of making a living, few people felt any desire to become an actor. Today, the social significance given to acting makes it a prized social goal—an aspiration which many hold as a dream.

sociometric: A means of recording patterns of social relationships within a group. A sociometric is typically a simple charting of friendships among people. For example, one might ask students in a classroom to write down the names of their three best friends. Given this information, one can then determine who is the most popular student in the class and who is the least popular. Lines of informal influence can be established from such data.

status panic: A term coined by Mills to refer to the problems faced by Americans in their quest for a sense of worth. Because the standards of worth in the American system, according to Mills, are ill defined, the American, no matter how hard he works, can never be certain he is a success. No matter where you stand in the system, there is always someone who can be looked upon as being better. Moreover, because American culture emphasizes a competitive relation with others, one is then obligated to match the worth of the person who stands above him. The fact that this is a never ending and uncertain enterprise induces a sense of panic—the constant feeling that one is on the edge of failing.

status quo: The existing order; the present way of getting things done; the established and accepted system of human relationships as it exists in the present.

structural-functionalism: As used here, a sociological school of thought (structural-functionalism is also found in the biological sciences and in other social sciences) which attempts to relate particular forms of social action to the total social system within which the action occurs.

sui generis: Literally, of its own kind; something unique; a thing apart; having special qualities. This term was used by Durkheim in his attempt to establish the social order as something having qualities of its own. Just as life, though dependent on the physical order, is different from inert matter; so is society, though dependent on biological beings, different from biological matter. The term is a call for recognition of the special understanding that is required to comprehend the nature of social activities. A social system has dynamics of its own (*sui generis*); it is not a simple manifestation of individual human needs and character.

supersensory: A term coined by Sorokin to refer to the capacity of the great thinker to transcend the limits imposed by the senses.

symbiotic ecology: (See "ecological.") Referring to mutually sustaining life systems. A symbiotic relation is one in which several life forms provide reciprocal benefits. A prosaic example of a symbiotic relation is man and his dog. The dog, in return for his gratification of the human need for recognition and affection, is given shelter and food. In some areas of the United States the dog is also given psychiatric care.

symbolic interactionism: As used here, a theoretical point of view in the social sciences emphasizing the symbolic nature of human social relations; the idea that human interaction is essentially symbolic interaction; the belief that one's sense of self arises out of the capacity to view one's self as a meaningful entity apart from others—this in turn is based on our capacity to evaluate ourselves symbolically. A very simple demonstration of what the symbolic interactionist is trying to put across can be carried out with an ordinary television set. First, turn off the sound and watch the picture. Because this reduces the symbolic content of the picture drastically, the meaning of most of what is taking place is lost. Next, turn off the picture but retain the sound. The symbolic content carried by the physical action in the picture is now lost, but this is the smaller symbolic element. At the level of pure symbolic inter-action we can retain a good sense of what is taking place. Human social interaction takes place at a symbolic level and this makes it distinctive. When we interact with a person, we interact with that person in terms of the values which obtain through the symbolic meanings we attach to him. The symbolic interactionists, in the classical formulations of G. H. Mead, made much of the fact that not only does the individual have the capacity to interact at the symbolic level with others—he can also interact symbolically with himself. The individual can assume the role of others and then either praise or castigate himself from the perspective of these other people. Symbolic interactionists see this as the most essential aspect of social control. Any biologically and mentally normal person is highly vulnerable to the symbolic evaluations that others make of him. We have no physically determinable and sensorily observable self. Therefore, what we are is what others make of us. We uncritically assume the symbolic evaluations of self that others give us. If enough people tell us we are bad, we come to accept this evaluation. Conversely, if enough people tell us we are good, we also accept this. Our self, therefore, is located in the external evaluations imposed upon us. For this reason, society and self are only different manifestations of the same process.

symptomatic behavior: A term coined by Goffman to refer to behavior which validates one's right to act out the content of a particular role. Such be-havior is symptomatic of whether or not one "really" is what he is trying to appear to be. For example, a professor who has a deep British accent, every-thing else being equal, will be more acceptable to his audience than one who has a strong Arkansas accent. The British accent is viewed as symptomatic of a man of wit, dignity, and learning. I was once told by a colleague of mine that he mistrusted the work of a certain man because he had seen him at a meeting and the man was deeply tanned. No *real* scholar would be tanned. As Veblen pointed out, a suntan is symptomatic of a frivolous life in an age of office workers.

tautology: Circular reasoning; saying the same thing in different ways; re-dundancy; redefining a condition and then using the redefinition as an explana-tion. For example, it was once fashionable to define an immoral person as spiritually corrupt. Spiritual corruption was then used to explain immorality. All that was being done here was to claim that someone was immoral because he was immoral.

testocracy: A term coined by Sorokin to refer to the tendency in modern Sensate cultures to rule people by subjecting them to such various tests as those for IQ, aptitude, personality, and the like.

tradition-directed: A term coined by Riesman to refer to cultures in which individuals are strongly influenced by traditional as opposed to rational considerations.

transcendental: Going beyond the limits of normal human experience; transcending one's natural abilities; extending beyond normal physical awareness.

tripartite: A threefold classification scheme. Riesman's three character types exemplify a tripartite classification.

typology: A classification scheme; an examination of types.

usury: The practice of lending money at very high rates of interest.

utilitarian: Having utility or usefulness.

Utopia: An ideal community; a place in which men achieve their most noble conceptions of life; literally, no (*ou*) place (*topos*).

value system: A structure or ordering of actions which are highly esteemed by a people; the assignment of worth to different activities in a manner which reveals an underlying common basis of evaluation of such activity. In this text, Sorokin's ideas most clearly illustrate a means of comprehending the nature of value systems. In a Sensate society the relative value of an activity is determined in terms of the extent to which it attains Sensate criteria of worth. In such a system chastity would be assigned little value; sending an astronaut to the moon would be assigned great value. These disparate activities are valued in terms of a system which ranks them according to the extent to which they can be ranked in terms of Sensate criteria of worth.

volition: A concept implying man has the capacity to exercise choice; will; decision making. See the discussion under "determinism."

weltanschauung: Literally, world view; a conception of life and the universe; a way of seeing the world.

xenophobia: Having a fear (*phobia*) of that which is strange or foreign (*xenos*); a hatred of the foreigner.

Index

A

Adaptation, five modes of, 82–84
Advertising, 73, 74, 259–261
Allport, Gordon W., 322n
Alpert, Hollis, 162n
Alternation, 204–206
Altruism, 298
Altruistic love, 250–253
American Negro, 210, 217
Anomie, 45, 46
Arendt, Hanna, 291n
Arkoff, Abe, 302, 304
Art, 242–245

B

Barr, Stringfellow, 5n
Barzan, Jacques, 64, 221n
Becker, Howard, 64
Behavior, cynical, 180–183
  sincere, 180–183
Belief, 199
Benedict, Ruth, 227n, 237n
Bendix, Reinhard, 63n
Berger, Peter L., 16, 22, 154, 194–213, 219n
  and alternation, 204–206
  and American Negro, 210
  and belief, 199
  and capital punishment, 210
  and existentialism, 208, 211, 212
  and fraud, 200
  and freedom, 207, 209
  and lack of character, 204–206
  and man, 196
  and nonconformity, 206
  and occupational control, 201

Berger, Peter L. (*cont.*)
  and ostracism, 200
  and ridicule, 199
  and social control, 196, 197
  and social roles, 203, 204
  and sociological determinism, 206
  and sociology, evaluation of, 210
  and violence, 197, 198
Berle, Adolf A., Jr., 68n
Berne, Eric, 297n
Biologism, 46
"Black box" problems, 27–28
Blue-collar worker, 140, 141
Boulding, Kenneth E., 115n, 127, 127n, 298n
Brace, C. L., 255n
Bronowski, J., 15n, 17, 17n
Broom, L., 71n
Burdick, Eugene, 7n
Bureaucracy, educational, 64, 66, 68
  essential features of, 63
  technical competence in, 67
Bureaucratic organization, nature of, 59–60
Bureaucratic power, 62–69
Burnham, James, 68n
Burroughs, William, 243

C

Caldwell, Robert G., 275n
Calvinism, 55–57
Cameron, William Bruce, 134, 205n
Capital punishment, 36–37, 210
Capitalism, 60, 62
  and church, 51
  growth of, 54
  and morality, 57